LIGHT YEARS

D1616145

LIGHT·YEARS

A *Spiritual* Memoir

Barbara Du Bois

2011
Laughing Vajra Press
Prescott, Arizona

Designed by Walton Mendelson
Cover Design by Sue Favia

Photo credits
Front cover: Barbara at 45, by Catherine Noren
Back cover: Barbara at 70, by Amanda Amos

Cover photograph of "Hubble's Deepest View of Universe": NASA, ESA, G. Illingworth (UCO/Lick Observatory and the University of California, Santa Cruz), R. Bouwens (UCO/Lick Observatory and Leiden University, and the HUDF09 Team.

Laughing Vajra Press
P. O. Box 10192
Prescott, Arizona 86304
www.laughingvajrapress.org

Library of Congress Control Number 2011912397

ISBN 978-061551118-4

Manufactured in the United States of America

Homage to the True Nature, the Primordial Purity!

Homage to all who awaken,
Homage to all who realize,
Homage to all who protect,
Homage to all who gather,
Homage to all who teach,
Homage to all who practice,
Homage to all who hear and contemplate,
Homage to all who yearn,
Homage to all who seek,
Homage to all who have never heard of that to be sought
yet resonate to its echoes, within and all around.
Homage to the One and to the Ten Thousand,
Homage to the One in the Three
and in the Eighty-four Thousand,
Homage to the Five, to their immanence and radiance,
Homage to the Six, to the high and the low.

Holy, holy, holy!
Praise, praise, praise!

Contents

PROLOGUE

Intimate with Error and in Love with Truth

U NDER A TABLE IN MY ROOM I keep a box filled with old books. From time to time I take one up to glance through or to ferret out a detail, but mostly they are at rest there. Many are simple, utilitarian; some, from China, have black covers with red spines, and pleasing, heavy, lined pages. One is covered in bright orange brocade, and two were gifts from the friend, long dead now, who made their papers of herbs and grasses. There are a few slim, elegant volumes, but most are sturdy, serviceable, and worn, like little scuffed grade-school leather shoes. And hovering in the box, in the books, is the slenderest intimation of fragrance: something between must and incense.

These are the journals I wrote in from about age forty to sixty, my first twenty years on the formal spiritual path in this lifetime. They are the raw material of this book: the stuff of my experience and my probing of it.

•

I was an American woman studying with an American woman teacher in an American spiritual community in the final quarter of the twentieth century. My life was unfolding in the "jungle of worldly concern"[1] that most of us inhabit, and I brought to this teacher a full cup of mind, the brew of a complex, textured life—its richness, its troubles, and especially its elaborate structure of elaborations.

I have had much to unlearn in opening to the natural state, to simple *being*. The process has been sometimes joyous and sublime and sometimes dense, bewildering, terrible. The naturally free, the stainless, is here in these pages, and also the confusion and suffering that obscure my view

---

1. Jungle of worldly concern: our conventional, self-bound samsaric existence, and the realm or condition most propitious for awakening from its repetitive dream. See, for example, Dharmarakshita, *Wheel of Sharp Weapons*.

of it—arising simply from grasping to illusion: the habits, dramas, and fixations that we think of as "I" and "reality."[2]

The deepest suffering in my life was my sense of separation from the absolute, from truth.

Morning fogs disperse, revealing the open sky. It is never not there—as we are not, have never been, can never be separate from truth ceaseless and all-permeating. The relative is inseparable from the absolute, from essence. They are indissolubly one, from the beginning of beginningless time. And we are that.

Not to see this is suffering. To long for it is aspiration. To walk toward it is spiritual path.

•

Suffering has one supreme virtue: it can bring us to the path. Discomfort, mild or extreme, focuses our attention and we seek relief, answers, change. With great good fortune we may meet teachers who can shine light on our path, but no one else's answers will liberate us, not even those of a buddha, unless we also discover them for ourselves, through our own direct experience—compelled by our own need, longing, and aspiration. Compelled by the wisdom alive within our ignorance.

We misunderstand the nature of reality. We're like underground explorers following maps of the skies, or worse, like people eagerly jumping from airplanes, taking clouds for continents. There's always a possibility the folks below ground will find a way to the surface, but the jumpers are doomed. Like us, they apprehend transitory phenomena, impute to them some kind of solidity or "selfness," and cling to them—leap into them! It's not that we and things don't exist; we do, just not in the way we think, as with the mesmerizing clouds. It's the thinking that's awry, not the phenomena. The appearances we cling to are impermanent and ever-changing, empty in essence while vividly, dynamically appearing, like our dreams, our thoughts, our emotions. Like the clouds. But our nature is not this. Our nature, and the nature of all things, is like the clear sky itself. This is the penetrating insight that cuts the tree of suffering at its root.

---

2. Suffering as I use it in this work does not always mean agony, torment, misery, although sometimes that is exactly what I am talking about. It often refers simply to the general unsatisfactoriness of things: the boring, repetitive, infuriating, unscratchable itch of phenomenal existence. Of both kinds of suffering, some I longed to relinquish, and some I strove mightily to keep.

It is so simple, but for most of us not so easy. Sense experience is convincing and compelling, the illusory "I" defends its illusory territory, and when the afflictions of thought and emotion are thick, as mine have been, the defense can be frantic and the suffering of life and the path intense. Yet how insubstantial is this suffering, how lightly it can be borne! Yes, we all have mind's condition: attachment, aversion, ignorance, and their outflows—*and* we all have mind's *nature:* primordial purity, truth itself, puissant, irresistible, all-conquering. A chamber dark for æons is illuminated in one instant when the lamp is lit. Just so, in every instant we perpetuate confusion or awaken in truth. In every instant suffering can arise as awareness.

When we recognize our personal suffering nakedly, without story, simply *as suffering,* we understand this as the experience of all beings— and this allows us to tolerate and care about others who suffer, even to the point of holding each one more dear than oneself. This is the foundation of the *bodhisattva* intention. Upon this ground we commit to awakening—for ourselves, for all. [3]

•

Stepping onto the path—that first step! So unlikely, so precious! Bhagwan Shree Rajneesh poignantly wrote, "A Buddha is not a miracle. He is capable so he reaches. . . . But when someone comes to me with all his desires, with all his longings, with all his limitations, and thinks to begin, it is a miracle. If I have to choose between Buddha and him, I will choose him. He is a miracle—so incapable and so courageous." [4]

I was that person at the beginning of the journal years, and in the journal pages are those very longings and limitations: all my aspirations, all the evidence of my incapability, all the reasons I needed courage. I did not write in my motley journals for anyone but myself; they were a private place to which I repaired for respite, to sort through and clarify

---

3. *Bodhisattva:* one who cultivates and gradually becomes solely motivated, throughout the succession of lifetimes until full awakening, by the altruistic intention: to liberate all beings from suffering, into their true nature. This motivation, this radiant quality of mind, is *bodhicitta.* In its relative sense bodhicitta is the fine flowering of the natural qualities of compassion and love; in its ultimate sense it is the natural radiance of *being* itself: awareness and love impartial, nonreferential, limitless, unimpeded.

4. Rajneesh, *I Am the Gate,* 36.

my confusions and to explore the inner landscape to which were opening my eyes and heart. I have asked myself if exposing this evidence,
so personal, so raw, might prevent another from taking that unlikely,
precious first step, or from generating the courage to press on. I have
also questioned whether those relying upon me might feel deceived in
a spiritual friend so nakedly, sharply revealed in her flawed and fallible
humanity, and perhaps falter or even turn away from the path.

For several reasons I share this history. First, it seems possible that
seeing my confusion and its gradual release into clarity might allow
another to understand how we all have both confusion and clarity—
and thus give rise to love and compassion for both self and others.
Further, at a certain point in my history I saw this: "We don't have to
have perfected our personalities in order to realize enlightenment, so
apparent personality glitches and faults are no obstacle to enlightenment
and no justification for discouragement. They are simply displays of
pure awareness, occasions for piercing the veil of appearances to reveal
What Is." If personality is no obstacle to enlightenment then we must
use it *for* enlightenment, for ourselves and others. I am not the sole
individual whose self-grasping is strutting around as the Personality Kid,
so perhaps observing how spiritual aspiration and practice gradually
allow my outrageous, frantic Kid to relax will encourage another to
persist with confidence.

However, the principal consideration that brings me to expose my
experience in all its rawness is precisely this: its rawness. Most spiritual
biographies I have read highlight the saintly qualities of their subjects
rather than revealing the process that ripened them. When I was in
the worst of it (which only much later could I see had actually been
the best of it), I found such stories inspiring but at the same time
oddly disheartening. [5] They tended to say, essentially, "I was born, I
wandered in confusion for twenty years, and then I awakened." But
they didn't show me the twenty years! They didn't actually *lay bare the
details* that could convince me these holy people had once been like
me. If I couldn't believe they had been like me, how could I believe I
could become like them?

5. The best of it and the worst of it: see Milarepa, "The Song of a Yogi's
Joy," in Chang, *The Hundred Thousand Songs*, 74–87. In this work, see "sacred
sewer," 341–42.

•

When we first meet a spiritual master we may not know how to be helped. We may not even know, consciously, what we are really there for. In no way is this an ordinary meeting. It is our heart's deepest longing and highest aspiration—for truth itself, for authentic, holy *being*—from which this meeting arises. The relationship with the spiritual teacher is a relationship with one's own sacred potential, for which the teacher is a quickener, magnifier, and elucidator and the relationship an alchemical retort, burning away the dross to reveal the primordially pure.

It is easy for Westerners, perhaps especially Americans, to have confusion about this relationship, trained as we are to idealize individualist and rebel. Even our car bumper decals exhort us to Question Authority. Well, so did Shakyamuni Buddha—wedding it to the injunction to assay all spiritual teachings in the medium of our own experience, to test them for ourselves and then to take up what works for us: what helps us wake up. This testing must inform devotion and transcend skepticism and rebelliousness; if it does not engender full self-responsibility and inner authority it is a mistaken relationship, a faulty path. My principal teacher in these twenty years worked me with vast love and close stringency, according to one purpose only: to awaken me to my true nature, to the true nature of all beings and phenomena, to the true nature of reality.

The dance in which the practitioner engages with a true teacher is both a dance with the teacher and a dance with one's own mind. The spiritual teacher can be the most terrifying person we will ever meet, standing before us as a mirror that reflects both our condition and our nature, both our smallness and our greatness. Certainly I have been more deeply alarmed by intuitions of absolute majesty than by evidence of relative limitation.

•

Quite early in our relationship my teacher told me, "Write down what you observe." So I did. My journal observations focused on my own process of inner inquiry and reflection, and on events, circumstances, relationships, and other people only as they related to that process; such information is sparse in the journals and even more sparse in this chronicle. No living persons other than me are named or identified in this book (except in two dreams); the same is true for most places, organizations, events, and times. For more information about the principles and methods by which this narrative morphed from raw journal notes into its present form, see "Combing the Precious Teacher's Hair: Notes on Method" at the end of the book.

During the decade or so in which I was transcribing, cutting, and shaping the journal record into this chronicle, I often erupted into laughter or tears, grief or gratitude; ejaculations of astonishment; amused, wry, rueful, or reflective commentary, and sometimes expressed these responses on the page. This interaction with the material appears in the form of italicized comments in brackets: my conversation with myself and with you.

I recorded many dreams in my journals and include some of them here. The symbol ❖ marks the beginning and end of dream sequences.

Every error in this work is a remnant of my own confusion; flashes of wisdom are radiance itself; and any scant sign of understanding is a happy artifact of karma, sparkling in the light of my spiritual masters' love. I bow to them.

•

While the process of spiritual awakening is timeless, since awake is what we primordially are, for us it takes place in time, through time. In each lifetime's magical, dreamlike display we must awaken in *this* particular, precise, specific, unrepeatable moment—to see what is always already here to be seen.

Contemplating my days and years herein, even I who lived them can now—*now*—perceive the workings of spiritual aspiration and practice and the alchemy of relationship with an authentic spiritual master. What do I see? The conditioned self seeking its own transparency and dissolution—and intrinsic awareness flashing through the experiences and events of daily life, gradually transforming both context and content. Proud, self-centered, rebellious, I clung to my identity and suffering, swung wildly between love and fear, confidence and doubt, surrender and grasping. The journals show this process even as they elucidate the steady quieting of the selfish clamor, radiant bodhicitta slowly gaining sway.

I offer you now the grainy negative, the proof positive—proof not of this individual's perfection but of perfection's immanent potentiating light in us all.

Perfection's immanent potentiating light in us all—that is the shining thread to trace through this history. As I read it now I see vividly what I most often could not in the density of lived experience: those flashes of light signaling "Here it is! Here, look here!" Right here in the mad swirls, the terrifying storms, the wild dance of appearances, truth itself is whispering in our ear, "Here, look here! Here it is! Here you are, in all your perfection! Here you are, perfection itself!"

We already are what we aspire to become. We are templates of truth, to be laid bare by love.

•

Book·One

Breaking Light

BREAKING LIGHT

*I*T WAS LIKE A LONG-ENCODED SIGNAL *sounding within me. "Catch your students before they turn forty!" my teacher told me years later—and in the spring of my thirty-ninth year I began weeping. I didn't know why and I couldn't stop; I seemed to have sprung a leak. A psychotherapist myself, I had intuitive certainty that this was not psychological malaise, but what it was I didn't know, and I continued to weep. I looked as if I were mildly breaking down, but I felt as if I were wildly breaking open.*

While sorting the papers of a friend who had recently died, I came upon a letter from a woman named Ruth, describing her experience of life-threatening illness; she had approached it as spiritual inquiry and spiritual practice, and it had transformed her life. Something in the tone of her communication said to me, "Try on these lenses." So when I sprang my leak I went to see her. [6]

I used to call Western psychology "3-D psychology" for its blindered focus on deficit, dysfunction, and disease, but while I had been unsatisfied with that worldview I had also been influenced by it, both personally and professionally. Ruth introduced me not just to a new worldview but to a new world, redirecting my attention from issues, problems, and materiality to energy, wholeness, subtlety—son et lumière. My brief work with her began opening me to the radical truth that it is love, not grief, that heals sorrow; love, not anger, that rights wrongs. After a few months Ruth sent me to her own teacher, who became my first spiritual master in this lifetime: Beloved, with whom I studied, practiced, and contended for the next twenty years.

I was at that time teaching psychology, social science, and feminist studies at a small northern college. Single by choice, I lived with my cats, Sassafras and Spidercat, and later also Amazing Gracie and Lucy, in a small brown house with turquoise shutters set in a country meadow at the edge of dark woods, looking west to mountains and skies. I loved living there, heating with wood, shoveling pathways through the deep snow, running in the shady, dusty lanes. To have a small house

---

6. Ruth was a true spiritual mentor and friend to me. She stood by me when I stumbled, cheered when I soared, shook me when I huddled in my ignorance, and rejoiced in my times of clarity. She was this kind of spiritual friend to many, and to our motherly planet herself.

of my own in the country had been the only material goal I had consciously held in life, and I was peaceful and happy in its modest accomplishment.

Indeed, in spite of my apparent lack of worldly ambition, up to then I appeared to have been successful at everything I had attempted, including working with refugees in Africa, international development work with the United Nations, disarmament and other sociopolitical activism, art, writing, teaching, psychotherapy, social science research, and clinical theory. My doctoral work at the nation's premier university had been an intellectual high point for me, as my research joined with the work of other feminist scholars and writers of the era to push back the conventional boundaries of scholarship and understanding of women in every discipline. "Passionate scholarship," I called it: very heady stuff.[7]

In my early years of college teaching I poured myself into helping others engage their own intellectual and moral imperatives, to expand lives, to change societies. Some five years into this work, though, the journal in which I begin recording my new process of spiritual inquiry reveals serious dissatisfactions arising. In both love and work I am edgy and restless, something within me demanding attention, urgent to express itself, maladroit and jarring. In the earliest journal entries its call is compelling, and will resonate through the coming years and the journals that chronicle them. Even now, more than three decades later, it is the experiences and insights of this early period—some of them true markers in my spiritual landscape—that are some of the most vivid in my memory and far reaching in their impact on my life, on my mind.

I was a spiritual seeker from childhood, oriented to inner experience, by nature a mystic, not an adherent. Not that I, and others on my behalf, hadn't tried. Baptized Methodist in West Virginia and brought up Episcopalian in New England, I found relief from an unhappy family life by going away to a Quaker (Society of Friends) coeducational boarding school in Pennsylvania at age fourteen. In my early twenties I even enjoyed a brief flirtation with Catholicism. While teaching in Africa after college I had fallen in love with a hardheaded, soft-hearted Irishman, dashing in his Roman collar, whose own religious certainty and bedrock love for me suggested, briefly, a possible path. But most influential, perhaps literally lifesaving, had been the Friends school, my first experience of respect and encouragement for my spiritual inclinations. It was like balm and like oatmeal: healing and sustaining. Quaker observance felt very natural to me, simple, unencumbered, direct; and Friends'

---

7. See Du Bois, "Passionate Scholarship," a paper delivered to the American Academy of Arts and Sciences and the National Women's Studies Association (January and June 1979). The published version contains a number of editing errors, the most important of which changes *eductive*, describing my inductive research method, to "educative," a misleading substitution.

testimony to the inward light, that of God in all, struck chords of recognition and love deep within, authenticating my own sense of direct relationship with the divine.

When I was nine or ten my mother asked me what I wanted to do in life. Without hesitation I said, "I want to understand mind." "Oh, you want to be a psychologist," she replied. "Uh . . . okay," I responded, uneasy but not knowing why. It was philosophy, not psychology, that initially attracted me in college. I was exhilarated and then gradually put off by academic philosophy: the study of others' ideas, not the book-lined room with deep, inviting shadows in which to probe and develop my own. And it was to be awhile before I would discover afresh what "understand mind" meant: realize mind itself—the true nature, the absolute. I knew what I wanted and I knew the name, but that was all.[8]

From very early childhood, then, I already had the essence of spiritual path: I longed to be a good person, I longed to serve, and I longed to know God, to know truth—not by rumor or report but immediately, directly, personally. The Hound of Heaven has been at my heels my whole life long. But I never knew what to do about it until I met my first teacher, Beloved.

The spiritual journals begin in the summer of my thirty-ninth year, shortly before that meeting.

•

---

8. Many years later, giving Dharma teachings, I recounted this story about my childhood intention to understand mind and its misdirection into the study of psychology. Afterward a woman came to tell me her story. She was a dramatist, had made the theater her career—and it was only upon discovering Buddhism that she realized she had made a slightly dyslexic error: it wasn't Drama she wanted, it was Dharma!

YEAR ONE

How to be? · Meeting Beloved
Marianne · Here in my life

I am learning to speak my pieces, to inject into the living world
my convictions of what is necessary or what I think is important
without concern (of the enervating kind) for whether or not it
is understood, tolerated, correct or heard before. . . . The world
will not stop if I make a mistake. [9]

July, August, September

I love the way Chevy's face changes in desire. Sexual power, animal
hunger. Frightening, yet I love her in it. What am I afraid will happen
if *I* loosen up and flow sexually? That I'll be vulnerable, "wanting"?
That I'll be *powerful*?

"There's a tone of voice you have that pushes me away," Chevy said:
derisive, mean—yes, *mean*. With Mother, getting along better when I
place my own needs first—but it's my mother! And I'm coming to
face that this teaching job is no longer good for me. I need and want
to be focusing more on my own health, growth, and happiness, less
on taking care of others—and this college's ethos is that we should be
"all there" for students while at the same time it uses us up.

If other people are important to me, *treat* them as if they matter.
Yet I am not taking responsibility for *myself*, for my own feelings, needs,
perceptions. For my own life. It seems that I can't take care of myself
and be in relationship.

[With lover, mother, and work, I am trapped in conflict: confounded by thoughts of
self and other, strung out between engagement and withdrawal, disturbed by the anxious
thought that I am not realizing my own potential. I am needing fresh air: the fresh

---

9. Audre Lorde, speaking at a feminist studies conference (not documented
in my journal notes) on her experience with breast cancer, about which she
later wrote extensively and powerfully in *The Cancer Journals*.

air of inner *engagement. At a deep level I am here asking how to be—and "how to be?" is a question about authenticity. It can be answered only from within.]*

Chevy and I are at her house tonight, companionable before the Franklin stove, a fire merry in the grate. When I arrive the horses come trotting down—lovely to hear the sound of their hooves, see them come over the little knoll. Bugs and Erica *[cat and horse]* nuzzling each other, Bugs rubbing against her leg, she pulling his ear with her mouth. It's very sweet and peaceful here. Daily grateful for our good friendship, this sweet, rich loving.

Meeting Beloved.

[She is beautiful and mysterious, definite and indefinable. The air around her seems still, conscious, pregnant. When she speaks I hear her as if from within a watery globe, her words stirring my long-sleeping mind like a hand moving undersea grasses: they sway dreamily, yet quicken. I feel lightly mesmerized, fixed in place, unable not to listen with great interest and respect, as if to an emissary from outer space. That she has wisdom and power, and these of a different order than the ordinary, is unmistakable. That with every word and gesture she is pointing me insistently toward my own wisdom and power, which I yearn for and fear, means I resonate deeply to her very first words. I am receptive and uncritical—rebellious and nonconforming as time goes on, but very open here at the beginning of the precious, perilous journey.]

She said that my work is important, "opens people to realize themselves." And, "I recognized your voice, I have known your spirit before." *[To be recognized by my voice means that my voice must ring true. "How to be?" is a question about authenticity.]*

October

Too much to do, too little time, feeling threatened and impinged upon by people, demands, Chevy and I suffering under the strain of my busyness—*and* from my desire to be alone more: for quiet openings in the mornings, running, silence, reading, meditating. Hurt her feelings in the morning, saw her sad face all day. Tonight weeping and talking, then kisses and sleep, holding each other all night long.

Beloved singing for me, to help me find my way home, my connection to the Source. "I felt a cool breeze rise off your body," she said: "your death wish leaving you." I felt her drawing down to me the Mother energy, myself open to receive it.

I feel I once was one with the Source, and now I'm separated—and oh, how I long to be one again, to go home. I sense that I block knowing what my life purpose is, for if I know I shall have to do it and won't be able to go home. Beloved: "You must stay here anyway." I laugh. All my dreams and visions of God tell me the same thing: "No, you can't come home just yet." So there *is* a reason for my being, I *do* have a purpose in this life.

Chevy's lovely ways of seeing. She went out onto the rocks, came back with a starfish. "Were you meditating?" she asked. "There was a silence around you." And later, "Did desire just come into you? It filled you and you seemed to be floating." Feeling vulnerable, open; wanting this love to deepen its roots, hold in good soil, nourish us.

Meditating, I go to the light, don't want to come back. How to bring the light back with me? How to come back and be here without the pain? Ah: seeing that the pain can come up—and I can let it go by. *[An important early insight—but it is one thing to see it, another to practice it. Willingness is key. I am not just "attached" to pain, I am closely identified with it; I do not yet know I am not my pain. There is curiosity here, and a tentative willingness to consider that it might be possible to let go of mental and emotional habits. Beloved will soon step in to help me with this.]*

November

Really tired, physically and mentally; wanting to stop and hanging on, just, till the college intensive is over and I can reclaim my own rhythm, my own life—yet also aware of the energy of health and wholeness ready to buoy me up, carry me along.

[Here, now, brilliant and precise, two shafts of light illumining the path:]
Beloved says things are moving quickly: "Truth is all around you." At the moment I am in willful removal of attention from spiritual work, partly in reaction to my recent session with her—in which I recognized that in order to take my next steps I might have to *give up* some very dear attachments, things that I think are essential—simply in order to *see* clearly. *[I cannot overstate the implications of this insight—into*

the nature of consciousness and awareness, and into willingness. Let go, see right through.]

Sense of loss, dismay, in recognizing that what I've always called "spiritual" may just—just!—be *natural*—that there may *not* be that longed for "other" plane—that it may be *in* me—and in others, too—that I'm not special, that I'm not "chosen," any more than anyone else—that the light shines for each of us, not specially for or on me.

Beloved: "What do you long for?" Barbara: "Union with God, the divine." She: "How?" I: "At the moment of death." She: "Why wait? *Do it now.*" Powerful shift: *Now* I am one with God, *now* I am whole and real—it's *now* and *here*—*I Am Who I Am.* *[Breathtaken:]* Jahweh's words! I don't blaspheme, I am divinity, too (as I've always known, as a child asking both self and others: "Why is Jesus any more God's child than I?")

[Potent, profound, penetrating shift. This is where I turn in the right direction. This is where, in this lifetime, consciousness opens to the path of union, and I step forward.]

•

Sharply, Beloved this morning: "Negative, hurtful energy: transmute it," she said. "Discharge it not as pain, anger, but as joy, light. *Change* it, *consciously.* You have the choice, you are responsible. *Use* the disciplines. Stop reacting like an adolescent, always asking why, why, why. *Choose* light, wholeness, joy. Energy is consciousness. No intellectualizing. Just deal with the energy."

["I step forward"—so then immediately encounter the next challenge: a completely new teaching, for a very old pattern. Could her instructions be any more direct? "Deal with the energy." Apply antidotes; every system has them. Transform, transmute; every system teaches ways. Later, much later, I understand that "deal with" can mean simply "be with."]

Awaking at 4 a.m., very aware of fear in relation to Marianne. Tried to lift and transform it. Not altogether successful.

[Ah, Marianne. What shall I tell you of Marianne? Dear wife of my graduate school classmate Manny, and herself my dear, dear friend. Intense, loving, smart, funny. Devoted to Manny and their two vibrant, bright, laughing girls, April and Alisa (Leesy). Marianne and Manny met as teenagers in New York City, both highly intelligent and creative, Marianne the child of a German mother and

Chinese father, Manny a Manhattan Puerto Rican. They married very soon and made their own little universe, taking safety and comfort in each other in a society hostile to love between races and to love between youngsters, in a city raw with energy, opportunity, and risk. Manny attended college while working as a tool-and-die laborer, and earned a full scholarship for doctoral work in psychology; we met as graduate school classmates.

We were intimate, loving, and laughing, this little family and I, but as the years went by Marianne became increasingly reclusive. Manny was taking up his profession and the girls, smart, energetic, creative, were growing, reaching out to life. Marianne made sporadic attempts to step out into the world herself, but gradually some fault line began to give way. Not two full years before this entry in my journal—oh, right in this instant my eyes are closing, my hand is heavy, a sickening paralysis is infiltrating my mind, I do not want to write these words: Marianne murdered Manny, April, and Leesy in their beds, with the shotgun he had given her for protection in his absences. She shot herself, too, but not immediately, and not lethally.

I was heartsick, crazy, frozen with grief, horror, and rage, and, briefly, suicidal myself—thinking I had failed them, failed them all, by not being able to protect them all. I had recognized danger, by the ghastly chill that Marianne's recent flat, soulless communications about her family had placed in me, but I did not then know how to give full credence to my inner state as a valid, though visceral, cognition. I summoned the help I could, living far away; what I wish I had done was go to their city, drag the police in, hide the children. I did not withdraw, but I did not engage extensively or effectively enough. Neither did anyone else.

Marianne was tried for murder, acquitted by reason of insanity, committed to the state mental asylum—and, unbelievably, escaped. At the point of this journal entry I am certain she is coming to find me, either to seek forgiveness or to kill me, too, for not having saved her and her family. Either prospect terrifies me.

For years to come my love and grief for Marianne will toll through my life like a great bell, at first heavy, portentous, gradually lightening, pealing like a carillon to lift sorrow—to reveal, finally, only love.]

I've given myself three days to fast (autumn apples and cider), do spiritual study, and practice. I've never done this before. It is a step on the climb to the mountain retreat. *["Mountain retreat"—the image of my longing for spiritual succor and solitude, for realization.]*

I don't, actually, feel a conflict between this spiritual work and my feminism. *[Ha! Preview of coming attractions!]*

December

> Purpose recedes like the sun on the horizon as you approach it. [10]

What am I doing this for? Started with concern for health, then for wholeness, then for spiritual transformation. *[Wonderful progression—from the densely material through the psychospiritual to the spiritual. I'm seeing this principally at the level of intuition, but the intuition is correct—and later will arise in the form of a healing mantra that touches the three dimensions: I AM HEALTHY, I AM WHOLE, I AM HOLY.]* And now? When I ask, "Why am I here, what is my purpose in this life?" I see only light. Is this "it"? Is there something more or other I'm "supposed" to experience? Ah, my paradigmatic question: Is it here, now, this, or is it elsewhere, then, something else?

My sense of estrangement in spiritual groups. Because of my feminism? But of course this is *always* my issue in groups: that I am different, other, outside.

About my alienation from men, Beloved told me, "That's a sickness in your soul, Barbara; it means you are refusing the Father. You must struggle with this. *Don't withdraw.* Withdrawal is also a withdrawal from consciousness, and will make you sick." I felt invalidated, pained that what I see and experience as a strong, healthy, healing part of who I am in the world—feminism, my choice to give energy to women—she was seeing as a manifestation of cosmic sickness. But I didn't withdraw; I stayed with it—and oh, kept weeping, the tears flooding my face, such pain, like a hurting heart. By the end I felt heard and understood.

Don't go to the mountain retreat. Live *here in my life* the sacred, the consecrated, the mindful, the conscious. *[This sweet and challenging note of truth rings for me again and again.]*

•

10. Khan, *Mastery Through Accomplishment.*

YEAR TWO

To be present in love · "Do it in the supermarket"
Initiation · Forest retreat · The absolute within the limiting frame

January

> [Don Juan] said that if I really felt that my spirit was distorted I
> should simply fix it—purge it, make it perfect—because there was
> no other task in our entire lives which was more worthwhile. [11]

I have to laugh: I decide to tell Beloved I want a private space for my
sessions with her—then today, with that resolve clear in mind, I arrive
and there are three *men* in the house!

She spoke today about my attachment to pain: "We can go deep to
change the old patterns completely, but you are very sensitive; better to
peel away the scar tissue bit by bit." *[And how many times later did I wish
she had chosen the first route, even at the cost of my life or sanity, saving me, her,
and all around us from the effects of my suffering and confusion.]*

Broke my fast after a long, cold walk and a meditation with cats and
Brandenburgs. When I first sit, I relax into a "place" I feel joy in
returning to—then the chatter and buzz of my mind that even for
an instant won't still, consciousness of my body, my thoughts and
"worries"—and always the recurrent morbid images: death, violence,
ugliness. Reminding myself: replace the old patterns with the abundant,
healing, transforming light.

I think that much of my life I have been feeling *Weltschmerz* as my own
pain. Beloved keeps asking me, "Are you sure the pain is yours?" and I
keep claiming it. But earlier she had said not "your *pain* has penetrated
your etheric body" but "your *attachment* to pain" has done so. Then it's
not the pain itself that is deeply a part of my being—only the habit of

---

11. Castaneda, *The Teachings of Don Juan*, 108.

it. *[This critical distinction: not even a wedge, just a tiny sliver, holding the door to the Sad Sanctuary of the Solid Suffering Self now very slightly ajar. It introduces into my mind a glimmering of doubt about the interpretive paradigms I hold so close, with such certainty.]*

"The pain is the pain of separation, of estrangement from the light, from the Source," Beloved tells me. "Be still."

•

An exciting walk this morning—sun, cold air, strong wind, grasses and trees blowing and shining. I fill my lungs with bright air, my heart with bright joy, my mind with bright light—and then ruckus with Chevy, who says, "I don't know if the amount of time we're having together is enough to sustain a relationship." She sees me withdrawing from her; I can see why. I am feeling impinged upon. What do I want? Pause. There's a part of me that would like to have all my time alone, to work, read, study, meditate, walk—yet I think this is not permanent, that it's a time of adjusting to this exciting new venture: spiritual inquiry, spiritual practice, my energies all caught up in it. *[Here I take the time actually to look within, to see what my impulse to withdraw means—and find both a self-protective reaction to demands and conflict and also a spiritual longing for solitude. This longing, inchoate yet unmistaken, is for the stillness that is at once aim, method, and gift of inward attention: natural wisdom. Not understanding this, I am drawn to withdraw.]*

Really, the most interesting things occur in meditation. Spontaneous image of plumping up my cells, electrons, molecules, as with a down comforter—to give them greater "conductance," greater capacity to conduct energy and light. And then tonight the top of my head actually opened, as if on silent, gliding hinges, and through me beamed an intense and focused light, as strong as a spotlight. I was a little frightened at first, but after all, I've been praying, "Perfect light, shine through me!"

•

❖ Dreams filled with broken things and cutting. ❖ Just before bed I had been writing a letter, but it was severe, without love or light; in it my edges were sharp—and I got it back in my dreams.

Oh, I have fallen into doubt, into skepticism. Is Beloved for real, is this all true? I do not really doubt—but I am now, here, doubting. Reading *Initiation*,[12] I find warnings about the dangers and responsibilities of attuning the body to a higher vibration, becoming conscious on this higher level. I feel queasy, frightened. Am I taking this on lightly? Am I able to make that commitment? Will I sustain it? Do I want to? *[These are critical questions for me, presenting repeatedly, even far along on my path in this lifetime. Much later I will see how important it is to recognize such questions in the spiritual aspirant or practitioner not only as signs of doubt but also as markers: choice points for authentic aspiration and commitment.]*

Dismay at the multilayeredness of time, space, reality, the Self: their complexity, immensity, boundlessness—and dismay that there probably *isn't* an end point, a "better time/space," a "spiritual" plane, beyond what we know here. *[If someone had said to me, "You're clinging to the idea of a heaven," I would have laughed. But am I not? Dualistic fixation: material vs. spiritual. Compelling. Illusory.]*

After the murders, in not—oh, these words are so hard to write—in not moving toward Marianne in love and care but in pulling away from her in fear *[and anger, my own murderous anger]*, did I incur a karmic debt to her that will weigh very heavily on me in another life? I remind myself that I will have another opportunity, I am not doomed never to be able to repay that debt, and I can discharge it in love, not fear. Perhaps she will reincarnate as my daughter and I will love and care for her.

How strange to find myself thinking these thoughts. They are utterly new for me; these are not the *ways* I have thought of things before.

And how to understand and work with such traumatic events? Maybe my lesson is about *not withdrawing*—about *being present in love* with others.

•

[The inner work begins to reveal its purposefulness and order now. Recognizing "being present in love" opens immediately into a period of complex work on manifestation: voice, expression, creativity, life purpose.]

To speak is a potent act. One that creates or destroys worlds, makes the seed grow or the rain come, brings or drives away the winds, brings the loved ones, and delivers to our ear the voice

---

12. Haich, *Initiation*.

of the divinity or opens our voice so that it may be worthy of being heard. To speak is a potent act. It brings life and opens the way to the land of the dead. When the word is true, when it has been strengthened in the interior of your heart, when it has grown in silence. [13]

Yesterday, great sadness, like the sadness that follows grief. Sense of entrapment in my college job, my financial straits, my craving for time and space in which to nourish my own mind, my own creativity, after all these years of putting my creative energies into nourishing other people's work. *[One sentence, six "my." That is entrapment.]* I want to create, articulate, manifest myself more directly in this life—not to make a mark, but to have the deepening, the joy, of expression.

❖ I am focusing on the men in this extremely heterosexual dream scene, feeling charming, beautiful, desirable, very alive. ❖ I awake with the thought that in the ideal world I'd be able to be close to both women and men.

Evening meditation. Meandering thoughts of how nice (meaning still, calm, ordered) it would be to live in a contemplative community—then: not yet, not until you've learned to "do it in the supermarket," as Beloved puts it. *[Leitmotif.]*

So many of my behaviors are subterfuges for withdrawal. Even meditation sometimes seems just a way to get some solitude, and my spiritual focus in part a flight from sexuality and intimacy. Smiling: I recognize myself in these maneuvers, yes.

February

Even my "spiritual" intention to become one with the light, with God, is self-serving. Light comes to shine *through* us in the work of love and service. I won't be enlightened just because I want to be, but only if and when I am ready to commit my light to love and service. My yearnings are still about myself. *[Here, a slender intuitive understanding of what is required for buddhahood: bodhicitta, the altruistic intention.]*

A week of crisis. It is *grief*—for my lost potential, for the ways I have

---

13. Bellesi, "Human Word, Sacred Word."

crippled and restricted the energy, intelligence, and creativity I didn't know how to discipline and channel, and that are now being depleted in my job—in a system in which the only faculty members who can be full human beings, creative professionals, and good teachers are those who have *wives.* I have nothing left. If I were offered a research fellowship right now I'd be unable to take advantage of it. Burnout. And the way to deal with *burn*out is to *get* out. So I'm going to take a leave from the college. First a real vacation, then begin seriously to work on developing alternatives to this job.

All is vibration. My inner work yesterday about Marianne: caught in a moment of terror, transformed by literally singing out a song of love. Terror is a pattern of energy, a vibration; love is the opposite one—and working directly with the love vibration *breaks up* the energy pattern of terror. So this is what is meant by "working at the subtle levels," and what I'm doing, too, with Beloved. I haven't really understood it till now.

A little trembly this morning, interpreting it as tiredness and illness residue—and just realized that it's really vibration. When I first awoke I felt feeble and "new." I am. I'm pulsing with life, feeling newborn.

The work is going so fast now, it's disconcerting, exhilarating, takes my breath away. My process of refining is rendering me so much more sensitive. I need to strengthen, too, in every dimension I am refining in. We must pass through wholeness of self on our way to union with the One. [14]

I've long said of myself, "I seem to lack some membrane others seem to have." Beloved asks me again, about my pain, "Is it yours?" and again, "Are you sure it's yours?" Of course it isn't all mine; tonight I understand that. All my life I have probably been just as sensitive, just as permeable, as I am now consciously experiencing myself to be.

[So many of these early entries record the learning of new concepts, ideas, vocabulary—and beginning to apply them, to see how they actually work. I am querying "how to be" and probing the relations of self and other, called forth by the commitment to be present in love. And I am sensing—tenderly, yet—the subtle. These are the ponderings of the nascent wisdom of discernment.]

•

14. See Wilber, *One Taste,* 128–30, for a pointed discussion on the relationship between spiritual and psychosocial development.

OY! All I have to do is be ready for a lesson and it comes to me. A colleague was hurt by something I said. I don't see other people getting into these kinds of stews and wrangles with each other. What is it about me or what I do that is so provocative to others? I seem to go around hurting people, out of unconcern with or insensitivity to their feelings. Well, in fact I don't *want* to be giving a lot of my attention to other people's feelings and needs—because I haven't yet learned how to do that without denying my own! Oh. Okay—I said "yet"—so maybe this learning is what's on the agenda. Part of "doing it in the supermarket." *[Beloved said, "You don't want to pay much attention to feelings and emotions because you know they're not real." I thought, "Huh?" I didn't know then that I knew that.]*

Whew. Chevy is hurting, too. The brilliant, precise intensity of our early loving—I feel threatened when we seem to be getting close enough for that intimacy, sensuality, and focus to shape our relating again. I don't know how to be intensely with someone else and intensely with and of myself at the same time. Oh, can I say this? *I want not to be interrupted.* What I'm doing with myself feels more important to me right now than my relationship with Chevy. And that is exactly what she is saying to me.

March

I learn to draw in the light. I am light, perfect, incorruptible light: *manifesting.* I know myself divine, love the body, the world, the human spirit that my light shines through—feel an immense, soaring gratitude and joy, sing praises, let my joy and light flood out into the world, into the universe, my thoughts becoming aligned with the One Thought. I am so blessed, I am so blessed.

Tomorrow I'll see Beloved again, after more than a month. I feel that now I am more ready really to work with her. Will reread my journal before going, to see what I've traversed, and how. In the old religions dolmens traversed the landscape; my journal is one of my dolmens now—it helps me orient, keep focus and vision. [15]

---

15. Dolmens: prehistoric stone monuments; I had seen them in northwest Bretagne (Brittany), standing like sentinels.

Later. All she saw was my "-ism": feminism and its "negativity."
Teacher, I found you harsh today, you flung *charges* at me: "You have
no control over yourself; you're in a rut; feminism is just jive, *nothing.*"
I'm being challenged to let go of attachment—to a *thoughtform.* I want
to wail, "*This* thoughtform is a *good* one, let me hold on to *this* one"—
but she says no, "Let go of your attachment to forms." *[Right from the
beginning, giving no quarter: let it go, let it go, let it all go.]* Such resistance I
felt to her, so separate, such pain. I wanted to have "done well" so my
teacher would be pleased with me. She was far from pleased with me.
She is saying that I'm stuck—until I let go of attachment to a form
that means separation. [16]

In timelessness, in the All-in-All, feminism is irrelevant, or something—
but here on the mortal Earth plane, where women suffer abuse daily,
it is relevant. *Feminism* doesn't separate—it is the *reaction* to separation
and conflict.

A flash of fear: she will send me away if I am not obedient and
quick enough to follow her.

Still smarting, still feeling separated from Beloved, I meditated,
reconnected with the light. What I saw: she and I are *both* rays of the
One. I do not need to fear what she has to say to me or to see the
issue as one of validation-invalidation. My own small, perfect light will
burn clearly, strongly. It will illumine my way. *[Over and over again this
true teacher will give me occasion and encouragement to see this truth. Sometimes
I see it, sometimes I don't.]*

•

16. When we contemplate letting go of attachments, it's the seemingly solid
things of the material dimension that we usually think of: house, money, children, spouse, job. However avidly we cling to these material things as "ours,"
we know we are not really our money or our house, not even our child or our
spouse. Our thoughts, on the other hand: no space between us and them—
until we see them one with the space-like nature of mind itself. Meditators
are sometimes astonished, even frightened, when first perceiving that we are
not our thoughts—but this fear vanishes, moment by moment, in the fierce,
liberating joy of recognizing mind's natural state, in which all thoughts arise
and dissolve. It turns out that not only are we not they, but they aren't even
any of our business! And this is not even to mention our attachment to attachment itself, which is where we are heading, dear friends on the path: we
are going to let go of attachment itself.

At the opening of the new college semester, I saw the room filled with light, each individual a shining ray—and together, how bright we were! Yet I'm so exhausted that I can't function, today the second day without meditation, I feel it like a headache. I don't want to do any more of other people's work! A leave of absence is a break but not a solution. It is *essential* that I create an alternative, a way to do holy work, right livelihood, without destroying my well-being and creativity. I feel drained and ashamed, yes, *ashamed*, to fall into in such disarray, as if I've learned nothing in all this time if I can be so unnerved, so overwhelmed.

❖ I dreamed that I was going to die of cancer, and in that dreaming I was robust, filled with light, health, vitality. ❖ Somewhere in the course of the day a quick flash of recollection, of a message while I was sleeping: I am to seek solitude.

Have begun a new meditation practice from Beloved. Felt that I couldn't lose my way with such light filling my eyes and understanding, that I could eventually see *all*, filled with that holy light of understanding. I am spiritualizing the body—becoming fully incarnate. *[So sweet, this innocent time of discovery, childlike and open, without preconception, seeking to understand, awed and wondering.]*

Told Beloved my disappointment that she hadn't seen how much work I'd done during her absence. She said, "Of course I saw it. That's why I pushed." For the first time I feel I am working *with* the teacher.

April

A lesson in the irrelevance of anger. I arranged a meeting with Beloved for my college class; five people came, three did not, and I was annoyed. We arrive; the room is arranged so nicely: five sitting mats. I give them the oranges I've brought: exactly five. All is as it is, perfect, whole, in harmony. From attachment to my idea about how it "ought to be," I chafed at how it was. Caught in the Ten Thousand Things, I missed, till later, the One.

Climbed up and into the woods to talk with my father *[who died when I was seven]*, my stepfather *[also dead]*, my mother, my sisters: acts of acknowledgment, forgiveness, appreciation. My father's gaze was like Beloved's, who said, "Only if you think you're separate from others will you be unable to hear, see, know them when they're dead."

May

Ah: I can choose, even when with others, to stay in the light. All I have
to do is choose—but *will* I? *[Willingness is key.]*

The vortex of energy and light draws me into perfect attunement,
into stillness and silence, where even my open-eyed gaze at another
seems like meditation. Exploring this new focus and concentration,
increasingly filled with knowledge of the oneness of all created things:
the Ten Thousand and the One are one. Meditating with Beloved, for
an instant I knew the bliss of stillness.

•

> I am
> beneath the wing
> of a great white bird,
> slow, measured
> beat,
> amber eye.

I seem to have passed some initiation; Beloved is working with me at
new levels. "It is my nature to bring unclarity to the surface," she said.
"I've been giving you some hard tests. I *know* you: after what you've
been dealing with, nothing is impossible for you!" Today, for the first
time, experienced partaking, with her, of the mysteries. "You are
making contact now with your soul nature," Beloved says. My teacher
is pleased with me.

*[From the time of our first meeting I am aware that Beloved knows more about
me than I know about myself. This inspires me to understand myself more deeply,
to look beyond appearances and into the subtle for understanding. It also orients me
to her wisdom voice as a source of validation. This may be a necessary phase in the
student-teacher relationship, securing a foundation for genuine devotion—but it must
be only a phase, for the entire purpose of spiritual development is the individual's
direct, authentic, unmediated realization.]*

The western sky is alight, mountains purple in silhouette against the glow
of the setting sun. How timeless a journey this is. It is the evolution and
perfecting of my soul and of the world that I'm about here. Yet how
time*ful*, too—for I've been rushing (and why not, after all: if all time is

now, then *do it now*), and the rush contains the assumption that I can "get there" in this lifetime. Is this just arrogance? Am I not to reach as far as I can, *now*? Am I not to believe, and act on the belief, that the wholeness and perfection of my soul *is, now*, and that I have only to lift aside the veil of form in order to realize and live this knowing? Am I not to believe that God is here with me *now*? Am I not to believe that I can be fully realized in this life, this body? I shall continue to hold this thoughtform of the immanent light, the indwelling radiance of my wholeness and perfection. All of heaven is shining through this evening's sunset . . .

["Lift aside the veil of form"—a mistaken notion, but one that persists in me for a long time. It is not the apparent veil of form that must be lifted but the illusory veil of ignorance. Absolute truth (emptiness) and relative truth (phenomena) are mutually interpenetrating, as the Prajnaparamita [Heart] Sutra sings: "Form is emptiness, emptiness is form." There is no veil.]

•

❖ I am in California, on my way to see Lola and Robert Redford. Their house is ordinary, on a shabby strip of highway outside Hollywood; the land is scrubby and bare. From the side door children rush out, one slightly handicapped, and a large dog. Much Sunday morning commotion, Robert frying pork chops and tomatoes, he and Lola enjoying each other, welcoming me casually, warmly. At one point Robert cuts Lola's hair, which, like his, is bleached and brittle; hers is mostly short, with a pony tail in back for Robert, who likes long hair, and she has a fairly pronounced stoop, as if she has for years made herself shorter for him. The view is of rusting cars and factory ruins, slag heaps, burned-out buildings. I realize that these people are here, in this ugly, blasted place, out of conviction and service. The life and beauty and warmth are *inside* their house, in how they love and laugh and care for each other. ❖ *[This dream stayed with me for a long time, and when I discovered it again upon first reading through the journals it touched me as it had in the dreaming. It is a dream of love, and love is what now begins to reveal itself.]*

Yesterday with Chevy I felt sorrow for the pain, and possibly the irreparable damage, done to our desire and delight in each other, through the fall and winter, the time of my closing off to her. I began to weep, intensely, deeply, almost keening. The image: "the breaking of the casing."

In meditation I began to cry, couldn't stop—saw an image of the universe, and I, another universe, identical, "as above, so below"—and of unconditional love as "all the atoms in these universes are just that: atoms in the universes." It seemed a sharp, precise moment of unconditional love: *letting be.* Maybe that's more neutrality than love—but—I don't know, even now, what I'm saying—no words . . . *[I had experienced isness, thusness: reality, inseparable from love.]*

Sitting by the lake with Beloved. My eyes dazzled, I begin to see lights as a web, and the faint suggestion of a path. Beloved, hand warm on my shoulder: "The path is always there. Are you ready to follow it?" "I don't know," I reply. She takes her hand away. Some doubt or hesitation in me. I feel regret, then interest and curiosity: if doubt, then something to learn in the doubt. *[When I am certain, the Teacher Mirror reflects certainty; when doubting, doubt.]*

This little illness is letting me be alone. But I don't have to be ill to justify doing nothing, seeing nobody, lying in bed, sleeping a lot, not cleaning the house: being alone. It is all, and always, about how I accept or resist taking full responsibility—for truly *being* who I am. Taking the time and space I need and want for myself, in relationship and out; taking responsibility for my own welfare, not subtly trying to give over that responsibility to others. *[How poignant is this intense struggle with myself about solitude—as if I have no right to it, as if it is somehow wrong, means taking something away from others. It is to be with myself, to be who I am, that I need to be alone. How wonderful! And how freeing—once I disentangle from my habit of withdrawal my authentic need for solitude.]*

June

> The mystic is ever conscious of duality. He is the seeker in search of light, of the soul, of the beloved. . . . He is a devotee and one who loves the apparently unattainable—the Other than himself.
> Only when he becomes the occultist does the mystic learn that all the time the magnet which attracted him, and the duality which coloured his life and thoughts and which gave motive to all he sought to do, was his true self, the one Reality. [17]

Struggling with what I sometimes perceive as the impersonality of the

17. Bailey, *Esoteric Healing*, 117.

universe and universal love—the endless, ever-changing continuingness of it all—that my being is forever, does not have a home, a destination where I may finally come to rest.

But I *am* the flux of all things, and contained in all. There is the "rest": that all *is*, that I *am*. *[Yes, but it is a long time before I can take rest in this. "Letting go of heaven" is indeed what this sounds like: letting go of attachment to the idea that truth, peace, love, oneness with the divine, are to be found somewhere else, somewhen else, not here, now, within me, within all. Though I "know" the immanence of the sacred, have glimpsed and recognized this truth, I have not yet integrated this knowing, and continue to struggle, to grasp, and to strive, for that which is realized in nondual presence.]*

•

"He guides me and the bird."[18] Here, the answer to the problem of evil, victimization, oppression, exploitation. So simple; such a completely new understanding for me.

Running this morning with the large, amiable neighbor dog, we startled a grouse by the roadside. The dog threw herself after the bird then dropped it at my command, the death already dealt. The bird lay at my feet, torn, her feathers scattering. I knelt and sang over her until her eye closed, breathing ceased, then lifted her into the brush and went on my way, no longer angry at the dog for its wanton, sportive destruction of that bright, free form—for I remembered the Browning poem, and said to the dog, "He guides both you and the bird."

Pain with Mother tonight. She says to me exactly what I feel about her: "I'm always wrong to you, you always criticize me," and hangs up on me, weeping. I feel rage, tell myself I must let go of my expectations and accept that she will never be emotionally direct and honest with me. *[It is shocking to see here my density, my lack of compassion. Nothing could have been more "direct and honest" than the hurt she expressed in that conversation.]*

I have accepted Beloved into my heart as my teacher, but I still fight her, too—in my refusals to treat her "importantly," to recognize her as master and us as her followers. I have only to truly love and accept

---

18. Browning, *Paracelsus*.

her in my heart, mind, and spirit to be one with God. *[I begin, here, to explore the critical, profound, perplexing question of spiritual devotion and surrender, although it will be awhile before I conceptualize it this way. I am intuiting that truly loving my teacher is the necessary, beauteous doorway—not at all understanding yet the relationship of self-responsibility and spiritual devotion: that surrender to the teacher is not about the teacher. I am also recognizing Beloved's spiritual authority, her spiritual power. To this I am deeply drawn and before it I am reverent (if not always outwardly respectful). And I am fighting this very power—power to draw me in, to dissolve me. I fear losing my self. No fool, I, at least not in this: the constructed self is exactly what is at stake.]*

The day began with the death of Colby *[Chevy's horse, named for a crisp, sweet apple]*. Shocking, how she fell suddenly to the ground as the vet administered the shot and jumped back: her mouth opening, her eye stilling, the life ebbing from her beautiful, suffering body. How hard it is for us to let go of the material form. In our bodies it is bodies we love, and oh, faces, bright, particular faces—how hard it is to have our last glimpse of a face we have come to expect to see.

Loneliness, feeling cut off and unconnected from Beloved, from other people, from the light—and tonight, ah, tonight I see that I have not been cut off at all. Ever since I last saw my teacher there have been friends in abundance: small red lizard, turtle, hummingbird milking the bleeding heart on my deck, Amazing Gracie, little calico cat, entering our lives on my birthday, wolf strongly crossing my field into the woods, grouse brought down by the dog and dying at my feet as I sang it on its way, Colby, at whose death I am privileged to attend. I am filled up, not empty, not alone, cut off, unconnected, but amply, radiantly filled and plugged in and joined and one and full of love and comradeship. How holy and sweet a moment is the one in which I understand this.

❖ Dream of fishing with pole and string. I play the fish on the line, feel it gradually lose its strength. It is trying to get under a submerged blue car. *[Blue is the color Beloved flashes in the subtle, like a signature.]* I hear it crying and say, "I'm going on with this anyway." I sense there's something I'm supposed to learn here, something like "love isn't an idea, it's a living reality." ❖

Am aware of love in me. Working with *love*. Only just beginning.

•

I begin now to sense the great spiritual family around me, behind me, with me.

A gathering at the ashram *[Beloved's residential teaching and retreat center]*. All day very much in a sense of separation. Instead of experiencing the fullness of Beloved's presence I preoccupied myself with pain at not being close to her, not being "special." *[So clear, here, the dance of transformation, how invoking the light brings up what blocks it—to be resolved, purified. To realize love I must walk through the illusion of separation.]*

I ask the Earth, What is my lesson from you? "Be gentle and tender with the form." ~ What is my lesson from you, Air? "Breathe deeply, I am life." What is my gift from you, Air? "Life, and oneness with all." ~ Fire, my old healer, Sun, my old friend, what is your lesson for me today? "Be still." And your gift for me? "Warmth and light, in the stillness." And what gift shall I give you, Fire? "Your open heart." ~ Water: "Motion, all keeps moving." Isn't that a little obvious? "Not to you!" From all, the next lesson: to open, to open, to open.

Ah, recurrent freshets of tears these days, longing for closeness with my teacher—oh, be honest, Barbara: *recognition* from her. Clearer now that all this pain is process, clearing out—and resistance to letting go, opening the heart, the step long guarded against—but this is the next step—I can go no further without an open heart—so it *is* happening, I *am* opening my heart, my *soul* is opening my heart.

Chevy again feeling insufficiency in our relationship—as usual, I then choose to feel impatient and burdened. Opening the heart, Barbara, opening the heart. If my personal love is insufficient for her, at least freely and fully channel the large, abundant, impersonal love.

"The person who goes on erring in the search for truth is always forgiven. It is a promise from the very depths of existence." [19] These words drop into my mind like rain. *[And still today they moisten, they solace and renew.]*

In my run this morning, the holy child standing in the road, brown and naked but for shorts, about seven to nine years old, gazing at me,

---

19. Rajneesh. Ambiguous journal notation; I have been unable to find the quotation.

gravely. I keep running, my heart suspended between fear and love: awe. And in one movement the child becomes God's holy deer, leaping away into the woods.

I am in the process of opening my heart (whatever that means!), and I observe how I . . . make this difficult.

•

A day of silence and sun—very slow, very lovely. If I go without words long enough the mind does begin to still.

Alice Bailey emphasizes that as the soul begins to "grasp its instrument, the personality," there will inevitably be a great increase in disease, disharmony, and distress. [20] Apparently all is not inevitably tending to perfection—there appears to be great *danger* inherent in the path. It is hard for me to conceptualize that the spiritual search could be "dangerous," or how. So I begin to think, well, if it's all so complex and dangerous, then I probably am not up to it. This isn't skepticism but self-doubt.

And yet I trust. I trust that the universe is basically ordered and creative, that the life energy of all beings and all things is the same, that love is the name for this order and this energy—and that it is possible to be one with this, one with God, creation, life, and love, in will, spirit, mind, consciousness . . . and in flesh. *[Credo.]* It is this oneness, this wholeness, which I seek to realize in myself. *[Et facio.]*

Ah yes, of course: the heart will open in its own time. My work is not to push, but to prepare and be ready. That is enough.

July

A deer goes all around the house, calm and beautiful. As I walk down the hill, a single deer suddenly in the road, waves and patterns of energy moving between us like a tunnel, spiraling, and I inside the tunnel with her. At the end of the morning a deer circles the house once again, love and quietude in that protective circle.

---

20. Bailey, *Esoteric Healing*, 193.

It was my arrogance and egocentrism that last night made the barrier between me and the visiting swami. As I prepared myself to meet him I was anticipating seeing God in him. That was quite right, but when actually in his presence I wanted him to acknowledge me as a seeker—so instead of meeting him with open heart and mind, ready to learn and receive, I met him with my will and desire engaged. *[Cautionary tale.]*

So, Barbara, why do you think you were given this remarkable perceptiveness, acuity, clarity of understanding that enables you so often to "see into," to know what is going on with other people? So you could be *compassionate*, that's why.

Paramahansa Yogananda's *Autobiography of a Yogi*—a very important book for me. I steeped in the world of devotion and practice, openness to the guru, wholehearted discipleship. Why am I not completely open to Beloved, why have I not wholeheartedly embraced her as my "guru" (besides the fact that she doesn't, in some ways, invite that)? Recalled her saying "I recognized you by your voice," recounting to me some of the circumstances of prior meetings in other lives, just as the masters did in Yogananda's book. She recognized me, but not I her. Truth is to be found within me, yes, but I want a guide, a teacher—I *want* to open my heart wholly to her, to her teachings. There is nothing she has taught or said that has not proven itself in my heart.

Yogananda's teacher: "[She] who rejects the usual worldly duties can justify [herself] only by assuming some kind of responsibility for a much larger family." [21] And this:

> Young yogi, I see you are running away from your master. He has everything you need; you should return to him . . . What one does not trouble to find within will not be discovered by transporting the body hither and yon. As soon as the devotee is *willing* to go even to the ends of the earth for spiritual enlightenment, his guru appears nearby. . . . Are you able to have a little room where you can close the door and be alone? . . . That is your cave . . . That is your sacred mountain. That is where you will find the kingdom of God. [22]

21. Yogananda, *Autobiography of a Yogi*, 288.
22. Yogananda, *Autobiography*, 161.

Tonight I am very aware of my oneness with Chevy, the evening we have agreed to be lovers no longer. Whatever problems our relationship has had, the fact remains that I just didn't love her enough.

•

Yesterday I heard the story of "The Mouse Who Went to the Sacred Mountain."[23] On the way to the sacred mountain the mouse meets a buffalo and a wolf; they are dying, can be saved only by the eye of a mouse. The mouse serves these "greater beings than he" by giving them his eyes; in return they help him on his way. Finally, he is blind and alone atop the sacred mountain. He hears the death-dealing eagle coming, feels its wings and shadow, its claws lifting him—then, rising into the air, he realizes with amazement that he is not dead. The eagle tells him to open his eyes and see. The mouse opens his eyes—and he has become the eagle! In meditation after hearing this story I rise up and fly above the mountain . . . and this morning I awake to a sky the color of grief.

It seems that it is possible to see God and fall again. I have the strong, strong sense that I have at some time "been further" than I am now. Why was I sent back? For lack of charity and love in me?

I think now that opening my heart is connected with knowing, forgiving, and releasing some great wrong I did in another life—the occasion for my fall, my separation from the One, my resistance, all my life, to *being here*, my yearning for God, my dream of being told, as I stand on the threshold, about to see God, to "wait a minute." Ah, now I understand my doubt and fear better. If I was once one with the One and became separate again, then how to accept myself as ready, trustworthy? Have I learned the lessons, have I paid my debts?

Meeting with Beloved at the ashram. She's late, we go to the shrine room where she leaves me, instructing me to "meditate on the open heart." I sit there alone for about forty minutes. Where has she gone, why did she leave, will she come back, this is ridiculous, what am I sitting here alone for? *[This isn't the open heart—more like the gaping maw!]* When she comes in—with her next student!—I flee, holding off tears—and,

---

23. "The Mouse Who Went to the Sacred Mountain" is a version of the story of Jumping Mouse, recounted by Hyemeyohsts Storm in *Seven Arrows*.

driving home, see that *in each moment* there I had the choice: to perceive sufficiency or lack, fullness or emptiness, her presence filling me with her caring and wisdom or her absence leaving me alone and in pain. *In each moment* I can choose to be open or closed, to be fully present, to let go of blame and shame and guilt, to align my consciousness with oneness instead of with separation. Driving home I was aware of wanting to close my heart: "She's not my teacher, I have to do it alone, no teacher is more important than direct experience, etc., etc." And I *choose* to keep my heart open, to ask for and receive her wisdom—I accept her and her teaching, and seek each time to learn from the confusion and disarray that I experience with her. *[Aspiration-doubt, longing-resistance, trust-mistrust—dancing, dancing in the light and in the shadows, and all reflected in the Teacher Mirror.]*

At the ashram, meditating, I am off in the cosmos, drifting calmly, blissfully—no time, space—the beginnings of sound—then, suddenly, the sun! so bright—and the high field grasses I'd bladed in the morning now swirling and spiraling around, forming into solar system, galaxy— then moving out of form again into shimmering bright colors. Beneath a tree I stretched out on my back, mind clear, body open, exposed and relaxed—awaking with surprise, pleasure: I fell asleep just like a baby—in the arms, on the bosom, of the Mother.

At lunch, suddenly, in his blissful reverie a Sufi focuses his gaze on me briefly—and like a shock wave I am taken by a surge of joyous excitement, catch in the throat: the wondrous is at hand. His "God-madness" has gone right into me. Moments later I am aware: my heart is opening. It is a beginning.

I just received the initiation of the opening of the heart from Beloved, in her glance, smile, gesture—confirmed by her words that initiation can occur just like that.

She is the dearly beloved, right before our eyes. Today she talked about the work that she has been doing for centuries, in a sequence of lives she told us about—but always, in whatever body, her work is the same: to bring us to a consciousness of our oneness.

Dear One, so much more your student and your servant now than before—imperfect in my self-concern, drawn to perfection, grateful and deep in love for your wisdom and love and generosity. Last night she looked across the shrine room at me, her face filled with love, and said, "I love you, too, Barbara, shining," after I said, "I love you, Beloved," right there in front of everyone. She praised me for "opening and growing." Her praise is inspiration to me, I breathe it in as an elixir of love, bask in it like sunshine—and then go right back to work.

When a friend cautions me about "guru-izing," seeking or seeing authority outside myself, I say I am submitting myself for the first time, consciously and freely, to the discipline of the teacher-student relationship. Yet she called me to recognize the ways I am indeed seeking to submerge my will and responsibility in a will "higher" than mine. It's good that I am opening myself more and more to Beloved—and good that I live elsewhere, good that I not throw away the checks and balances I have for being always reminded of my own responsibility for what I am doing. The teacher can teach me, but only I can do my own learning.

Large Group Retreat

Tonight, meditating: I am light, perfection, timeless, whole, God/divinity, essence—and with this affirmation, a surge of energy as the members of my subtle bodies arouse and recharge, flashing in a great arc around my physical body, violet, white, pulsing, waving—I am a *column* of energy, immobilized and in constant motion all at once, trembling and utterly still. Now I can't recall what produced that blinding/end-of-blindness illumination, now I don't *feel* any different—but illuminated I was, thoroughly.

My joy in loving Beloved is very great. The more I am joyful, the more of the beloved I find. I learn to trust myself more and more, little by little. Yes, yes, yes. Say yes to what is and it becomes *filled* with light.

Facilitating the large group, I knew a blissful, joyously contemplative experience of energy spiraling, bright with light and color, dancing, rhythmic, and lyrical. And oh, the singing at the end, music, song, passing *through* me. I, too, can make a joyful noise unto the Lord.

In class she said, "The imagination of the poet is the imagination of the heart, and the eyes of the poet become the eyes of the seer." And to me, tonight: "Where are the poems? I see them in your eyes."

In meditation, suddenly, in the Great Light, Christ appears to me—

gesture of expansive benediction and love—such delight and appreciation I feel: Ah, that's the Christ! I'd recognize him anywhere!

Met a young man in the group this morning who, when asked his name, said, "All." Thinking maybe he'd said Al, I repeated, "All?" "All," he said; "that's short for Everything." And his girlfriend, Miracle, said that everyone in their household had chosen such names and then one day took the *reverse* of their names for awhile—so All became Nothing and Miracle became . . . Nothing Special.

Off in the field, the near horizons shimmering and dancing—*le coeur content, la voix qui va bientôt chanter sa note, dans le coeur une grande paix: je reviens à mon* être [24]—I am coming home. First I thought I'd find the gift in the Earth, then in the sky, then I realize I'm finding it in the *meeting* of Earth and sky, in the shimmering where field and trees and sky meet. [*All my life it is in the intersections, at the borders, that I find the gifts. In painting, where two textures or colors butt up against each other, singing or shocking; in human endeavor, where aspiration and limitation dance, lyrically, fiercely, or chaotically; in working with people, where ignorance and wisdom reflect and refract in light and shadow; in war and illness, where life and death meet face to face; and in my own spiritual life, where conditioned-I and awake-I mirror each other and meet as one.*]

This morning I saw clearly that I came into the world "knowing" and then withdrew from manifesting, communicating, *being* fully my knowing. [*Ah, so that is what Beloved meant when she told me, "Don't withdraw. Withdrawal is also a withdrawal from consciousness and will make you sick."*]

Oh, the discoveries! Energy rising as light and sound within and through and around, all connected and pulsing as one beat, one heart, one thought, one mind . . . the ecstasy of oneness, oneness with other beings, oneness with All, the oneness of All. For the first time I actually *know* the experience of love and light and sound and energy moving in me, flowing through me to others. Ah, indescribable, how even to try in words—I want to sing and dance—I am drunk, mad, intoxicated, spiraling and whirling—

---

24. "Heart happy, voice soon to sing out its note, in the heart a great peace: I am returning to my *being*."

Godmadness: Spirals

Dervish whirling
Hasid dancing
Lover touching
Leaf swirling
Thought rising
I, coming home

Extreme vulnerability and receptivity now. *[This powerful time with my teacher has markedly intensified my energetic receptivity and I am now experiencing a subtly burgeoning awareness of permeability, interpenetration, intimations of self-lessness.]* Quavering, shakiness: am I going to disintegrate? Beloved says don't stop the energy, remain mindful that all is process: in the continuing flow all can pass through and I can sit in stillness.

(End of Large Group Retreat)

August

> When you do not realize that you are one with the river, or one with the universe, you have fear. [25]

Home again. Running, attuning with the land, the bees, loving Sassafras and Spider, those sweet, silly cats, picking black-eyed Susans and Queen Anne's lace for the house—aware of the energy in the Earth, in the sky, in me, in all I see, vastly more sensitive, the light and energy spiraling. Running, began feeling shaky, so walked, then felt really shaky, quivering, trembling, nervous. Aware that I was trying to stop the energy instead of letting it move through me, heard Beloved saying, "You can't stop it anyway, all you can do is block your awareness of it—so let it go, let it be."

So what am I afraid of? Dying? Yes. Oh. There is nothing to fear—so in meditation I gently, slowly, let the energy move through me—no dramatics, just let it be—and welling up in me: a gladness of trust, a softness of being—I am, we are, it is, we are one, *let it be*—

---

25. Suzuki, *Zen Mind, Beginner's Mind*, 94. Suzuki points to the direct experience of oneness as the resolution of fear. I was at a more primitive stage; intimations of oneness were arousing anxiety and fear in the experience of self's apparent solidity being revealed as illusory.

What I've been experiencing as fear-trembling is really just the universal vibration in me. It is *life*.

I am learning that the block or pain is precisely the door through which I move into the next level of wholeness. So this week, experiencing pain, grief, in working at the throat, I know it is the pain of growth. It hurts, so this is where I am opening now.

❖ In the dream Beloved smiles and dances while still—and by the vividness of her presence, her eyes, and her smile, I know I am really in her presence, not psychologically dreaming. ❖ I heard sound, in sleep consciousness—like wind, but way out in space, a wind/air that carries time and consciousness.

The beginnings of a poem about fear, but I don't know what to do with it yet (hmm, metaphor as metaphor):

> The light glints
> on my fear: it shines
> huge, without form,
> bigger than faith, & has edges
> that tear me
> apart. I am
> stricken, I want
> only to trust and here's
> terror again

I keep running into fear in the gut, solar plexus, bowels, icy, in head and heart. Beloved: "Transmute fear with light. Call the light down, surround and irradiate yourself with light." I ask her what it is I'm afraid of. "Of falling. We all fall; it's nothing." I ask, "Did I kill someone?" "We all do; no reason to get upset about it." Ah. No attachment, no ego.

Oy! It's about *giving up the fear!* Of course. The pain is the door.

•

The beginnings of my new growth phases are pretty spectacular, as in this work with Beloved—each phase introduced with full fanfare and then slowing down, sometimes almost to the point of immobility. After the extraordinary heights of sensitivity and awareness that I experienced while with her at the group retreat, now I am aware of the phase that follows the "preview of coming attractions": the steady, consistent work that will enable me to be conscious of, fully responsive to, and responsible for those powerful energies and sensitivities.

Aware of the gradually increasing impersonality of my love for people. She is teaching me detachment even from myself, from who I imagine "myself" to be.

A burst of laughter at the end of meditation: "Enlightenment wants to happen in me all of a sudden, if I can just let it!"—for tonight, again, I am flooded with energy, again directly to and in the heart—so powerful, as if I were quite literally bursting open. Felt frightened—opened my eyes, focused on the candle, and called aloud for the light to come down, to surround, protect, and irradiate me, to help me stay open to the great surge and pulse of love, life force, within me—and sat through it as it gradually diminished in intensity. But just look—this keeps happening—I keep saying, "a little bit at a time," but God keeps hitting me over the head! Oh, the flooding into my heart, so intense, I thought I was going to pass out—the opening of the heart, the filling of the heart. I am sought, even as I am seeking.

> However great a person may be in holding the thought firmly in mind, [she] cannot bring about as great results as a person who loves the object [she] holds in concentration. Love is all powerful, and it naturally gives power to one's concentration . . . Whatever one loves one gets, small things or great things. [26]

I don't need or want to be special to Beloved in a personal way; from her what I want and need is precisely what she is giving me, her guidance, help, and challenging: her teacher self, her bodhisattva self. If she loves my person as well, terrific—but not necessary. *[And how I will suffer, as the years roll over me, from grasping for her "loving my person."]*

●

26. Khan, *Mastery through Accomplishment*, 17.

Jct. Rtes. 202 and 15

Leaf settles.
Tall grass leans,
rises again,
bearing its new weight
lightly.

A bit of light coming in now. This past week has been a swamp. I scared myself more than I thought with the power of the energy and light as I opened so fully at the group retreat and afterward—instead of slowing it down I actually closed down, battened down the hatches. It sure felt dark and tight in here all week, yup.

August

Love's too humid for me
right now. I look for the crisp,
the dry—moss crackling
beneath my feet, buzz and tick
of noon meadow, wine-crisp
air on tongue, throat
ready, anticipating, stars,
each distinct,

separate,

in a night that promises
no rain, no fog. Lover's touch
is moist, breath moves air
around me, voice slides
through my thoughts that want

space between them, pulsing,
silence, everything open,
potential.

The rich belly,
the heat of the gravid
breast—no, let me be
alone awhile, I want this:
precise solitude,
whir of planet,
click of beetle,
this particular self
in its time.

Forest Retreat

Yearning for solitude, for quiet rest in nature, I sit now in a wilderness lean-to, rain playing a gentle tattoo on lake and roof. Some small woodland creature goes about its nest building in one corner of my little three-sided home, a candle burns before me, I have offered prayer and song at lakeside and sweet sandalwood incense here in my shelter, napped briefly in the stillness, fallen into the water and so had the short dip I thought of. I have read a little of Hazrat Inayat Khan, who speaks of finding one's purpose and accomplishing the purpose one finds, no matter how small. [27] I have meditated and am peaceful. I settle into the evening, into the solitude, wanting to find the sacred within me in this place I am finding sacred—small temple, very still. And here comes the rain now, a curtain for me, a veil of silver in the silvery evening light, individual drops silhouetted against the flat pewter of the lake.

Ha! The power of thought in oneness with all: the *instant* I committed myself to being warm and reached for my sleeping bag, that *instant* the reluctant embers burst into flame!

A gentle morning, but night was filled with wakings, violent. Thunderstorm and heavy, strong rain; a tree fell nearby in the forest, with a great crash, and loons cried, one close by, another at the far end of the lake, wild hoots, then a rhythmic call back and forth. I awoke in the night, tossed awhile before sleeping again; don't know how the wooden *banc* that is so hard and narrow during the night is so spacious and cozy in the morning! Today is cold and gray, a good time for this little fire that is now murmuring merrily as I eat my apple.

---

27. Khan, *Mastery.*

Don Juan told Carlos: "We choose only once. . . . We choose either to be warriors or to be ordinary men. A second choice does not exist. Not on this earth."[28] I think I made that choice in my childhood *[well before that, more likely]*, and have been confused ever since about how to act on it, until I began to work with Beloved.

A flock of ducks, circling once toward the setting sun, then rising, wheeling directly above me, the dry thrum of their wingbeat thrilling my blood in the cool, bright evening air—heading south, as our winter approaches.

It was *cold* last night, and this morning has the distinctness, the specificity, of goodbye. A hawk appears silently above the center of the lake—gyres up, up, and up into air, minute adjustments of wings and tail—then moves off, easily, slowly, directly to the northwest.

(End of Forest Retreat)

•

The visualized meditative forms: I am now attuning more with their universal qualities, and with that which contains me, is beyond me, of which I am a part. Though I am still questioning what my work is, my purpose, it's no longer my own creativity I'm seeking to give expression to but the Creative for which I am seeking my own expression—and the work I want now seems more closely allied to service, less ego-directed. But I am so good at sounding high-minded. In the interest of honesty: yes, there's a part of me that says, okay, no ego—but let my work be prominent, shining!

September

Tonight, *fear.* With each great creak in the house the fear starts up abruptly, a leap in the throat: center of manifestation, creativity. Does the fear come up to block me here, or is it with fear that I have blocked creativity, blocked bringing the thought, the inspiration, into manifestation? This is intellectualizing; the point is to get through it. I know what I have to do right now: put the pen and journal down and get back to meditation, like getting right back on the horse. Here goes.

---

28. Castaneda, *The Teachings of Don Juan*, 271.

I have been judging myself for the ways in which I still want to be "there" instead of "here," in nirvana instead of samsara. Even if we are all *now* God, now I am God in a body, in a limiting form. It is my oneness with God, my perfection and divinity *without* limitation that I seek. Oh, as I began to write these words I saw what I am really seeking: full God-consciousness, oneness with God, oneness with my own perfection and divinity—*while* in the human form. To know the absolute *within* the limiting frame. *[This insight pulses through the years. It is Immanence speaking.]*

Meditating late tonight, I am overcome with the sweet surge and draw of the light and energy, feel frightened, keep it moving. In the meditation a cow comes to visit, large, palpable, warm: hello, cow.

•

I want my light back! What can such a cry mean? How is it that I so waver in my consciousness, my awareness, of the ever-presence of the light? *[Aha! That is the question. The "light"—truth, awareness, so many beauteous names for that which cannot be named. It is unwavering. What wavers, just for an instant, is our recognition of it.]*

Meditation with the remarkable clarity and fluidity of consciousness that I've come to associate with the Heart Sutra: expanding, mobile, transparent. This evening a friend told me about *bardo* after-death experiences, where all one's projections appear, the things most feared, most desired. He said that in preparation for conscious, choiceful reincarnation, not forgetting one's level of spiritual development, it is important to master these fears and desires. Working with them before death is one way: I could, in meditation, work directly with the terror energy, get to know it, take its lessons, dispense with its forms.[29]
    ❖ In my dreams there was something terrible, something frightening. I reminded myself that only God is, that this was just a projection, that it had no reality, no power, other than what I gave it. ❖

Trying to be mindful of silence and speech. I talk too much, too freely,

---

29. *Bardo* (Tibetan): "gap," here referring to the intermediate state between death and rebirth. See especially Padmasambhava, *The Tibetan Book of the Dead*.

about my "spiritual" or "healing" experiences; I am abusing the power in doing this, it is a way of attracting attention to *me*. *[This lesson is long in coming.]*

Elisabeth Haich, on learning to keep silence:

> I learn to keep my urge for communication . . . carefully . . . under control . . ., and through this constant self-observation, I gradually form the habit of listening inwardly, whenever I want to say something, to be sure I have authority to say it. . . . And I come to recognize two beings in my self: a personal ego which is often inclined to chatter, without control, purely for the sake of communicating and attracting attention to my person—and in the background of my consciousness a higher self which restrains my personal ego, telling it when and what it is to speak or do, and when it is to remain silent or passive. The important thing is to pay attention and obey the orders of this higher self. Merely to hear its commands is not enough. [30]

With a new friend, climbed Pate Hill for the setting of the sun. A deep, dusty rose suffused the western sky, the woman-form mountains silhouetted against the changing colors and then against the translucence of early night—the rising of the full moon from behind the lovely mountain a brilliant white glow, then the moon, freeing herself slowly, delicately, from the topmost tendrils of the tallest trees, flooding us and the landscape with a clear, powerful, mysterious light, our shadows stretched out long and thin behind us across hilltop and meadow.

With this friend's visit I learned how confusing and insulting my controlling behavior is for others. That I can be deeply honest, honor my own feelings and act on them, my own needs and take them into account: I can *be who I am* when with another. That with another person, too, I choose from moment to moment whether to be separate or one with. That I have not been a sexually or emotionally honest person, not even with myself—*because* of not being so with myself, because of *not knowing* what I felt, what I wanted, what I thought. Denying desire, my own desire—that's more serious than giving over my body to someone else's desire that I didn't share.

Tonight I saw again that my purpose is to *be* the light. Literally. The first

---

30. Haich, *Initiation*, 237.

answer is the one to heed. I asked what my purpose was 'way back last summer—and the clear vision, the answer, was this: *to be* the light.

October

> In the spiritual disciplines, the person who has developed direct, *experiential* knowledge of spiritual realities is the real authority, not the one who has not had the experience but has done a lot of reasoning about it. And the function of the real authorities is not to tell others what the ultimate nature of reality is, but to teach people how to experience it for themselves so that their knowledge will be direct. *[This is the work of the master. This is what Beloved is doing with me.]* [31]

Sitting quietly, phone off the hook, a bowl of rice steaming, feeling good about giving myself time and space for clearing work—and my dear neighbor arrives, deep in tears for her dying father. I was first dismayed at being interrupted then glad I had done some clearing, so I was ready to be fully there for her. *[Signs of movement in my struggle to balance being with self and being with others. "I can be who I am when with another"—I am trying this on. In the medium of spiritual practice, the self-confusion is beginning to break up a little.]*

I am beginning to recognize that enlightenment demands *total devotion* to the path. Ah, how far I am from making that choice, even though I say that "oneness with God" is the only thing I want. *[I love seeing this recurring note: recognizing what is called for, recognizing my current state in relation to it. These periodic observations reveal the clarity that many years later will help me understand how spiritual despair can root, but doesn't have to, in the gap between aspiration and realization—and begin to see and take responsibility for the missing link: sincere, sustained, selfless engagement. Until then I suffer, more sharply as the years go by, in the thought that I am characterologically incapable of enlightenment, despite the depth and intensity of my longing—and of my subtle certainty. Very gradually I acquire and work with the blessed understanding that the necessary character is created by the practitioner, step by step walking the path from aspiration to accomplishment.]*

Second day of drilling the water well here at home, now down more than

---

31. Tart, *Transpersonal Psychologies*, 91.

two hundred feet—and dry. I feel upset, then attune with the water running deep beneath the Earth. She's a lady, swimming, sleeping, dreaming deep; she sings a low, quiet song, a dream song of watery consciousness, of watery sleep, of the massive rock ledge above her, the deep, still, dense matter around and below, the sky she has never seen—but she is sister to rain, to snow, they dream one another, they are one in the skies, in the depths of the Earth. I call you now, dream sister, watery one.

Well (so to speak), the waters came. The deeper the drilling went, the harder I had to work at letting it be easy! There was weeping this day, and the sky sent water, too. I laughed out loud: water coming from and to everywhere but where I was asking for it.

❖ I am lying on a large rock, suddenly see that it has the immanent shape of a woman's face and body. I break off a piece and her face is revealed. I bring my lover to see this beautiful rock sculpture. We reach the rock place—and the rock is gone! I look about, more in wonder than in disappointment, and see, standing against the horizon, the rock woman, beautifully etched against the sky. ❖

Reading an article on Christian mysticism, I know again that my connection has ever been to God, the ground of my being, never to Christ as my way, my path. As I read materials in the Eastern traditions I recognize my more open response: this is language that I can hear, these are ways of knowing the absolute that I apprehend. Though as I write this I also recall the intense experiences of my adolescence that were more akin to what I read of in the Christian tradition: the emotionality, the highly colored, subjective intensity, the extreme longing, the anguished sense of separation from God, the painful search for humility—but perhaps those who follow Buddhist paths know these kinds of states, too. *[We'll see . . .]*

I am in the process of some subtle shift in consciousness now, or in awareness, conscious intent—shifting from immersion in the experience of energies and light toward something more . . . austere? Aware of calling on my own buddha nature, visualizing this, referring to it—something about being more "pointed," somehow—"one-pointed"? Something different in meditation—nice to have the strong flow of energy, the lights, but these are not the *point*—the *point* is . . . is . . . is . . . ?

"Letting go of the teacher to receive the teaching"—knowing the next step is from seeing her as a buddha to seeing myself as a buddha.

Becoming fully who I am means taking on *my* buddha nature, too. The point is: to embrace fully my own divinity. Now.

•

At the ashram. Going deeper into the silence. Still calling attention to myself—but less.

The main thing I learned from these four days at the ashram: I am mostly ego—bloated, inflated, self-seeking, posturing, affected, judgmental, petty, vain, self-serving, rigid, controlling, pretentious, arrogant, deluded, hypocritical. I could go on and on. *[And do. This is what I call a "negativity litany."]* [32] So different from how I experienced myself in the recent teachings, love flowing through me freely and sweetly for others.

I feel that I am responsible for absolutely every *contretemps*, misunderstanding, unpleasantness that occurs between me and another person. All the discord or disharmony I was aware of while at the ashram was somehow initiated by an act, word, or attitude of mine. I wonder how

---

32. A note about these occasional negativity litanies, in which I probe and apprehend multiple textures and qualities of the negativities I identify. Beloved had told me, "What you focus on you magnify," and indeed I see how focusing on negative qualities of self magnifies grasping both to illusory negativity and to illusory self. Good to see our faults so we can *abandon* them. But these litanies of mine—sometimes painful, sometimes comical, sometimes both—are not just ejaculations of self-loathing or disgust; they also show that I am beginning actually to search out and to *perceive* the operations of ego, the conditioned self. This is a sign of clear intention, and a sign, small but certain, that the process of ego-dissolution has begun. When we're completely identified with ego we don't see it at all.

I didn't begin to understand what negativity really meant until I began recognizing, identifying, and naming my negative thoughts and emotions, individually, specifically, precisely, accurately. For example, understanding that anger is a "negative emotion" can allow us to take responsibility for what is obvious, overtly recognizable anger. It does not mean, however, that we understand "anger" to include even the subtlest flutterings of aversive reaction that, unrecognized and unresolved, can become the overpowering waves of rage and hatred that we ascribe to others' pathologies—because we don't see their seeds in our own mindstreams. My negativity litanies were like data from microscopic assays, allowing me to see the seeds and their stages. Very, very useful in my inner work. Until we recognize what we are experiencing and seeing for what it really is, we are unable to take full responsibility for our own minds: to tend well our seedbeds of cause.

I could ever have thought myself innocent of any of the difficulties, from slight to significant, that my relationships have known.

Have a little humility, Barbara. I don't want to energize this self-disgust and self-condemnation *[this focus on* self*]*. Going into the silence now is a *necessity*. It is time for me to go to the *source* of speech and act: to the void, the stillness. In my solitary practice is the humility my public practice so missed last week.

Meditation tonight—sweetness flowing through me. Felt my body *simply being* while I floated around inside it—wondrous. But I chickened out yet again, feared to let the experience just take me. Barbara, it is time to keep going.

•

I like it when the karma gets back right away. I hung up on Chevy yesterday, and last night in my dream: ❖ I saw the neighbor's two big draft horses and another bay in my field, hindquarters to, while I was talking on the phone with Chevy. I was excited, they were so beautiful, then they turned, wheeled, and came fast toward the house. I said, "Oh, they don't destroy houses, do they?"—laughing at my sudden fear, saying, "Chevy? Chevy?" as I realized there was no response from her—she had hung up on me! ❖

While I was standing outside, between the house and the car, my dead stepfather came to me—filled my whole heart to overflowing with love—our first loving connection ever. *[A sudden, subtle event, unbidden and without external referent, that changes the nature of my relationship to him completely and permanently, such that even my memories of our unpleasant historical relationship are free of even the most subtle negativity. Not only the interpenetration of what we conventionally think of as the separate realities of life and death but also the illusory nature of phenomenal experience itself are apprehensible in this event that lasts less than one second.]*

•

I haven't yet made the final commitment to service—have not (in this life) taken the bodhisattva vow. Very focused on self; even my thinking about teaching is about me, not about helping others. Saw this morning that the way to release my creative energies is to put them into *service*. If I think only of me, I won't budge. If I call myself back to sharing something of value with others—ah, then there's a possibility of movement.

> A story of the Baal Shem Tov, the Master of the Good Name, founder of Hasidism, a spiritual leader in southeastern Europe about 200 years ago: The day after Yom Kippur, he drove out to the forest, stopping when he came to an inn in the middle of the forest. The innkeeper, a Jew, greeted him: "Oh, Rabbi, I have been wanting to see you. I have something terrible to confess." The man lived isolated in the forest with his family, far from other Jews; he had tried, but failed, to find a way to pray together with other Jews at least once a year, on Yom Kippur. This Yom Kippur he was determined; he set off with his family. En route, remembering that he hadn't locked the door of the inn, he sent his wife and children on and rode back. As he was locking up and preparing to leave, customers started coming in; soon it was too late to go and he saw that once again he would have to pray alone on Yom Kippur. But he was even without his prayer books, which had gone on with his family! He told the Baal Shem Tov: "I am an ignorant man and all I know of Hebrew is just the alphabet. So what I did was to stand up and face Jerusalem and I just recited the alphabet, *alef-bet-gimul-dalef*, a-b-c-d, and I said to God: Here, God, here are your holy letters, you put them into the right words and put the words into the right order." Baal Shem Tov put his arms around him and said, "It was revealed to me in a vision that on this Yom Kippur your prayers had opened the gates of Heaven, and I came to you to find out how to do it." [33]

Although I am attracted by and interested in the "energy action" during meditation—the *son et lumière*—I am headed for something else: union with the One, with God, realization of my buddha-self. Tonight aware of Lord Buddha, Beloved Buddha, and Barbara Buddha. *[Increasingly one-pointed, because increasingly allowing myself to know what I know.]*

> As the personality comes under the sway of the higher Self there is a corresponding tendency to view other people in the light of their higher potentialities and to evaluate them less in terms of their overt behavior as personalities. [34]

33. Kaplan, "Hasidism and Zen-Buddhism."
34. Srigley, "Hamlet: An Esoteric Approach."

Every now and again I have a glimpse of the nonreality of me, this personality, this personal identity that I construct and cart around with me—and, increasingly, of the nonreality of other people's personalities, also. The trouble, of course, is that neither my personality nor anyone else's likes to be not taken seriously—so the question is how to take the personality seriously . . . as a manifestation of the being it is striving to realize. *[Taken as practice, this points to sacred outlook, pure view.]*

I awake in a sweet peacefulness, Spidercat curled into my belly, Sassafras on the back of my head; we all curl and purr. The house is chill, the fire wakes right up; I wash with water warmed on the stove, and meditation is punctuated with bursts of sunlight enlivening lavender mountains and brown-green field, a floodlight for the valley floor.

Invited tonight to serve on the ashram governing board. First reaction demur, but Ruth said, "This *is* the work. We need those who are in the light, who have consciousness, and your energy and clarity are rare." That was more persuasive than the slight guilt trip; get me in the star trip and you've got a good chance of getting me!

[This juncture brings me into a landscape alight with potential for waking up from the dream of self; I will find myself at some points turning toward the light source and the waking, at others seeking the relief of shadowy sleep. On this crucial evening, although I have promised myself not to, I step into close involvement with Beloved's activities, organization, and community: no more "safe distance." Such closeness is both an opportunity and a danger for the practitioner.[35] The opportunity: that one's defenses and pretenses—the "I, me, mine" that we often name "ego"—may be incinerated in the revealing, annealing fire of the teacher's purifying love. The danger: that one will blame the fire for being hot, and recoil from the blessed burning.

I fully experience both the opportunity and the danger, starting that very evening. I decline a particular task and Beloved rebukes me for it. She has confronted me before, and sharply, but this rebuke is caustic, mocking, and I am shaken, distrusting both my discernment and her harshness. Instead of voicing my disquiet I cover it

---

35. "Staying near an enlightened teacher is said to be like staying near a fire. If you have enough faith and confidence in him, he will burn away your ignorance and obscurations. But if your faith and confidence are inadequate, you will be burned yourself" (Khyentse, *The Heart of Compassion*, 77–78). The acute danger is not that the disciple will feel pain but that she or he will turn away from the path, from bodhicitta, from the potential to awaken for all.

over—and with it an opportunity to clarify my confusion about the distinctions between dependency and respect, self-responsibility and devotion, submission and surrender. Here, when Beloved shakes me in my slumber, I open my eyes, recognize the shaking, but do not rouse myself to meet the moment.]

•

It seems different now, with my practice, a new phase: working directly with *qualities of being*. With a little rush of tears I see, this morning, that I am working, not with the heart center, but with that which the heart center, open, reveals: compassion. I feared I never could, never would. And always, gratitude for all that is given—so simply, so directly.

Yesterday I saw something about how other people respond to me, the many who speak of my "great power." It's not about personality, it is about a quality of *being*. Beloved says of herself, "It is the nature of this being to bring to the surface whatever is unclear." Now I can say of myself, "It seems to be the nature of this being to call into full presence those who engage with her." *[When this call comes principally through the personality vehicle, it can be clumsy, harsh, tendentious, importunate; when through spiritual clarity, in love, it is clear, liberating, truth calling forth truth, love calling forth love—as Beloved had said early on: "opening people to realize themselves."]*

❖ Vivid, lively images of people being "blown away," over a cliff. Walking near the cliff, I know fear, great fear. Coming toward me is a group of women, holding on to each other to protect themselves from being blown away. They are lurching along, making some headway in the ebbs of the wind and just barely managing to stay on the ground during the gusts. I plan to throw myself into a roadside ditch if another dangerous gust threatens to blow me away. ❖ *[Cliff: frequent image in my dreams and self-reflections, powerfully evocative and attractive. Terrifying threat, terrifying freedom.]*

November

Marianne is dead. She killed herself, in Greece, about a month ago. Completion of a tragic cycle. Marianne. Sister, friend. *[This is all very well, but what I remember is sitting in a field at the college, the pitiless letter in my hand, staring blindly into space, my heart an empty cave, my tears a waterfall.]*

❖ Strange, detailed dream about a young woman lost, caught, or abandoned in a large house—on an island?—left there by a man she'd gotten involved with. The house is high, at least three stories; perhaps just a summer house but very sumptuous. I feel her mounting desperation and panic, then her despair, as she realizes she has been left and will die there. In the bathroom are bits of letters she's been writing; one, to a girlfriend, is a scrawled scream. Has she perhaps been very ill? Is that why she'll die if she's abandoned here? I see a downstairs bedroom, very lush, a bed unmade. Does this mean the girl might be found, that someone's been here recently and might soon return? Much later, I see that the house is on an ordinary residential street, and to have escaped the girl would have needed only to walk out the door. I realize that she has in fact died in the house. I lose sympathy for her plight, am angry that she didn't save herself—and then I realize that for her the house must have indeed been on an island or of course she would have saved herself. ❖ When I awake it is early; the sky gradually lightens, reveals nothing, I see nothing: the window is blank and white, the world has disappeared in a massive fog. I realize that this is what the girl saw when she looked out the windows of that house: nothing at all, no matter where she looked. I think this must have been a dream about Marianne. *[The bell tolls quietly here, in this dream that allows me to experience as Marianne experienced, breaking down separation and judgment, opening me to greater understanding and compassion for her.]*

In the night, aware of the flu-like illness in my body, instead of fighting or giving in to it I simply let it be—my consciousness not in the illness feelings of the body but in the self that was neither body nor illness.

•

Meditation. Calling for help, calling on Beloved, on all my teachers and guides, on Mother Mary—petitioning for help in putting aside the veils of ignorance, doubt, conflict, ego that separate me from . . . from Beloved, from service to her, from my oneness with the light. I saw Beloved in pain, being broken, and wept.

Seeing sharply how great is the gap I place between commitment and responsibility, capacity and will. Beloved told me many months ago that there is nothing I can't do, but tonight I couldn't even clear away my own inner agitation to give her a space for rest after teaching. This is the first time I can remember sorrowing for not loving another well enough to forget *myself* for her.

She told me that I'm only recently become a woman, suggested that if I looked into my past lives I would see why I became a woman this time. *[She and others told me that formerly, as a man, I had been abusive with women, shaping this lifetime's experiences as a woman in relation to men.]* Later, to myself as a monk in past lives I posed the question, "Why did I come as a woman this time?" The answer: "Because the world needs *active female energy.*" *[One question, two answers. The first is about karma, pushing us from behind, the second about spiritual aspiration, drawing us forward.]*

•

Oh, I'm finally really understanding it: When I'm hurt I'm to give love, when I feel scarcity I'm to offer to another, when I'm sad I'm to bring joy. I think someday I'm gonna be a grown-up—and then finally young, really young, for the first time. *[Yes: new.]*

❖ I'm sharing a room with a male colleague at our faculty retreat. As I bathe in a huge tub, we are both filled and flowing with desire—I *crave* his body, want him inside me—we acknowledge these feelings to each other but we don't make love. I'm aware, in the dream, that this sudden sweet flood of desire must be why this man sleeps with so many women. In the midst of my own luxurious, compelling desire I am no longer feeling judgment about this—only sweet regret that *I'm* not going to make love with him! ❖

Meditation. Oh, all I have to do is *be*. Again I've been trying to *move* the light and energy, the healing flow. All I have to do is *be* in it, *be* it.

December

Beloved has expelled several students for trying to undermine activities at the ashram, told me that to work there is a privilege: "Those who work against it won't be able to stay." I felt so sad, my heart went out to them—and, yes, admit it, an instantaneous alarm: So one *can* be kicked out. I, too, could be kicked out! Oh, what would it be like to be living in the world rejected by Beloved? *[Not seeing, then, that it would be not rejection but correction—and that their expulsion came not from Beloved's rejection of them but from their rejection of her.]*

Fiery dreams, fiery temper flare-ups, fiery sexual feelings, compulsive eating, "feeding the furnace"—all this characterizes the past few weeks. And many images of fire burning down my house, so I go to the ashram to live. Ah, but this is not the way to do that. Beloved: "The fire is the fire of purification and transmutation. Greet it as a friend; do not energize the form of it burning down your house." So now I am making friends with the fire, beginning to work with it at the subtle levels, imaging the fire purifying my ego, my pride—"burning down the house" I've been living in so the essence can be free.

It certainly is hard work being really honest with oneself. I recognize my perceptions; the hard part is to bring them to the forefront of my awareness—and to act on them. So incredibly risky: to act on what I know to be true. Even when I don't know or understand why, how, what it means. *[Sometimes "to act on" may mean simply to see, to recognize, and not to react.]*

I want to record a good lesson. Beloved's closest student had been in great pain and one day Beloved just said to her, "I haven't slept for two nights because of what you're working with—so now would you please sit down here with me and *just do it.*" Oh, let me take that as *my* lesson. Maybe *my* work, *my* blocks, are part of what she is always working so hard to transmute—so let me take the responsibility for myself. There is no reason to wait and every reason not to. Don't even need to know what it's about, more specifically than ego and ignorance, and no need to—just clear it out, clear the way.

"You were stifling your creativity," she said to me some time ago. And now Paramahansa Yogananda: "You have choked with doubt and laziness the fountain of creative power within you. Clear it out!"[36]

•

Loving Earth, all her beautiful moments and places, sights held dear in the heart: tree, ocean, mountain, sky, meadow. Cradling Earth in

---

36. Yogananda, *The Movement Newspaper.*

my arms, solacing, loving, caressing. Aware of all given, wanting to return it in full. And my relationship with my own human mother, so confusing and conflictual: giving to her simply out of respectful recognition of her as Mother, the one through whom I came here this time. With these seeings came tears welling up from deep inside, deeper than the heart, way down in the belly, seat of my relatedness with Earth and Mother.

First-ever reading with a spiritual channel. [37] I am to release the sense of unworthiness of the self, accept God's plan for this plane, release sorrow and disappointment that things and people were not as I wished them to be. Spontaneous imagery during the session: I shout in anger, frustration, and disappointed love at Mother. *[These three emotional reactions will surface again and again to show me the poverty of self-clinging and wounded entitlement]*. I see her turning away, going to God, and as she becomes filled with light my love can flow out to her. I grieve for my father, for my loss, for never having been able to say good-bye to him; know I've lost him over and over again in every man I've loved; see that his going had nothing to do with me. His was the core of love that nourished me as a child. The medium advises letting go of the great burden I've carried in the heart; just like a bag of stones, simply put it down and walk away. *[Her advice is so simple. I have no idea how to follow it.]*

❖ I'm out in the wilds on a journey, come to a great craggy cliff, know I must go over it. The only way is to jump. There is a high, strong wind blowing; it may slow my fall. I jump—and find myself wafting down the cliff face, slowly and safely. ❖

Eucharist at the Episcopal cathedral. I enter the chapel, I sit, I am astonished: an intense, powerful, sustained, upward moving energy. I am contained, elevated, in this movement—the God of my childhood is here, the Named God. I sit meditating, in almost-bliss of reunion, contemplation. I experience the service itself as interruptive, so patriarchal

---

37. I rarely consulted trance channels. Someone who is not wearing a body is not necessarily wiser than someone who is, and even the wisest of discarnate beings using a human channel is relaying information through an imperfect instrument. But this woman was remarkably clear and compassionate, the beings she channeled had a deep and precise understanding of spiritual process, and she herself had great respect for my teacher.

is it, fixated on sin, negativity, and death. But the *energy* here is very clear: straight to God, straight to God.

These journals—I am a pebble dropped into a pond and these notes are the rings of my surface-breaking, the bubbles of my descent, my tracks into the deep. The deep, still pool: God, the Nothing, the All—the only place I have ever wanted to be.

•

I must take responsibility for myself, not expect someone else to tell me what I need, not abdicate responsibility for my own life, well-being, choices. There must be a big part of me that wants to!

Trying not to be attached to Beloved's irritation with me yesterday. I sensed she felt I was disagreeing, challenging her. I could do something just because she says that's how, or when, or what—but all her work with me has been about my taking more responsibility in my life, not less. Perhaps there's something I'm not seeing, some way I'm not under-standing? *[Visible here, the confusion I already had about "the distinctions between dependency and respect, self-responsibility and devotion, submission and surrender." It isn't* Beloved's *behavior that contradicts my authentic self-responsibility.]*

Meditation. I see a shimmering lake, molten light, circular currents. Beloved is there, in a boat. "Oh, *you're* here!" I exclaim. "Well, who'd you expect?" she asks, smiling. I am chanting the Heart Sutra: GATĒ GATĒ PARAGATĒ PARASAMGATĒ BODHI SVAHA. "Take me to the other shore," I say to her. "No, you must go there by yourself. All I can do is show you the lake, and point the way."

•

❖ In a large conference room the issue of child care is up for discussion, and men from a fundamentalist group speak out strongly, tyrannically, against women having any help with children. Many of us, feminists, thought we were in a group where such issues were at least granted validity for discussion; we are thrown back, dismayed, momentarily stunned and without strategy. One outspoken woman is especially bearing the brunt of this, becoming identified as the focal point for the feminists. In a later scene, having been branded a witch by these fundamentalists, she is found dead outside, a wooden stake through her throat. (This is connected to her actual recent experience. She has a "Witches Heal" decal on her car bumper; she heard that the men at her trucking school were "praying for her soul" and, very frightened of being in moving vehicles with men who saw her as evil, satanic, she has quit her trucking classes.) I see that these are people I'd easily mistake for like-minded with me and feminists: they "look normal," as I said about one of the men the day I was so shocked by his hostile anti-abortion bumper decals. ❖

Oh, my friend's decal! Oh! Oh, it's all the same thing! Separatism is the disease, no matter who, no matter why.

Aware of having dreamt tender, gentle, strong eroticism with men, thinking, "Oh, I must be moving out of being a lesbian, I seem to be desiring connections with men." It is with relief that I take off some of the armor, remove some bricks from the walls, let love flow—it is an *inner* healing.

The current proliferation of books and articles on how to love, how to feel better—all dealing with the *emotions*. Reading my college student's manuscript on love I suddenly see: Ah, all these people are addressing the ways we deal with our feelings because that is what needs to be addressed right now, to prepare the next transition in human evolution—from emotions to impersonal, universal love. *[How beautiful in my heart is the sweet recognition of this insight as I read it today. How happy I am that I saw this so long ago, this magnificent portent!]*

•

Beloved, of me: "She's the hardest person to get over to the other shore I've ever met!"

In a spontaneous reverie, I see Beloved and me, again in a canoe. I'm paddling, she's sitting.

"What should I do?" I ask.

"Stop paddling."

We are still. The boat is a lotus flower, in a still lake. Suddenly she bores a hole in the surface. It is scary, black and red. She says to look down. I look.

Beloved: "What do you see?"

"Nothing."

"Ah. Go down there."

"Down *there?* Down the *hole?* Into the *nothing?*"

Down I go—and out the other end, feeling light first at the top of the head. When I come out what I see is: lotus-canoe on still lake, Beloved . . .

•

YEAR THREE

Shaking the frame · Beyond right-wrong
Journey into the Deep Valley · To acknowledge majesty of being
I came here out of love for you · This, the emptying · Mother and child

January

> Enlightenment is a precious gem and must be bought at a high
> price. Methods to teach *tharpa* [supreme liberation] are many. . . .
> If it is easy it is a wrong one. [38]

Out across the valley it's like a dream of mountains, snow-bright peaks
floating in the haze, the surrounding mist the same color and texture
as the sky.

Beloved speaks of "crazy wisdom," throwing away all limitations of
culture—then "ten degrees of bodhisattva." I say, "It never ends, does
it?" She replies, "Oh, yes, it does."

Once again some change is preparing itself in me. In meditation I ask
to see the divine will for me. "You're not ready yet," I hear.

Nighttime, ill at ease, reading, I come upon this and weep with yes,
yes, I know, I know: "Love fulfills the law. Do you not realize that all the
emotions opposite to Love violate the law and you work against all creation
instead of with it?" [39] I want to let go of this burden of ego, pettiness,
and meanness of spirit, to enter into my true largeness of being, to *be*
love and harmony and compassion—not abstractly but *with* others.

Much weeping: dry, jagged, harsh, abrupt, momentary—*old* stuff, I
know it, though no idea what; doesn't matter. When it comes it shakes
me, body and emotions; I forget to call in the light till later.

Amidst grieving, incanting, "Let all the small griefs, the gentle griefs,
the great griefs, flow, bubble, flood, pour, wash out from within me,

---

38. David-Neel, *Magic and Mystery in Tibet*, 163.
39. Caddy, *The Spirit of Findhorn*, 4.

into the light." Meditating, entered a deep underwater cave, saw a tall gold screen: "the mask that covers the Mystery." At the end, aware of a calmer, surer *faith*.

I am so aware of my tasks now: learn to love, live without fear, serve, discover and fulfill my spiritual purpose. Align myself with God, become one with What Is, attain enlightenment in this lifetime—and help others to do all this, too. And I think this strange work I'm doing now, this weeping and letting of griefs, is part of it. *[Yes, sluicing the way. And though I am still saying I want to "discover" my purpose, is this not it, all along: to become one with truth and help others to do the same? Here, I am not yet ready to see and accept this vastness of purpose as mine.]*

•

Awake before dawn. Working on fear. Without fear there will be room for love. And I see that releasing the fear is to be done minute by minute, in all my activities. Oh, I am going to *change* this deep, archaic pattern—I am going to be without fear! *[An early intuition that the task isn't principally to release something stored but to change something habituated.]*

I have been kept free of permanent, intimate human ties for a reason: "Here am I, send me." *[Later I will note, "the seeds of service are deep in my heart." Now they are pushing up against the surface crust, impelled by love.]*

❖ I and others are on a lawn. Ram Dass is seated on a dais. Looking at me the way Beloved sometimes does he says, "You are meant to be a teacher—so give up the last attachments to ego and *do* it." ❖

[I can feel, reading these entries, the extreme tension I am living with in this period. At age sixteen I had pressed my flesh into the rough bark of an old, gnarled tree and called out to God, "Show me my purpose, show me my service!" I am calling out again, honing commitment, like an arrow nocked in the bowstring, taut and trembling.]

•

We are in January thaw, the air gentle and light, western sky warmly luminous, snow melting all around: spring promising. And I, longing to be outside, running again. I've been cooped up, slowed down, have used winter as my alibi for stopping my own flow. I don't want this alibi any longer, I want truth: energy moving through me again, my breath fresh with sunlight.

How easy it is for me to slip into comparing, comparing. Myself little, others great, and hating them for it; or myself great and unrecognized, gloating about that "hidden greatness" which if only they knew . . . !

I am to follow my own path. The work becomes ever more inner. I am quieter, calmer, less needy, seeking less to draw attention to myself, to be important—not done with that, but it's less—and thus freer with my regard for others, less judging, less controlling.

Ah, but I *want* there to be God "outside" me! Tears spring when Beloved says no, God is what's *inside*. [*Desiring outer reality and authority: resisting full responsibility. Longing for longing itself: clinging to the illusion of duality.*]

At the ashram, falling down the stairs, deep cut in my hand. Much loving attention from others—the heart greatly opened, in a new way: *receiving*.

I love—

February

> "Out beyond ideas of wrongdoing and rightdoing, there is a field. I'll meet you there." [40]

[*Here begins a deep burnishing of my commitment to truth. In appearance it takes the form of a professional and ethical drama; in fact it is a trial and an initiation, great in its impact on the quality of my mind. It begins with Beloved telling me she sees me engaged in "right-wrong" thinking. I look within, see what she has seen, and immediately commit to expanding my consciousness beyond right-wrong—not yet even knowing what this means: that I must release judgment based on duality into love beyond duality. The purification begins instantly.*]

We are all one, so fear and anger—not necessary. Not "we are all one so we *shouldn't* fear or be angry at each other," but "we are all one so there *is* nothing to fear or hate."

[*Seems as if through the months and years just about any one of these light-filled*

---

40. Barks, *The Essential Rumi*, 36.

insights might have sufficed, doesn't it? Because here it is again: inner awareness of /
nonduality—yet look at the pages still to turn!]

A heavy day. Started in beauty and joy, a walk in the cold sunlight. But the college, it seems, is going to join the army. I am pained at the lengths to which our institutional apprenticeship in demoralization will let us go; longtime faculty are so poor and desperate they'll do things now that they would have organized demonstrations against ten years ago. Some even spoke of how this could be the college's new mission: influencing the military! *[In financial crisis, this small, private, pedagogically and socially progressive college has decided to sell some of its viable programs (including the program in which I teach) to a military school. I—social activist, feminist, grounded in Quaker practice and the disarmament movement—am shocked, dismayed, sad, and angry. I protest in college community meetings and faculty councils, raising my voice against this choice. Then, over the coming weeks . . .]*

In the middle of the night, strong coughing: "choking on my anger"—and still choking on it most of the day. But tonight I see that not only am I morally outraged at the college, I'm also angry at myself. I, too, had been entertaining the thought of conveniently teaching in the new situation until a colleague pointed out that it's a military school—*then* the NO began rising from deep within me. I am angry at my collusion, my own lack of integrity. Now to transform the energy from anger into light—and *get the lesson.*

Whew, what learning! I awake clear and bright. What I began to see yesterday, and worked on, it seems, during the night: all judgment is projection, all anger is projection. I awoke with such gladness and sense of *newness.*

Lingering doubt. I choose not to teach in a military college, but what is this choice coming out of? There might be circumstances in which I would choose to work with the military—if this were World War II, if we were invaded, if the army were rebelling against internal totalitarianism, fascism, etc. But now I see the military power of the United States being used to support totalitarian régimes of the right in Third World countries, the heating up of militarism in this country, the warmongering of government and media. I do not want to support these movements and tendencies. Is this again "right-wrong," judging, separativeness?

Still wanting greater depth of choicefulness, I brought the situation again into meditation. Wept, seeing that one of the deepest impulses of my being has always been nonviolence, the knowledge that we are one.

With this recognition my decision about the military school moved from automatic—positioned—to choiceful. I choose *to be who I am.*

I have resigned from the college. Shaky; grounding myself in my decision by telling people. Know I will need to trust all is well, through doubt and fear. In some way I'm not yet completely *clear* in my words and acts about this. *[I had been considering resigning my job even before the military college drama, but am now subtly tempted to use this situation as my pretext.]* Oh. I was afraid I might just ride the event for its moral outrage, feared I might not behave with integrity. What follows from this clearer seeing isn't visible to me yet, but now I know it will be. I *can* trust myself. I *will* be honest.

> At bottom the whole concern of both morality and religion is with the manner of our acceptance of the universe. Do we accept it only in part and grudgingly, or heartily and altogether? Shall our protests against certain things in it be radical and unforgiving, or shall we think that, even with evil, there are ways of living that must lead to good? If we accept the whole, shall we do it as if stunned into submission . . . or shall we do so with enthusiastic assent? [41]

This deep searching for integrity is burnishing me, brightening my edges, sounding my depths. I trust myself more now: I can recognize the place where I am called to say no, and I can respond. And I can see that I am at the same time being called to say yes—to trusting the inner knowing. I give thanks for the "military connection," challenging me to this deep probing, this deep searching out of myself.

❖ A large group. Laughing, I suggest we start a "yin over yang" movement—if we're going for imbalance, by all means let's go for the yin! Later some people sing one of our meditation chants in a comical way. I object: "It's sacred sound." ❖ It is now, in this writing, that I see the two events are the same—and that I was on a different "side" in each of them. The lesson carried through the night into waking consciousness: I have done all things, been all things, so: no judgment.

Pain and sadness at the confusion of *maya [illusion, delusion, the world of appearances (Sanskrit)]*—wanting to be pure enough just to see things as they are.

---

41. James, *The Varieties of Religious Experience,* 172.

As I wake I have this message: "There is a time of fear and a time of doubt, when every favorite ray of light . . . " *[interrupted by Sassafras, that slinky black cat]* " . . . is momentarily dimmed or obscured—but have no fear, the light is there, and you are moving in it, with it." Not Beloved's voice, more like my own. Ah.

March

Felt literally *called* to go into the woods behind the house, so I went—trudging through the deep, heavy snow, following the tracks of the electric linemen to where they had cut "right o' way": pine, birch, beech, black cherry—an *abattoir [slaughterhouse (French)]* of trees, still fragrant, their brightness preserved in the snow, but dying, dead. I walked that line, holding the light, feeling sorrow and remorse: on the day of their death I, like the linemen, had electricity more in mind than the life of the trees.

Reading Mishra[42] I see that I'm just at the beginning of learning the control of mind needed for real meditation. Up to now I've just been "sitting" most of the time. At some level I've thought that *samadhi [meditative concentration, absorption (Sanskrit)]* would just sort of "happen" when I got "pure" enough!

❖ A child, very young, who the adults think is retarded or mentally ill, but he's really only living in both worlds at once, the gross and the subtle. *[Many of my dreams in these years point to this: living at once in the gross and the subtle.]* I meet him for the first time; he says, "I've seen you before, I see you in the night—we go flying together." ❖

Violence and degradation in Latin America: a sheet of tears on my face. Guns, starvation, rape, assassination—and the U.S. is helping—force, violence, raw might. And the light? What do I do with the light? Keep holding it, keep directing it, *keep believing in it.* The dead, violated women sprawled on the ground—seeing them in the vibrant, all-embracing light of infinite love, then seeing the men with their guns, holding them, too, in the light. *["He guides me and the bird."]*

I am only now becoming able to love—and it's not about "personal" love.

---

42. Mishra, *Fundamentals of Yoga.*

Saying to a close friend, "I don't know what my purpose is." She is very surprised: "I see your purpose so clearly, I see you doing it all the time—being clear for others." She says my very presence is a mirror for people to see their fullness of being, to experience deep honesty. Tears come in relief: I am to *be* as large as I am. I am not to make myself smaller in order to "fit."

Then tonight, in a lively group of friends and colleagues, artists and writers, a discussion about racism at the college. Painful dissension, some talking about African Americans being racist themselves, I speaking to white responsibility, not just for racist wrongs but for our own lives, in our own lives—and I was hurting, afraid, yet wanting to say what I saw: the "us-them" behavior *[us-them, right-wrong: same]*, the refusal to look inside, the necessity to do so. I spoke of the erasure of difference by dominants, the need to allow and pay attention to difference, affirming the right of the erased to speak their/our reality and experience *in their/our own terms.* Trying hard to say it clearly and simply, no judgment, just say it. Feeling strained, pained, thinking I was behaving badly, ruining the party, alienating people. At the end, some say how important and exhilarating the discussion was for them, stimulating new and necessary thinking about issues they'd thought they'd already dealt with. Later, alone with our hosts, I say to them: "I see that what I was doing is a *work*. As your art is your work, that is my work: to speak what I see and know as clearly and honestly as I can." In the moment of doing so, what I experience is the intense pain of struggling for truth in conflict—going all the way in to get clear, coming out again to speak clearly. This is a *work* in the world. It requires enormously of me in clarity, integrity, courage. Tonight I *see* it as a work. I am doing my purpose—*being who I am. ["Being clear for others," for my and their deep honesty and presence. This and my inner work in the college drama: same.]*

And at the college, the pain of choosing to *speak myself.* In the meetings where the military issue is being discussed, I wait till the very end, to see if someone else will say "life-death," "war-peace." It is so *painful* to me to do it, and to have my words erased, fall on deaf ears. But I think the pain is really the pain of manifestation *[of "speaking myself"]*—and the pain of seeing myself as separate, which I am not.

After writing all this, a heavy, wracking storm of weeping, shaking my whole body, *shaking the frame*—calling out, "Shake the frame, break the form, let the essence shine clear." It's about manifestation, somehow—some work is accomplishing itself within me—I don't know what it is—I weep, I weep, I don't know why—tears all over the page—

I went to the college filled with light, sensing the *love* flowing in me, ready to do its healing work. Had still been feeling some inner conflict I couldn't figure out, intense pain, sense of separation from my colleagues, guilt at my own firebranding, wanting not to cost them their jobs by my acting on principle. Nothing seemed to come clear till I said to a colleague, "I have to tell you my guilty secret: Really, at some level I *want* the military deal to go through—so our faculty can have their well-paying, secure jobs that they need." I had finally spoken from my *love*, not just from my principles. It was as if I had made my colleagues and me separate in order to differ from them.

Unblocking the love. The pain was in the process of manifesting, yes, but also in the blocking of my love. Ah, I see: This is part of fully manifesting—making manifest *all* that I am: truth *and* love.

Beloved tells me, "The act of speaking your own truth, whether others want to hear it or not, is deeply aligning."

I am uprooting from within *myself* the roots of war.

•

[The college-military drama and the acute conflict I experience in it, my willingness to be pushed beyond right-wrong, my fierce determination and persistence in clearing my own inner way for honesty and love—these efforts usher in the next piece. Manifestation: bringing forth in mind, speech, and action the indwelling truth. Being who I am. This is lifelong work for me, perhaps for us all. As Beloved had oft reflected to me, I had long been ignoring (for this whole life, for many lifetimes?) my inner knowing, subverting my own wisdom, quelling my self-expression. In the college-military drama I commit to finding my voice, standing my ground—and find that I must do this not in opposition and separation, as an adversary, but in love, as a lover. Now conscious work on the Father, on sexuality (generativity), and on voice become important elements of this "bringing forth," in clarity and wisdom, through the principles of activity, receptivity, and union.]

Morning meditation. Transmuting hot flesh to clear, open heart and mind. Bringing sexual desire into my meditation in just an open, easy way—no urgency, no need to transmute the desire: I can play it out, run it, toy with it if I choose, but I can also let it become light, as it is in essence. Seeing myself and partner in the tantric embrace, the flow of desire gradually becoming the flow of energy. *[I would enjoy being able to say this notation reflects understanding achieved in actual relationship, but, oh well, it refers to activity in mind only.]*

Male energy. When it's "good," it is very sweet, pure; when it's "bad," it is violently destructive—but it's not necessarily one or the other. I'm to be learning something about "male energy and me"—to observe it, not to get attracted to it or repelled by it. I've been thinking and behaving as if I needed to sexualize this return to openness to men—as if the lesson is about sex, which it is not.

At the Celtic music performance, aware of pure male energy—and loving it. And as these virile, laughing men played and sang, I saw, vividly: If you do what it is you love, do it with your whole heart, and wholly, that is holy work, that is service; that is a spiritual devotion, offering, and path. *[This beautiful insight has guided me since that very evening. It addresses not what my purpose may be but how I am living my being—that question burning in my heart, drawing me deep within and then again out, to the domain of manifestation:]* Now, what *is* it that I love, that I do with my whole heart, that I do wholly?

Out running, calling on my father to guide me in this next work: opening to the Father, letting love in. In meditation, working in the light of the father, sensing a great inflow of *power.* I AM THAT I AM. And the rainbow bridge opens from my crown. 'Way, 'way back, to before I was born—seeing my parents, young and shiny-bright—and I wasn't open enough to them. I tell my about-to-be-born self: "It's okay, you can come through them—*just stay open to receive their love.*" They turn to leave, shining like suns.

•

At the ashram. The energy is dense, radiant. I sense friends nearby and relatives, beings in other dimensions, Beloved, students, cook in the kitchen chopping for our supper, the late afternoon light thin and shimmering around me. I allow waves of confusion, frustration, and sadness to move through me, over me: lives not lived, whole worlds of information never encountered. So how to understand these refined, subtle teachings: crystal structures, musical intervals, cell morphology? They are foreign languages, their concepts slide by me, gone into the air, notes too high for my ear, vibration too fine for my understanding. I toy with judgment: I should have taken science, I should know this or that—and give it up; it's a labyrinth. I try reassurance: Oh well, there are other things you're good at; let's see now, what were they?—and give that up, too; it rings hollow to my overstimulated ear. I try humor, I try pain, I try annoyance, and give them up: dead ends, bramble bushes, pits. In my corner, sitting in silence, confronting all these concepts I don't grasp, I am forced into the heart, deep into what I *know*:

I am	We are	Star light	In your heart
We are	The same light	Rings with sound	In mine
We are One	As the stars	Hear it now	In us all

Epistemology, language, and silence. Words are my tool and my joy. They come at my call, they dance and sing for me, they enlarge my visions, color my dreams, pipe for my fancy, delight my friends, and seduce my lovers. They even make money for me and please my cats. What words now, though, for this quiet knowing, this knowing that is eye and heart and womb and star?

When I reached home yesterday, this note from Beloved:

> Is the chalice
> Half empty
> Or is the river ever full?

Ha! A koan from the master! My response:

> Filling and emptying and filling again,
> the river knows neither beginning nor end

•

Beloved: "How do you know you are *not* the Buddha? So speak your truth, girl!"

During the recent group retreat, going down after receiving negative comments about how I was guiding the chanting. Oh, how awful it was to go there, up against not trusting myself. And of course: about voice. All my life being teased for being unable to carry a tune—always laughing when they made fun of me, but such sorrow, so much music in my soul and unable to make music—and oh, my great joy when, in learning to chant, I knew myself strong, clear, powerful, and *sure*: I can use my voice to help others, I *can* sing out. I, too, can make a joyful noise unto the Lord. And all in an instant felled, brought into a heap: "You're off key, incorrect notes and intervals, people can't follow you, they stop singing, they talk about it later." And from then on I'm afraid to lead; I silence my voice, neither speak guidance nor sing it. I ask Beloved; she says, "You're *good.*" Momentarily reassured but feel myself muting, dimming. I am being tested, fear I won't meet the test—self-expression, manifestation—that this one I'll back away from, that I'll stop here: "Oh, it's all been very wonderful, very high, but I see I can't go any further." Later, meditating by the river, I see I am *not* going to back away. *[Over and over I see this crisis of confidence: "Oh, I've peaked, this is as far as I can go, now is the time I'll stop, this is the test I'll fail." And over and over the saving insight:]* The river empties only to fill, fills only to empty. This filling and emptying and filling, this *is* the river.

April

Sense of wanting something from outside, from men—not just approval but "to be chosen." Feeling an empty space inside, filling it up with food, tiredness, activity—I who have long said other women, not I, felt empty and needful of men. There's nothing I've disclaimed that I'm not to see is mine. *"Je suis humain, et rien de ce qui est humain ne me demeure étranger."*[43]

❖ I am lovers (or trying to be!) with the young Einstein. He's experimenting, sending light through a spectroscope onto a grid, forming geometric shapes, trying for a perfect square; every now and then a perfect square will flash for an instant, in the blue. A concert is about to begin; people are filing in, getting comfortable. I kiss and nuzzle him behind the ear; he has an erection in his maroon sweatpants. We are lying together covered by filmy, transparent gauze netting and I am amused: "the young Einstein under gauze." ❖

---

43 "I am human, and nothing human is foreign to me." As a college freshman I first read and was stirred by this statement. Coming upon it in a volume of writings by Michel de Montaigne, I long thought it was his, but it is commonly attributed to Terence, Roman playwright (190–159 BC). What I translate as "human" was *homme* (man, human) in the French version I read. I was an early experimenter with gender neutral language—and gender-specific, too. Especially entertaining in French, which has all nouns either feminine or masculine. Note, for example, *le vagin* (vagina), so much lusher as *la vagine* . . .

What is resistance? Energy/consciousness that is blocked—and mind/ego does the blocking. How to deal with resistance? Remember perfection *[fall back on what is true, undistracted by the momentary display of emotions, thoughts, phenomena]*. In meditation I ask to see what resistance looks like, instantly see a violet double tetrahedron—"as above, so below." Resistance *is* transformation. *[A powerful, liberating insight that helps me help both myself and others.]*

Growing sense that the quietism of past contemplative lives, a strong pull for me, is contrary to the direction I'm being called to now: full, active manifestation and self-expression. I am still—and increasingly willingly—in the process of making the transition from devotion as *contemplation* to devotion as *service*, but have not yet decisively made the shift. It is perhaps the work of this lifetime. *[Yes.]*

The seeds of service are deep in my heart.

Even my mother is in on this! "You must write and publish; you need a bigger setting than these small regional colleges." Oh, oh, oh—it's so *demanding*. I've resisted this all my life. Now it's time.

Oh, I can *sing*, the conservatory teacher says I can *sing*! I can match pitch, I have a two-and-a-half-octave range, true tone, good breathing and projection, I do *not* change key, and I *can* carry a tune—I can *sing*, I can *sing!*

Journey into the Deep Valley

Oh my, Beloved seems to be telling me to come correct. In my dreams she is sharp, stern.

[The teacher now acts to heighten the tension—to precipitate the spiritual crisis that brings the student, with free will grounded in understanding and discernment, to choose wholeheartedly the path to full awakening. Commitment—to love, to manifestation, to fulfilling my spiritual purpose through service—has prepared the difficult way ahead. Later Beloved will tell me, in a dream, that there are two kinds of trials or tests, the high mountain and the deep valley. Here, signaled by the exigent dream teacher, now begins a rigorous, perilous, inner annealing that she will call my Journey into the Deep Valley.]

Finally went for medical help. *[I have been experiencing months of increasing fatigue, exhaustion, and allergic reactions and have resisted seeing a doctor, thinking*

I should be able to bring myself to balance through spiritual practice and "right thinking."] Diagnosis: adrenal exhaustion. I am shocked at how deeply I've been blocking, so deeply as to disturb my glands in their functioning. The energetic block is at the throat; "You are cutting off the head from the body," the practitioner said. I think my fear that I would block has *become* the block. *[Perhaps it wasn't so much that "I" was blocking as that the next level of purification and realignment was now under way. I could neither make it happen nor make it not happen.]*

Sensing the energies beginning to move through the blockage—a blind, mole-like creature emerging from channel between heart and throat.

Last night's meditation: saw demons, fiends—and *did not react.*

[Many years later the memory of this moment will help me greatly as I seek to recognize the true nature of mind. What I will have to see in that process are the actual contents *of my mind, everything, including fiendish and demonic energies. When we are able to observe,* without reacting to them, *all the horrific, unspeakable things that await their fifteen minutes of fame in our minds, they absolutely lose their power over us. So this early meditation experience became a touchstone in my mental pocket, reminding me: the fiend and the demon are what I am seeing in my mind—but* they are not I.*]*

•

Panic at the thought that I might not make it, might not fulfill the task of this lifetime, might not fully realize—then perfect trust: the way is open before me; I have only to go forward, one step at a time. *[Beloved had told me once, "You get it then forget it." I learn, only to forget and relearn as if anew.]*

If I were feeling clear, focused, quiet, and in good movement on my path I would not be fretting over, comparing, competing with, and feeling ripped off by anyone else. Jealousy breeds in the medium of a sense of insufficiency in the self. [44]

❖ I see a man speeding on a bicycle, small, wiry, dark, his face intense and intent. He is on a mission for help. I wonder what the emergency is,

---

44. When I encounter jealousy, in myself or another, I call upon the wisdom of Amoghasiddhi, Karma Buddha sitting in the pureland of enlightened activity, action accomplished to liberate beings. That is the key: call forth our skills with that intention and our gifts will flower to benefit beings.

come 'round a corner and know: I am on Beach Street in Frances Harbor *[my family's home after my father died and my mother remarried]*, and our house is burning. I must be lucid dreaming, for I tell myself, "Have no fear, let the fires of purification and renewal burn right through." But it seems difficult; the fire doesn't feel ethereal or subtle, it feels like physical-plane fire—I smell it, feel its heat, hear its thrum and drum, the wood of the house being devoured. ❖ *[These images of my house burning will recur at points of intense transformation, and later they will make me laugh, but at this moment they are still scary—because I am still so identified with illusions of materiality. What would have been* really *scary, though: knowing in advance what I was going to have to go through in order to loosen my grasping to those very illusions.]*

May

A stormy, upset day—and then a night of fear, perhaps proving the point that to indulge the emotions merely strengthens them. I awoke at 2:30 in the old gut-wrenching, mind-spinning fear. Men's brutalizing, violent acts toward women and children and animals and the Earth and themselves and each other are in my mind, but my fear seems really to be about getting violently attacked or killed myself: fear for my body, and *fear of the fear* I'd feel then. When I went outside I was immediately no longer afraid. Inside, behind locked doors, fear of what might get in; outside, open to and a part of it all, no fear. It is separation, the *idea* of fear, that brings fear.

    ❖ Dreams of fear and anger, both seeming improbable even in the dreaming, but very vivid. Seven or nine deer in the field, two stags, some fawns. Coming out the door I suddenly see them—they are startled—one of the fawns, confused, runs toward me—a huge stag comes between us—and I am *frightened*—because of *their* fear. And even in the fear, in the dreaming: What am I afraid of, *deer*? ❖ These dreams—showing me that my emotions are irrational, useless, don't bother to do them anymore.

This morning Kwan Yin appeared, just for an instant, near the glass door—a flow of robes, her form and face . . .

    ❖ A dream of crystals shaped like fishes. One, long and segmented like a Japanese decorative fish, I placed up high on a wall molding; immediately it began moving and in the morning was gone. Another, blue and green, I placed on the top shelf of a triangular what-not mounted in the corner over my bed. All these crystal fishes: Beloved, fisher of souls, precious friend. ❖ *[Like Kwan Yin, fishing beings from the stormy samsaric seas].*

Instead of grief that I am not indistinguishably one with the source of all light but a flame out here, see it as *joy*. As I hold the incense to the candle it catches—and as I draw it away slowly I see: ah, two lights, more light. We are in the world to bring light into flesh, into form: *to bring more light.*

Overwhelmed by life in its physical details, wanting someone to "take care of me," Beloved, my father; feeling like reaching out to people for help, feeling needy, deeply exhausted, so old and tired. *[I was forty-one.]*

June

> It is so difficult to work in and through you / When you are weighted down by self-concern, / Regrets, / Worries, / And anxieties. / You know this because I have had to remind you of it over and over again. / Why not do something about it, / Instead of resenting the times I have to repeat these things to you?[45]

❖ An overall plan or scheme is unfolding itself, in which each of us has a specific part to play, however peculiar or incomprehensible. Beloved is orchestrating, but even she can't *make* things happen or protect us from the consequences of our acts or omissions. ❖

What was that hot weeping during the movement work this morning? I, all stiff and large and white—some sense of "burning off," purifying, for white women and women of color: the separations among us.

Aware of a tendency these days to trivialize the teachings, to secularize it all; impatience or skepticism at the extreme complexity of what Beloved says sometimes. A rebellious energy in me, and self-doubt: "Oh, what the hell, I'm so selfish, have so far to go—why bother, why even try?" Looking for reasons to leave. Oh, the *negativity* rising up in me. So much ego: me, me, me. Seeing I've been closing my heart to her, *willing* my heart to open to her.

---

45. Caddy, *The Spirit of Findhorn*, 62–63.

❖ I am in the open bed of a truck, throwing something from the truck as we move along. It has something to do with my rebellion against Beloved. ❖

I am hungry ghost and rebel in alternating current.

An allergic reaction, to wild strawberries. Trying to move it through simply as energy; it's intense, coming up in waves, compounded by anxiety. What is going on here? All tells me this is purification: I am burning off something with this intense heat.

Knowing that all is a manifestation of What Is, I call upon that everlasting stream to wash me clean of all illusion and distraction—a great humbling of myself—to acknowledge *majesty of being*.

[In these brief entries now surfaces a deep-seated, recalcitrant inner conflict between recognizing and denying "majesty of being"—the sacredness of myself and all things. The conflict is hissing and spitting here in reaction to the real-life, flesh-and-blood, in-my-face teacher, confronting me at every turn with the possibility and necessity of dissolving the conditioned self in the light of that potentiating majesty. Her action on me quickens me, stirring up everything in me that resists quickening, that curls back into lethargy, to fester and sleep. The conflict: wake up or don't wake up, be who I truly am or turn aside. It is my choice. The quickening is to bring me to the choice point, that I may choose. My defiance is to avoid seeing the choice, to subvert choosing. The teacher is essential here. I project onto that unyielding mirror my self-clinging and self-hatred and my refusal to give them up, and thus come face to face not with her but with myself. Left to my own stratagems I would not see—and could not choose.]

❖ My crown opening markedly. Is it safe to have this hole in the top of my head? ❖ No matter, it's certainly closed again this morning!

July

Meditating, I saw the Aztec dancers dancing, and it was *[actually, literally]* the movement of the stars. *[A strange, beautiful marker event, showing me that it is actually, literally true: as above, so below.]*

Oh yes, I am still in the process of choosing service, my practice, my prayers, all still directed to my own spiritual evolution. And my attachments, still so identified with the physical body.

Awaking ill—straight to the catastrophic fantasy, right into the clammy, cold bowel of fear. Today's is old, fear from other lives. Time to release it, come fully into this time, this life, *be who I am.*

Increasingly aware of the importance of meditating with eyes open now—*to see things as they are.*

I want to learn humility as realism, not as self-negation. Oh, am I ready to begin learning humility now? What a strange, circuitous, odd journey is mine. *[Having at an early age recognized my prideful nature, humility had been the spiritual aspiration of my youth. I had no idea how to attain it, although here I do seem to know what it requires: seeing things as they are, seeing what is.]*[46]

❖ Taking care of someone in a hospital. In the elevator I turn the lever for the seventh floor, we zoom upward, much too fast to stop, out through the roof—we are in space, in free fall—I am terrified, then let go of the fear. I see that there are two different kinds of controls on the panel, brass levers on the left, ordinary buttons on the right. I used the brass lever, but if I had used an ordinary button we would've simply stopped at the seventh floor, in ordinary reality. ❖

•

With Lama *[receiving Dharma teachings, empowerment—happy, oh, so happy]*, reciting the Vajra Guru Mantra: OM AH HUNG VAJRA GURU PADMA SIDDHI HUNG.[47] Afterward, in the kitchen with a sangha companion, a sudden heat flush and intense fear, then up and out came fear held for lifetimes, surging through me, from legs, back, lungs—saw myself in Africa, abused, tortured *[in countless lifetimes there and in the Orient, but especially in Africa—my friend and I both saw these images so clearly]*. Great release; even the physical body feels different. What will it be like to live without

46. The formal denotations and connotations of humility reference meekness, lowliness, and so on. I look, though, to humility's relationship to *pride*—overestimation or overassertion of the significance of oneself (whether positive or negatively valued)—and see humility as correct apprehension and valuation of self in relation to others and phenomena.

47. The mantra of Guru Rinpoche, Padmasambhava, also known as Pema Jungne (Lotus Born) and Guru Pema. In this book I refer to him by all these names at various times.

that? I experiment, imagine going to edge of high cliff, flying over deep ravine, falling, falling: no fear.

When I released that fear, I really knew it was not just for me but for all beings. All day reminding myself: I am a person who is not afraid.

Meditating, I see a house on a hillside—I enter—a dark, cool room—up near the eaves, a dark bird—it flies out the door, soars into the sky, a *hawk*—I ride up under its belly, carried in a wind pocket—the hawk becomes an *eagle*, soaring ever higher—we fly far and far, over a smoky mountain, a volcano—a moment of fear, I don't want to land on a fiery mountain—the eagle suddenly becomes a *ship anchor* ⚓ and plunges downward into the ocean, immediately rising again, the form inverted: a *phoenix* ⚓ .

Beloved has no time for me, nothing more than the occasional smile. ❖ On the phone I tell her I have been sensing I shouldn't ask for attention or help from her but that I have been feeling needy and sick. She laughs, as if laughing at herself, and says, "*I* can't need till the end of August." I ask her, "Does this mean I, too, am not to need until the end of August?" "Yes, if you can do it." ❖

In meditation I see: It is a *thought* of insufficiency and limitation that gives me dis-ease and depletion—a *thought*. My path is simplicity itself; I need nothing from outside, I am to find all within. *[This penetrating insight I receive over and over . . . because I forget it over and over.]*

Disempowerment. At the level of consciousness, two forms: "I don't have enough" and "I can't let myself receive." My adrenal depletion perfectly manifests the first and my allergic responses perfectly manifest the second. As my feelings of rejection by Beloved reflect my bad feelings about myself. To the precise extent that I think I don't have it, I will give away the love, abundance, power that I crave. *[Thinking I don't have means I can't receive. Paradox? No. Beginning to see the active, creative relationship of mind to manifestation. And to spiritual integrity. Down through the long corridor of my apprenticeship to truth, three times I will hear this specific note sound.]*

August

There is nothing wrong. Imbalance is caused by the *thought* of imbalance.

It is time for me to be working *at the level of the thought*. "Embodying the form" means embodying the thought. I see how I do that with the thought of imperfection; now it is time to do it, consistently, constantly, with the thought of perfection.

Today I begin a new level of practice, seeing how my own cleansing cleanses for all, acknowledging my responsibility and capacity to transform energy for the entire planet in each act of transformation I embody in my own small sphere.

You are leading me a rigorous apprenticeship, Beloved; I thank you.

[Beginning to recognize the nature of the work as training allows me to take greater responsibility for my part in it. For a long time I saw it more as "spiritual therapy," which perhaps it was—bringing me carefully to the point where I could become an active, informed participant in my own spiritual process. As I begin consciously to recognize the interrelationship of individual with all, I come gradually to understand the work as the bodhisattva's training, dedicated to the liberation of all.]

Oh, wonderful lesson! Jealous of a sangha companion invited to the Dalai Lama's audience, I suddenly realize: She swept and scrubbed all his rooms, cooked, donated her linen, dishes, silver. All I did was entertain my ego.

This Shantideva makes me laugh out loud with his imperturbable logic that fits my case so impeccably:

> Having generated the Awakening Mind
> Through wishing all beings to be happy,
> Why should I become angry
> If they find some happiness themselves?
>
> If I wish for all sentient beings to become
> Buddhas worshipped throughout the three realms,
> Then why am I tormented
> When I see them receiving mere mundane respect? [48]

Exhaustion, illness, allergic reactions—today, an offending peach. The immediate inner guidance is just to *be*. So tomorrow I leave for the coast.

---

48. Shantideva, *A Guide to the Bodhisattva's Way of Life*, chapter six ("Patience"), verses 80-81.

A sense of proportion restored to me in the ceaseless ebb and flow of the sea, her waves slapping and hissing, her gentle reminder: *I am that I am*, I continue through time, I exist beyond time. Sudden rush of tears each time I finally reach the water—the sea calling forth the salt seas in me—to open, heal and soothe: salt of the Earth, calming the fires of my mind and flesh. "Ghost horses, I am like you . . . my heart strains forward too: / Heavy with salt, the blood leans like a tide. . ."[49]

The energy available to me, through me, is so powerful now that even the slightest block or distortion of it will deplete me. I am to be *completely clear* now. And I am not—I am *imprisoned* in the ego—can hardly breathe—

Shantideva: "When Bodhisattvas greatly suffer they generate no negativity, instead their virtues naturally increase."[50] This sentence *stopped* me. So one could suffer, then, without sending it out into the world as negativity. [*Truly a new insight, a point of mental discipline, inspiring me then, inspiring me now.*]

Last night, sudden weeping—so many lives, so many births, so many deaths—*I want to go home.*

Spontaneous reverie: I sit on a rock above the ocean, feet small and strong against the rock, at ease, creature of sea and stone, hovering above the Earth and below the sky. Yearning to "go home." Suddenly: I want to be free to *choose* to be here—not because I have to be, imprisoned on the wheel of existence, but free to *choose* to return, *choose* to serve. I see: My own growth is service; when I experience peace in my heart, all the world, all of being, receives it. Without forethought I stand up, dive into the water, surface, shake off like a sea animal, climb onto the rocks, sit a moment to catch my breath, then get up and go. Said, innerly, "There's more than one way to get there, that's the message." I can scrape and agonize and exhaust myself or I can move into and through my life flowingly, easily, like swimming in the salt sea.

My new kitten, Lucy, is up in the woodshed eaves riveted by something she sees, Spidercat staring fixedly in the same direction. A raccoon platoon

49. Thanks to Katha Pollitt for permission to quote her poem "In Horse Latitudes."

50. Shantideva, *A Guide to the Bodhisattva's Way of Life*, chapter one ("The Benefits of the Awakening Mind"), verse 35.

is lumbering across the field—like a wave they keep coming, noses and eyes bright, intent upon my cats. They don't stop till they see me, even then appear unafraid. I greet them several times—"Good morning, good morning"—before they all turn and undulate back into the woods.

❖ I am sitting on the edge of a precipice. A fat woman sits down next to me, mistakes her balance, falls onto me. We are both in danger of falling over; somehow I manage to get us anchored again. Am distressed by my panic: saw that I would sacrifice her, give her a little shove over the edge, if it would save me. Don't like to see that degree of panic, so I test myself, lean out over the edge and look down, willing myself to let go of the fear. But I fall over the edge, plunge down, down over the precipice—the fear chokes me, I am totally gripped by terror—then I say to myself, "Enjoy the ride," remind myself "there is no ground." Fear goes. ❖

•

"Thinking of structure as a composition of 'things' [is] meaningless. We have now come to a point of appreciating the true meaning of the word nothingness . . . a dynamic process of vibrating energy states. And the essential nature of this process (which, remember, *is* us), is its total interconnectedness, interdependence and interpenetration. . . . Energy can fully convert from one form to another *but* the total amount of energy never changes. Ever." [51] So when I feel I have less or no energy,

---

51. Postle, *Fabric of the Universe*, 144–45. In speaking of "nothingness," Postle is talking about what, in English translations of the Sanskrit *shunyata*, is usually given as "emptiness." It refers to the *nature* of phenomena: that we and they have no inherent, independent existence, no actual self-nature, but come into and continue in existence interdependently, due to causes and conditions. This does not mean that nothing exists; phenomena, both inner and outer, do exist—just not in the way we think they do. To consider that there is nothing is the error of nihilism; to consider that what there is possesses or is possessed of some inherent self-nature is the error of eternalism. In Buddhadharma these are referred to as the two extremes. The teaching of the Two Truths cuts through these errors: absolute (or ultimate) truth is the truth of emptiness, while relative (or phenomenal) truth is the truth of apparent existence. The two truths are completely interpenetrating, nondual—but their laws are not the same. In the relative we exist in a field of karma, cause and consequence; in the absolute, nothing happens.

it's not so—I have—I *am*—as "much" energy always—what I am *doing* with the-energy-I-am changes.

[This point is a life raft for me during the time of extreme exhaustion and frailty I am now entering. I grow weaker and weaker, less and less able to care for myself, gently declining—until I can barely lift my hand from where it lies mute upon the bed. Frightening and mysterious. I persist, almost too long, in my commitment to working with it as spiritual process. That isn't wrong, but it isn't physical enough. Today, rereading this, I am amused to see how I take these profound insights into the nonmaterial nature of apparent materiality as reassurance for the "I." In the moment, that, too, isn't wrong, but it isn't meta*physical enough.]*

> "If I give this, what shall I (have left to) enjoy?" —
> Such selfish thinking is the way of [hungry] ghosts;
> "If I enjoy this, what shall I (have left to) give?"—
> Such selfless thinking is a quality of the gods. [52]

I go down to the brook to cleanse my crystals in the small waterfall. I quiet as I pray, acknowledging remorse for any ripple I make on the perfect Quiet, praying to be cleansed, to be cleansed utterly, released. I meditate peacefully, sitting on the large rock, gazing on the water. Then it is time to go. I see that I am to leave a gift, a crystal. "Oh no," comes the thought, "isn't the intent enough?" No, having thought it, it is to be. A tiny crystal comes to my hand, beautifully faceted. Maybe a less exquisite one will do? No, this one having come to my hand, this one is it. I see on the opposite bank a good place to leave it, in the soil under a tree. Oh, but it might get washed away in rain or flood; if I put it somewhere else I can come back to see or retrieve it someday—barely a thought, an impulse of the mind, but definitely there. Suddenly I see: I am to throw the crystal into the water. Oh, no—gone forever! Oh, yes—to give is to *give*. It is there in its perfect inevitability; I can no more turn aside from this than I can pretend I haven't seen it. I touch the crystal to my heart, throw it gently, lovingly, firmly into the pool. Letting go, letting go. I am to learn generosity by being generous—and that all is ever filling and emptying by myself filling and emptying. *[Small occasion, immense lesson, never forgotten.]*

All my life, I think, I have been running on fear energy, adrenal energy.

---

52. Shantideva, *A Guide to the Bodhisattva's Way of Life*, chapter eight ("Meditation"), verse 125.

It's as if when I am to do something, anything, even something I like, I rev up for it—fight or flight: adrenalin. So now what I have, in this adrenal exhaustion, is both danger and opportunity, a veritable crisis. The danger, that I shall go on the way I have been and really get sick. The opportunity, to get the lesson: I *am* energy, let it flow.

A bee is right in front of me at the bedroom window. I decide to kill it. Adrenalin releases, heart pounds, energy mobilizes—fight or flight. I apologize to the bee for taking its life, explain why I am making this choice *[thinking I am allergic to bee stings]*, pray and chant to transmute the energy of fear/anger into love/unity. *[Lovely—but I definitely killed the bee.]*

As I read Alice Bailey on the qualities of the First Ray, Will or Power, "The Destroyer,"[53] I recognize myself here: destroyer of forms. *[The habitual mental formations, not the bee.]* Slow unfolding of my understanding of purpose.

•

In meditation, an image of my dying. I call on Beloved and she is there with me. As I look back on my body I breathe a sigh of relief. She says, "That wasn't so bad after all, was it?" I smile—it's so—but, "I feel bad for the people; they are so sad." She: "You were much loved." I acknowledge this, wonder aloud why it was so. She invites me to look at the lives I have touched—and across the country, the continent, the planet, I see lights aflame, so many lights. I am astounded. "And now see the lives they have touched, and you through them"—and more lights spring up, the world is lighted up by these lights. "Oh, if that's how it is," I say, "I want to go back and do more!"—and see that this is a step toward becoming a bodhisattva in truth: seeing one's power and responsibility to bring light to all beings. *[And the power of the choice to return, again and again.]*

I am very aware in these difficult weeks of a wish to be living with other people, so hard to be doing all this illness stuff so alone. *[There are human contacts from time to time during this period, but not many. One young woman, previously unknown to me, appears as if from nowhere, just to help me. Both her arrival and her selfless generosity are unexpected and irresistible. Even today I*

---

53. Bailey, *Esoteric Psychology*, 62–65.

remember her open, unadorned face, lit up by her kind smile—and by a second smile, a childhood horse-kick scar, hovering on her right cheek, like the fainter second arc of a rainbow.] Tonight I look up on the hill and see my neighbor's little light, feel comforted, companioned. Perhaps it is coming time for me to change my life.

Sitting deep in a field of grasses, amid much release, amazement—my soul speaking:

> I WANT TO BE HERE.
> I CAME HERE OUT OF LOVE FOR YOU.
> I PUT ON THIS BODY SO I COULD DWELL AMONG YOU AND SERVE YOU,
> ALL MY RELATIONS.

I never saw this before in my life. I am filled with thankfulness for this seeing.

[No event in my life, not even my birth, has until this moment been more important than this first conscious apperception of my nature and purpose, and the understandings resonating from it.]

Visit with a splendid doctor in a tiny village south of here. Fear: "Release it, let go of it," he says; "It's some wrong message about seeing things as threats. *Work with what you recognize as alien.*" These words went into me like light. Work at the level of the thought—not "this is alien, dangerous," but "I am one with all that is, I love, these are my relatives." "I am whole" *means* "I am one with you." All the ills that trouble us are manifestations of the thoughtform of separation.

   Even my name, Barbara—the alien, the stranger, the foreigner—is emblematic, initiatory, for my path: to find unity, to find our oneness. I think of H. *[my college mentor, wise and beloved old friend: the first to show me that the blemish is the beauty, and the first to hold up to my face the mirror of my ingratitude. Later teachings, from others, told me that gratitude is the doorway to the spiritual dimension; I began to practice gratitude when H. told me that I lacked it.]* He told me I had the gift of being able to find the human connection with anyone, no matter who, no matter our differences. I know it's true. Now just expand this—to the bee, to the penicillin, to the car coming toward me, to the person newly entering the circle, to the question that startles, to the invitation that offers but that I think demands, to my mother, to everyone, every being, all of life: find, smile with, acknowledge, affirm, praise, celebrate. The bee and I, all living beings, breathe the same breath: *we* are the body of God.

Meditating last night, a strange, wondrously easy, deep, full breathing —Earth and sky breathing together, breathing through me, I the channel for their breathing.

 Compassion comes in knowing I am *one* with. It is a "breathing with."

In the context of this change in my seeing I understand better my current desires to be with family—my spiritual family, my mother and sisters. When I see a big farmhouse I think of lamplight, cooking, squabbling, generations, and people working out their lives together.

❖ I am in a car, going too fast around a curve on a precipice, a great green steel bridge ahead. I shoot over the edge—fear pours through me, adrenals drain, heart pounds. This is *physical* body reacting to *dream*. I remember, Oh, I can do this differently, without fear, replay it. Car shoots off the edge, I say, "Here we go!"—car falls, I rise free, watching, while the physical body goes down with the car. ❖ Oh! Twice, dreams of falling—and twice I've mastered, let go of the fear—*in the falling*.

There's something just the very slightest bit different, hardly enough to notice, and like a wisp it's gone if I look at it directly. I feel cleaner, clearer, purer—the light moves through me more easily—I as only one of many, many channels for the light, my radiance helping to light up the world, my energy helping to heal the Earth. Just that, nothing more. Very clear, very direct. Simple.

September

I see that we are one, yet I live as if I am really separate. *[So now the archaic patterns will present again, available for choice when seen in this clear, direct light of expanded conscious awareness.]* Time to look more intentionally at my connections with people. I am more isolated now than I've been in years. Probably for the first time in my life acknowledging that I long to be cared for, taken care of, by a man. *[Don't I say that repeatedly? Seems it takes me by surprise each time—apparently the longings aren't as deeply buried as is my recognition of them!]*

Ruth, on the phone, gives me a message from Beloved: "Tell Barbara to relax in the light." I have been *fighting* my exhaustion, as if I shouldn't be feeling it. *[But "relax in the light"? I don't know how. And I tend to materialize the very concept of "the light," to imagine substantial light, to try to see what is the very medium within which we be. It is the absence of something to see that reveals the nature of spiritual light.]*

Mother calls, asks me what I'm planning to do professionally "if" I get better! Should I be doing some professional planning now? *[I'd been living on savings since leaving the college and falling ill, until in this period my mother offers financial help.]* How to earn money without working too hard and stressing myself again? What work is like play for me now? I'm thinking I should just be at ease, let direction reveal itself. But I'm asking myself the wrong questions! I need to be asking, What is my next step in serving the light, the planet, the people?

I see one thing I really like: I have such a willingness, now, to hear other people's suggestions and advice for me.

My solitudinous self-sufficiency—I can not do this alone; this week I have so needed people to take care of me, physically and emotionally. The body says STOP. Now I'm beginning to learn what "stop" means. God, give me the courage to live this cheerfully, relaxing in the light.

I am so weak. If I weren't to make a real commitment to being here in the world, living, vital, radiant, I think I would just fade away. I am so weak.

Humility? Here's how!

Becoming glad to be just another grass in God's wide meadow . . .

This, the emptying.

[Back and forth, up and down, strong and weak, fearful and courageous— "filling and emptying and filling again . . ."]

Another phone message from Beloved: "This extended illness was precipitated by your standing up to the people at the college." *[Near the end of that crisis she had said, "The act of speaking your own truth is deeply*

*aligning." It isn't that the crisis has made me sick, but that its "deep burnishing"
has evoked deep purification—and purification can sometimes look like, indeed
manifest as, illness (as in a cleansing crisis). Many years later my Tibetan lama
will tell me, "Be grateful for every sign that your karmic predispositions are being
purified—and especially be grateful for every experience of physical illness."*[54]

The beautiful angelic being I see channeling light to me—her smiles
are becoming brighter and brighter. And today, when I contracted with
fear, in my mind I saw Beloved laughing at me! I laughed, too. It is only
my *fear* that is dangerous to me.

Thoughts of giving up and going to the hospital, just letting them
have this body. Thoughts of dying, wondering if this is my old escapism,
fantasizing surcease, my "real" life beyond this life. Struggled a little with
this, then looked at the "will to live." What will is that? I want whatever
is for the greatest good, either way, live or die. Let the fevers burn away
what is to be released and transmuted. I hear that so many are sick—we
are the kindling being used for the fires of transformation—so I am
not to take my illness personally, it really has nothing to do with "me."
"My" growth is not the *purpose* of my being ill.[55]

54. Reading this, I recall Bailey saying that as the soul begins to "grasp its
instrument, the personality," there will inevitably be a great increase in disease,
disharmony, and distress. Bailey, *Esoteric Healing*, 193.

55. As in this extraordinary experience under ether for surgery, reported
by a woman to William James, whom I was reading during this period: "A
great Being or Power was traveling through the sky, his foot was on a kind
of lightning [pathway]... made entirely of the spirits of innumerable people
close to one another, and I was one of them. He moved in a straight line,
and each part of the streak or flash came into its short conscious existence
only that he might travel. I seemed to be directly under the foot of God,
and I thought he was grinding his own life up out of my pain. Then I saw
that what he had been trying with all his might to do was... to *bend* the line
of lightning to which he was tied, in the direction in which he wanted to go.
I felt my flexibility and helplessness, and knew that he would succeed. He
bended me, turning his corner by means of my hurt, hurting me more than
I had ever been hurt in my life . . .

"He went on and I came to. In that moment the whole of my life passed
before me, including each little meaningless piece of distress, and I *understood*
them. *This* was what it had all meant, *this* was the piece of work it had all been
contributing to do. I did not see God's purpose, I only saw his intentness and
his entire relentlessness towards his means. He thought no more of me than a
man thinks of hurting a cork when he is opening wine, or hurting a cartridge
when he is firing. And yet, on waking, my first feeling was, and it came with

October

Picked up by friends and carried away, to the city, for treatment with a Korean acupuncturist.

Ah, so I *was* dying. He saw it instantly, he told me.

Now comes a new learning process: how to be *alive* effortlessly. He says the healing requires that I be "dumb," no thinking, no planning, no worrying. "Everything is a moral issue with you," he said. No more fear, no more judgment: peaceful heart, calm mind, glad eyes. *[For me, transcending right-wrong sometimes seems like ripping a hem one stitch at a time.]*

•

> You must learn to be served as well as to serve, for in so doing, your personal will is broken and the higher good substituted. [56]

At home, getting weaker and weaker, I moved into surrender to the divine will about whether I would live or die *[in the journals, my first utterance of the word "surrender" in reference to myself]* but now that I become stronger my little personal will starts to kick and struggle again. Here in the city, I am full *in* the difficulty of this surrender among people, events, circumstances: staying in others' homes, relying on others for care. When it's a matter of whether I'll have a ride to the doctor, whether food will come when I'm hungry, it doesn't feel like surrender to the will of the divine so much as surrender to the wills of other people, such as the friend I'm staying with now. If I'd come to someone more pliant, less stiff-necked herself, I wouldn't see so clearly the operations of my *own* will.

tears, 'Domine, non sum digna,' for I had been lifted into a position for which I was too small. I realized that in that half hour under ether I had served God more distinctly and purely than I had ever done in my life before, or than I am capable of desiring to do. I was the means of his achieving and revealing something, I know not what or to whom, and that, to the exact extent of my capacity for suffering.

"While regaining consciousness, I wondered why, since I had gone so deep, I had seen nothing of what the saints call the *love* of God, nothing but his relentlessness. And then I heard an answer, which I could only just catch, saying, 'Knowledge and Love are One, and the *measure* is suffering.'" James, *The Varieties of Religious Experience*, 301–2n10.

56. Bailey, *Discipleship in the New Age*, 241.

A big release tonight—something about family—seeing I've never let myself have or be in a family, not even my family of origin—letting go of these old thoughtforms. Aware with each menstrual period that I am nearing the end of my physical fertility, so there's some bodily letting go to happen, too.

•

I seem to shift focus from "spiritual ~~purification~~" to "physical healing" and back again. As I write this I see that of course they are the same. I think a part of my task in this purification process has been to engage the body more intentionally ~~and closely, commit~~ myself to it—and with love and compassion. *[And to place intention correctly: at the level of the thought. ~~At this point the body~~ process seems the necessary vehicle for learning something about how to do this, perhaps because my extreme physical vulnerability during this time so compels my attention.]*

I must let go of the drama with which I have invested the process of moving toward death.

•

In the moments of illumination, when the veil parts for an instant, all is revealed as simple and luminous, utterly clear, perfectly obvious, and I know I am *seeing* differently, that it is a moment of irrevocable change, that from then on all will be different—and then the moment passes, the veil once again covers the light source, and all is, again, not different but the same—and yet not the same, for I never can forget the moment of enlightenment, nor its lesson. So, then, this is how it happens that one is enlightened? Moment after moment, an eternity of instants, each one rendering the veil infinitesimally yet ineluctably finer, more ~~transparent~~ . . . . *[There is no veil.]*

I've stormed the gates of Heaven—let *me* in, *me*—ego seeking not God but itself. My practice has been rigid, even violent. I hope I am learning now, through illness and weakness, to be gentle with myself. Resistance to ego only strengthens ego. Just lie back on the river of life and trust its unceasing flow: that's the lesson now.

Today I *thank* the body as it begins to feel weak and trembly during my walk, thanking it for showing me how to take good care of it. *[Such a simple, subtle shift, but it begins to change my life, through changing my relationship with myself—from fear and hatred of my weaknesses and failings to compassion and love for my humanness, my condition as a living being. I know of no other way to open the heart to compassion for others.]*

The beautiful park down the street . . . since the last time I was able to walk that far the ground has become blanketed with the golden leaves of the great maple tree. My heart is heavy at the coming of winter, the passing of the open, blooming seasons, especially the passing of autumn, so full of glory in the northern countryside—and I am here in the city, marking autumn's artistry on a few particular trees and bushes. I watched spring open, summer bloom and throb—from inside my bedroom, from inside my body, missing deep draughts of spaciousness, airiness. It is hard to go abruptly into a far-north winter; we need our autumn to help us slide down into the cold, long months. I shall return home to hibernate in my crystal cave, to come out again in the spring, quiet and strong.

Didn't feel well cared for in childhood and youth, and now, in this collapse, needing and wanting to be cared for, physically and emotionally. My intense sadness at winter coming: I didn't live my youth.

"I didn't live my youth." I *am* in it now: now is all there is, all is within. Go back, comfort, teach, and cherish that girl-child, the youngster, the adolescent, the young woman—teach her what she needs to know. *[This is a powerful practice of repatterning: rewriting the past, transforming present and future.]*

I awake wanting a child.

Endocrine tests confirm early menopause! There is some mourning of this loss of body vitality, all my children not born and loved in this life—yet I see that I have been a mother in other lives, and will be again. Then, meditating, I see myself as Holy Mother and Holy Father. One function of not having biological children: to know my parenthood to all.

•

Thomas Merton on spiritual pride; I laugh in recognition: "He thinks his own pride is the Holy Ghost." And: "I will never be able to find myself if I isolate myself from the rest of [humankind] as if I were a different kind of being." [57]

Feeling that only now am I beginning to relax and let God's love heal me. "Your job is to feed me, Lord, and my job is to praise You." [58]

The line between hope and discouragement is thin for me these days—one hour I feel stronger and healthier, hours later I am down again, weak, chilly, uneasy—and there it is: the struggle to stay alive. The choice to be here, to be alive, is made over and over again.

•

Reading Isherwood, about the young man who will take monastic vows in a Hindu order in India, I am wishing I, too, could enter an order, take vows, have clear focus and discipline. [59] Then see: Oh, I am; it's just a different kind of order. That it sometimes seems more like *dis*order only reflects its particular nature, time, and circumstances—and its teacher, and her message: "Be *in* the world. We are not recluses, we are bodhisattvas. The planet cries out for our active help now—don't withdraw, don't withhold your resources. *Be all you are.*"

November

❖ Beloved and others are together, laughing and talking. Somehow it is made evident to me that I am not wanted. I ask why. She says, "You lower the vibration." I am hurt, but I know it's true. ❖ *[I wonder at the precision of some of these dreams. Today I understand this one as frank recognition of the tidal conflict between longing for divinity and refusing it, that old undertow. If I refuse to rise on the full tide, it is certain I'll fall on the ebb. I cannot see this at the time, though it is right there to be seen.]*

Fear is completely absurd if I really know and believe I am in God's care.

57. Merton, *The Seven Storey Mountain*, 50–51.
58. Dallas, *The Book of Strangers*, 135.
59. Isherwood, *A Meeting by the River*.

I need an index of some sort so my sense of progress isn't so vulnerable to my immediate state. *[I am speaking of my physical condition, but as time goes by that index will really be needed for my spiritual condition.]* And I am being too damn serious about all this, forgetting to see its humor and drollness—my body flapping around like a big fish, frustrating all my efforts to exert my own will.

I seem to see and feel everything as an observer—sun, breeze, leaves, people. In the park I see the season of the year change, am struck by the seasons of human life. These old people tottering along, chatting busily, moving slowly but determinedly down the street, and the teenagers in twos and threes, breezy, quick, noisy—they are moist, the elders dry; darting, to the elders' tentative steps; alert, eyes bright, lips parted, the elders dreamlike in gaze, eyes dimming, mouths compressed in concentration, effort. The whole range, walking before me; I observe them from some place in between. I watch the elders, some so infirm they can barely move, day after day out in the air, moving their frail old bodies, and I think, What infirmity is this of mine, that cripples the body only by its own incorrect thought? Out into the air and sun with you, my girl! LIVE! *["The choice to be here, to be alive, is made over and over again."]*

A strong affirmation arises from within: I AM HEALTHY, I AM WHOLE, I AM HOLY. *[This grounding, empowering pulse of truth continues to resonate in my mind as a mantra in times of difficulty as in times of strength.]* [60]

•

It seems to me recently that I am only beginning, now, to learn about being a woman, that in other lives I have long, long been a male. The strangeness, alienness, of my physical body, the "uselessness" of its womanly features . . .

How little I know. I don't even meditate yet; I mostly just sit and stew.

I am just a beginner on the spiritual path. The sense of "spiritual identity" I've always had—an intuition, only, and used by the personality to confirm its uniqueness, separateness. My soul has been calling me

---

60. All three words—healthy, whole, holy—derive from common roots in Old English and Old Norse. (See www.etymonline.com)

for a long time; intuitively I have sometimes heard, sometimes even answered. But not until very lately has my mind begun to respond, and my heart, with any degree of consciousness or intentionality. This journey is one humbling or humiliation after another to the personality. For which *I* rejoice, but with each one of which "I" cringe in chagrin and discomfort. Oh well.

I am now doing the work relating to the mother—and this work that I have feared even naming all my life, I am not afraid of it. Last week, for the first time, I said to and from my conscious self: I wanted my mother to love me. Now I shall learn to love myself, to accept both the lovable and loving child within and the loving mother within. *[My mother did love me, showing it not in speech but in every deed, small and large. I couldn't see it, couldn't feel it. Repatterning, learning to mother myself, I will come to compassion, forgiveness, and love for my mother—and face the challenges of love coming to me from others.]*

•

Reading Alice Bailey is helping me relax. I see how long the journey is in human time, a single lifetime but a moment in the evolution of a soul. I see that I am fine, my development and evolution proceeding just as they ought: I am doing my best. And I'm seeing that to be always looking for results is not just counterproductive but futile. Bailey's "The Tibetan" *[a principal teacher in Bailey's works]* says the ordinary human personality and brain are actually *unable* to know what the soul is doing. Too, the disciples all have personality faults and spiritual blocks, most of which I could claim as my own, and seeing this helps me see that I'm not so bad after all. And for all I know each person I meet might be a disciple, serving in a way I can't even see. Simply be true and faithful, learn to love, and service will flow. *[I must have written this last sentence simply from intuition. It turns out to be true.]*

All this time I've been trying to *grab* my soul—as if she's floating some-where above my head, like Mary Poppins, and I'm trying to catch her by the feet, haul her down where I can get hold of her! This morning: Oh, if I just sit here quietly, open and expectant, she can simply reach down and gather me up to her.

❖ About possibly coming to live at the ashram, Beloved says that by March I will be ready to "discharge my responsibilities." ❖ *[And I arrive there in March, to stay.]*

•

[Beloved comes to teach in the city where I am recovering:] At the possibility of seeing Beloved tonight, desire for personal recognition came bobbing up, gleeful and importunate, but I was too weak to go to her talk. My longing for her to pay attention to my personality will only get burnt off as long as it is not reinforced, so what she is doing—not calling, not coming to see me—is exactly what I need.

Some people have nowhere near as much to work with as I but make full and rich use of everything they've got—while I, who have so much, use it, when I do, virtually exclusively for my own ego gratification, bring few of my gifts into manifestation in the world. When and how will I finally take responsibility for my *strengths*?

Ah. The resolution will be through service, without thought of self.

> . . . you have never yet served as a soul—possessing nothing and asking nothing for the separated self. [61]

In Bailey I read that physical devitalization is often due to not expressing on the physical plane the reality that one is—not bringing through into manifestation. "Vertical growth and horizontal growth must parallel each other." [62]

And Bailey's repeated emphasis on *knowing* as more important than feeling or believing—this has helped me know that which I have long known, at some level: There is in me one who knows, even while there is another one flapping and flopping like a fish on a line, seemingly hopelessly caught in illusion and emotion. Pay attention—do not let old thoughtforms become reenergized!

Ego grows to fill the spaces love was meant to fill.

[Decades further along, I will call out to my precious lama, "How will I ever dissolve

61. Bailey, *Discipleship*, 570.
62. Bailey, *Discipleship*, 534.

this egregious ego?" Instantly I will hear in my heart, "Your ego will dissolve in your love for others." This knowing is bedrock, absolute, unmistaken: to be lived literally. Instead of trying to dismantle ego, generate true, warm, generous, compassionate, open-hearted love for others—always recalling that each of us exists within and is never separate from absolute love, the Great Love: unconditional, nonreferential, unwavering, timeless, all-pervading.]

•

❖ With Beloved in a large group. I am holding some kind of appliqué work. She takes a piece of it—a blue cloth bee—gently, smiling, buzzes it toward me and stings me with it in the neck. I fear nothing, know the sting is healing, feel the strengthening energy flowing into me. ❖

The teacher in Bailey's works: "I beg you not to handle force so powerfully. Learn to approach yourself and your life problems, your work as a disciple . . . *with less intensity.* . . . [T]he achievement of an inner stillness is the way out of all your problems . . . [Your intensely active mind] *must* learn to rest quietly in the light. *[Just what Beloved had told me: rest in the light.]* It must learn simply to *reflect,* both in the sense of quiet thought and in the sense of a quiet radiance."[63]

Spontaneous reverie while listening to Sachdev flute. Still lake, mountains on the far shore; a pavilion, two flute players playing together, a man and a woman. At the edge of the lake, bamboo reeds, laborers working in rhythmic cadence; sometimes I am one of them, sometimes a flute player, sometimes the lake. The laborers are scything tall grasses by the shore, gathering and tying them in bundles. Two yoked bullocks wait for their loads. It is evening. The overlying greenish light and the water become calm and still, the *Raga Bhupali* sounds from the pavilion, *tabla* and flute carrying coolly through the air to where the laborers put down their tools, sigh, and settle themselves by the lake. Tea, a light meal, the *raga* easing the end of the day, the lake receiving all care and sending back the last light of day. Quiet radiance.

I am deeply loved by so many—it *must* be that love is coming through me, too, to others, not only that I am receiving love in this life because I have been kind and loving in some other life.

---

63. Bailey, *Discipleship,* 576.

A personality spasm: infantile, archaic stuff coming up. Intense loneliness (who, me?), and when alone all the time I feel parched. Such an important thing for me to see: I do need people; in just a simple, human way I need to be around people. Then, dreaming: ❖ A little girl, covered with blood, walking home along town streets, seen by many, no one ministering to her, taking her in to see if she's hurt. She gets home, to where I am. I pop her into the tub to clean her off; she's not really hurt but is drenched in blood. ❖

There are regressive as well as potentially transformative aspects to this whole experience. Sometimes I feel I am using it for the needed transformation; sometimes I fear I am just acting something out, stuck and staying stuck.

Seeking to become receptive. I have been pulling and tugging—at Beloved, God, my soul. Now, learn to be still and *listen.*

•

We have all—disciples and initiates of all degrees—to enter the secret place of initiation with a sense of blindness (or loss of direction) and with a feeling of complete destitution. The disciple . . . ascends towards the Hierarchy and assumes the correct spiritual attitude but, at the same time, he descends into what he erroneously regards as the depth of human difficulty and iniquity (if necessary), preserving always his spiritual integrity and learning three important lessons:

1. The recognition that he shares all human tendencies, good and bad, and hence is able to serve. [*"Je suis humain et rien de ce qui est humain ne me demeure étranger."*]

2. The discovery that the thing which he most despises and fears is the thing which exists most strongly in him, . . . unrecognised. He discovers . . . that he has to explore and know these despised and feared areas of consciousness so that they become eventually an asset, instead of something to be avoided. He learns to fear nothing; he is all things. . . . And—because of all these acquired states of consciousness—he becomes eventually a Master. He has "mastered" all stages and states of awareness.

3. The uselessness of past attitudes and dogmatic ways of looking at life and people . . . when they separate him from his fellow-men.

When he has really learnt these three things, he is initiate. [64]

Thanksgiving Day. I see that all I am experiencing I have asked for—purification of ego, opening of the choice to serve, to be here. Yes, and yet . . . sometimes I feel just numb with pain.

It's in the personality that I'm hurting. In the soul I am serene and joyous.

Preparing for dental surgery, I couldn't let go of obsessive fear-thoughts so just went with it, began a mental list of all the things I'm afraid of—and I'm afraid of everything! When I saw that I started to laugh. It's the opposites I fear: life and death, pain and pleasure, hot and cold, loneliness and people, food and hunger. [65] In Bailey, the teacher says we must

> learn to move forward in spite of the activity of the pairs of opposites, paying no attention to the reactions of the senses and standing free and unafraid whether the experience being undergone is one of high import and of spiritual satisfaction, or is one of the "dead-level" happenings, where nothing brings joy and where only pain, fear and suspense are to be found. You must learn to move forward steadily *between* the pairs of opposites, saying to yourself: I am not this; I am not that; eternally, I am the *Self*. [66]

In extreme weakness I am pliant, quiet, open. How to bring these qualities into my *strong* times? Deep weariness: I don't know *how* to "let go," to "accept," to "stop struggling," to "surrender." NOW I need God to help me do it, grace to help me let go, relax in the light, trust. I keep trying to learn the lesson—I don't know *how* to "stop trying." I feel like an alcoholic who finally acknowledges she can't control her drinking, is *unable* to stop. Will to live not very strong—feeling again: oh hell, let them just *have* this body.

___

64. Bailey, *Discipleship*, 708–9.

65. Speaking of surrender! In this dental surgery the acupuncture anesthesia failed, they gave me gas, and I had a full-blown near-death experience right there in the chair: tunnel, light, voices, the whole thing. As I slipped away I heard my voice, eerie, sepulchral, informing the dentist, "I. Am. Dying." He ripped off the gas mask, tore out the tooth, and I lived to tell the tale—and to remember the lesson: let it go, let it go, let it all go. And to speak up when necessary!

66. Bailey, *Discipleship*, 664.

I don't know *how* to let go and *just be.*

Spidercat died last night at home while I am still here in the city. Spidey, Pie, little Pie-dough, Spidoodle McCroodle, Spydor, Pidey-Doodey, the greatest cat jumper in the world, little engine kitty, funny little scaredy-cat . . . *[And when I received this news I instantly knew that he had carried my death away from me.]*

I am really hitting the wall. This is *the time* to let go of the old form and pattern of personality—I am flailing and thrashing—I don't know how to do it—and I'm terrified I won't be able to do it—this is the crisis point—all has led to this—now please, God, lead me through.

Early morning. Somewhere in me I know now that it will be okay. I am in my little boat on the river but I am no longer the pilot. ❖ In my dreams, Beloved and I are by a river. I see that she is always with me. ❖ Walked toward the sun, played on the playground swings, prayed to become like a child again, to start afresh, trusting and free.

•

I've been letting go of all the *external* structures of my life; it's the *internal* structures I need to let go of. I'm like a beetle whose carapace is coming off; it is brittle and dried out but still attached, so the shell catches and snags on twigs, grasses, other insects' wings and antennae. I can see now how unwieldy, clumsy, and ugly a thing it is; how it has been so awkward, unpleasant, and sometimes damaging for me and others; how it has gotten between me and free movement in the world—and most of all, how it has hidden my true beauty. When it still fit me tightly I never even noticed it! But though I now wish it gone, now really *choose* to be rid of it, I can't rid myself of it by an act of will. It seems that it must scrape and catch on things until it gradually falls off by itself.

Or will the new growth under it, beneath this dry shell, eventually dislodge it for good?

Talked with Beloved by phone. She said the work has been completed this weekend. "Now you know the full power and meaning of mother-hood. I know how painful it has been, and I also know how strong you are. Time now to acknowledge the pain and the trial, and to carry the gifts forward—acknowledge the blessings of the valley and now begin to climb the mountain again." And said my time of solitariness, monastic-like living, is coming to a close: "Come on home, girl!" she said.

Beloved told me, "Your gifts are too great to be wasted by going into retreat." [*Ah, how little I understand this, and how loath I am to accept it, for so long. Thinking that the most profound practice and realization are to be found in solitary retreat, I long desire to make that my most pure offering, my service to all. In essence my longing for retreat is my longing for liberation, but in my attachment to this particular form I am still dualistic and escapist, still focused on self, thinking, "Oh, in retreat I will be free of life's demands, able to realize, to awaken fully." But I think it is just as Beloved said: I must "do it in the supermarket."*] This must mean I am indeed freer for service now, as I have prayed to be. "Look at your effect on people," she said. "You are more of a nature to give than to receive."

And she said to me, "Don't you know how I love you? In my love for you, you are like my daughter."

(End of Journey into the Deep Valley.)

December

Today, feeling the first steps out of the valley, up the mountain. Beloved confirming "a job well done" gives me energy, hope, confidence. No longer am I looking out for the next trial, now have a sense of walking from a dark room into early spring sunlight.

Aware of the love that is the Christ consciousness, the love that enables true service. But perhaps even he wasn't automatically always aligned with God's will, for in Gethsemane he first asked, "May this cup be taken from me"—and *then* said, "Nevertheless, not my will but thine be done." He, too, had a human will that must be schooled, in love and devotion, to surrender?

The trials have been the path of wisdom, and it is this perfected path that leads to the open heart of love.

A wild, snowy, windy night, sleep disturbed. ❖ A huge machine running swiftly and inexorably in a big groove in the Earth, pushing before it droves of Earth's wild creatures, lions, elephants, giraffes, and her tame ones, sheep, goats—so they are easier game for the hunters. I am shattered by grief: they are killing all these my relations. I call out, "We must do everything we can to stop them!"—but not only do I not know what to do, I am immobilized by my grief. And by my long habits of laziness. ❖

•

I am home again, after this long, long time. *[Three months. Felt like a year.]* I felt strong and capable the last two weeks in the city, confident about coming home, being on my own; now that I'm here I can't imagine I felt that. Now I have to *do* it—learn how to *live* not separated from others.

Oh! Reading my journal notes I see that in my dreams I am taking care of my little-girl self! And in meditation I see that both mother and child are within me, I have become both mother and child. That's what Beloved meant.

My blood family is in my dreams these days. ❖ My aunt brings an infant girl to introduce me to. I immediately love her, deeply, take her in my arms. Then she is older, still a baby but able to talk like a child. I ask her name. "Euritum" (pronounced "*your*-ee-tum"). She explains that her mother died before she was born, and this was either like her mother's name or the month in which she died; it is also the name of the disease from which her father died when she was very young. As she tells me this I sense that her grief and loneliness are not yet resolved; she will need to do the work of mourning. Then I am told that Euritum is dying. It is as if her death has been expected, for she has some "condition of life" that means she is to die very young. I am walking with some people on a street; we pass a church where a service is going on—I ask if it is Euritum's service, am told that now it seems she will live at least another year. ❖

In evening meditation I am offering my resistance up as a gift to my soul, knowing it is the gift she is happiest to receive from me right now.

❖ I am reaching up to grab a tiny, wiry, filthy little girl who, like a monkey, is coming in the window of my New York City apartment. In the dream I register: Oh, another image of a little child who is me. But here the predominant feeling tone is not pity or concern for the child, but annoyance, frustration: she is *always* doing this, climbing in the window uninvited. ❖ *[Thank heavens she does, too! She is to be one of my most faithful and significant teachers, this grubby little girl.]*

Still and warm inside, a walk in the blizzard, and in that walk an instant of utter fullness: right now, in this moment, I am completely happy.

•

❖ On the upper floor of an old building, the office of a shoemaker; I am here for something, clearly not for shoemaking. I lean over the back of his couch, kneeling on the cushions. The man jabs me hard in the ass with his shod foot, then assaults me, or seems about to. I leave, fast, and once outside tell all the women I see not to go there. In a later scene, a friend and I go to a room that is dark, cushioned, Middle Eastern in flavor. We sit together on a long *banquette*; the man we're to see comes in and sits on a smaller one at the end, facing us. He is the "shoemaker"! I startle, want to leave, my friend prevents me. Into the flesh of our right thumbs and palms he presses a wire, with two needle-like ends, and a medallion. Again I want to rebel, protest, leave, but it is clear from my friend's reaction that what we're experiencing here is not an assault but a privilege. I have the impression, from her greater pain, that this is a practice in which she is more advanced than I, hence the greater severity of her discipline. This man is some kind of spiritual teacher. I try to tell him about my physical condition, exhaustion, the acupuncture treatment. He says treatment like that is quite primitive compared with what he's now doing to me, and could do. ❖ *[This dream, too, calls me to see through dense appearance to subtle meaning. I need repeated reminders, as I think we all do, for the world of appearance and sense experience is compelling, convincing—until we learn to see its actual nature.]*

A rough night. I panic, thinking maybe I'll just go downhill again, thinking maybe I can't get along without my Korean doctor, thinking maybe I should go back to the city. Thinking, thinking, thinking. *[Especially "thinking maybe, thinking maybe, thinking maybe." Debilitating.]* I awake to glorious sunshine and a cold, clear day.

I wish I could feel confidence about caring for my body physically, healing myself, no longer feeling like a victim to illness and doctors; people assure me that as I come through this healing process I will learn that confidence. *[I really don't, though, not for a long time, panic still arising with illness and injury. A sense of not understanding a body, not knowing how to work it, how to be in it, continues into age, rendering bodily experience mysterious and somehow alien, unpredictable, out of control. Only deep, continuous practice on impermanence, gradual detachment from self-grasping, merging with the Great Love, and the permeating experiences of direct awareness allow me to begin to "relax in the light."]*

My heart and mind contract in pain and helpless rage over the killing of the deer, the whales, the seals, Earth, her air, her waters. I can't protect them. Like my dear friend when her son was killed in a car crash: "I couldn't protect my own child." Asking to have the boundless love and compassion of God and the masters, who look on us through the countless ages of our mindlessness and ignorance, our wanton cruelty and destruction of ourselves, each other, the little ones, the planet. They see it all—yet go on loving us. But how *do* they bear it? The "unbearable compassion" of the bodhisattva: this I must learn.

As I walked outside in the cold, bright afternoon sun I saw: Of course—it is that they have learned to observe our pain and ignorance *without* the contraction of heart and mind that I experience. Learn to keep the heart and mind open and expanded in the face of fear, pain, ignorance, violence, cruelty, sorrow, my own and others'—so love and light keep flowing, and the harmony of What Is manifests through the suffering.

Now I understand better what Beloved told me about the different paths: the Hinayana teachings of renunciation, discipline, and egolessness—certainly the valley I was in; the Mahayana path of openness and compassion—certainly where I feel myself moving now.

Yesterday, thinking of how this path is the path of mastery, I felt a pang of alarm: Oh no, that means I must master *everything,* all states of mind and being—oh yo, can I really choose to go through all that? *[Again this alarm at a point of choice. But it often appears that by the time the alarm flashes I am already choosing or have already chosen. The alarm seems to call my attention to the point of choice, that I may affirm it consciously.]*

Lord, what a gift this is for your service, this strong will of mine! Only teach me to give it over entirely to you—and what a will is here for your work!

❖ An old high school auditorium: wooden floors, a stage. A large group gathering for initiations—with Jesus! He's shining away there in this fusty old auditorium. Beloved is presenting her students; there are candidates from other groups, too. The testing begins with people playing an old upright piano on the right side of the auditorium; Jesus attends with much graciousness to these performances. He touches some in a fatherly, reassuring way, stroking their cheeks as one does to a baby. I imagine that when I go up to him we will both giggle at how long and silly all my struggles have been, his fish that has finally let itself be reeled in by surrendering. He could have reeled me in whenever he chose, but it had to be that I gave up my will to his. ❖ [*Surrender! Happy surrender!*]

Today my first day alone. Full and peaceful. Tired—and committed.

•

BOOK·TWO
RAKING LIGHT

RAKING LIGHT

*R*AKING LIGHT, A TERM FROM ART SCHOLARSHIP, *is a method for studying a painting's surface using extreme cast shadows. Illumination angling sharply across the surface of the canvas highlights painterly gesture, material defects, earlier paint layers, and so on, bringing the observer close to the artist in the act of painting. This method can be used to trace provenance and to discern true from false, for "under a raking light" the hand of the painter, how she or he actually placed the marks on the canvas, is strikingly apparent.*

As I emerge from the deep valley, the inner direction is now to move to the ashram, to live with and serve my teacher and to join my life with the lives of others in spiritual community. My long orientation to solitude and separation will make this a challenge at once arduous and rich. These next years were surely marked by extreme cast shadows in the steadily intensifying light, and both my own and the Divine Painter's hands are here vividly revealed.

"First the perfect light draw down": a primary principle of spiritual transformation. When we invoke the pure light it floods the inner landscape—and our task is then to manifest fully the perfection revealed by this inflowing light. What we may not understand when we set out to "fulfill our spiritual potential" is that spiritual work is work. It is noble work—and sometimes difficult, slogging work. There is nothing unintentional about profound purification.

Not long before moving to the ashram, I dreamed of a man who was a morphologist. In my dream he opens up a huge bin of words, which he rakes and scrambles like curds, the rake turning up and sorting words of particular structure. The dream was detailed and vivid, but its significance escaped me. Decades later, working with my journals, I came upon the dream again; musing upon it, in curiosity and for my own pleasure, I jotted these notes:

> Morphology, across disciplines, relates to the study of form and structure—of organisms in the biological sciences, of language and words in linguistics, of rocks in geology, of narrative and symbol in folkloristics. *Morphe*, the Greek root, simply means form or shape. The mysterious, magical *metamorphosis* means a *change*

of form or shape; metamorphic rock, for example, has been changed in form specifically by heat or pressure, or both. Profound transformation is suggested by the word "metamorphosis" and the image of heat and pressure sufficient to change the very structure and form of rock itself.

From the beginning of my work with Beloved—and especially as I move to the ashram, to deepen formal practice, to live, love, and labor with the teacher and the community—I am doing exactly what my dream morphologist is doing: "raking" forms and concepts to study their underlying structure and nature; and undergoing exactly what creates metamorphic rock: the transforming power of great pressure and heat.

Most important in this transformational process is the increasing clarity of purpose. These are the minutes, hours, days, weeks, months, and years that I shall experience as the refining fire, freeing from impurities, freeing for love. Shining through the obscurity, brilliant and unwavering, are the love of the teacher, guiding by inspiration, instruction, and example, and the true nature itself, irresistible force, indestructible beacon.

•

Year Four

January

Green wood can be bent;
When it is dry, it is only straightened by fire. [67]

❖ I'm in a classroom, knowing I'm supposed to be in a more advanced class, yet recognizing that now that I know how to *just be* wherever I am, it matters far less where I am. ❖ *[This is a "pointing out" dream—a pointer to where to look, how to see. In my actual lived reality I am far from knowing how to "just be," and certainly not "wherever I am"—but that is where truth is, and somehow, from a very early age, I know this and seek it.]*

I am not yet to be relieved of the consequences of my solitudinous life. This evening I am wanting contact and no one calls, I call and no one is home. Others' lives are full of others, not of me, and I, loving my solitude, now also need some dailiness of engagement with other people, the tapestry being woven together.

Beloved spoke to me of planetary transformation, the great sadness and fear rising from the Earth, many people going through pain and illness, as I am. "Now is the time to call on your discipline," she said. "Remember the power of the thought for good or ill, especially at the level you're working on. Hold the correct thought." *[The thought of inherent perfection.]*

Sometimes just being in her presence brings out the worst in

---

67. Saadi of Shiraz, in Shah, *The Way of the Sufi*, 85.

me! For me to *see*. Yet I keep doing the same icky things over and over again—seeing the negative, being critical, looking at the *im*perfection. *[As in this very comment.]*

Ah, it is about unconditional love. I am to love *myself* unconditionally, whether ill or well, weak or strong, good or bad, productive or *just being*. And to let myself *be* loved unconditionally.

I see that my mother has loved me unconditionally all my life. It hasn't felt unconditional, but I know it has been: nothing I could do would make her stop loving me. *[That I cannot register this viscerally, emotionally, is from my side, not hers: akin to refusing her love. The Teacher Mirror will show me this refusal very clearly as time goes by.]*

Aware in these months as never before of the nature of human life, being in a body: pain, fear, death, vitality, pleasure, love, life. Will someone please tell me what it all means? Silence. The Wheel of Life, the endless cycle of becoming—no, of *being*.

I seem more continuously aware now that "I" am not "real"—that this form is but a manifestation of an essence, which is light, consciousness. And that the real lessons being learned are being learned by my soul, not by this personality.

Beloved is calling me to the ashram. I go around touching my home, sad to think of leaving this peaceful, serene little temple, place of beauteous solitude, leaving friends, countryside, neighbors. *[I lived tenderly there, bathing in the wild stream, running in the dusty, shady lanes, looking out on the large western sky. It was a pivot point for deep change.]* The times they are a'changin'—my teacher is calling me—I am answering.

February

Barbara, you're so funny—you always think you have to "do something." *[Oh, my goodness: decades later a friend says these exact words to me as she lies dying and I get all busy about it.]*

Coming down the hill to my house at the end of my morning run, I remembered how it felt to be a strong, healthy person—open, clean, lungs expanded with fresh, good air, muscles vibrant, skin rosy and tingling, body alive, alive: happy, full of joy. And a sense of *relief*. Healing comes from inside, not outside; wholeness is the essence, always immanent. God is in the cell. Hallelujah!

Asking to learn how to follow the gentle path, the path of joy—because I am knowing now that, as Beloved said, "Suffering is not necessary." *[Know, forget; forget, remember.]*

Slight, tender intimations: gifts devoted to service—an opening place in my consciousness.

❖ We baked Beloved a big Valentine cake shaped like a heart. I asked, "What have I done to get a guru who's a red hot momma?" ❖ "Speaking words of truth," she says when I tell her this dream.

Seeing, again, that dealing with Beloved's humanity will require me to deal with my own divinity.

In teachings, slightly bored. I want to be out *living* it.

March

"I want one of those," as I see a solid, bearded man driving his farm truck. *[Not the truck.]* I see how selfish I have been in my relationships with men, ask to be guided in transmuting those patterns of fear, despair, competition, anger, possessiveness. Walking in the magnificent spring snow, tears and little-girl words: I miss my Daddy. Good that this comes more clearly into focus as I go to live at the ashram *[where the daddy, the lover, the brother, the son, the friend, the bully, and the protector will in turns great and small be spinning me around the dance floor of my mind].*

> In learning how to learn from a Sufi school, the intending student should take note of this admonition, which indicates his difficulties: "If you are too soft, you will be crushed; if you are too dry, you will be broken; if you are too hard, you will cause hurt; if you are too sharp, you will inflict wounds." [68]

I live at the ashram now. [69] Needing to walk steadily in balance, one

68. Shah, *Learning How to Learn: Psychology and Spirituality in the Sufi Way*, 288.

69. The ashram was a place for teachings, ceremony, and retreat; Beloved and her staff lived there and in the vicinity. Not lovely but serviceable, the building looked out on woods and a large beaver pond. In autumn we heard wild geese; in spring the geese again, followed by cacophony of peepers and frogs; in summer black flies and mosquitoes; and in winter silence, occasionally shot

within the many. Pressure, external and internal, to do more than feels okay; very tired already. Scared to say no to the work demands, though I make a big thing out of being able to: "Oh, they won't love me, they'll send me away." *[We've already seen in the first years the thought of being sent away, and here it is again. Now I know how to look directly at a thought; then I did not. Seen directly, without elaboration, thoughts self-liberate, return to their nature; looked at sidewise or avoided, they create karma. This particular thoughtform's karmic seed falls into fertile soil that continues to be well composted, and it fruits up right good in the coming years.]*

My gifts today: God's little chickadee bathing in the crystal stream, a bright sky, the warming sun—Earth beginning to wake and move again, her mantle of snow softening and melting.

[And speaking of softening and melting:] Asked Beloved how my light is; she hesitated, then said it's better but still sharp, pointed, and "everyone's looking for the soft round." She said I "down the energy." *[Exactly as she had told me in a dream some months earlier.]* I wonder if I'm strong enough to take the next leap. She says it's my soul that's tired, that I am in "error saturation," working on this for many lifetimes.

Seeing different lives, different bodies: so many forms, so many forms. In the middle of weeping I *yawn:* so tired of all this—error saturation—*get* the lesson.

I have learned in these first days here something about hierarchy and place. I'm not "special" here because of attainments or qualities of personality; here I have no attainments, and the very qualities of personality that have won me prestige and status before are impediments, now, to my unfolding and opening. *[It is of course not the qualities that are impediments but my attachment to them, for their identity reinforcement.]*

Stuff seems to get transmuted very fast here: yesterday moved something through just by chanting in the temple. *[Purification by sound—an entirely new kind of teaching about voice.]*

Feeling trapped, like a prisoner, and seeing how I can erase and demean myself in relation to a man. Oh yes, now I remember: I *asked* that it be given me to release and transmute my old patterns in relation to men!

Quiet sitting on a pail behind the goat shed. Seeing the fruitlessness

---

through by tree limbs cracking in the deep freeze. My staff jobs were varied, from teaching to sweeping, but in general I served as Beloved's assistant.

of negativity, how the patterns of limitation and separation perpetuate themselves.

April

Service, huh? If I can't even serve Beloved by cheerfully answering phones, writing letters, staying in on a fine day, how can I say I seek to serve God? I've been in full resistance: *my* thoughts, *my* feelings, *my* wishes, comfort, convenience. Seeing Ruth's gradually increasing impersonality, knowing that's where this path leads—yet, I don't want to go there! Full resistance—to giving up the emotions, the little comforts, the self-indulgences, the entitlement to a "personal" life. [70]

I am a stone in a tumbler, being jostled, abraded, rounded in the vortex and action of all the other stones. *[It's the abrasive effect that's salient at this point; the polish and shine reveal themselves only very gradually.]*

Visiting Mother in Florida. Pelican, cormorant, kingfisher, swift, some small dove-like thing, very pretty and soft—and the little lizards darting about, as in Africa, their orange throat-bags puffing in and out.

Grief for my mother's aging—and anger, for I'm as if brought to a mirror, showing me how I learned the ways it gives me such pain to change now: the fear, the unremitting negativity of thoughtforms, the constant alert, nose in everybody's business in moralistic surveillance. Compassion and forgiveness—for both of us. And what will *my* aging be like? Feeling I've lost everything, am empty—yet empty means open, open for God to flow through. What matters the rest if I am filled with God?

Yesterday, for just an instant, crazy, giddy, trembling in love with God.

May

These strange yearnings for community, family, mate, ordered life, my needs provided for, I having only to *be*—this is information about myself, about being a human being. *[And about inchoate knowing*

---

70. Impersonality, in these journals, doesn't mean indifference; it refers to caring (compassion, love) that is not based in personal, self-referential attachment or self-interest, thus free to be dispassionate, nonreferential, impartial, inclusive, universal.

that has not yet reached the level of insight. At the heart of these "strange yearnings" sounds not the clang of laziness or selfishness but a very subtle tone: just being.]

[Beloved had told me that many of us were "ready for our next vows in the Buddhist boat," having followed that path with her in many lifetimes. And now:] Buddhist vows with Lama in our temple, in Beloved's presence. Taking refuge in Buddha, Dharma, and Sangha. And bodhisattva vows: accepted into the mandala of all buddhas and bodhisattvas. The awakening of natural mind. *[Natural mind is awake, already and always awake. What happens on this day is a slender intimation, not quite even a glimpse, of that: awakening to natural mind.]*

Teachings on compassion: I see that it is *difficult* to be compassionate, not just for me but for everyone. It's not something one either has or hasn't but something to work at, as Lama says, "slowly by slowly."

Aware of a new energy since the initiations—easier service, fuller generosity, fountain of joy, steadiness of compassion. And after a morning's meditation on the ridge, as I began to walk down I could feel my light bodies streaming out behind me.

June

> You sentient beings who seek deliverance, why do you not—let go? When sad, let go of the cause for sadness. When wrathful, let go of the occasion for wrath. When covetous or lustful, let go of the object of desire. From moment to moment, be free of self. Where no self is, there can be no sorrow, no desire; no I to weep, no I to lust, no "being" to die or be reborn. The winds of circumstance blow across emptiness. Whom can they harm?[71]

In an ashram ~~nothing is ab~~out one's personal life.

Desire is a thoughtform of separation: I only desire that which I think I am not or have not. Let attachment know itself for openness, desire know itself for union. Unify the apparent opposites; own every quality, every aspect as what I AM.

I seemed, last night, to be right *in* my "stuff about men"—with

---

71. Blofeld, quoting an anonymous Chinese teacher, in *Bodhisattva of Compassion.*

two here, one calling to my higher self, the other bullying, and I, caught between love and rage—almost I can *see* two pillars of light, or two racks, and I between them, caught on both.

But the personality pain is just an old coat flapping in the wind, a little ragged around the edges, fraying and swaying when it's touched or handled—not who I AM. I am creating a new reality for my relating to men.

My desire for intimacy of body and heart is pouring up through the layers under which I've hidden it, knocking me off center, bringing up my defenses. With a man, wanting to be mother, teacher, lover, little girl—but not yet knowing how to *just be.*

How to love impersonally when feeling needy? Oh my. Yet I am more aware of fullness than of emptiness, of love than of lack of love, of joy than of pain.

"Hopeless love"—my father dying, that abandonment—and something earlier, about my mother. "Go deep," said Beloved. "Meet mother and father and forgive them." *This* the wound in my heart that I pray to have healed now: let my heart fully open to the union within.

Just working and working and working on unconditional love. Let me move on, oh please, into abundance of love.

July

Two are in vigil up on the ridge, their energy a holy mantle over us all, their faces huge and all-seeing.

Let personal will subside. Living with others now, I see the operations of my mind, its frantic, self-deluded clinging to territory and power.

Last night I spoke affirmations that I now see were vows—and today very shaky, emotional. *[Vows entrain purification of all that obstructs their realization—and so we practice.]* Beloved said, laughing, "You're not stuck, you're doing great! Deep psychic issues, working through. *Be* the teacher you are," she insisted.

August

Oh, here they are, the ashram group now expanded, offering me the chance to be who I am *with* others, to love and be loved, to learn and work together in sharing and intimacy. A flash of excitement and gratitude. And . . . I need to watch my maneuvers to remain separate.

I sense some dry, fibrous husk, like a coconut shell, breaking open in me now, another husk of ego—shattering to release more light. Ricocheting emotionally: connected then separate, happy then sad, loving then critical. Many moments of willfully breaking connection. For me there is such a strong subjective element that I am often quite caught in separation consciousness. Simply *hold steady in the light.*

Retreat on the Ridge

[A little solitude out in the wild, longed for and delayed by work demands, my frustration intense and now my joy intense. I continue for decades to knock up against this frustrated longing for retreat. It is, absolutely, the longing for the natural: just being. And its frustration, by my karma, by the wisdom of my teachers, and sometimes even by my own willingness, keeps me in the world, apprenticed to love.]

Bored. Staying with it.

The most powerful act for good is simply to *hold the form.* See it, do it; don't talk about it, just do it; don't tell others to do it, just do it yourself. Mind your own business.

[The journals highlight some of the entangling threads: a personality tendency toward bossiness and criticism, heightened by perceptual acuity, intellectual precision, moral conviction, and idealistic fidelity, all wrapped tight in a package labeled "If I Can't Be Loved I'll Be Right." Yet character and history—fruits of karma—are not determinant. Aspiration, spiritual practice, and bodhicitta—authentic love— powerfully impact the field in which karma ripens, even purifying the karmic seeds themselves. "Be the teacher you are," Beloved insists. When the instrument is refined, the personality inclination to "tell others what to do" becomes easy generosity, the offering of teachings and methods to the student who seeks. In this, both teacher and student are freed in their loving connection dedicated to the liberation of all.]

A sweet, quieting day. Found a bird grove on the far side of this ridge, much whirring and whooshing, fluttering of leaves overhead. *[Noting the recurrence of bird references in these journals, I recall Beloved telling me, "When your heart becomes happier the birds come around you."]*

I sat up for a long time in the quiet beauty of the night, Lady Mountain brooding over us all, then awoke to a great wind—and fear, fear of blowing free, blowing wild, blowing strong. Sister Wind, I am like you . . .

(End of the Retreat on the Ridge)

September

How energy is magnified in efficiency and one-pointedness when I am minding my own business! This morning a sense of joy in this new learning—oh, very new. It is effortful and easy to forget. Every *instant* I see my mind slide over to what someone else is doing or not doing—and then I just call it back, trying to be gentle and loving with myself, and firm. *[A fruit of retreat practice: the inward attention stilling, gathering.]*

Brief, sweet visit to my former home and friends on the other side of the mountains, visiting the "personal," and now resistance to returning to the ashram. It is important not to attach any significance to this. *[During my visit "home," I walked into a restaurant and everyone stood up, clapping and cheering, just happy to see me. No such juiciness in the ashram, where indeed "nothing is about one's personal life."]*

Energy of dedication and commitment in the group—seeing range upon range of great beings clad in white: "We are the shining band. We offer ourselves for service."

Don't ask for anything. The opportunity is to master the flows of energy, not to gratify the desires of the various vehicles.

Tired and a little sad now, late at night. *[The continuing pulse of expansion-contraction.]* This transition into impersonality is happening—but so far, more aware of what I'm giving up than of what will come afterward.

Beloved said to another student, "You should ask Barbara what kind of teacher I've been to *her*! Everything she has held dear I have taken away—especially concepts. Sometimes I've thought I've gone too far, but I knew her strength." And spoke to me about seeing the "bright diamond" I am, my "great love shining forth."

•

Tired, tired. The lesson ~~for me in this degree of~~ exhaustion always seems to be about "trying to make something happen." *[The thought of "I."]*

The wondrous, mysterious unfolding of the plan here, in this time, in this place, among us. The great acts of service Beloved is offering to the planet. Immense gratitude and wonderment at being close to and directly in the service of this realized master. That I have such abundance of opportunities to serve in this lifetime—I am deeply happy, deeply grateful.

And so I see that all self, all arrogance, will be purified. She has mentioned the different life goals people have—for enlightenment, for service, for material achievement—as different paths of learning. I know my goal to be enlightenment, and I feel confident that I shall reach that goal in this lifetime. And if I don't? Oh well, drop it down the Oh-Well.

An autumn leaf on the ground, droplets of water from the morning rain, each distinct and sparkling—and I *saw*: the leaf, the ground, each droplet, the air, the light—all God.

The "we-consciousness" coming forward. Oh, the efficacy of prayer: three days ago I see my resistance to moving into the impersonal—and here it is!

In this weekend, assisting Beloved at a teaching, pure intention birthed acts, words, and energies that were clear, strong, economical. I knew myself to be holding the form, able to carry it at the correct level, and I knew myself to be *nothing* in the process, in any personal way. I also see the ego/personality reaching up to claim this new power for its own, but I attach no charge to that: it's just the old coat flapping a little in this new, fresh breeze. [72]

October

"Awareness moving in me" is the phrase moving in my mind.

I am speaking of *impersonality* to my friend in an attempt to elicit his *personal* response to me! So many subtle tricks the personality has in its old coat pockets! And oh, I am receiving Ye Olde Feedbacke from folks here about my sharpness, my abrasiveness, my "edges." My reaction is annoyance tonight, while last night it was pain. I call on these others to take responsibility for *their* part of these interactions—I, too, am a mirror.

---

72. "A hard won truth and a principle of reality can be grasped, and then around it the disciple can build the easily formed illusions of the mind which is just beginning to find itself. The glamours of an emotional nature can emerge and gather about the ideal." (Bailey, *Glamour: A World Problem*, 95).

Long talk with Beloved tonight. She confirms that I'm on the First Ray, the ray of Will, the Creator, and that yes, the energy of will is to be tempered by compassion—in this lifetime.[73] *[I am still tending to think of compassion as a lofty state rather than as an intrinsic quality to be freed by practice. It is as if I think that someday, when I am "pure" enough, compassion will somehow be "conferred" on me—and that until then not only am I incapable but also actually* unworthy *to practice compassion. I don't yet understand that compassion is not only a goal of spiritual work but, principally, the very means itself.]* "The path of Will is a long path, many, many lifetimes," she said. "It takes a long, long time to shatter the shell of the ego so the individual can make a conscious choice. Individual personality, emotion, issues are not important—it's the patterns of energy that matter: cause and effect." She told me it was important, for my own "elucidation about human relations," that I see the consequences of choices, adding, ". . . and the patterns people get caught in, in relation to the opposite sex, the brother or sister, are very hard to change; they repeat over and over again."

I felt alarmed at the possibility that I might be allowed to get close to this teacher and make the same mistakes others have made, but she said I won't make others' mistakes: I'll make my own!

And as usual, I talked too much and didn't listen enough.

How odd it is: This level of responsibility with Beloved is not remotely what I sought in coming here—and yet at a deeper level it is what I've asked for, in seeking to become ever more available for service. I am doing what I'm doing now *simply because it is being asked of me.* This is the time in which I am becoming more aware of ego not as an obstacle but as a vehicle for the work of God in me. Though I still want recognition for service, underneath all else a hymn of praise and gratitude fills my heart. Let mind be clear, heart open, hands willing. And mouth *shut.*

Driving the Notch Road—a tunnel of color, tawny, bronze, gold, an almost erotic confusion: I couldn't quite tell what was inside and what outside, the leaves and the evening light like the phantasmagoria of color and light within, leaves giving back now the light they've received all summer, in this great ongoing cycle of reciprocity and life-force.

---

73. First Ray: See the works of Alice Bailey. Several are listed in References; see also www.lucistrust.org.

•

Snow!

Keep silence. Conserve energy. Release critical mind, the Judge, the Fault-finder. Mind my own business. Be alone more. Read, study, reflect, contemplate. Now needed: greater consciousness of the *group*: its needs, potentials, tasks.

I am aware of my reluctance—not really fear, not resistance: reluctance is right—reluctance so often to be the lightning rod for reactivity in the group. [*The more Beloved puts me out in front, to convey her directions, to inform and guide the community, the more reaction there is to me. Partly it is to my lack of skill, compassion, and kindness, which makes me a very challenging administrator and sangha companion, as well as an easy target—and partly I serve as a buffer. The teacher is faithfully, unremittingly showing us our ignorance, insistently calling us to "transform, transform" whatever obscures the indwelling perfection. I am her spokesperson; the shock waves of resistance break first upon my shore. Beloved is giving the sangha a buffer, so people's frustration (normal, as everyone's ego is being abraded) does not focus on the teacher, impeding receptivity to the stream of blessings. And she is giving all of us repeated opportunities to love one another: to love beyond prejudice, preference, and pain.*]

I remember my heart cry as a teenager: "Let me *serve*, show me what, show me how." I begin to become useful—ever to be less and less *who* I am, ever more and more what I AM. All has been preparation, all, all, for this time of beginning.

•

I am sensing some vague shape of the impersonality of this work, seeing that many of the experiences of last year's inner journey in the deep valley were *specific spiritual events*, some having to do with initiatory processes, all seeming to be registrations or impressions on soul consciousness of distinct, particular aspects of or stages in *knowing*.[74]

---

74. I was beneficially instructed during these early years by my readings of Alice Bailey, whose works directed attention to the level of mind, to "soul" mastery impressed upon mind. I was doing plenty of feeling and had no inclination whatever to belief. I wanted to *know*. Bailey gave me, over and over again, keys to understanding both the intense inner challenges and the subtle accomplishments I was experiencing on the path, and I found bracing and

The perfect autumn day, bright, crisp, and cold. I climbed partway up Lady Mountain, singing and drinking in the beauty and giving thanks for this good body I am wearing. How resilient, forgiving, and generous it is.

A great male being stood before me as we chanted—Padmasambhava. He bowed to me and gave me a deep blessing, somehow "included me in his being" as he moved toward me. *[And he still does exactly this.]*

Consulting again the spiritual channel, who comments that for me this lifetime is a review class, something all must undertake at a certain point in their development. My choice to do it in manifestation is rare, more difficult and intense, she says, but the lessons are firmly ingrained once mastered. *[This information helps me very much through the coming years, giving me encouragement—and also a scaffolding on which I can hang two strikingly irreconcilable facts: I have great resources of wisdom and love within, and I repeatedly fall into great disturbance of mind, emotional confusion, and stupidity. I laugh now, writing this: Sometime later, when I am bemoaning yet another excursion in the swamps of samsara, Beloved will tell me, rather dryly, "Human condition: very interesting."]*

I am to willingly sacrifice pain and attachment so that I may fully love, love without limit of thought or emotion. Each time I meet another's walls I am to love more—love each brick and stone in the wall, love the mortar, love the pain. Beloved says, "See the many ways you can nourish the people. See yourself as the Divine Mother birthing the light in others."

She told me last year, "Like all true healers you will always give more than you receive." This is true only at the personality level; spiritually, I receive in an abundance that staggers my mind.

> A medicine man shouldn't be a saint. He should experience and feel all the ups and downs, the despair and joy, the magic and the reality, the courage and the fear, of his people. He should be

challenging the teachings that required of me a focused, meticulous, conscious understanding of spiritual experience. As my perceptual and conceptual paradigms were shifting, expanding, simplifying, the insights Bailey's work offered continued to stimulate and inform—and today, reading these journal notes, I find that they still do.

able to sink as low as a bug, or soar as high as an eagle. Unless he can experience both, he is no good as a medicine man. . . . Being a good medicine man means being right in the midst of the turmoil, not shielding yourself from it.[75]

Whew, there is such rapid movement I can hardly keep up with myself!

In working with ashram staff, I feel resistance and reluctance to move to each new level of responsibility, pain in the process of moving to a larger perspective. Beginning to work more out of something approaching "group consciousness." Feeling very new and untried in this. Something, too, of that old pain in relation to naming what I see, feeling as if I'm therefore *causing* conflict or disharmony.

I am to mind my own business. But how do I know when I'm meddling and when someone else's business is also my business? *[Decades later my Tibetan lama will teach, "Never interfere with another being's karma." "But isn't that what a bodhisattva is supposed to do?" I asked. "I wasn't referring to you," he replied, smiling.]*

•

A little sadly, but mostly just factually, I recognize the spiritual development of these my peers as greater than my own. I am valuable here in our work, but I think it's for my intellectual and organizational skills, not for any spiritual gifts. Alice Bailey's work emphasizes the importance of recognizing exactly where one is in one's spiritual evolution, of seeing precisely and without glamour *[illusion or delusion]* one's position on the path—and this *in relation to* other disciples. *[Beloved had told me, adamantly, "No judging or comparing! Throw away the measuring stick!" I didn't ask what the difference was between these two instructions because I intuitively understood it: Recognizing is factual, while comparing is fictive, even when accurate, because it arises from projection.]* The glamour in my seeing is just this sadness: seeing the comparison as indicating insufficiency in me.

I have reached out from my loneliness to many people this morning, seeking connection and no one choosing to be with me, so I come away up onto the mountain, to sit alone with the western sky. Driven back into myself. Deep feelings of separation, aloneness, my emotional,

75. Lame Deer and Erdoes, *Lame Deer, Seeker of Visions*, 68.

physical self wanting connection at a bodily, intimate, loving level. *[I know I must have felt this because it is in my journals, repeatedly—but I am laughing as I read it: it is so far from my memory of myself! And I'm laughing at the "solitude irony"—how I had longed for solitude before and how I long for connection now. Seems it's the longing itself that's the problem!]*

Seeing, all through this intense week, how retention of speech, conservation of creative energy through silence, drove me inward, fueled, focused, and intensified the inner work. This morning, reenergized, I watched how I dissipated the energy in talk and interaction. Returning to silence in the afternoon and evening, I see the rhythms of silence and speech more clearly. I shall learn the rule of silence yet; I feel it coming. *[Still coming . . .]*

November

Was planning to stop smoking today, then remembered Beloved saying, "You don't need *any* prohibitions in your life."

Energies in the group flowing more joyously, organically. I really see a difference when *I* am not being antagonistic, contentious! And something else is moving for me—about being true to what I am though others may reject or disagree. To learn this solitary way without falling into separation mind: that is new for me. To be as I AM, what I AM, while holding the form of love and oneness with all. *[If the noisy college drama of war and peace with its quiet lessons of love had been one form of initiation, this present learning of a "solitary way without falling into separation mind" exemplifies one of Bailey's teachings: "After initiation the work is to make that expansion of consciousness available as practical equipment for use by the personality, and in mastering the path not yet traversed."]*[76]

Something is definitely Going On Here—some old pattern by which I have withheld myself is beginning to lose ground, to break up, some new energy wanting to come through. In meditation I chanted strong

---

76. Bailey: Initiation *marks* attainment rather than bringing it about. "In all cases it is preceded by a burning, through the medium of the inner fire, and by the destruction, through sacrifice, of all that separates." And, "Every step up is ever through the sacrifice of all that the heart holds dear on one plane or another, and always must this sacrifice be voluntary." (*Initiation, Human and Solar*, 18, 82.)

and sure—*with* my group sisters and brothers—praising all that is holy and divine in us and all of life. When I felt separate, I imaged the light pouring down through me, like a great searchlight beaming out, and such a palpable radiance shed from this vehicle. I saw how the heart can open when the light is drawn down from above, *for others.* Let me hold nothing back, so the light finds here no obstacle, oh Mother-Father God—even I, this proud, contentious, First Ray daughter of yours.

A larger, more inclusive vision is seeking its place in me.

[A key presentiment comes to me in these words visible in the limpidity and luminosity of mind—no explanation, no elaboration—just this—like a teaching. Again and again I shall recall these simple words as the frame shakes and cracks, slowly opening for all.]

•

I'm feeling somewhat better—and am aware of *resistance* to that, of actually wanting to stay separate, miserable. ❖ Beloved leads a procession into my room, smiling, to cheer me up. ❖ *[Weeks later this actually happens, Ruth carrying a cupcake with a candle, to cheer me up.]*

Meditation and chanting this morning, with me leading, were awful, disharmonious. Beloved: "See conflict as energies seeking harmonious resolution. Don't take either your own responses or others' reactions personally." What happens is really about *energy.* I can work with the emotions and understandings as they come up around the personal issues, but the main point is just to hold steady in the light. Keep breathing, let everything move, hold the heart open and the mind still, be receptive and responsive without being reactive—and continue to love and serve. *[If today I were to hear such words from a teacher for the first time, I would think I had received a profound pith instruction—so I say to myself and to you: Please, please cultivate the inward attention, hear your own wisdom, discern and cultivate it so it becomes available to you, useable. And follow it, so you become certain, so you walk your path with confidence, true to yourself.]*

SILENCE—and then the Good Word: speech that manifests the good.

Beloved can say things that go straight through the veils of obscuration and people feel jarred out of their rut but not personally wounded. I am to learn to do it with the same perfect compassion that she does it with, not to stop doing it.

This afternoon, six wasp stings in the back of the thigh. I see that the six are the six I live with here—my own "stingingness" returning to me in the healing venom of the wasp, to release and transmute the waspishness and venomousness of my own character. Cosmic acupuncture.

●

Anxious fear. The tenor of last night's dreams: me on the point of withdrawing energy or presence, dropping out of these relationships and activities. It scared me because I associated it with lacking energy, being sick, like last year. *[That is a superficial association, though. The "anxious fear" really reflects the enormity of the challenges being spoken of in these journal entries, the profound spiritual transformations being called forth, while full in the vortex of the human maelstrom. Life, work, and practice at the ashram are spiritual quickening and service. We are serving the teacher in ways great and small, serving her vast, timeless vision; this, our meditation practices, and her spiritual presence are quickening our positive potentials, purifying our negative ones. All of this also makes the ashram a house of mirrors, the faults and potentials of each one reflected by all. And just as in the wildly disorienting circus fun house, at every turn I am confronted and confounded in my perceptions, conceptions, preconceptions, misconceptions; in my sense of identity; and in the deep-seated, habitual, dualistic (thus divisive and separative) patterns by which I make myself and others right or wrong, loved or hated, chosen or rejected, worthy or unworthy. In my life to this point, this is surely the most difficult task I have ever undertaken:* the willing dissolution of the constructed self *in the excellent—and ceaselessly, minutely challenging—field of merit that is the sangha, the community of practitioners.]*

"Working with the thought" is a sham if I don't invoke the will to bring the thought into manifestation.

These days I am—oh yuck—fully in my personality, filled with poison-ality, feeling secular, resistant, rebellious, negative. Beloved tells me, "Focus not on the imperfection but on the means of perfecting it." Each exposure to the higher vibration jangles and realigns the being. *Know* this, Barbara, in all moments of doubt and ignorance. *Life and Teaching of the Masters of the Far East.* Know that what you pray for, for

the good, you receive instantly, in the very moment of asking for it. [77]
*[Far-reaching, powerful insight, changing my life both then and now. Pray, offer,
supplicate with absolute confidence for the good of all . . . then relax: it's already
done.]*

My first public teaching since the deep valley. All day I remembered to
"see with the eyes of God," to see the perfection of the original form,
not to get caught in the apparent imperfections of its manifestation. And
in doing so, I am learning of the power of the symbol. The symbol *is*
the thing it represents. Its qualities fully imbue our minds as we embody
the forms. The mandala, the sound, the dance *are* the universe, called
into balance and harmony. The representation of each element on the
altar *is* that element. The symbol holds and radiates all the power of
that which it stands for; as it "stands for" it, it becomes that very thing.
So a good work for peace was done this night.

So much resistance I am. Innerly I recognize: "it's just vibration."
Very tired, and several times, yesterday and today, a sudden rush
of weeping—releasing tension, resistance melting in the flow of the
salt sea within me. I don't really know what these sudden storms were
"about." Whatever blocks the free movement of love and light within
me, let it break up and wash away. I am tired of illusion & glamour &
resistance & weakness & self-indulgence & grief & separation & anger
& jealousy & resentment & attachment & pride &&&&&&&&—weary
of all that blocks the light—and tired of my petty, small vision, seeing
no further than my own runny nose, caught in my own reactions &
emotions & mind traps, barely able to see the world and its needs.
Today, Thanksgiving—and here I sit complaining. Let me lift my
vision beyond these limits. I'll go to the temple.

Weeping, weeping—calling upon Christ, my brother:
> The perfection that you see
> in me:
> let it
> *be.*

•

---

77. Spalding, *Life and Teaching of the Masters of the Far East.*

As with other major lessons, so with this one: seeing that I long for love is all that is needed. The point is not to realize these knowings on the material plane: it is to become whole within. *["Don't ask for anything,"* *Beloved had told me. "The opportunity is to master the flows of energy, not to gratify the desires of the various vehicles."]* So the longing for love, the yearning to be chosen as the beloved—this, now acknowledged, is to be joyfully sacrificed on the altar. *[Ah, how insight and confusion dance together in me! While the insight is authentic, I tend to use it to "spiritualize"—thus to suppress, not to lift—my longing for personal love. Which must, eventually, surface—so it can be offered, consciously and fully, for the love and liberation of all. Ultimately, we are already and always the beloved, who recognizes and chooses each one as the beloved. That is the liberating Great Love.]*

❖ I dream that Beloved has just returned from a dangerous trip to South America. ❖ I awake apprehensive, lock my door, am unable to sleep again, Holly Near's song about the *desaparacedas* of Chile running through my mind—*"Hay una mujer, Desaparaceda . . .* and the Junta knows . . ." My thoughts go to Beloved's last death, also in war. I realize that coming back in a body time after time—to *serve*—means going through such things over and over again. Where the people are in need is where the server must be. Feeling a shrinking from the task, a wish for a peaceful life.

December

Error saturation.

This is not just "one more piece" of letting go. The whole thing is dislodging a little more, the whole carapace.

I am right up against it. I am completely at odds with myself, scraping off the patterns of my old being like skin. I hear in my head "Jacob wrestling," but it's not so—I am not wrestling with angels: the real I is wrestling with the old excrescences of personality. I'm trying to get out of my own way, out of the way of the I AM. I don't know how to be or do in my relations with myself, with others. I don't really want to make a fuss about it; when I'm up against the wall I know it's because the wall is going to come down, but meanwhile it is very, very, painful and humiliating. I am so needing love and care, and I don't know how to get it. And my vision is so limited, so narrow, so *self*-absorbed. I know we're all doing this together, but I don't like these people very

much right now, and they don't like me, either. It's all just part of the
process and yet I feel lost in it, bewildered, incapacitated.

Whew, I am really OUT of kilter, OUT of whack, OUT of control—as
well as OUTrageous and acting OUT. And left OUT. When not included
tonight in a social gathering I definitely let it all OUT, my tongue stuck
OUT and the door slamming as I went OUT. And today, too, my tire
went flat—my escape car! *[Couldn't get OUT.]*

Last night's storm of hurt and anger has swept me back into myself;
I am in withdrawal, stiff, sore, and numb. Where is love for me, the
person? I feel outcast. Say it: I suffer, I am alone. I suffer, I am alone.

*[Again the surprising note of loneliness. I have few memories of ever in my life
being lonely—alone, solitary, isolated, yes, but not lonely. So it is very strange to
read these recurrent plaints, thinking that the journal record, written in the moment,
must be truer than my memory, looking back. Who is this person who feels lonely
but who doesn't store it in her memory banks?]*

I keep coming up against others and being cut to pieces or shattered. I am
breaking all apart. ❖ I am in the shower; the tiles of shower, walls, ceiling
are all buckling, about to come loose. It looks like an Escher print.[78] ❖

Others here at the ashram consistently articulate their understanding
that what looks like individual dynamics is really a co-creative group
process, while I am still in the illusion of separation, of individuals in
their own worlds of emotion, motivation, intent. Where some see the
Mystery and its unfolding fabric, I still see but the threads. Theirs is a
vision of cooperation and harmony, mine one of confrontation and
conflict. When, how, will I move beyond these fetters to clear seeing,
to vibrate to that higher pulse?

I don't know how to "do it" with people, must keep approximating—but
I feel as if my vulnerability has crystallized, hardened. Oh, this is quite
a time, quite a time. Beloved, I feel I am poisoning the atmosphere—I
can't find the things I used to know, how to bring my confusion into
the light, how to lift, release, transmute. HELP!

---

78. M. C. Escher (1898–1972), perplexing, diverting master of graphic
art, meticulously rendered intricate structures that are hypnotic, convincing,
impossibly logical and logically impossible. Often I think of his work and see
it in my mind's eye when experiencing "inner-outer" confusion, confabulation,
dissolution—duality pointing to nonduality, nonduality peeping through
duality.

Then I heard Beloved's voice: "The heart opens and closes, opens and closes—it's a pulse; you're okay."

•

It takes far more energy to stop love than it does to let it flow.

❖ Beloved: "You seem to have a need periodically to enter your soul's cavern and to go through your trial as if you are alone, cannot reach your Master." There is somehow the suggestion that she is not necessarily referring to herself as my Master. ❖

In meditation I sensed that my old coat was no longer attached to me! Startled to find it missing, I checked—not there! My back felt open, strong, unencumbered, not needing that coat anymore. So works the inner light, so burn the fires of transmutation: the turmoil and pain of these last weeks—groping and stumbling, bumping into people, feeling my way, half-blind, unsure of each step, sure only of the direction and trusting the I AM to guide me—and days later I discover I am touched with grace.

We empty ourselves, little by little, as if for the light within to have room to expand—and we *become* liberated: we become what we already are.

Beloved to another sangha member: "Barbara is a feather in our cap!"

My prayer today: "God, thank you for letting me be useful and well used—but please, God, don't make me indispensable!"

Yesterday I felt, not tired in the usual way, but *weighted*—with the full weight of the future of our work. I know I do not bear anywhere near that full weight, but I felt it descend onto my shoulders, felt pushed down, prostrated, flat on the ground. I am a small person sharing a large job. My prayer is for the strength to fulfill my sacred duty, to carry my responsibilities.

Beloved's tears. How is it that one who is enlightened can feel sad and fearful, lonely and overborne?

Assisting Beloved in a teaching. The city feels vibrant, open; I feel at home. Standing outside as night falls, feeling the immense, throbbing vitality of this island like a teeming hive, a wondrous, alive, creative energy; seeing the panorama of the city before me, lights, skyscrapers, charging traffic, technology, energy and light, vibrant and powerful. Aware of the poverty, the violence, the despair in this city, yet without judgment. I felt myself a generator of love there.

Yesterday, tired, in a "secular head," things seemed empty of spirit, and then at one point I looked up and saw the beautiful faces of the people listening to Beloved, their openness and light, eyes like stars, shining and clear, radiance filling the room—and once again was deeply moved by the return of the people to the light, and Beloved's wondrous grace, her strength to go on, day after day, month after month, year after year, city after city *[and lifetime after lifetime]*, reaching out to touch the people, singing out their divinity, shining out the light to mirror their perfection, to call them home. And gave thanks for being able to share in this great and holy work, and for the strength needed, in every moment the strength sufficient to the need.

Saw an old beau tonight. He made me laugh, as always—told me his son is now thirty years old—I was flabbergasted—"Your son is old enough to be my lover!" "So's his old man," he replied dryly.

❖ Conversing with Beloved in a large old house. By color code we paint the furniture—blue for beds, white for chairs, orange for bookcases—and laugh about how we'll be able, by knowing the colors, to avoid going to sleep in a bookcase! ❖

•

Florida, visiting Mother, who asks, "Are you going to stay at that ashram forever? How will you live? You won't have very much money when I die." In the night I awake—her anxiety fills the room—I try to hold myself clear, in the light—I am shaking and cold, feel as if I'm sliding into a dark pit, as if the universe of love and abundance has turned hard and cold and empty. *[Stifled by her anxiety, as in childhood, I am unable to recognize and be nourished by her love and concern, as in childhood.]*

Returning to the ashram shaky, weak, labile, cold: adrenal strain again. Nine days of recoil; this is the result. It occurred to me to laugh at myself, eventually: Mother was so much more relaxed during this visit that I could in no way avoid seeing *myself.* I have much work yet to do. *[These seem to be the lessons I take from every encounter with my dear mother: I lack compassion and stability; I have much work yet to do.]*

•

YEAR FIVE

Gift of holy power · No great leaps
Stretched taut · Vigil · "Shake down forms"
Certainty and uncertainty moving together in me
The Gully of Not Good Enough
That I be as I AM

January

"Many paths appear, but once the way is taken, it must be followed to the end."[79] Form and essence. So what vehicle is it, for me? I believe it is enlightenment and the bodhisattva path.

Projections catch on the hooks of our unresolved issues, feelings, disappointments. All that I see is a reflection of my own consciousness. Soon after I feel critical of something someone else has done, I see that I myself have done that very thing!

Today we played broom hockey on the frozen beaver ponds. In the molten golden light of late afternoon I watched Eric flying in great silvery spirals across the ice, dancing, soaring, graceful, and happy, bright flashes of red winter underwear signaling his turns as the flap of his torn trousers caught the wind of his movement. I could feel him glad to see me out playing, one with the mêlée of shouting and laughing.[80] *[For I am always working, working, working in the office, which I love for its usefulness and moments of selfless service; enjoy for its intellectual stimulation; resent for its confinement and dryness; resist and need for refuge from group life; cling to for identity and ego. What I really miss isn't play but meditation.]*
    Intensive spiritual practice is as important as "productivity." We

---

79. Matthiessen, *The Snow Leopard*, 46.
80. Eric: dear friend of many lifetimes, met again here in our little community, where we resumed our loving, challenging, supportive, provocative, tender, faithful spiritual friendship. We laughed a lot as we worked, chafed, and ruminated together—a priceless gift for me during these years.

have done one day of silence since we formed in the summer, never yet a whole day of sangha together in the temple—and today the staff postponed group meditation in order to continue talking! I feel shattered. Day after day I put work before meditation. Beloved says that silent sitting is "personal" meditation, to be done in the evening—when I am too tired or still working. She also says "work-is-practice-is-study-is-practice-is-work." Yet I think I *need* the silent sitting. *[Karmically I need the work, but mentally I need the meditation: I don't yet have mind stabilized in its true nature, so the daily rounds are taken in conventional attention, not radiant attention.]* Oh, there is so much to give up—even what I think is the essence—no, sitting is just another form, the essence is to be One. And here I am in my room, separating myself from the group, not going to the temple—where they are now, finally, about to meditate. Well, it all is just as it is. My lesson is not to react. Let go, let go—see all in its "suchness." *[Of course I have no idea what that means.]*

I can't stop crying.

Desirelessness. To desire nothing, not enlightenment, not stillness, not even desirelessness, for within all desire lies the thoughtform of separation and lack. Yes, *let* me shatter, let this encrustation shatter . . .

Beloved: "Three a.m. is when the Masters are up talking to each other. If you should find yourself awakened at that time, consider it a blessing." So last night when Sassafras knocked over the water and I sprang up, muttering, at exactly 2:55 a.m., I gave thanks for the blessing, and spent a luminous, spacious, elevating half hour in the energy field of the Masters. I entered quickly into a deep meditative state; chittery thoughts kept running discursively but I was somehow deeper than they were, the stream of meditative awareness running in a smooth, unbroken course. Felt my consciousness clarifying and vivifying; "ascending," as in an elevator, saw a great single Eye, geometric shapes, pillar of light. On a dark screen, two words flashing—registered their meaning and impact, no conscious awareness of what the words were. I talked with the Masters, there with them in a generous fellowship, in a state of equality, accepted as one with them.

"Patterns of energy" and the "consequences of choices"—Beloved's points of emphasis for me to study and reflect upon. *[Study of karma.]*

This "larger, more inclusive vision that seeks its place in me"—it sure is a long time *taking* its place in me, replacing partiality, exclusiveness.

This morning, aware of ego striving to claim for itself the territory newly opened, I remind myself that one of the most important things in the recent conversation with Beloved was this: She confirmed my responsibilities, position, skills, and gifts as rendering me useful, useable at this time, in this place—that for this reason and for no other I am here doing what I'm doing. It is neither a matter of "spiritual development" nor of "specialness," but simply a matter of function: I am able to get the job done.

Feeling anxious at going out to teach again—last year I was too full of ego, burned my circuits, almost died. That association is still in my mind. *[Still materializing and dramatizing a process that I have already apprehended in its subtlety as spiritual purification and initiation. Habitual patterns of thinking are recalcitrant to change, and yet not one of those patterns, mine or yours, however entrenched, has any substantiality whatsoever.]* "I'll be safe if I just stay here in the office." (Two months later: HA! See how safe it is here—ego found me, though I was hiding in the office!)

Our co-creative planning for the teaching worked magnificently, revealing two absolutes that we humans usually treat as relatives: the absolute truth of the truths the teachings reveal—and the absolute truth that we know these truths already, have immediate and profound access to them, to all that we are shown. This was very evident in the movement mandala. I saw the group one living, breathing organism, intent and focused, beauty radiating from the ordered precision and grace of the movement, the selfless concentration of the dancers. I stood with tears flowing, deeply stirred by this universal perfection in human form.

Getting somewhat better at being simply an observer of my lower nature. It floats up, all claws and gaping maw, in the moments of highest potential.

•

I'm very, very tired, up against something that wants to be moved, another letting go of ego, and not sure what it is.

It's about *love*. It's all hollow, all that I do and say, if it isn't done in love, with love, for love.

Uh-oh. I have been in negativity again, critical mind grabbing hold of discriminating wisdom. Let me release the idea of the separated self. Let me learn to *love*.

Beloved points out that being and becoming a loving person is a discipline, a *practice*—and I realize that I'd had an image of a mystical "opening": "Abracadabra, now you are a loving human being!" Just as Lama said about compassion: you become compassionate by *practicing* it, and "slowly by slowly" it becomes the more powerful idea form, the dominant energy.

[Certainty and joy in spiritual practice and accomplishment come with bodhicitta, activities and practice given with love for all. Love is not an emotion but a quality of our being. We practice not to create it but to reveal it.]

•

Sadik Hamzani was asked: "How did you come to succeed, by his own wish, the sage of Samarkand, when you were only a servant in his house? He said, 'He taught me what he wanted to teach me, and I learned it. He said once: "I cannot teach the others . . . to the same degree, because they want to ask the questions, they demand the meetings, they impose the framework, they therefore only teach themselves what they already know." I said to him: 'Teach me what you can, and tell me how to learn.' This is how I became his successor. People have cherished notions about how teaching and learning should take place. They cannot have the notions and also the learning." [81]

I ask Beloved, "What spiritual boat am I in, your lineage or the Dharma?" No answer, and a question back to me: "So you think you're not a 'this'—are you a 'that'?"

But I am not really engaged by *any* of the forms. I seem to resonate to the inner teachings that are beyond form. *That* is my dilemma. *[And my medicine, my gift of holy power, its vastness and transcendence difficult for me to accept.]*

She said, "In the Buddhist way there is a consciousness that 'self' does not exist, while in many other traditions very few are called to that fullness of consciousness." "But I am," I responded. She nodded.

I think of those who do rituals as "spiritual" and of myself as "nuts

---

81. Shah, *The Way of the Sufi*, 148.

and bolts," having no real sense of the sacred. What *is* "sacred"? It feels to me as if it is all sacred—or, it is all *just as it is.*

"Remember Ananda," said Beloved. "He was the codifier of the teachings while the Buddha went off into the forest; he was closest to the Buddha because he did that important work. Ananda delayed his own enlightenment in order to serve." It was at this point that I said, "I will do whatever is needed—I just want to learn to do it with love." Beloved responded, "Maybe it is not that the love is incomplete but that the communication is incomplete. Don't hold back. Express your point of view, say what you need to say. It is very important to do so." *[Over and over she reminds me that I must speak, regardless of whether others want to hear me or like what they hear. Over and over I speak—but not completely. Often I confuse myself and others by speech that seems forthright but that is partial and thus manipulative. I doubt myself, fear rejection, hostility, disapproval. But, more deeply, I fear my own clarity and potency.]*

February

Beloved keeps correcting me on the distinction I make between intent and effect. They are one, she insists. *[She is telling me that the effect of action reflects the intention of the actor—speaking of this to underline our responsibility for clear intention and to undercut the whining "I didn't mean it" with which we try to evade accountability—for our* minds. *Motivation is everything, everything. Because everything arises in mind, from mind, of the same nature as mind.]*

On personal suffering, Beloved teaches: "Offer it up as a sacrifice, that your own obscurations may be cleared, that another may be reminded of the seed of wisdom within." *[This simple teaching changes lives in one instant.]*

❖ I have been clawed very deeply, right near the heart. ❖

•

No request for real aid must ever be refused . . . Nothing should stop your service along this line, not even the realisation of limitation and of ignorance. . . . Above everything else in life: give to all who seek your aid the fullest measure of *love,* for love releases, love adjusts and interprets, and love heals. [82]

---

82. Bailey, *Esoteric Healing,* 352–53.

Well, she certainly has me in the perfect position for all my faults to come up in glorious Technicolor—the job *[administering, managing, directing]* that hooks all my drivenness, controllingness, right-wrongingness, judgmentalism, critical mind, élitism, pride, arrogance, sense of estrangement. And I'm getting it all flung at me in our staff meetings. The stone tumbler is working full tilt.

I have asked to be clear: here's every opportunity. I can't not see what needs correcting in me, yet I know I don't know how to do it. I pray for guidance and help, that I may continue to do my job here in the face of so much evidence that I do it so very imperfectly, and in the face of so much dislike for me.

❖ Beloved advises that I do some needlepoint, asks if I can do it free-form then suggests I begin with a pattern. She draws on the pattern, making curves where there had been angles. *["Everyone's looking for the soft round," she had told me.]* I am aware that there is an energy transmission and an occult teaching occurring in this pleasant exchange. ❖ *[If we can't do it free-form, begin with a pattern: this is the occult teaching. And this is the way the masters teach, first giving us truth naked, unadorned—and if we are unable to realize directly, giving us structure, form, pattern by which to approach it.]*

At the waterfalls last week, the ice still intact all across the stream, the flow and rhythm of the water visible beneath the ice; this week the ice receding, the water can be seen moving freely. This interests me very much these days: this story is the same as my own.

Something I must record so I never, never forget it: I know now how it is that we can use ourselves, even our sacred skills and implements, for killing, hurting—out of anger, the refusal to own it as the creation of one's own thought, the continued illusion that one's anger is caused by another person's acts or attitudes rather than by one's own choice. I said something hostile to Eric and he immediately zapped me with a crystal, as with a gun. I said to him, "A crystal is not a toy, especially not a toy gun." "Neither are your words, my dear," he quietly replied. *[Is he not the best of friends?]*

•

The Mirror turned toward me these days is closed, stern, cold, forbidding. A shift. Some biggie coming for me. Not to speak of it; just hold steady in the light.

March

Erotic feelings and stirrings in the flesh—

Eric is cutting away at me with a sword of light, love and consciousness ablaze in his face; he brings the blade down, thrusts it deep into
me.

I am fully *in* my pattern of alienation, the "separated self" experienced
here and now in this group of people. But in morning meditation, mind
steady in the light: this personality stuff is not all that I AM.

I am to be *all* that I am—say what I see, know and believe, simply
and directly, without energizing my fear that others will not love me,
my anger that I feel alone. And I am to accept "separateness" from
others in form and personality while holding firm to my knowledge
that there is really no separation.

Error saturation. I am trying to do what is "right"—but it turns out to
be "wrong" in relation to other people. Oh, I want to SCREAM! And
I am afraid: she will "fire" me. *[The recurring anxiety about being fired, as
in rejected or ejected, is really anxiety about being fired, as in a kiln, a chemical
retort. She definitely is firing me, and the fire is getting hotter all the time. The
image of being fired from the ashram, though, is projection: I feel trapped in that
hot furnace, want to flee in panic.]*

Nowhere to hide. I see it, everyone sees it: the me that's trying to
cover up the me that's afraid to be seen. I can do nothing but change
and I don't know how to change—I feel as if I'm trying to rub my
skin off—as if I can just *take off* what must go—but it doesn't work—I
don't know how to let go of it—

Beloved: "Don't separate yourself and then say people don't love you—I
don't want to hear that." How shall I heal this wound within me that
I keep laying at others' doors?

I am holding this vision: I stand clear on the mountain peak; around
me on all sides falls away all that is not needed, the pairs of opposites,
the "this and that."

Fasted till evening, then joined the group for popcorn—not for the
popcorn but for the group.

•

With gratitude I see that the very slow process of my enlightenment is the greatest of gifts. I am to see every rock and pebble, the smallest and most subtle of obstacles, stumbling blocks, pitfalls, and obscurations. I am to skip over nothing, take no great leaps. I am to know the path by heart and *sole* as well as by soul—for I am to help others, and the guide must know the way intimately. Some relief, poignant and bittersweet, arises in me. I am not slow and stumbling because I am inept or unworthy; I am slow and I stumble because I am worthy. My work is to do it all, *all*, so that I may safely, wisely, compassionately serve others on the path.

Now I see the path more clearly, see my own way more clearly. To see in the instant *how* "the obstacle is the path" is quite different from just knowing intellectually that it is so. It doesn't feel glamorous to think I am to learn the path in every bend and obstacle and pitfall so that I may guide others; it feels accurate. It is the path of mastery, the way to come into Knowledge.

As I walked down the hill today in the stiff spring wind, I laughed aloud at the sheer joy of the spring waters running down, down the mountain, freed from their freeze, each tiny drop joining with others to form a trickle, then joining again to become a rivulet, a stream, a brook, a river—the *joy* of it, the delight! "Down, down, we dance and sing, the One in the many, the many in the One." On to the lakes, on to the ocean—no obstacle can stop the flow, it leaps and flows around and under and over and through, the Earth drinking in and giving up the waters all in the same moment. The *profligacy* of it—nothing is wasted—and I am not separate: I am in and of the flow. What beauty there is in this world, this school of life. Only *see*, and joy rises from within like the dancing waters of spring on the mountain.

[The insights of these moments: a torchlight for my whole path. Ever wanting to leap right to the end, ever reminded to bless my slowness. Ever grieving my faults and failures, ever reminded to offer them for all. Ever tempted to regret, ever reminded to praise, praise, praise.][83]

•

---

83. The sequence of inner events in these last pages exemplifies what Alice Bailey writes about initiation—how it is preceded by collapse of meaning: "We have all—disciples and initiates of all degrees—to enter the secret place of initiation with a sense of blindness (or loss of direction) and with a feeling of complete destitution." (*Discipleship*, 708.)

The first day of spring. I sense myself increasingly transparent. Will-less. Flowing. God, Allah, Sweet Mystery. Chanting silently, for an instant I went through the window.

❖ A dancer and two other women are above me in the sky, on an A-shaped wooden frame. The dancer is sure-footed and calm, as is the young girl she is teaching; they seem to have no fear. The third woman reminds me of myself: she knows the correct steps and posture but in her fear and anxiety she loses her balance, almost makes the girl lose hers. ❖ It is fear that is unbalancing, not lack of knowledge. In lack of knowledge one can simply *be*. In fear one is trying to protect oneself, disturbing the simple flow of what is—where, indeed, there is nothing to fear.

The geese are homeward bound, eager, eager.

April

Beloved has been quite ill. Wishing I could "do for her" in a personal way, but all I can do is just what I do do: burrow into the office. To do my job as well as I can is the only service I can offer her. And I am often perplexed these days, contemplating her humanity and divinity—and ours. How *is* it that one can Know and still be fully human?

In the temple this night of Christ's crucifixion I felt such loving compassion for the man Jesus, who did indeed suffer and die upon the cross—as each of us must, on the cross of humanity. "We fall into matter," said Beloved. The cross: the four directions, the four earthly elements; the person standing in the world, arms outstretched in invocation and blessing; and at the center the heart of the matter, the heart in matter, the heart of Mater, Divine Mother, giving birth with spirit to material form, the human being who seeks ever to realize in form the essence of spirit. In the sacred dance I was "dancing the cross," transmuting matter into spirit and spirit into matter as I danced.

•

Aware of how I have more care for "the universe" than for those right here next to me, I offered prayers, very focused and attentive, for each one in this ashram family.

I begin to see that the painful transforming work of these past months has come to a place of pause in the light. Hallelujah! Have been working on transforming separation mind and that old "charge against the self"—the "I'm not good enough." I *am* good enough. We are *all* good enough.

Sensing more clearly now the activation of that "larger, more inclusive vision" that was "seeking its place within me." Knowing myself one with the circle has been necessary to prepare the place for that larger vision to take root and begin to grow. *["One with the circle" is the large, inclusive vision, my dear.]* I begin really to see that inclusiveness has more power than exclusiveness—more power for good, more power for love, more power to magnify the light, more power to build the form.

What am I to go through yet, before liberation? I know now that I shall not fail. I also know that I shall once again doubt.

•

In the bright sun I walked down to the small waterfall—today huge, roaring. I lay on a rock, entranced myself listening to the sound till it became no-sound, the flow and the sun lulling my mind to quiet. What I loved was the play of the tiny drops leaping in the sunlight, as if playing catch with the light, then falling back into the torrent—still water in air, still light in stream.

In our staff meeting this morning I spoke of Beloved and we being one—and I see that it's not just that I now *identify* with that but that I am at the beginning of the process whereby I *am* that. I am making myself available to serve the group, the planet, in just that way—to take on the karma and transmute it, to let the confusion and suffering pass through me, to find resolution of conflict through my own transmutation of conflict. I am now consciously "one with."

And last night in the group I observed how Beloved turns each thing to good—greets each comment with positive energy, transforms limit to opportunity, pain to gratitude, self-pity to joyous rededication. I'm sure I've seen her do this a hundred times, yet last night I really *saw* it—because now I am ready to learn this myself.

I've always sensed that I was missing some "membrane" others seemed to have between themselves and the world's pain. Even as a child I was aware that all this was somehow my responsibility—but I

didn't know what to do with it. I didn't know how to hold the energy
of love, oneness, so I was wracked by conflict instead of drawing it
into resolution.

Signs of change in our family life—playing in the snow, laughing at bug
stories of Africa, Mexico, Hawaii, the Ozarks, after a lunch of pasta al
pesto on this cold, snowy day, warm with food and comradeship. I believe
that in the fires of transformation we are welding our bonds of light.

•

Beloved just told me this is the summer of my prayer vigil. I realize now
that the vigil began that very moment.

Wondering if I've been slightly scorched by Beloved's energy—feeling,
"Okay, that's enough Beloved for a few days."

Aware of the violence within me. I'm actually *seeing* myself trying to
impose my will on a person or situation, seeing how my frustration brings
up anger, images of "knocking people's blocks off." *[Better to dissolve my
own blocks!]* And just now I learn that a good man I once knew, in the
village where I used to live, has gone and murdered someone. Oh, let the
violence cease, let the warring stop—in the hearts, among the people,
on the planet. And in me, Creator—let me become peaceful. *[In reading
this I am struck again by the recurrence of violence around me, remembering Beloved
telling me that such circumstances may reflect one's not having fulfilled one's spiritual
purpose, having seen truth but not realized. This helps me have great compassion
for my underlying anxiety that I would fail my spiritual task or test, be unable to
fulfill my purpose in this life.]*
    "Each pilgrim on the Way is worn and tired. All are sincere. Forget
this not." [84] I am weary, so deep down.
    Beloved: "There comes a time when one needs to go inward."
Awoke with an image of a long tube through which the light is spiraling,
creating a vortex into which all negativity is ineluctably drawn. That's
me, that's the process I'm in right now.

❖ I am "swimming" through intense weather—it is tangible, a substance,

84. Bailey, *Discipleship*, 534–35.

swirls and spirals of energy; it takes great effort to move through it—but I'm doing it. ❖ I awake at dawn, go out into the beautiful morning, meditate in the field overlooking Lady Mountain. Back in the temple I remember that for as far as you go out, just so far must you go in. For as high into the light, into ideal form, as I recently went, just so deep again into the dark, into material form, must I then go. I realized myself as free, an effortless, flowing sweetness, and then came crashing back in a full arc of the pendulum, caught again in the body and its limits, entangled again in negativity, critical mind, bitterness. This morning I prayed for *mastery* of these vehicles.

I still have such self-reference and self-orientation—but okay, that's why shifting to a mind that is one-with instead of separate-from brings up so much stuff. That's *good*—get it up, get it out, let it go. Know that you *will* come through: you *are* the light you knew yourself to be two weeks ago.

And then Beloved tells me, "When you're doing everything you usually do to come clear and it's not working, do something outrageous. Have a stiff drink!" So after a good long cry I drank some brandy and went to sleep.

Frankly, I'd like to get laid.

May

❖ A grubby little girl climbs into the van in which I am trying to escape. I grab her by the shoulders, wanting to shake her. She is bewildered: "Why don't you want me to get in?"—as if she has every right to force her way in. "I don't like you," I say, and yet realize that I do love her—then it is I who am bewildered: What do I do now? ❖ *[There is no way I am going to escape samsara, escape suffering, without learning to love unconditionally, and this grubby little girl—myself, abandoned by me—is going to teach me how.]*

My mother's here, visiting me at the ashram. Greeting her, Beloved said, "Barbara really knows how to make people feel good." That was surely a description of my next step, because it certainly doesn't describe how I have been with my colleagues here!

The Circle of Cause, or: I Create My Own Reality, or: What Goes Around Comes Around. A few days ago a co-worker and I were talking about friendship. I was saying the spiritual work calls for unconditional love and I don't have to "like" everyone in order to love them. Two days later I am hurting because I am not "liked" by my sangha companions. Moral: when you feel something lacking, look to see whether you are withholding or giving that thing yourself.

Lightning!
Storms!
Stretched taut.

❖ A gathering of the community. Everyone is to choose the one whom they want to take care of and the one by whom they want to be taken care of. I neither choose nor am chosen. ❖

> If you are despised by others and are about to fall into hell because of your evil karma in a previous life, then because you are despised by others the evil karma of your previous life will be extinguished. [85]

[When result arises, necessity ceases; when the fruit of cause ripens, the seed of cause is no longer. Throughout these years at the ashram I am engaged in intense karmic purification, although I don't really understand that this is what is going on. The process is both sweeping and minute. When it is sweeping I tend to experience it as expansive, liberating; when it is operating minutely I experience it as agony. Who sows the seed will taste the fruit—when dreaming and sleepwalking, as I still am, bitter or sweet; when awake, one taste. But when we really understand and have faith in karma, its most precise and most challenging activity arouses us to fierce joy—for each tiny degree of freedom we are thereby attaining.]

I am writing what Beloved is dictating, the words coming naturally to me. I laugh and ask her, "Am I just learning the lingo or is it in my heart?" She replies, "It's in your heart—I can tell by the light in your eyes."

I posed one of my "technical questions about enlightenment" as I looked at a child, wise and innocent in her blanket, making mudras with her lovely, graceful hands: "Once you reach enlightenment, then take a human body again . . . ?" "You do it over again," she said,

---

85. Robert Aiken, *The Mind of Clover*, 72, quoting Huueh-tou's *Blue Cliff Record* (an excerpt from the *Diamond Sutra*).

"because it must exist in the moment—but you do it faster, you remember sooner." So *every* lifetime is a review class!

•

Thinking about the path—that one sacrifices *everything*, even down to the bone marrow, when it is called for *[as Ruth is then doing, offering a bone marrow transplant for her critically ill brother]*, and thinking, Oh, do I *really* want to do that?

❖ Beloved is speaking of enlightenment—then I find an "occult clue": the letters "TL," and I awake. ❖ *["TL"—"and I awake!" And this is before I know about Tsawai Lama, my root guru.]*

Mists rise from the valleys and disperse in the clear, bright air. Even so disperse the veils of ignorance obscuring the bright sun of clear mind. In my fantasy my birthday was forgotten or neglected, but in reality not so—and I had the opportunity to observe the mind wanting to hold on to the fantasy, resist the reality.

I see how the pattern is: I say NO first, then gradually let the yes come through. No wonder they find me negativistic! The project now: hold speech until the obscuring mists have cleared through the power of correct thought, and *then* speak. This will be the way I learn conservation of speech and right speech, not as an end in itself but as a discipline to correct thought. And then in the circle Beloved spoke, looking directly and steadily at me, of exactly these things.

June

Amazing experience with Leo. [86] Deep openness, almost a trance state. I am a young woman named Phillippa. A colonnade of columns or palm trees, the avenue empty of people, though I see boats on the sea, each with six men rowing. At the end of the avenue, low, wide steps

---

86. One day I heard footsteps approaching my room, saw the incense smoke suddenly cease swirling and rise straight up into the air, and knew it was Leo coming. Beloved said of him, "The inner sacred space is pristine." At the ashram, we had a foolproof way of getting Leo to take on something he didn't want to do, like washing the dishes; we would just tell him, "This will benefit sentient beings," and he would hasten to the task. That's Leo.

rise to a domed temple on a mound. I see on the temple a golden
crescent that resolves into the form of horns on a rectangular base;
Leo is wearing this symbol also on a medallion. I resist seeing what's
at the top, tell myself I'm just inventing it—but then I am there, at the
sacrificial altar—my head is pulled back—my throat is open, is cut—it
is a ritual sacrifice—I have been trained for this from childhood, *it is
a loving act*—loving for me and for he who cuts: Leo, in this time my
father. I know no fear—just the open throat, the ritual knife, the welling
forth of my blood for the people. Later, as Leo and I go further into
the scene *[and all this unfolds virtually in silence: we are seeing and experiencing
simultaneously]*, I receive this teaching: "People the avenue"—bring the
mysteries to the people, bring the people again to the Knowledge. And
this: If I could give my very lifeblood then, I can give all I am now.

Beloved thanking me, so many times, so beautifully, so gratefully, saying
that she really appreciates "the consciousness with which you prepare
the people for the work, the way we work together."

In the recent teaching I was pained that I was not thanked by my
teaching colleagues or the students—and then saw that I had *erased* the
moments when that did happen.

Some veil seems less dense—I am seeing a little differently. ❖ A
dream about replacing red velvet draperies with bamboo curtains.
Beloved was there with me and said very clearly, "I'm so glad you're
doing this, Barbara." ❖ Now I see: replacing the heavy, dense, opaque
velvet with the airy bamboo that lets in the light.

Several days ago Sassafras brought in a live chipmunk, which I saved by
scooting Sassafras out the door. I thought the chipmunk had gone outside
or died in the wall, but I was awakened in the night by the patter of little
feet—loud!—the chipmunk dancing before my little shrine. Set out seeds
to catch him; they were quickly gone and later I saw him running across
the room. Either the chipmunk was going to get caught by Sassafras,
be trapped in the wall and die, or I was going to set a trap. I accepted
the responsibility of choosing to trap him, told him, prayed—and this
morning found the bait taken from everywhere but the trap trigger, and
the chipmunk drowned in the toilet. Felt it was still my karma, as I'd
chosen to kill him, but Beloved and Eric both said, "No, he saw your
intent and walked right by it, took the karma on himself."

A sangha sister tells me, "I see you in the realm of the Ideal—that is where you *are*—so in terms of difficulties in communicating with others it's not just that you are holding the form but that you are always holding the *ideal* form." No wonder I come off the way I do: add this to separation mind, critical mind, and the Judge and you get a heavy dose! Beloved: "Finer and finer all the time—just keep refining." *[See how she looks not at the confusion but at the clarity? That is the teaching on transformation.]*

July

The lessons these days are about simplicity, peacefulness, humility. Observe the seasons; in each do what is to be done. In summer plant seeds of good cause; in fall bring in the harvest, prepare for the quiet time; in winter send roots deep down; in spring come forth with the waters, cleansing and renewing. With self be true; with others be careful, have respect, be kind. *[So simple and pure, these instructions. Reading them today, as if for the first time, I am wishing that in that long ago moment I had known how to live them, simply, purely.]*

Everyone else is preparing for ceremonies and tending the garden, while I do my work in the office—and their joy, the transformation of energy from the caretaking of the sacred places, is a burning fire, a flowing river. Let me dare to sit apart, holding silence about pain, holding love in my heart.

My attention is caught by something I do not understand: am I to learn that I do not need personal love?

My longing is not about sex but about connection—I keep wanting to write "completion"—not completion in the sense that I am not whole and need to be "completed," but in the sense of "completing the circuitry." There, that's it. So now I am consciously working to call sun and moon into balance within. Sitting on a friend's porch I see the moon, remember my prayer that she teach me her ways, woman ways. And I take inspiration from the great clouds moving silently across the sky, majestic, dignified, resisting nothing, flowing and changing with the wind.

In ceremony: "I am walking in the sky, I am walking in the sky."

Full moon vision—I stand on the mountain top, arms downstretched, and the clear light streams down me to the world.

With intensification of fast and other preparations for vigil, I am very inward. It's a cleansing time—no cigarettes, almost no food, feelings close to the surface. It all smells so good, I long to indulge my oral senses: potato chips! popcorn! garlic! pasta! peanut butter! toast! cheese!

August

Vigil

[This I see as I crest the ridge: the two doors of the sky closing. And I know what it means: I will not step through the hole in the sky this time. Self-doubt, transmuted by love into calm confidence. Then, arriving at my site, I panic as I see bees using it for their complex communication patterning. The source of the nectar is a little bush right next to my sitting place. I don't want to write this, but I must: I cut it down, I cut it down. From fear, of course.]

The beauty of the night—clear sky, great canopy of stars. Trying to keep the fire going, wood sodden from two days of rain. Met the Giver-upper in me and moved right on through. Dawn this morning an astonishment—a slow, subtle increase of light and then, suddenly, "Oh, there you are!"—the sun. Early, early dawn; the most delicate of morning stars over Lady Mountain, three in a vertical line, reminding me of Christ.

Her instruction: "Listen!" The first thing is to let my mind still enough to hear.

The stilling is happening—wheels had to run down. Weak, shaky, dizzy—longing for some of the fruit hanging on yonder tree, but don't know if it's need or desire. Don't act. *[Good life instruction.]*

The inchworm works its way up the dead tree. At the top it stops: no branches, no leaves. Reaches out into space for contact with something to indicate next move. Nothing. Inches back down the tree—at bottom seeks another tree, contacts the tree it has just descended—and up it goes again. Same result, same response. I feel compassion, consider moving the worm to a more fecund site, decide not to interfere—then feel superior: "that's programming"—and see: no different from us humans, no different from this one, me, who weeps with frustration at finding herself continually climbing the same dead tree.

What do I give energy to, seek others' acknowledgment of: debility or strength, incapacity or power? I'm seeing the Excuse Maker, and she's full of "I can'ts." My "negotiations" with others—for time, attention, love—are often, perhaps even usually, based on my *weaknesses*. A whiff of honest pride at having made it through these days on total fast.

This is an intensive on the human condition: Form Life 101, vigil as metaphor for life. Physical discomforts, not extreme but incessant, impossible to ignore. Boredom beyond anything I've ever known. *Entrapped* in this body, and in time. Physically aching, the sun moving an inch in what seems like hours. Supposed to listen to wind, fire, songs in the Earth—all I hear: mosquitoes and flies. Supposed to meditate—every three minutes needing to do something with the fire. Supposed to chant—the voice wants to be silent. Oy! The vigil *is* an ordeal! Of the most mundane, petty, inglorious human kind: human body with all its desires, needs, limits, cravings, ideas, attachments. *[Excellent: arrest the ceaseless activity and see how mind craves it—craves any distraction from simply* being.*]*

The highs are high, the lows are low, and mostly it's just in-between, just like life. The main thing: keep the fire going, just like life. If you lay a good fire, subject it to a constant high heat, eventually it will burst into flame. If you form a clear intention, subject it to constant energy of purpose, will, and skill, eventually it will manifest.

I *need* vision. Not for glory, not for glamour, not for brilliance, but just so I can *see*—see clearly, see far, see true.

An intense, dark night. Knowing I would be leaving in the morning, it was a struggle to keep on keeping the fire going—reminding me of when I was sick, the struggle to keep on keeping on, not to die. I sat with the open sky, the mountain's shadow in my vision, the night forest open and breathing all around me—then put the tarp up against rain—it was like a cave, where I chanted, prayed, slept, and worked the fire in the company of the ancient women. At first I was deep in self-doubt, then offered it to the fire—*all* people's self-doubt. Finally found the voice to chant—strong, long, calling on the mothers and grandmothers, the sisters and the aunts, to bring their ancient women's wisdom. Then I heard, as a pulse in the Earth itself, the drumming of the ancient ones, the women, and their chanting, and I chanted and drummed with them, the two firesticks my drumsticks. Self-doubt, frustration, and sadness offered to the fire as a gift for the people. I am ready to go.

(End of Vigil)

•

Beloved really zapped me today: "Argumentative: too many words, always words, you hear only my words. I'm trying to teach you to hear essence. Western Mind Disease: the mind that argues with itself. You must transcend it." I felt stung, am in mild perplexity still. "Think on this phrase," she said: "Shake down forms."

So much seems so different since the vigil. I am happy, calm though busy, relaxed and at ease. We have accomplished a good summer, have harvested seeds of peace and unity and sown more good seeds for the coming year. The struggles seem nothing when I see the results. Mind of judgment seems to have relaxed its hold somewhat. I am more open and loving; no regrets, no ifs or shoulds or maybes—just see all things in their suchness. *["Shake down forms."]*

September

Skepticism, rebelliousness in relation to Beloved, my Mirror Teacher. Last night in my meditation I heard her say, "I am showing you your own mind." "Is this chaos my own mind?" "Yes."

On the inner plane I have no doubts: this is the one who is guiding me to enlightenment, to realization of my true nature. On the outer plane . . . ? Part of my doubting is again about my relationship to her tradition. When I question why I'm not as involved in the ritual work as some of the others, this is a good reminder: It's not that I am not accepted, it's that I myself am holding back full acceptance. How is the essence to be realized if not through form, that which makes manifest? So why is it that I hold myself aloof from the life of these forms?

[I see three things happening here—and one teaching for them all. First: I am always being called to what informs, animates, and transcends form, yet self-doubt inhibits my acceptance of this vast, profound way. "Shake down forms." Second: I love the beauty and power of all that is being given through Beloved's teachings, through her spiritual lineage, but I often feel foreign in the practice and community. "Shake down forms." Third: Although I do not write about it extensively in my journals, I am in this period experiencing anxious, disorienting stirrings of doubt and confusion in my relationship with my teacher. The rebellious energy to which I make occasional reference is pride rising up. It

isn't choking me yet, but it is stirring the swamp, and the gases are starting to rise. "Shake down forms."]

A co-worker said to me tonight, "Barbara, *you* are the biggest block to this community being harmonious and realizing its ideals." *[I don't contest his view, and . . .]* I am angry at his charges against me, laying at my door his own dissatisfactions. Is it possible that my recent frustrations have been partly *not*-mine, but also his and others'?[87]

I seem to be in a time where I don't know much, don't understand much of what is going on. "Shake down forms." In the temple I brought her me, just as I am, filled with doubt, uncertainty, skepticism—felt her love and clear light, and sensed myself a crystalline vessel, luminous. *That* is what is real, not what is momentarily *in* the vase. "Shake down forms."

Vigil and reconsecration seem to be taking place naturally, in the dailiness. "Shake down forms."

[Certainty and uncertainty moving together in me. Confusion, doubt, pride, skepticism, rebelliousness—and, running right alongside, clarity, ease, certainty.]

•

My prayers so often are just thank you, thank you.

Leo's excellent Buddhist teachings on pride—every point applied to me.

October

When doubt is transformed it is certainty that can flower. Aware this day in meditation, and yesterday in reading the newspaper, of ease in focusing light to places, people, events—effortless, sure, precise. In the

---

87. Reading this, I am reminded of Dorothy Day, cofounder of the Catholic Worker movement and the newspaper of that name (in 1932, with Peter Maurin), that inspiring, outrageous, uncompromising voice for total, radical abandonment of self in service to the poor, to peace, to God. She was a terrifying and compelling figure to me when I was young; I never met her and I never forgot her. In her diaries, Day describes over and over how those she worked with and served assailed her with their charges against her, laying all at her door. As many times as Day recounts being the target, she acknowledges her own shortcomings—and affirms how *loving more* was the only possible response. See Ellsberg, *The Duty of Delight: The Diaries of Dorothy Day.*

temple more power coming, compassion and goodwill flowing from me in the light—easily, directly, abundantly. I seem to be growing into my responsibilities these days, leadership more wise, loving, graceful. And I see my metaphoric language changing slightly, working with more concrete images of material things, speaking less abstractly.

This morning in meditation I saw how I have been lacking in compassion and love for Priscilla. She has never been unkind to me, and I have held this stony-hearted, punishing-parent attitude toward her. All her small acts of love, kindness, and caring—in the divine scales those weigh in like gold, while my "rightness" is dross, dead weight: the scale goes "clunk" but registers nothing of value. [88]

A generosity ceremony—to offer "something that means something to you" to be chosen by another. I think of this thing and that—and then I see, standing in the corner of my room, the prayer staff taken on vigil. Instantly I know that is the gift—and yet all day I am dancing around the choice, trying to get out of it. "Something meaningful," yes, fine—but not *that* meaningful, surely, not *that* something. And the resistance is the clincher, the attachment the sure sign that I have understood *[as in the early lesson when giving a crystal to the stream]*. The staff is my gift to the circle, with my prayer that it give strength to another's walk on the path. And it was Priscilla who chose the staff!

I have begun running again—out on the open road, in the wind, in the bright, fresh morning.

Something odd this evening—very tired, trying to sleep in my room during meditation time—began to cry, not really my own pain, more like unstressing—aware of the pain and confusion of us all, then specific people, specific situations—it wasn't that their pain was moving through me but that I was aware of *all* as energies seeking balance and resolution—aware of how our attachment to ideas—good, bad, like, dislike, who we are, what should be—stands in the way of the free flow

---

88. Priscilla, the beauty maker: a vessel of compassion, generosity, and loving kindness for humans, critters, and the Earth. I loved her like a sister, a younger sister who annoyed me very instructively and who continually touched me with her grace, her ageless wisdom, and her depths. I have never known anyone at all like her and when I think of her I am surprised by longing: I still miss her daily presence in my life.

into balance, into harmony. I was letting go of some of my ideas of what might be right for anyone, any situation—and my transmuting such thought-attachments in myself was itself a prayer, a blessing, an opening of the energy channels in *their* lives. One of the group later said that at about that time she heard my voice singing her name, calling her to come to the ashram, to be together with the family.

> First you identify the principle, then you practice it. Gradually you understand the principle, . . . you become one with it. When you become one with the principle it responds to your will. [89]

My heart is opening like a great lotus flower. As we chanted with Padmasambhava this evening I was in Tibet, then India, then everywhere, the waves of sound generating all-embracing light, flowing out to touch every suffering person on the planet, especially the children; the light giving birth to a being of compassion whose every sense and action is an eye, an ear, a hand, to see, hear, and touch those who are lost, alone, in darkness, doubt, fear, ignorance, or pain. For this work a strong mind is needed, to hold the light steady. No flinching in the face of pain. The grimace at the open sores of suffering might be just an involuntary reaction, not to be ashamed of; the mind, though—this can be *directed*.

•

Awoke this morning to a moonset that abruptly, for just an instant, turned the world upside down—an instant of absolute bewilderment, almost panic: a bright red orb setting behind the mountain, exactly where I am used to seeing the sun set. I knew what time it was, I knew it couldn't be the sun, and yet I knew it wasn't the moon—so I knew nothing. For just that instant I thought perhaps it was the end of the world. *["Shake down forms."]*

Three wonderful hours out tramping around in the woods alone, over across the beaver ponds to Charlie's Snag, bright dead white birch blazing away on the hillside like a beacon fire. Found it on the second pass, after going all the way around the bowl and orienteering back from directly opposite, cutting straight across the swamp—the snag itself, a very peaceful place, where the woodpecker soon came *[when*

89. Boyd, *Rolling Thunder*, 71.

I'm in the right place, the woodpecker comes]. Then an inhabited cave—bear or mountain lion—where I was literally *stopped* by an energy that simply commanded: *Go no further.* So I made an offering and a detour. My walking sent up great gusts of ducks from the ponds, three times, arcing away into the sky.

November

Keeping the fire tonight. Nothing transcendent, just simple: be there, keep the fire hot and strong, keep a clear mind, make offerings, don't be afraid, go slow, be sure. Big wood, high flames, hot fire, strong Barbara, giving thanks.

In the act of prayer in behalf of the people and the land I am transformed. Prayer is my sacred path, the way I know is true and direct, straight to the Source. In prayer I am pure, pure, wholly open to what is, asking not for the self but for all. In prayer I lose myself, give it over wholly to Creator. It is the moment of my holy power.

Just when things seem at their most ordinary and mundane the veils part again. My eye looking out and Buddha's eye looking in—same eye. And this afternoon I experienced inhabiting two planes of reality simultaneously: liberated mind and ordinary mind in ordinary body, eating lunch. Liberated mind saw all the activity, preoccupation, nervousness, agitation of ordinary mind as fitting and at the same time as empty. Ordinary mind, eating its lunch, saw liberated mind seeing it from a vast and spacious perspective, found that fitting, and continued eating its lunch. *[Ms. Absolute and her ditzy Relative, the ladies who lunch—but Absolute knows something her cousin does not: liberated mind is ordinary mind.]*

Directly experiencing that the One to whom I pray is *within* me, the seed of pure mind that is activated by the power of prayer. I AM the Source of my own perfection.

And today, with almost everyone away, I got a lot done, and done well—and feel happy that I am doing a good job.

•

The thing about being with Sassafras is this: with him I am a *kind* person.

The Four Vows

All beings, without number, I vow to liberate.
Endless blind passions I vow to uproot.
Dharma gates beyond measure, I vow to penetrate.
The Great Way of Buddha I vow to attain.[90]

Let me attain enlightenment swiftly, swiftly—it is *time*—time to be done with these illusions, these obscurations of clear seeing, full loving, whole serving, these obstructions of heart and mind that spread ripples and waves on the surface of the lake. Reading Zen enlightenment stories, I see that I have attained *kensho*, the first awakening or opening of the gate. I *know*, yet I do not live what I know. I have not yet "grasped the ox."[91] What are these blocks, these old hooks, these deadly habit patterns of thought, emotion, and behavior that still master and govern me? How can I transform them, break through them? In the midst of painful weeping I held open and serene, simply seeing what is, in its "suchness"—even as the "separated self" was weeping in despair. *[Deep sigh of relief, reading this, for it shows that a gap is opening—a gap between my ignorance and my identification with it.]*

Beloved: "The mind of 'am I getting something back?'—this isn't the place if this is the mind, for here we are doing it for the people and the planet, not for self." Tonight I really called my own motives into question. There are so many rewards for the work I do that it doesn't at all seem as if I *could* be being selfless in doing it. *[The altruistic paradox.]*

A very weird experience while teaching. Energy sloggy, messy; one of our teaching team described it later as a dark gas, another saw heavy, gray humanoid forms. It seemed to rise up from the ground, had to be dealt with then and there, no waiting. I had the people stand; we drew light up through the feet, ringing chimes, wafting incense. When

---

90. Kapleau, *The Three Pillars of Zen*, 365.

91. "In the Ten Ox-herding Pictures a little child and an ox are depicted. The ox is the essential self which we are seeking. The little child represents the self of the phenomenal world which wants very much to grasp the essential self—not through concepts and thoughts, but as it really is." ("The Ten Oxherding Pictures.") Many years from this time I will ask myself, as if I were someone else asking, "How did you do it?"—and I answer, "I never let go of the tail of the ox."

the light reached the heads, still more clarification needed, so brought the light spiraling down around the bodies. Finally all was bright and clear, and the group's subtle work was the strongest, most focused, most efficient I've ever seen. Afterward I could hardly stop laughing, it was so unexpected and perplexing—Leo puffing away, doing his best to clear it but it wasn't clearing, and Eric just built himself a pyramid of light and stayed inside it the whole time! I'm still laughing as I think about it—it was *ridiculous*—there we were, doing a beautiful, luminous meditation, and it was like sewing light-stitches in dryer lint!

Once again feeling self-doubt after teaching. In the midst of it calm, confident, happy, and now a little fearful, wanting reassurance, asking the team, "Was I okay, was it good?" "Yes," they said, "only you don't give yourself enough credit—you said they were Beloved's words." Well, they are. *[And then this dream, with the same message:]* ❖ A national magazine notifies me I've won a contest for women who've achieved high or distinctive expressions of creativity. Beloved says, "It's for the dance." I object: "But it's *your* dance." She shouts at me, "WHEN WILL YOU WAKE UP?!!" ❖

•

I'm confused—not understanding what's happening—with me, with the work—something has shattered, some tight holding on to a sense of competence. Maybe I should be demoted or reassigned; I'd be a pretty good cook, I think. The shakiness of the day emptying in painful, deep weeping—feeling the load is heavy, yet knowing it's not—feeling incompetent, inadequate, yet knowing I can do what is given me to do—feeling as if I can't trust myself, yet knowing I can. Very confused, in the space between my self-perceptions and others' perceptions of me—yet aware: something is releasing, discharging. I'm confused. *["Shake down forms."]*

I'm confused. Residue of pride, control, arrogance, separation mind—something in that old lexicon coming up to be transmuted. Leo as "jester" tried to dance me around in the temple—I was confused yet found it funny, half-played, half-resisted. Beloved: "He's telling you about pride." Misheard her, thought she meant I was to tell *him* about pride. *Confused.* Just keep watching.

I awake sad—in the Gully of Not Good Enough. All morning I've been hearing, "There's a little devil in here—open the door!" I need to do just that: banish the little devil, banish self-doubt and self-pity, move forward with confidence and generosity. Out with the little devil! "I am not good enough" = "I am not *God* enough." But I AM.

For days (and nights!) I have been sexually preoccupied. The desire is for a man, for sexual and loving companionship. Not for belonging or having, but for *being* with. Specifically sexually—to live that vaguely remembered sharing of energies flowing freely, the dance of the two, the arc of energy between the poles. And for the sweet, languorous melting of time and boundaries, slowing of time, swimming in time with another—playful, grave, exploring—opening, softening.

When Beloved touches an object or a person it is a blessing—recognition of the essence. I wish to learn that full presence, that clear seeing, that mindfulness.

An episode of depletion. Attachment to the idea that "I" am "giving," "I" am "not receiving" puts "me" in that channel, so "I" get tired, "I" need to be acknowledged, given to, replenished. If no "I," then nothing to tire, nothing to need, nothing to want. This is what I glimpsed when teaching recently: that "I" was absent while teaching. But then—oh, I see it now—again the personality reached up to claim that new space for itself, and "I" inserted myself into the channel once again. Who is this "I" that is so importunate? Who is giving, who receiving?

December

I move through serene knowing to profound self-doubt, all with the Eye open on the forehead and the joy ever increasing—yet the challenges of Don't Know Mind are still with me, and the Gully of Not Good Enough (ha! "Not *God* Enough"!) ready to engulf/engully me if I should slip—

Oh dear, I slipped. I'm back in the Gully.

I seem to have a *hole* in my heart, that lets the vision, creativity and energy leak out: the hole of not-good-enough, not-worthy. *[No hole in the heart, no leak in the bucket. Habit has created strong tendency to think these sad, self-demeaning thoughts, so over and over that is where attention goes, as to default position. Functions like a hole.]*

Oh, oh, oh—feel as if I'm falling apart—fits of irritability—feels like another spasm of personal will—let go, let go—no need to cling, all is unfolding, perfecting—the people are here to help, they are helping—let go, let go. But if I let go, don't push myself so hard, and it shows, finally, that all I do is quantity, not quality, she'll let *me* go. She said, "No, if you fall apart or can't do it we'll just find something else for you to do—you'll only have to leave if that's best for *you*." *[Remember this, Barbara.]* Image of Beloved cradling me, comforting me—makes me weep—no time with her for weeks and weeks. When I'm in self-doubt she stands steady, and it's I who recede.

[One of Beloved's greatest gifts to me is to show me, over and over and over, my self-doubt. Until I come to certainty. Then she shows me that. To those who are certain she shows certainty, to those who are doubtful she shows doubt, to those who are miserable she shows misery, to those who are joyful she shows joy. She shows us our own minds. There are times I love her for it, there are times I hate her for it—as she tells me I shall.]

In the book of Don't-Know Mind, this is the chapter of Transformation of the Gully of Not Good Enough into the Delta of Divinity, the Bay of Beauty, the Plains of Perfection, the Avenues of Amplitude.

Each spasm of this intense confusion and distress is remarkably brief—and afterwards I'm in cheerful equanimity once again.

Beloved reiterated: "To take bodhisattva vows and then think about what *you're* getting, that's not the way it works"—and my "what am I getting back?" is jerking me around this morning. I'm remembering the spiritual medium telling me to drop the charge of unworthiness against the self: "Your soul comes up to this and falls away, again and again, failing to meet the test, failing to resolve it." And I wonder—am I failing it again, falling away from the test rather than meeting it and transcending? *[The leitmotif of self-doubt, anxiety about spiritual failure.]* Though who knows—sometimes the test seems to be simply endurance, rather than blazing light.

Beloved said, "You are a very good teacher. When you stop doing whatever it is you do to yourself you're a very clear channel for the energy and light to come through." *[I remember the light slanting in from the back door as we stood facing each other there in her kitchen, teacher and student, in that homely setting.]*

Self-doubt is what I need to transform—it is this that clouds my channels, this that makes me defensive, rigid, arrogant, judgmental, driving, and controlling with others, this that makes me drive myself into the ground, this that denies the light. This last bout had in it some real self-indulgence . . .

. . . and then yesterday I found myself passing on to others the lesson I didn't realize I had learned: No matter what happens, no matter what you do, don't use it as a stick to beat yourself. In the worst situation, if you throw away that stick you are already transforming the situation. And if you do find yourself with that old stick in your hand, just look right at it—and change it into a prayer stick! *[This is the antidotal method for releasing an afflictive thought: change the* habit *of thinking it. Requires that we recognize both the thought itself and the tendency to think it—and that is what I am registering here, with relief, joy, and* confidence.*]*

Perhaps now I can begin to help others transform self-doubt, that root cause of blocking our own light, thus of denying others' light. Release self-doubt and self-negation and everything changes—the landscape, the path—everything.

[From time to time suffering and its transformation yield an insight so key to one's path that it transforms understanding of the steps already traced and illumines with the light of true purpose the steps yet to come. The early insight into the meaning of offering, received at the streambed where I take the crystals to bathe; the soul message that I am here out of choice and love; the powerful, profound recognition that the slowness of my spiritual progress is entirely one with its purpose; and this moment, clarity gently penetrating the dank, obscuring swamps of self-doubt—each of these continues to steady and strengthen me, and to support those relying on me as they open to their own transforming, illuminating insights.]

Christmas Eve. Something wanting to break in me—some division of inside and outside, some barrier between inner and outer: that I *be* as *I am.*

•

YEAR SIX

A great clockworks · "Bye, bye, baby, go on home now"
It is being accomplished in me · To bow to majesty of being
Envy · Dharma shining continuity · Blowing my Knows
"Many will fall aside" · Assaying emptiness ·
Like a dry corn husk · That is her love
Wavering perceiver, leaning toward truth

January

I threw into the fire: DOUBT
I stand firm
I stand firm

❖ A city, a residential street, big houses set wide apart. I'm crossing an intersection; the street then becomes crowded, slummy, the houses ramshackle tenements. I'm looking for "1099 TURNS ST." ❖ All day what stays with me is the address—and the fact that the street is straight. *[To one still walking, the path may appear twisting and turning; once accomplished, it is seen as both relatively direct and absolutely nonexistent.]*

Beloved tells me, "Time to work on compassion, prepare to contemplate the emptiness. Chant for Kwan Yin's compassionate wisdom." Listening to the chanting, felt my heart struck like the gong, the light radiating out. "Twice a day and while going to the bathroom, throw all attachment into the fire. See things in their essence. Laugh, be joyous. Too many words—distances from what is. *Just do it.*" *[No TURNS.]*

❖ The ashram dining room. On the first table are two candles; one, in a draft, keeps going out. Beloved and I are standing by that table; she says, "This one must be kept burning at all times, it's the flame of will." ❖

She told me why crystals sparkle when I'm in the room: "Your mind is very orderly; you have built a very strong mental body; you know the emotions aren't real." *[She had told me the same thing several years before, and both times I am surprised to hear that I know something I don't know. However, I have not yet learned to see directly, in the moment, how emotions arise and dissolve in mind, like waves in water, with no nature of their own, and so the "strong mental body" has not yet the inner discipline needed to hold steady in the waves.]*

A doorway opened in my mind this evening. Beloved spoke to me of how the inner mysteries of her tradition can only be passed to one who is of that culture—"because that mind is very different, can't tell you how different." These comments lodged within me, catalyzed a process. As one door shut, another opened in my mind, and I saw: "I am Mother-Father of all. Every people, tribe, and nation is in my heart."

In meditation I saw this: large and small wheels in a great clockworks, my outer life like the small wheels, moving relatively fast, their movement visible, measurable, while on an inner plane something else is happening—the large wheel is turning, very slowly—and it is this that is engaging my attention and energy. I am aware that I am just at the edge of some major transition, something becoming different in my life, consciousness, work.

•

[In my journal I write down this pointing out instruction for the great compassion that confounds the mind grasping to convention:] Bankei's reply when his students petitioned him to expel a fellow student who was stealing: "You are wise brothers," he told them. "You know what is right and not right. You may go somewhere else to study if you wish, but this poor brother does not even know right from wrong. Who will teach him if I do not? I am going to keep him here even if all the rest of you leave." [92]

I feel as if I'm just a cipher, a function—am praying for light—whatever needs to crack, let it crack—so the light can shine through.

❖ Big conference, final meeting with Beloved. She verbally draws a picture that I see as a horseshoe-curve mountain trail, and says, "Now

---

92. Reps, *Zen Flesh, Zen Bones*, 42.

comes the most painful part": those who aren't making the final effort will be left behind, "because we're on the other side now." Steely-eyed, looking straight at me, in scathing tones three times she chants, "Bye-bye, baby, go on home now! Bye-bye, baby, go on home now! Bye-bye, baby, go on home now!" I am silent, appalled, chilled. Shall I leave? Is it over? Have I finally failed—or is it another test? ❖

I struggle a little between my desire to sleep and the need to write out these dream notes—this choice a small moment of what the dream is about. In that semi-waking state, this thought: I could go on as I've been going for a long time yet before it would become obvious that I was on one side of the curve and everyone else was "on the other side now." I could still work, they'd still find me functional—but it would be empty, empty. I wonder now, as in the dream: Is it over? Or was she issuing a challenge, throwing down the gauntlet?

[This dream remains searing and vivid to me for a very long time, portentous and precise. The moment itself, as the dream reflects, is a turning point, for those going up the mountain and for me, about to spiral down into confusion—with essence of awake mind ever flashing through, flashing through. Disturbing conceptions and the powerful afflictive emotions come and go, rise and fall, momentary appearances only, like clouds drifting or scudding across the sun—while the light, the light, the light itself shines in unbroken continuity.]

February

I made a serious and possibly dangerous mistake. I'm looking right at it. I can only pray that my action cause no harm. I recall Beloved saying, "A warrior acts with good intent—and does not look back." I am seeking to discipline my mind, to not look back, to keep moving. This experience shows me that my awareness of the subtle, the sacred, is still rudimentary. Also, surely, a great opportunity to learn compassion: my mistakes are so much more serious than those of others.

Maha: "What a wondrous opportunity! This is the year we'll learn to be overjoyed at our mistakes!"[93] And now today Beloved acts as if nothing happened! As if I didn't do anything wrong, as if I'm okay! One part of me says, "But doesn't she *see* me? Doesn't she see what

---

93. Maha: Medicine Basket Woman, sifter of stars. Seer, healer, majestic mother to children and mothers, true teacher to me and many. We long shared warm, robust, vast love, huge laughter, absolute dedication to absolute freedom for all.

I'm really like?" And there's a small voice answering, in a tentative tone, "Maybe it's I who don't see me clearly . . . ?"

A small but significant gain: I think I've gone through this latest crisis without generating additional negativity. A step on the bodhisattva path. *[Loving, and now honoring in practice, Shantideva's teaching that "when bodhisattvas greatly suffer they generate no negativity."]*

Again in a time of just moving forward (trusting it's forward!)—not knowing what it is I'm working on, or why, just trusting in the process.

❖ I am reassuring a group of people, old and young, that there is nothing to fear, the necessary shifts in consciousness are indeed occurring, little by little the people are "coming over." I say that the change may not be visible in our lifetimes but it is happening, nothing can stop it, there is nothing to fear. ❖

Out walking in light, fresh snow, came upon cardinals pecking in the road—red-breasted, soft, bright, fat. They flew away as I passed and I entranced myself with the lovely prints of their wings where they had rested lightly on the surface of the snow, like a visit from a bird in the dream.

Some small openings of vision. I have long found it ironic that I am placed in a work role here that accentuates verbal activity, intellectual qualities—that this is the context in which I am to meditate, empty my mind, come to stillness. After all the releasing of form, structure, and role that led me here, I find myself in much the same kind of situation as before! This has seemed to me quite an enormous obstacle to my enlightenment, for it calls up all my patterned, habitual patterns of mind and behavior. *[Well, of course: I'm certainly not going to face them until they're in my face.]* Yet some days ago I suddenly saw this whole situation as an enormously rich and wondrous opportunity for enlightenment. If I can come to stillness and emptiness here, in *this* kind of work, then it's the real thing! And for just an instant, instead of the pain of impossibility I experienced the zest of the challenge—seeing once again how the obstacle is indeed the path. And for just a fleeting and welcome instant I saw this personality as such a *blessing*—so much here to clarify, transform. If I can come to compassion, clarity, emptiness through *this* vehicle, it is the real thing!

And I shall. I shall come to enlightenment through this vehicle, in this lifetime. The bodhicitta grows and grows in me. It is to better serve and love that I seek enlightenment now.

March

I am now having to hear, really hear, people's reactions to me. Threatening or strengthening: my choice. I'm functioning. That's good. This is surely a serious, sobering challenge for me: just to stay here and try to fulfill the responsibilities in my hands as best I can while being so aware of my shortcomings and confronted with them by others. It's as if I'm inside some Thing, trying to melt it from the inside while it's being hacked at from the outside. A co-worker today: "Hey, we weren't put in these positions because we're *perfect*, you know!" *[Plain truth, kindly spoken, from one who shares some of my challenging personality traits.]*

And, paradoxically, this is also when I am beginning to make a conscious assay into the waters of emptiness. Not a paradox, really. Have been stirring my consciousness with agreement to look at fear of emptiness, fear of not doing *[fear of not doing same as fear of just being]*—and at root it is surely this that stimulates my controlling behavior with situations and with people. In meditation, contemplating emptiness as a sea of clear light, felt myself as a young woman standing just outside a collapsed mountain—still not venturing away from the solidity of the mountain but aware of looking out onto the clear light.

Clinging to forms—this ashram, this teacher. The small-I seeks to be contained, the large-I knows that it contains all. *[The so-solid mountain has already collapsed! "Shake down forms."]*

Delightful visit to the Temple of Records. [94] Easy flight over the mountains, then the forest, wet, dark, sun-dappled, small white flowers, the perfumes of spring, new growth, running water. From the path I see the sky *[this is it, this is it—from the path we see the sky!—ah la la!]*; near the top this ravine becomes clear, almost bare; to the right it drops sharply away, to the left the mountain rises steeply. I'm approaching

---

94. Beloved spoke of the Temple of Records as a repository, like a library, for the books of each individual's spiritual history, lessons, purpose. Once having learned the way to the Temple it was possible to go there at any time to pose questions and consult one's book. I think this repository is called by some the Akashic Records.

an overhang, must haul myself up over the lip. The Temple is in a meadow with a lake. I enter, take down my book. On the cover is written my true name, in a hieroglyphic script I vaguely recognize: "AŠILA." I open the book, asking to see my purpose at this time. The page, like a report card, shows subjects and grades; three of the grades are "Ex" and two are "F." Did I fail? I ask to see the essence, see a pure, blinding white page with gold writing, but can't read it. Suddenly, two distinct, sharp, electric shocks—I am jolted out of my deep concentration, eyes wide open, fully back in my ordinary room, startled, uncomprehending. Have I done something wrong? No, no harm can come to me in the Temple; I shall return. I go now to a domed room of light, ask, "Why can't I understand what is written in my book?" "You're trying too hard." *[Ha! Pith teaching for me!]* So I take a trip—fly out over the land, swooping and soaring, an easy, playful flight—return to put the book away—see again both the report card and the white page inscribed in gold—and I laugh at the clarity and simplicity of the message: "Ex" = Excellent, "F" = Failure—and they are the *same*, neither means *anything!* The point is that I am to stop grading and evaluating myself: *just be.* I am laughing—it's so simple. Leaving, instead of walking decorously on the path I strip off my white gown and dive into the lake, cavorting and swooping like a dolphin, then again soaring through the air—anything but the dignified pilgrim, I am a child playing, a feather floating, a wind sprite delighting in sun and air, wind and sky, the beauty of the Earth beneath me. I waft down, twirling and turning—playing in the eddies of the breeze, teasing the wind. Instructed to land softly on my feet, I instead sail down smack into a glorious mud puddle, laughing and kicking my heels in the air like a happy puppy.

And then in another visit to the Temple of Records I was among the teachers and just filled with *joy* to be there: home. And, for the first time, I went to my book and wrote instead of reading. I wrote: "I AM HERE." And said, simply, clearly, with no adornment, to Beloved, "I am here, I am ready, use me as needed."

❖ I have a mala hanging on the back of my door. A teacher takes it and does something with it. I see fire flashing around it. When it's given back to me I know that whatever has been done to the mala has been done also to me. ❖

Oh, Compassion, I know, I see
your gracious flowering in me,
the ceaseless waves of your healing sea,
radiant heart of the Mystery.

It is being accomplished—the work of enlightenment is being accomplished in me.

•

Begin with yourself. Do not ask whether God exists; ask whether *you* exist. Do not ask whether love is an attribute of the divine; ask whether love is an attribute of yours. . . . Do not ask about grace; ask whether you have ever felt gratitude. . . . If you begin with the divine, then you begin with an achieving attitude. If you begin with yourself, then you begin with a losing attitude. Things will begin to disappear and ultimately *you* will disappear. And when you are not, the divine *is*—with all its grace, with all its love, with all its compassion. [95] *[The spiritual path is a subtractive process, not an additive process.]*

Oh yes, I aspire to emptiness—yet when I read Rajneesh on the discontinuity of mind-awareness from "periphery" living to living at the "center," I am aware of fear, distaste, resistance. [96] No matter what I say, "I" does not wish to give itself up. "The mind tries in every way to be closed, because to be open is to die. For the mind it is a death. So the mind will . . . find many reasons to be closed. It will find very absurd reasons to be closed." [97] *[And this mind does, oh yes, find very absurd reasons to be closed.]*

Vernal equinox, sunrise, a foggy, misty, silvery morning—branches limned in ice, pussy willows like silver bulbs on the bush, stitchery of little animal tracks quilting the crusty surface of the snow, the fire, strong and steady, sending flaming embers up into the morning sky, a tracery of light at dawn. Giving thanks for the new day, the return of the warm . . . and a spirit of laughter runs through me.

---

95. Rajneesh, *I Am the Gate*, 79–83.

96. This reminds me of an evocative description given by Swami Rama: "It is very eerie to attain Godhood: disconnect yourself here and connect yourself there." Swami Rama, *Himalayan News*, 1983.

97. Rajneesh, *I Am the Gate*, 121.

Whew, the energy sure steps up here when Beloved returns from a time away! We are a crystal, resonating to frequencies we're hardly cognizant of—and she's our tuning fork, ever stepping up the vibration.

The whole first day and night I was in the city with Mother, these lines from a Streisand song never left me, not even in my sleep: "We won't have tomorrow / But we have yesterday." Alzheimer's. Mother's future parts around her like a fine mist; her present is like water ever flowing, liquid moment to liquid moment, occasional eddies and calm, still pools. Only on her past is there a trace of her living: footprints on the sand. *[Lovely, lyrical reflection, after the fact, but in the actual situation I fall into impatience—and she is compassionate with me, saying, "You hurt my feelings, but I know it's because you don't understand."]* Tonight, back here at the ashram, finally I fell into compassion for my mother. To see her this way, living what she has most feared, facing it gallantly, gracefully, with courage, love, and humor. But I returned wearing all my spiky, sharp armor from the old days. Hope the time will come when I can be in touch with these high thoughts when I'm actually with her, not two days later. *[That time will come, a light-filled moment at the very end.]*

❖ A room with a fireplace, women sitting on a couch. Large slugs appear nearby and the women ask me to demonstrate the power that we have been discussing, to make the slugs go away. It would be an abuse of power to do that. I just stand up; I know they will go away simply because of activity near them. I give a talk on power: "We each have, and are, four different kinds of power: that which we have and are simply by virtue of our existence; that which comes through relationship in the whole family of life; that which comes to us from the stars and planets; and that which is simply, absolutely, an expression of consciousness." ❖

Last night Beloved spoke of dangerous energies, thoughtforms of war, severe tornadoes, lethal tides, volcanic eruptions. As I was preparing to sleep I experienced, awake but in a dreamlike state, *how* it is that through the practice of peacefulness within ourselves we create a vortex of energy that resolves into harmony the energies of conflict and war. Experienced myself creating, out of my very entity, a vortex into which the warring energies in the Middle East were being drawn and brought to resolution. It was a little scary—was I strong enough, clear enough to hold these powerful forces? But it was, simply, *happening*—I was learning that it *can* happen and *how* it happens by observing it as it *was* happening, within and through me.

Experiencing annoyance and resentment in relation to Beloved, in meditation this morning I acknowledge that it is her feet of clay I'm having trouble accepting, and the key is to love my own—so I take all the qualities I'm having reactions to in her, own them in myself, practice compassion meditation, become very still.

April

> Everything in the world is made of something, no? Of substance. Chickens, rocks, cars, dreams, thoughts, beans, shacks, feelings, tin cans, boots, even women. Even you. Made of Something. Our bodies came out of us, not the other way around. Bit by bit you made your body, like bees make a honeycomb. So [the physical body and the light body] are made of something. But the substance of one is finer, lighter than the other. One eats beans to live, the other eats air. It's not bound to the earth by as many laws as the first, but there are other dangers for it. Useless thinking that goes nowhere—what's right, what's wrong, who's good, who's bad, what you like, what you fear, deciding what you think so you can show that thought to the world. Pleasing others while ignoring yourself. You keep your attention collected now, girl. No more of that chewing, that daydreaming—it's very deadly for you now. A crazy devil. You have something of real value, girl. Keep it hidden. [98]

Feeling empty of meaning, confidence, joy in what I'm doing, who I am: "Oh, what am I doing here, I'm just nothing, nobody." Try to reassure myself that what I do is needed and useful, yet I really feel that only the "spiritual people" are the ones who are truly serving the transformation of the people and the planet. I feel so *not-valuable*. Useful, yes, as a brick is useful to a foundation, but not valuable, like the beauteous bird that soars in the sky. *[Shaken by a storm of weeping as I read this—oh, the sorrow, the courage. I'm reaching back to this woman, showing her now, this instant, the mirror that reveals her true face.]*

> All that came under *Preyas* [sense-bound, changeable pleasures] might be imparted to one who claimed kinship and equality of

98. Cravens, *Speed of Light*, 145–46.

status with the teacher. But that kind of relationship was not sufficient for bestowing *Sreyas* [transcendence]. The reverential attitude of a disciple was quite essential for it. [99]

Beloved asked me to read an article on spiritual teachers exposed for abuses, remarking, "It is said that at a certain point the spiritual leaders and teachers will be attacked"—asking me to be aware of that mindstream. But what I drew from the article was that those teachers had been rightly exposed, and that disciples not only need to "become the teachings" ourselves but also be alert to abuses and derelictions by teachers and poseurs. So just now she called me in again, told me I didn't get it, that it's not about "wrongly" seeing the teacher as divine but about *actually* seeing the divinity, the perfection. As she speaks I see how directly connected this is to the "clay feet" energy of rebellion and resistance I've been feeling in relation to her. I am *experiencing* the energy that gives rise to "attacks on spiritual leaders." In some way this comes close to the core of my pattern of "desacralizing," downing the energy. "When shall I see God?" I ask—and the answer always is: when I start *looking* for God in all I see. And indeed Beloved spoke of this as a *spiritual crisis* for me, the doorway to being able to see and acknowledge the sacred in all beings.

This crisis is making very few waves on the surface, it is so deep down—and what surface waves there are seem to be occurring primarily in my relationship, inner and outer, to Beloved herself. Once more she has seen the wave that is taking me under and tossed me the rope that, if I will, can help me learn to swim in these ever subtler, ever finer waters. *[And indeed it is about subtlety: sacred outlook, pure view, pure perception. This is the call for me willingly to pierce the illusory veil of appearances, to abandon enmeshment in materiality: to apprehend and bow to majesty of being, within, without, and all around. The teacher is a mirror; to see the teacher's perfection is to see one's own. This cannot be comprehended with the intellect; it must be experienced directly. The critical moment and its critical importance are reflected in the intensity of my confusion.]*

I do not love her enough. *Why* do I not love her, truly love her? What is it to "love Beloved" or not "love Beloved"? My relationship to her seems to me very *impersonal.* At times I feel a glow of personal love for her—when she's funny, or when she is kind and gentle to me or to

99. Chidbhavananda, Introduction, *The Bhagavad Gita,* 26.

another. Yet mostly I don't "feel" something for her that I recognize as the kind of love I feel, say, for Maha or Leo. It seems impersonal—a quality of mind, not of feeling. *[Yes, just so.]*

•

> The Great Way is not difficult.
> Only do not make distinctions.
> Take away likes and dislikes,
> Then everything is perfectly clear. [100]

I feel so confused. Everything I think, everything I hear, everything I read: What is this? What is she telling me? What do I not see? What do I see? What do I think? What do I understand? What is this that I don't understand?

It's like a koan, I can't understand "it" with this thinking mind. What have I got to understand it with? Where can I go where this mind is not?

This truly is a crisis.
Danger/opportunity, failure/success—
"like that,"
same thing,
just this mind
making distinctions.
What is she showing me?
My mind.
What am I seeing?
Only reflections of my mind.
What can I do?
Nothing.
I don't know how to do "nothing."
Who will show me how?
Beloved?
How will you show me, when I don't understand you?
What can I understand with?
Where's the hole in my mind for the light to come through?
    Oh boy, this is tough.

_____

100. Sahn, "Three Letters to a Beginner."

Not tough, not anything.
I'm just confused.
Mind talking to itself.
Where is no-mind?
Take me there, Beloved, *now.*

I'm like a caged bird, so long in this cage that I can't even remember flight. And I never see the wide, bright sky—only the bars of my cage, with something beyond, something unimaginable—I smell it, I breathe it, I dream it—but I don't know it's the sky, or that I can fly in it—*[Yes, we see, we do see. When we recognize, we awaken.]*

I've said, "I'll give up everything." What could I possibly have thought I was saying? What could I possibly have meant by that?

Would someone please bring me a hacksaw to this cell? I hear a rumor of sky, my shoulder blades are twitching.

S.O.S! S.O.S!

But: "The urgency of change is change, not urgency." [101]

Late last night, flat on my back, almost asleep, suddenly ripped apart by deep, violent weeping, electricity moving through me. It followed my saying to her, in my mind, "I surrender myself to you completely." Weeping suddenly at the thought of Christians being thrown to the lions—I felt I was one, felt myself waiting there to be torn apart. At another level, determination: just keep plugging. At yet another level . . . something I might even dare to call confidence? Confidence that this, too, is just part of the process—and a dim sensing: I am up against the wall again, as in that last, terrible weekend of illness in the city last year, and "I" have no way to break through—up against some furious defense by the mind of its territory, its domain, its dominion and control—and mind cannot will or effect its own demise—some other will, some other agent, must effect the transformation—I, the real I, have no recourse but to the Divine Will—and to the teacher.

While all of this is going on—a river raging in its bed—at the same time I am carrying on like an almost normal human being, functioning, talking (aye, there's the rub!), even teaching—serving the people, serving the light, even serving the teacher, as best I can.

What a quandary.

This is where grace comes in—if it does.

---

101. Krishnamurti, in Lutyens, *Years of Fulfillment.*

Deep, deep peace in my heart, even in the midst of struggle. The gifts are so beautiful, my heart is thankful. And yes, confident, almost serene. Some mountains have moved in my consciousness.

❖ I find the crystals I've been looking for and bring Beloved to see them. She is touching the top of a carved crystal; it is like a miniature tree stump, with wet, crumbling wood in the middle. She is peeling it away, pulling the pulp away from the center. ❖ *[Thank you, thank you, Beloved.]*

•

Beloved is home from her travels. The temple is fragrant and sweet with her presence.

> The hawk cries over me,
> her spiral alive in my eye.
> Had I her wings I would fly.

❖ I've driven down a long hill on my way to a village by the sea. On the way back up, the steepness and length of the hill are terrifying—it seems as if the car is barely moving, as if the slow forward gear is barely holding, as if any second I'm going to stall and start rolling backwards with no way to stop. Inch by inch I keep going, finally gathering some momentum as the hill begins to level off almost imperceptibly. I was staving off my panic by telling myself I had no choice but to keep going, that as long as I wasn't obviously going backward I must still be going forward. ❖ *[Then and now, so thankful for the message of this dream. Deep breath.]*

It *must* be so slow, so patient, this work of enlightening self and saving all beings from ignorance and suffering, through the free will of each one—yet it seems hard, sometimes, when I think: A flash of lightning, the single stroke of a sword of fire, one mighty sweep of great wings might do it all at once, and all be brought home, restored to the light.

[My mother is moving across the country, to live in a nursing home near one of my sisters.] A gentle sadness wells up in me, the sadness of my mother, losing her mind (yet isn't that exactly what I'm trying to do?—oh, the

irony!), and sadness for myself, losing my mother just when I'm feeling I've found her—for in this time of her gentle decline she is open and receiving, and for the first time I feel her accepting my presence and love.

May

Beloved very hot about envy, about people questioning what she does. But what is more to be expected than that we be imperfect? Were it otherwise we'd hardly need her guidance. Those were last night's thoughts. *[Definitely, defiantly, "questioning what she does"!]* This morning's: Whatever there is in me of these attitudes, let me root them out and transform them. I can muse forever on someone else's faults, but the only thing I can change is my own mind.

[And here is what she says about that:] "It is not the responsibility of the teacher to prepare the student's mind to approach the teacher and the teachings. That is the responsibility of the student."

Looking clearly at the face of ENVY, and everywhere I see how my envy has jerked me around, all my life. And I acknowledge that I have been envious of my teacher.

Inner seeing: I stand across a great fire from the teacher. "Only when you have sacrificed your envy to the fire will you be able to see me." I do. The fire roars up, consuming me. When it is over, where fire was is water. She commands me to enter it. I plunge down, deep, deep. I see a withered tree, a rock cave. I enter. In the cave is a young girl, alone, cowering. I gently lead her from the cave; as we rise up through the water, we become one. I break the surface into the light, step from the water, stand next to Beloved. She is a blazing light. I am not afraid.

Noticing some more spacious, clear vision of other people—seeing them as a "moment" in the continuity of their being, the light-path of their sacred purpose. And out on the land, an expansion of consciousness: my body sense now includes this whole terrain; I *am* this land—the bowl, an open plate, giving and receiving. I vibrate with the energy of all the large and small creatures living in, on, and above me, I sing with the waters flowing through me, in my veins I feel the energy of life coursing, know the gravity of my rocks, the tendrils of living things rising up through me, reaching for the sun. Tonight a great wind cleansing land and minds, the fire accepting offerings from my grateful hands, and now the gentle rains, washing clear the land, my body.

June

Outside my window the apple tree is blossoming. "Just like this." Can I see my own behavior "just like this," without charge of judgment or opinion? *[The gentleness in this invitation, balm to my mind.]*

Things—including me—seem a bit *simpler* these days. And I am very focused outward, too. Little introspection: I see, I act; I act, I see. Seeing more clearly, acting more efficiently, more effectively, more selflessly, more constructively. Yes, see all for its suchness. "Just like this."

•

Lama is here, meditated with us this morning. Some opening, some meeting, was taking place—letting go of attachment to some sense of loss or confusion, the thought "Why am I not a Buddhist this time?"—as I find that I am, that nothing is lost. Can't find words, don't need the words—something is healed, and my love nature, the compassionate wisdom, is finding expression in my thoughts, words, and deeds. *[This event: the transmission of Tsawai Lama's lineage. It sunders me, tears away obscuring veils, brings me into the Dharma in this lifetime, activates in me its shining continuity.]*

These days when Beloved corrects me I find myself laughing—then she does, too!

July

Beloved: "Doubt—the most poison of poisons, the most destructive of energies. *[And in this lifetime surely my gravest, most debilitating, most perduring affliction.]* Requires utmost diligence. Only way to come to certainty is to be still. It is time for you to hold a clear form with *no doubt.* Sometimes you are so senseless I can't believe it!" *[Me too, Beloved, me too.]*

I'm aware of a simple, straightforward determination: the use of *will* to transmute, or sometimes simply to pass through, the moments when the lower mind asserts. It's the consistent, dogged, faithful *practice* of mind mastery that allows me to call on it successfully when needed—not some "wish" for it, but its steady development over time, through small decisions made to be in right relationship, to hold and act on correct understanding rather than to give in to the flow of emotion or to continue energizing an incorrect pattern of thought. *[Wow! This is a teaching I need every single day!]*

❖ I, as a man, am standing on shore or in a boat, looking 'way, 'way up to the deck of what seems to be a Soviet ship. The captain is about to throw a person over the side: dead, dying, ill, or injured. I see the captain's face clearly: obdurate, adamant, unmoving. My companions are horrified; they are shouting, threatening, cursing—impotently, for there is nothing we can do to prevent this. I say nothing, my face is a stony mask; in my mind these words: "I will not permit harm to one of my own, a part of me, because of my inability to control my reactions." ❖ The dream message seems clear and pertinent, yet complex. His obduracy, his stoniness: choice made from compassionate wisdom *[like the one I have iterated at the end of the dream]*. Yet so rigid; surely that is not the way? But the content of the words—this *is* Beloved's message to me, is it not? That my ego reactions create waves of disharmony that feed the very disharmony to which I am reacting. It is my choice how I deal with my own reactions: to feed or to transmute them *at every moment.*

My thoughts about the need for change in my work here have become unhitched from the painful, debilitating thoughts of my own inadequacy. *[This apparently small shift is huge. It is a change in my MIND.]* For two and a half years I have been breathing out—constant, dedicated, efficient, and effective in building and holding the form *[in our spiritual organization and ashram]*: a good bricklayer, a good foundation builder. I am tired. Now it's time to breathe in—to deepen, to be silent.

•

Beloved: "It is time now for you to go beyond duality, to see without distinctions, in the emptiness. The foundation is strong enough now. You'll get there if I have it *beat* it into you!" *[Not yet realizing emptiness experientially, I am struggling about it. The struggle, even then, seems absurd. How can I not realize my own nature?]*

The first stirrings of "like mind." Sitting in the woods, listening to the wind: Ah, the sounds of people, phones, and machines are "like that"—life sounds, the vibration of the eternal. Hearing the mosquito buzzing about my head and at the same time an airplane: Ah, two wingèd ones, like each other. I sense that I am being, as she said, "beaten" into the emptiness. All that I am experiencing these days—all the pain and despair, all the overwhelm and heaviness in relation to my work—all this, I think, is just resistance. Emptiness *is*.

When will I really *act* on what I know to be true—that I can see things in their suchness, directly, and not react, simply *be* with what is?

[But I am not yet able to "simply be" with emotions, thoughts, events. Direct experiencing is obscured by reaction: grasping, pushing away, elaborating. I feel sad, writing this, because it describes precisely how we reify, and thus impoverish, our experience of this rich, brilliant, ever changing phenomenal reality in which we have our brief lifetimes. Phenomena are void in their nature, ephemeral and insubstantial, yes—and immediately, freshly, vividly displaying. We are not to deprive ourselves of this fullness of life, whether from fear or from mistaken notions of "spirituality." We are to live.]

August

Again today caught in arrogance, self-importance, in relation to Beloved. So much resistance to her. Very subtle. Clinging to my own ideas and preferences, attachment to the lama, competition with her. *Resistance.*

❖ "The Nod Blaster"—a very high Tibetan religious leader, like the Dalai Lama—"his slow, silent nod of encouragement, blasting ignorance." The present Nod Blaster: very old, very fat, very loving. ❖

Feeling the sadness of recognizing impermanence. *[Many who begin contemplating impermanence experience this sadness—because we cling to what we desire and like. But what we dislike is also impermanent, and it seems easy enough for us not to be sad about that, doesn't it?]*

With a pencil, Beloved bops me four times on the crown. I laugh: "I should have known the instrument of my enlightenment would be a pencil!"

My structures are collapsing. *["Shake down forms."]* Beloved: "What was the source of evil? It was pride, the thought of superior, power over, better than—that fallen light being. It *will* come to an end. And many of us will see it, in these bodies, even, or in our next ones." To me she says: "Barbara, it is time for you to make this turn. Transform the arrogance, which comes from fear. Let go of mind that has to 'know.' Experience directly, let it deepen."

And that evening: "Blowing my Knows," "Prophecies according to

Nostrildamus," "S'not what you think it is"—effervescent, hilarious, pretension-popping verbal play with a visiting friend.

I am finally having the giveaway I've been intending for so long—not formally, just giving away all the time, as the occasion offers. To beautiful Maha, my beautiful porcelain mirror, with these words:

> Herein see
> the Mystery,
> behold the face
> of compassionate grace.

September

[In my occasional musings on the mysteries and challenges of surrender, I now note:] I must clearly distinguish between *surrender* and *submission*. Surrender is opening to spiritual power; submission is denying responsibility for one's own power.

In the middle of a conversation suddenly Beloved says, "Barbara, you're trying to *dominate* the wave of thought. Just *ride* it." I feel as if I'm drowning, being carried away on a current. That's just my fear, the arrogance she says is the root of the impulse to control and dominate the energy. "Carried" is not "carried away."

❖ I discover the essence of a being near and dear to me: Sassafras, my dear cat, is really a . . . *zucchini*. ❖ *[An example of dreamtime insights warping into absurd forms as they filter through into waking mind. My favorite of these was years before, while still teaching at the college, awaking one morning next to my lover, in haste to convey out loud, immediately, before it faded, the profound insight I'd received while sleeping:* "Celery *is the vertical link between theory and praxis."]*

•

Ego bruised today, Beloved very critical of the chanting: ego, competitive energy. "This must change," she said. In everything I saw myself, and wondered how I could have gone on so long without facing it more responsibly. Why do I wait for the lessons to come from outside when I can see already the operations of my personal motives? Surely I have the ability to transmute what is impure in the very moment of perceiving it? *[This depends on attention and awareness, and on willingness. I*

have by now some ability to recognize my mental arisings but not yet the ability
to rest in awareness itself. The method needed is not yet in my hands, nor is the
willingness yet in my heart—willingness to drop my story lines, simply let them fall
to the ground. Willingness to give up the story of "self" for love of others.]

The little apple bobbing in the eddy: I and all of us, seeming carefree
and free, yet ever caught in eddies—while only inches away the stream
itself flows free.

Sloughing off this week—clinging to the personal—personal space,
personal time, personal gratification, personal opinion, personal will,
personal this, personal that. So today I really needed to read this simple
statement by Trungpa Rinpoche: "The bodhisattva vow is the commitment
to put others before ourselves. It is a statement of willingness *[yes, this*
willingness] to give up our own well-being, even our own enlightenment,
for the sake of others. And a bodhisattva is simply *[simply!]* a person who
lives in the spirit of that vow . . . in [her] effort to liberate beings."[102]

In meditation this morning I *saw* clinging, craving, grasping: ugly,
gluey strands, filaments sticking to whatever they touched, and stretching,
stretching, resisting release. And saw that this step, letting go of the
personal, once I take it, will render me more compassionate to beings
who are clinging, grasping, craving. *["Once I take it"? No, dear, you won't*
get to take this step just once—you will take it over and over again. This step will
become every step you take, until you realize your mind's condition one with your mind's
nature, yourself inseparable from the love that knows no self and thus no other.] And
saw, very graphically: Bodhicitta is not just the large, spacious intention
to liberate oneself and so to liberate all, but the daily, hourly renewal of
that commitment by liberating one's own mind from all these entangling
strands *[yes, that's it]*—so that each choice, in every moment, is made for
the benefit of others. And I see again these days how small the things
are that arouse the personal ego to desire, attachment, ambition—and
how great is the resistance to letting them go. In every moment.

[All this sincere, careful inner work—on non-attachment, abandoning self-concern,
gingerly assaying emptiness, the tender signs of increasing objectivity, compassion,
altruism—is lifting me into more authentic spiritual impersonality. At the same
time, resistance and reaction are building, setting the stage for flight, a headlong,
disastrous flight—into the personal.]

---

102. Trungpa, *The Collected Works of Chögyam Trungpa.*

•

> The pattern of the practitioner's progress through the three yanas is as follows: first [Hinayana], one develops extreme exertion in uncovering one's own neurosis.[103] This one-pointed mindfulness brings the sense of one's actual human quality. The second stage [Mahayana] is marked by gentleness, allowing one's energies to expand and be shared with the rest of sentient beings. Finally [Vajrayana], one develops fearlessness and a sense of joy and penetrating insight, filled with immense devotion to the lineage and one's root-guru. . . . In the Vajrayana [the guru] is the master— almost a dictator—who tells us what to do. The relationship must be very strong, definite and direct—one of great devotion.[104]

Beloved in class tonight: "In this time many will fall aside—and not even know it. In this time many will fall aside—and not even know it." Two times, turning to look straight at me. I was shaken. "Have I failed a test I wasn't even aware of facing?" I asked her. "It's about pride," she said—"pride, that keeps you from seeing." Later, speaking to me of my tendency to what she called "this source of evil," she said, "This must be changed." I wept. From childhood I have seen the face of pride in the mirror, in my mind. It is a burden. I seek to transform it. I *am* transforming it.

> Don Juan: In the strategic inventories of warriors, "self-importance figures as the activity that consumes the greatest amount of energy, hence, their efforts to eradicate it. . . . One of the first concerns of warriors is to free that energy in order to face the unknown with it . . . The action of rechanneling that energy is impeccability."[105]

I've been through fevers of the heart like this before, with their intense absorption, their unconditional love conditioning itself, their grasping and clinging, their haste and heat. How must this hot little heart of emotionality and desire feel to his clear, transcendent mind? *[This is me "falling in love with the lama"—confounding spiritual devotion with desirous*

---

103. The *yanas* are the three vehicles of Buddhist teaching and practice: Hinayana (also known as the Sutrayana), Mahayana (Bodhisattvayana) and Vajrayana (Tantrayana, or Secret Mantrayana). They can also be understood as three significant stages of spiritual development.

104. Kongtrul, *The Torch of Certainty*, 15.

105. Castaneda, *The Fire from Within*, 29.

craving. To nourish devotion calls for impeccability, "rechanneling" the energy of self-importance, as Don Juan describes it: rechanneling it through altruistic intention. Aspiration trumps appetite.] The lesson for today: Do not wait for the correction to come from outside. Now, today, stop this fantasy life, transmute the "hot little heart" into compassionate wisdom, love that seeks not for itself but to blaze for all creation. The function of this personal absorption at this time seems surely to have been to set up a "personal life" as a pole to the intensifying command to move decisively into impersonality. *[Yes.]* See it, do it. *[Yes. But this is just a prelude . . .]*

The fever is abating: I am letting go. What is there to hold onto, after all, but a chimera? I was, simply through the activity of my own thoughts, beginning to suffer. *[It is extraordinary, really, that I see this, recognize it, and take responsibility for it. Up to this time I have usually just seen, maybe recognized, and rarely taken full responsibility for correcting errant habitual tendencies of thought and action. This clarity, arising in love rather than self-concern, is what makes personal ethics authentic and reliable. Both my clarity and my ethics will soon be challenged, far more deeply.]*

Meeting my Tsawai Lama, receiving his blessing. Moved by his being, his gentle radiance—like a grandmother, so very beautiful. *[My one and only face-to-face meeting in this lifetime with this unutterably vast, profound, encompassing, penetrating buddha, precious root guru. He will give me teachings and empowerments mind-to-mind in the coming years, both before and after he dies.]*

October

I think I am beginning to light up—I sense my whole body subtly illuminating, effortlessly, and the temple filling with light: a pervasive, quiet radiance.

There is a young woman here in the midst of an enlightenment experience. It is humbling and inspiring to hear her speak and to see her. Am also aware of envy—for the purity and the *economy* of her experience: I'm chipping away at the encrustations and she's going at it all at once, cutting straight through. One thing she said last night really struck me: "I am not even to *think* something that's not true." *[That is taking responsibility for one's mind—genuine taming. It purifies will, tempers it to a keen blade.]*

Obedience is not the abdication of freedom but its *prudent use* under certain well-defined conditions. This does nothing to make obedience easier and it is by no means an escape from subjection to authority. On the contrary, obedience of this kind implies a mature mind able to make difficult decisions and to correctly understand difficult commands, carrying them out fully with a fidelity that can be, at times, genuinely heroic. Such obedience is impossible without deep resources of mature spiritual love. [106]

Again with unclear mind in relation to the teacher. It is pride that creates disharmony, judges, makes distinctions, attaches to its likes and dislikes, its opinions, its self-importance. Pride—that indeed goes before a fall. Before leaving on her current trip Beloved recounted to me (as if in passing, but she does not speak without purpose) what I heard as a cautionary tale. A student chose to go forward and then stepped back. "I had been holding her up," Beloved said; "when she chose to step back I had to let go of that string—and then she fell." In this tale I saw the wall that doubt puts up, as years ago when I sat with her on the shore of the bay: "What do you see?" "I see a pathway of light opening up before me." "Are you ready to walk that path?" Self-doubt spoke—"I don't know"—and she relaxed the dynamic tension on the cord she was holding me with. I must look again, to see how it is *pride* that gives rise to self-doubt. Without prideful mind one would come when the teacher called, step out upon the path of light when it opened.

It is very subtle. It seems to be pride, too, that has me *over*-defer to her: "See how good I am, how carefully I follow your instructions (even when they don't seem sensible to me)?" Approve of me, love me, accept me. Me, me, me. To think first of the good of the whole and to question her directives from that perspective might be quite different from questioning from pride, arrogance. Maybe guru yoga is meant to be practiced in monasteries; maybe the guru in that ancient practice is meant to be only the guru, not also one's organizational boss. Nope, guru yoga is guru yoga. It's up to me to find the clear light within that teaches perfect essential oneness with the teacher.

Late last night, huddled in my sleeping bag like a wounded animal, a twinge of longing for a father/mate to shelter and protect me, for Beloved to hold me like a baby. . .

•

---

106. Merton, "New Seeds of Contemplation."

Autumn

Cool morning
moon bright
lakes of mist in every hollow
leaves alight.

Yearning for the simplicity and directness of the Dharma teachings
and practices. The delightful visiting lama says: "The Dharma is non-
attachment. Nothing else is true Dharma, true Dharma is only this."
Chanting the Prajnaparamita with him—sweet, soft, like dawn light:
limpid. When I asked if he thought of reincarnating next time again as
the abbot of his monastery in Tibet he said yes, if that seemed useful
and necessary—though by then, he said, Mexico City will be the largest
city in the world, with 20 million people, and he might reincarnate
there: "Where there is pain and suffering, that is where I like to be."
[Unforgettable! What aspiration! What inspiration!]

Outside to run for the first time in many, many days. Am "edgy"—oh,
"edgy" means "on the edge"—something wants to open up, a gateway
in my mind. Emptiness: to see, to understand emptiness. Chanting
and contemplating as I walk and run, sitting in a field looking out
over the hills and Lady Mountain, curling up in a soft bed of dry pine
needles, weeping. *[I know, I know, there's a lot of weeping. Think of it as
sluicing, cleansing, lubricating, melting . . .]* Impermanence, no inherent
existence—this is bringing up pain—pain is just resistance to letting
go—letting go of *ideas* about what is—so I can *see* what is. Leaves
falling, everything changing; the tree gives up her leaves more easily
than I give up my ideas. It is simple to see Beloved and Tsawai Lama as
having no inherent existence in these forms—they are like "reflections
of moon on water," I feel their beings as continuous, without limit
of time or form. But the mountains, the Earth? Stream, waterfall,
running current, bright leaves on the surface, on the rocks, the very
contours of the streambed changed from when I last sat there. Placid
pool. Then a small vortex of violence: A water bug captures a fly,
swims with it—the fly still alive, its wings under water moving rapidly,
a blur, fighting for its life. And this violence, this cosmic struggle, the
ripening of the karma of these two beings, barely disturbs the still
surface of the pond. A little school of tiny, almost transparent fish:

my mothers. None of this having inherent existence: moon reflected on water. Sassafras calling outside my door: cat little dear, for whose well-being I make myself responsible. What is attachment? Lama: "Mother with child, *there* is attachment!" I have no child, I am free to let go of attachment to everything, anything. Including myself. What is "myself"? I have no inherent existence. What does this mean? Emptiness. What does this mean? How to understand this? How to let myself experience this? All this work we do—if no inherent existence, what is this labor about, this pressure? To help sentient beings—who have no inherent existence.

Does everyone else already understand this? No inherent existence—no "self" inherently existing, so no reason for "self-cherishing"—nothing to grasp, let it go, like the leaves falling from the trees in their season to fall, floating downstream in their time to float away . . .

I am chanting mantra almost all the time—MANI, GATE—[107]

Beloved states her intention: to take me into her mind, to "show me the emptiness." She went into the emptiness and I was left behind. Because of clinging to "I." Then I went behind the blanket. She asked each of the others in the group to articulate their experience, then asked me, "the old woman behind the blanket." She was so kind. Then she went around the circle again, giving each a lesson, advice, guidance, instruction. To me, the full loving brilliance of her smile, and just: "Let it all go."

I am to go beyond all form, all limit.

Twice today she has fed me: "I'm so happy we are together in this lifetime, I'm just so grateful to know you."

Third eye tight, body tense, jaw tense, dance clumsy, chanting uncertain, speech tight. Clinging. Just see it, name it, let it go. Clinging. Yet I have no inherent existence. So, nothing to cling to, no one to cling. Nothing to let go of, no one to let go. Where do I go from here, and how? No place to go, no one to go. No how, no way, no where, no when, no what. . .

---

107. MANI: short name for OM MANI PADMA HUM, the mantra of Avalokiteshvara (Sk.), Chenrezig (Tib.), the deity of compassion. GATE: short name for OM GATE GATE PARAGATE PARASAMGATE BODHI SVAWHA, the Prajnaparamita mantra, mantra of the Heart Sutra, wisdom of emptiness.

The Heart Sutra—"form is emptiness, emptiness form"—just glimmers of understanding. The door is opening, I am letting. Peeping through, recoiling a little, resisting a little, beginning to explore, to accept a little the concept of "no inherent existence." It is not nothingness, oblivion. Just *what is*, simple and direct. Even trying gets in the way: no clinging even to intention. Just *be*. Quiet mind, clear focus. Nothing to fear. Let it all go, let it all go.

Eat breakfast, turn off the phone machine, visit with guest, make phone calls. Breathe, see, feel, *be*.

Back in "doing" mind. I sort of forgot that I have no inherent existence. To enter the emptiness I must forbear filling it up.

❖ I hurl a 40 lb. crystal at my closet door, am appalled, filled with remorse, anxiety. ❖ Now I see another message in the dream: not trying to destroy but to break through my closet door! The closet, where I hide from the light; the closed door, my ignorance.

November

"Beloved, I am finally beginning to be overcome by your great kindness," I told her. I couldn't take my eyes off her, I saw her beauty, only her beauty and goodness and kindness—every contour drawn in light, her jewels merely reflecting the light of her. She was speaking in a way that would be accessible to our guests while working subtly with the rest of us, further teaching on emptiness: "I am not repulsed and I do not want." I experienced equipoise, touching the flow. Interacting with others this week, I see noncoercion, letting *be*, seeing things as they are. Confronted with one person's coercion, reminding myself that he, I, the objects or issues of contention, none of it has any inherent existence, and therefore practicing kindness, compassion, patience—for both of us, for all of us.

Beginning to perceive the "space-like nature of phenomena"—wind blowing through me; person, cat, and hug a momentary organization of energy; teacher and student like flows of light. No inherent existence. Just consciousness, manifesting—images on screen of mind, moon reflecting on water. Dependent arising—"my" thought giving rise to "me" and to all that I see.

Reading last night, got a tiny glimpse of how it could be *easy* to attain enlightenment: just correctly identify and realize the true "base"—Buddha mind and non-inherent existence. "Just." The teaching says that the Quick Path, if one proves unable to do it, must be let go of and the Gradual Path then followed diligently and carefully. Now remembering a moment with Beloved some years ago, sitting in the kitchen: "We could do it all at once, completely, but you are very sensitive: better to do a little at a time." Well, okay, it's obvious, even to me, that "I" am "doing it"—knees, hips, spine, head, heart, mind: come together now in realization of what is—let go, let go, let go—of all clinging, all grasping, all attachment, all resistance—just let go.

Though my frame still felt out of line, danced this morning for the first time in awhile. Studying dance as generosity and compassion, as offering; the "holding, grasping, clinging" that's made the dance a source of bodily distress and damage is simply ego. Today I offered my body, dancing: wept while dancing, hurt while dancing, prayed while dancing, danced for our lives and for peace.

•

Long walk up toward Lady Mountain and a sweet semi-doze in a field, looking out over the peaceable kingdom. Beloved has been saying to me, over and over: "The world needs us—if we don't do it, who will?"

Today, the impulse to withdraw from teaching until I am enlightened, or at least to take a serious retreat. With news of the election results, that impulse seems untimely. Instead, an intensification, a deepening of diligence in karma yoga, as an offering for the country, for the planet.

•

It is mostly from *pride* that I have accomplished things in this lifetime. Now, generating bodhicitta, the motive of compassion for others, there is no longer the old basis to act upon, so strong, driving, forceful—and I feel to withdraw from the action, for I mistrust my own judgment. I feel impaired, almost crippled. Oh, poor pitiful me, I don't know how to *be*. And yet—and yet—it has required courage, so often, just to keep on going, to continue working when feeling so imperfect, so ill-suited for my responsibilities, my faults so grave, my gifts so hard to see, for me. Let me walk gently, slowly, till I learn how to "do" from good intention, clear intention, to benefit all beings.

Feeling as if something is breaking open; feeling like a dry corn husk, used up, fit to be discarded. "See the dry corn husk falling to the ground to nourish new life," Beloved told me.

> Blossom for a hundred years,
> scatter your fragrance for all,
> but when the time for your fading away arrives,
> fall for the sake of all. [108]

I feel like a desolate landscape, laid low, parched. I want Beloved to tell me she loves me, that I'm only tired from long years of hard work and now I can rest awhile, yet her face is stern, closed to me.

She wants to take me through the door. That is her love.

•

Beloved: "Why do you cry so much? It's unhealthy. Laugh! JUMP—there's a mouse behind you! If you won't jump for a mouse then it's an old WOLF!" She says the next step is to master my emotions—yet I suspect she's really saying the next step is to JUMP through the door she's holding open right in front of me. *[And I don't jump: I step into a snare.]*

By the end of class I was a raw, frayed nerve-ending: shaking, rigid. The only time I can recall being in a similar state was after the murders *[Manny, April, and Leesy, Marianne's husband and daughters]*, then more extreme but similar—stretched to breaking point. Went for a walk in the dark—the sky dark, the trees darker, the land darker still—a black, silent tunnel—perfectly suited to my state of mind. And yet I saw the completely overcast sky filled with stars, above me and around me, points of light, many, many stars—it was very strange.

I told Beloved that I am censoring myself when speaking to her, fearing her rebukes. Her reply: "I am not rebuking you but offering correction." *[What I feel as rebuke? Were I blind to all but love I would know it for tenderness. What I take as humiliation? Were I deaf to all but truth I would hear it as songs of praise.]*

---

108. Swami Rama, "The Nature of Avidhya and Maya."

•

We must be still within ourselves, still and calm, and yet we must also, at the same time, be moving forward, moving further and deeper towards each other, towards the world. What is not useful for this endless transformation must be abandoned; anything that prevents a finer flowering of our spirit must be left behind; anything that hinders us from dealing with the world as it is, with ourselves as we are, in this place and in this time, with all the dangers and fears and sadnesses of this time and this place, must be renounced, and renounced, if possible, without grief and without nostalgia. Every truthful transformation takes us closer to the world, closer to things, closer to each other; the clearest and wisest man becomes the world, becomes Buddha, becomes "awake," enters without fear and without hope, and without any consolation or protection, into the full presence of Reality.[109]

Staff meeting. I was deeply touched to hear valuing of my playfulness, lightness, and joy, great warmth, clarity, integrity; process of surrender, letting go; willingness to hold the form even when it's not popular to do so. And from one person, this: "When I sit in meditation with you I feel your love just expand out, so *huge*, filling the whole temple." *[The Great Love. It is always there. I am never apart from it, we are never apart from it. It is this I am seeking, this that makes me seek, this that shakes away everything, this that sustains me, this the cause, this the method, this the result. It is stronger than "I," it is stronger than "you." Oh, how wonderful even to be speaking of the Great Love!]*

❖ I've shown a number of people a trail through the woods that has been very special to me, and now they all use it. I feel pushed out of my places where I can be private. ❖ *[Yes, this is the way. Our love for others pushes us out of our private places, where we cling to self. And that special trail through the woods? It is the path itself—and the work of the bodhisattva is just this: to walk the path, show it to others, help them walk it, in their own ways. "People the avenue."]*

Based on Buddhist nomenclature for stages of the path, Leo says, I seem to be a "wavering perceiver, leaning toward truth."[110]

---

109. Drukchen Rinpoche, in Harvey, *A Journey in Ladakh*, 182–83.
110. "Wavering perceiver, leaning toward truth"—splendid description,

Going back to basics: meditating on the great sea of compassion and letting emptiness, all that striving for emptiness, take care of itself. This path leads inevitably to emptiness, and for me compassion is the way to approach it. *[Not just for me.]*

Unwavering Teacher to Wavering Perceiver: "Contemplate emptiness as a mirror in the clouds."

December

❖ I am planting a small garden; right next to it is an apparently identical one, and I am laughing at the contrast between the two: the one lush and robust, a balanced ecology; mine scraggly and weak, filled with insects. Oozing through its swampy soil is an enormous, red, segmented worm, which gets larger as I watch. I move away, repulsed by the worm, but still laughing. I am told to stop putting myself down, that it's only a lack of knowledge and experience. ❖ *[Ah, the saving grace, the consolation, in many of my dreams: the wisdom voice itself, speaking, speaking—and I sometimes hearing. And also simply the laughter, that saving grace!]*

•

[Sitting in an airport cafeteria, en route to give teachings on the other side of the country:] Aware of yearning for the Dharma, for the lamas, for the Buddhist sangha—this thought that I need to or must follow these practices, that this is my boat to cross over to the other shore. Reminding myself that I am already in a boat and with my teacher, that there is nothing I need that is not already with me. Arising out of this disarray: strong impulse to fly like an arrow straight into her heart—the teacher who will guide me to the other shore, make me a fit vessel, teach me to become a bodhisattva.

❖ I'm in an elegant prison and not able to escape, partly because no one else will acknowledge that it is indeed a prison. ❖ *[Samsara, samsara.]*

---

pointing to three elements in my spiritual life salient at that time: my longing for truth, toward which certainly, and with certainty, I leaned; the fact that indeed I did perceive truth flashing through the experiences and appearances of life; and the fact that I couldn't keep truth in focus, couldn't "grasp the insubstantiality," as one of my Dharma students would later complain about her own wavering. "Intimate with error and in love with truth": that's *moi*.

[Gratitude: a doorway to the spiritual dimension.] Took to Beloved my long-considered request to let go of my administrative job. She said, "It's not time yet; there's still something for you to see, some obscuration to transform." I am dismayed—yet I trust the clarity of the mirror. My heart is thankful, thankful, that I am in the care of a teacher who will not let me fall aside. The opportunity for transformation must be significant or, seeing my distress, she would never have said, "Not yet, stay with it." And I am thankful for my thankful heart, for it is this, finally, that allows me to recognize her guidance. *[But later she will tell me that I missed the opportunity, did not want to see that "the doing is the jewel." Bodhicitta, the Great Love, empty of attachment and striving, empty of self-concern, empty of self—this is the jewel.]*

•

YEAR SEVEN

Freedom, then flight · I step into a snare
The Blade Sharpener · A prophecy
Pure lotus arising · The Great Unraveling ·
Love vs. duty · At the shrine of the Tsawai Lama
Cabin Retreat · This commitment cleaves the seas
I cut off all my hair

January

> A pain induced by the guru is the greatest of gifts. . . . One of
> the functions of the guru is to bring your karma right to the
> front, fulfilling something for which you ordinarily would have
> to wait for many years, maybe many incarnations . . . If you
> turn away from the pain, you turn away from the path. . . . Each
> time the guru within (or without) sees you becoming attached
> to something, he smashes it, breaks your heart in two, cuts your
> ego—if you are willing to take this step. [111]

In this time of karma ripening, a deep, archaic split in my nature is
coming up for healing: public-private, sacred-secular, altruistic-personal.
I can be clear for others, when teaching, especially, but have not yet
learned—because of not yet having made the *commitment*—to do it
in everyday life. It seems I have feared taking this step, for the great
responsibility it entails, and once taken there's no going back. Now I
am either preparing or actually in the process of taking it.

[This is really about the bodhisattva commitment: to live for all, to liberate
all. And of course it's not taken and realized all at once. It is the most vast,
the process of its fulfillment the most specific and precise, the most subtle and
all-pervading. Padmasambhava said, "My view is as vast as the sky, my behavior
as fine as barley flour." Everything is included. Recognizing the need to deepen,
expand, and refine the altruistic intention: this is the altruistic intention unfolding
in my mind.]

---

111. Usharbudh Arya, "Samkhya Philosophy: Meditation and Karma."

•

Beloved, in her great kindness, to free me for deeper practice: "It is time for Sassafras to go." He left about three hours ago, with his new person, a kind young man from the city. *[It was a mission for Sassafras; the man was facing eye surgery that would immobilize him for weeks, and our hefty, sinuous black cat lay on his head much of that time, helping him stay still.]* Immediately after, in meditation: On a mountain peak, the night ablaze around me, I am one with the deeps of space—filled with a kind of furious joy—I am free, free, free—I can go anywhere, do anything, there is no longer any worldly, personal tie. And the scent, the color, the taste of attachment cut through? It is like the heart of celery—crisp, young, green, snappy and tender, a little bitter, filled with fresh water. I am amazed at the power—stupendous, breath-catching—of what immediately comes: so soon after the letting go, the gift. Letting go of "particular attachment" allows expansion, toward being a Mother-Father of *all*.

And a visitor arrives for an overnight visit, sits in the back of the temple. His name? "CAT." Ah, Mystery—wit and wisdom.

Erotic attraction arising: Gregory.

[Right here: freedom—and then flight. Release attachment, know the blaze of freedom's fire, then turn around and use it as a hearth, to warm the self—*to avoid the great commitment: burn for all. I grab for the personal. I "fall in love."*

Gregory is a sangha member, a student of Beloved, and, at the time, married and the father of young children. He is beautiful, good-hearted, curious, direct, and unapologetic, earthy and sexual, with a rusty voice that pleases and grounds me. Our love affair is sudden, engulfing, shocking to me and to the community. Though we do not become lovers physically while he is in his marriage, we are certainly lovers. [112]

I fight it, I cling to it, I make drama of it, with the usual themes—forbidden love, longing, passion, tenderness, anger, grief, joy, beauty, tawdriness, and so on—and these play out as they usually do in the ceaseless rounds of our conventional lives, our minds occupied with self, sense experience urging conviction in appearances.

---

112. I think adultery's stark immorality is the adulteration or corruption of an existing commitment in relationship, which might or might not take the form of a sexual act, so to my mind the nonvirtue was no less because the bodies did not join. Perhaps the whole drama could have flared up and gone more quickly to embers if we had become lovers in the flesh, rather than cultivating for so long the entangling vine of desirous craving. While protecting our bodies from committing harm, we harmed our minds.

I have by this time some intellectual understanding of this imprisonment of ours, and ardently desire freedom from its sufferings—for myself, for us all. But I do not yet fully desire freedom from the prison itself. I have made efforts, even experienced some results—diminishing self-striving, expanding altruism—but I am still clinging to the illusion of self and the confusion of materiality. I am not free. Light has penetrated my mind, though. By the blessings of my teachers and by the beauteous rounds of teachings and practice, I have heard the words bodhisattva and bodhicitta and have generated the altruistic intention—to free myself, to free all.

This vast commitment requires that everything blocking its realization be purified. What I must come to see is that it will be my mind's clinging to duality itself, and thus its very enmeshment in materiality, which will have to be abandoned. Early on Beloved told me, "It takes a long, long time to shatter the shell of the ego so the individual can make a conscious choice." Everything that binds me, and all the ways of my binding, must come to conscious awareness, for conscious choice. Eventually one pledged to awakening must consciously *choose truth over falsity. In every moment. There is no alternative.*

So now, impelled by karma and by aspiration, I come to some very deep confusion, calling forth stringent and far-reaching clarification. Conventionally, this love affair is a crisis of morals and ethics. Spiritually, because of my intentions and sacred commitments already taken, it is a matter of life or death, of truth or falsehood, of meeting or falling away from the ultimate challenge.

I already know to give the crystal to the flowing waters, but here I cling to the crystal. Beloved tells me to step out of the snare, but instead I polish it to a high surface shine with my tears. She cautions me not to swim in the sea of causes, but I do, and nearly drown. She warns me, "It's about your pride, that won't let you see," and indeed I cannot see what I am not seeing. Right action and right relationship are direct, simple, unencumbered, arising from good intention: care for all. Everything else creates harm and the causes of harm.

I place myself in grave spiritual danger in this time. The outcome is very uncertain.]

The Blade Sharpener

[This ten-day retreat in a wilderness cabin in snowbound north country—where I break creek ice for water and mind ice for insight—sees my mind filled with Gregory and with the moral and ethical choice I think I am making: to cut through, with sharpened blade of will, this grasping attachment. I face up to it in the practice but when I leave my retreat cabin . . .]

Sunny, cold, blowy, the snow a crisply defined ocean, crystals in motion.

All is food for practice. Let me simply *be*.

Aware of the heat of the sun as fire in the seed, active principle awakening life in the womb. A spark popped loudly in the stove—a sudden image of the sun, with a face, the flames like hair, blazing. On the hillside I was the eagle, great wings lifting me high, high—straight into the sun. Calling on sun to burn within me, in balance with moon—*interior* balance, *interior* fire, not having to project it onto someone else. Let it be consummated *within* me, this marriage of male-female, father-mother, sun-moon. Like the sun, be there for all, impersonally, impartially—mother-father to all, give everything, unceasingly.

Seeing how fear comes up to block the easy, simple flow into emptiness. Rose suddenly up through a hole in the sky, glimpsed the emptiness of space—and kept descending again, pulled by thinking, craving, feeling, perceiving. Last night I knew that intense activity simply as clinging to self.

From fear of the stillness, I am active in every subtle and obvious way. This little stove's a sturdy but slightly leaky vessel. So am I.

> From fear of being too cold
> I feed the fire and am too hot;
> from fear of being hungry later
> I eat now, when I'm not.

Gregory, I cannot be your lover, for fear of losing all that has been attained, and knowing no relationship born of my deceit, plunder, and craving can be correct.

This clarity is preceded by compassion—for his family. Will still have to act on the choice, but chose, the relationship offered up for the good of all. *[Well, not exactly.]*

(End of The Blade Sharpener)

February

I say to Beloved *[the day before I renew my bodhisattva vows with her]*, "Tomorrow I shall bow to you." "What is all this vowing and bowing?" she asks. "It is a great wind blowing through me. On retreat I saw you arising from the black emptiness of space as Mother of Knowledge, clad in red-orange raiment. Now I shall bow to you and say, 'This is my teacher, the boat that takes me across.'" "You saw me as I really am and you didn't run away. That is very surprising; most people are afraid." "What's there to be afraid of? I recognized you—for the first time! It's your personality self that scares me, not your real self! I'm not running away! You've put up with a lot from me—now let me bow to you!" Much laughter.

[In the vow ceremony, Padmasambhava made his presence known, unmistakably, and Beloved spoke this prophecy:] "The door is wide open for you in this lifetime. For 23,000 eons your face will be seen in the sky, a Mother-Father for all. You can go all the way."

•

Yesterday I was praying all day, "Let Gregory and his wife come into right relationship." *[The one who needed to come into right relationship was Barbara.]* When I saw him today, his very manner seemed different and I felt, "Ah, your prayer is being answered—*now* what are you going to do, my girl?"

How to do right action *while* keeping the heart open? Oh, that old right-wrong lesson again, "love" vs. "duty." I will learn through this that I can love and still be ethical. *[Resolving this treacherous duality will take me to my knees.]*

> The nameless was the beginning of heaven and earth;
> The named was the mother of the myriad creatures.
> Hence always rid yourself of desire in order to observe its secrets;
> But always allow yourself to have desire in order to observe its manifestations. [113]

Image of shooting up through fire, fire through fire.

The desire nature asserts itself with each threat to its hegemony over will. It is hot, clamoring, importunate, grasping, without morals or compassion, greedy, insatiable. Here is the face of selfish desire.

No. I am *free.*

Barbara: "I release you from the bonds of my attachment and desire." Gregory: "I want to tie myself up in them."

---

113. Lao Tzu. *The Tao Te Ching*, verse 1.

[Like a two-sided mirror, flashing back and forth: love and attachment; others' well-being and selfish absorption; aspiration and grasping. Irreconcilable. Aspiration is giving what you long for; grasping is trying to get it. I have to choose between them. And though in this time the choice appears to be about this man, it is really about my whole life purpose, my whole being.*]*

Beloved: "When given the opportunity to go all the way and not taking it, life force diminishes, person may die." *[The stakes couldn't be higher.]* And: "Sometimes people create confusion in their consciousness as preparation for another transformation, but this is a very advanced practice." Feels as if this may be what I'm doing. *[Ha ha ha ha ho ho ho.]*

How come he's so much more patient than I? Well, he's mated, for one thing.

I feel strong again, though "bereft and sorrowing" is just below the surface.

It's all just distraction. I am seeing my terror of bodhisattva, enlightenment, the irrevocability and absoluteness of the sacrifice—and have been flailing around, making waves, running around in circles. The next step: getting quiet again—simply *be* where I am.

The woman-me, she longs for love—before the bodhisattva carries her away down the tunnel, through the doorway. *[The crisis is about self and clinging, while the tunnel is the true Tunnel of Love.]*

Water is pouring down the mountain, roaring with freedom.

•

Beloved says, "You are a jewel and I take care of jewels. Hold nondual mind, be nonreactive, contemplate emptiness." *[I do not know how, but my suffering requires and therefore must yield up the slow, painstaking learning of the liberating method.]*

More letting go . . . and ever subtler clinging.

> There is no greater joy than to strip yourself of all the stuff, to take virtually everything off. You can only do that when you have realized that which is indestructible—your true nature . . .

[T]hat which can be destroyed should go; that's what you want to get rid of, so let them take it. [114] *[In this time I have not yet realized the indestructible, that will allow me just to "let them take" what can be destroyed. But innerly this I know: To the true nature offer up identity, and only truth remains.]*

March

Images moving backward like a film strip in reverse. Suddenly the frame is frozen: two wolves, male and female, lifelong loving mates; he is gray and black, she white and gray. It is Gregory and I.

We won't sleep together so we stay up together, night and morning sweet and full with love, understanding, patience, and desire. Is this just selfishness? Greg: "We are meant to be together." *["Meant" to be together? No: karma, not teleology, drives this affair. This is relative love, entangled in attachment. It is the Great Love that is* meant *to be—meant to be our choice, our commitment, our liberating joy.]*

Beloved: "Your practice is the only thing you can be sure of; it's your parachute, when the ego is dying. Focus on the gift of love, be thankful. The passions are a vehicle; to make them so, one must remove obscurations. Let yearning be a vehicle to perceive truth. Offer your ignorance and tears as food and drink to quench the hunger and thirst of those in the abyss. Keep the heart open to see the vastness."

Am I ready for this, when all I feel is this personal longing and pain? *[Powerful encouragement: "the ego is dying." What I have aspired to and prayed for is happening. Yet, identifying with feelings, emotions, form, I feel as if it's I who am dying.]*

•

Amitabha Buddha initiation, mind filled with light, wave upon wave. Amitabha comes to me, large, immediately recognizable. My mind suddenly bright, I am looking down, down, into a tumbler of liquid he holds out to me—the wisdom nectar. And then this: ❖ The little hair on my crown spiral stands up, sticks out. ❖

Meeting with the visiting lama: "If no desire, then no aversion—just

---

114. Midwer, *Primary Point: Journal of the Kwan Um Zen School.*

peace. The only reason you have a body in this lifetime is to practice. Just go through the doorway. Nothing lose; only get more. If doubt, maybe something to do still in samsara, maybe not time yet to go through the door."

The one thing that's not yet done: to act in what I believe to be *Gregory's* best interests, to do what I believe is good for *him*. I may be able to do for love what I've been having much difficulty doing for duty. *[Aha! Intimation of the real meaning of "duty."]*

Whatever is to be let go of, if you don't give it freely, will be taken from you one way or another.

April

One of my Dharma names: "Morality Dharma Light." In my mind I'm a humping sow.

I who have prided myself on being right and doing right, look at me now: a moral weakling, a coward. A selfish, selfish woman. Fearing and resisting doing right because I will then be without my love. Yet I am already without him. And he's not "my" love, anyway.

[Fallen down all in a heap around me is the conscious, choiceful, attentive moral and ethical structure by which I have lived my life. I am in a state of shock. Who is this person who is willing—sometimes eagerly, sometimes in dismay—to engage in immoral, unethical behavior? How can I have fallen like this? Many had said of me that I was the most ethical person they had ever known, but now I am examining deep, subtle motivations, well below the personality patina visible to others.] Bubbling just at the surface of my awareness: the subtle, pervasive lack of ethics and integrity in all aspects of my life, all my life. Now, through the apparent nonintegrity, seek integrity. As I see the apparent dissolution of the *forms* of morality I've held, see now the opportunity to develop the *essence*. Let it grow from within, not be imposed from without. *[This deep prayer—an invocation—like a bright thread of purpose drawing me forward.]*

•

Am still being swept by intense sexual energy. Practicing, carefully.

What is this beauty I experience in desire, this bittersweet yearning? And letting go into desire-grasping brings up such primitive rage-aggression—the *other* face of passion, the other heat. Whether I call it desire or anger, same thing: hot passion, hot self. Do not let attraction turn into aversion. Cultivate equanimity, objective compassion. *[For the suffering of attachment and desire we feel attachment and desire; for the suffering of aversion and hatred we feel aversion and hatred.]*

Beloved: "You must examine *all* your thoughts of aversion and attraction, in every aspect of your life. This is *the* time in your life that these energies must be transmuted. There is no more play in your lifeline; it is all reeled out. You must cut out the nonessentials, all the ifs, buts, and maybes, or the life force will get very thin." I say that scares me. She replies, "You have created a fearful situation, where you are constantly suffering. This suffering is not necessary, it is neurotic! It all comes from 'I want, I, I, I,' personal-this, personal-that. You got caught in a snare—just lift the trap and leave!"

•

If I can keep the behavior correct the mind will follow—yet wouldn't real transmutation be the other way around, correction in mind with behavior following, actually *transforming* selfish desire into generous, expansive care? *[I think I have to resolve the inner issues in order to be able to behave correctly—not yet understanding that behaving correctly, for the good of all, is the resolution.]*

When I heard "The door is wide open for you in this lifetime" I thought I could go straight through, and now just see the detours, the confusions, the distractions I am creating. Pride, to think I could say, "Oh, yes, I'll go right through—in just a minute—first I'll indulge my passions, then I'll be right along—hold the door open—it'll only take a moment, and *I'll* decide when, *I'm* in control, *I* can indulge in impurity without taint." Not so—my very liberation in this lifetime is at stake with each second of willful delay. I'm fixated on Gregory, yet if I weren't acting this out in relation to him I'd surely be acting it out in some other way. I made myself a trap, went right inside, and the door slammed down behind me. Thought I could lift it anytime I wanted to—while still enjoying the bait. Can't. Must let go of the bait in order to lift the trap door and leave.

In my heart, "Oh, Beloved, take me back close to you, let me do nothing to separate myself from the teacher any more." *[For each instant of turning toward Gregory is an instant of turning away from the teacher—the teacher without and the teacher within. Not because I have to choose between the teacher and the man, but because I have to choose between clarity and confusion, commitment and craving.]* And in meeting with her: "I want to come correct, what do I need to do?" "Wipe your feet," she said. "Take a shower, too. Think of your life purpose. Work with the fire of transformation." She also said, "Don't worry, you're okay."

The opposites are the same. In the moment, be still—let all movement come from the center.

•

[The ethics thread, continuing to weave:] ❖ I am on horseback, passing something from one person to another. When I come to Greg I am confused: How to pass this precious thing to him without touching him? ❖ *[What is "this precious thing" I am to pass to him without touching him? The most precious: the Great Love. Is this not the essence of the spiritual opportunity and challenge of the meeting with Gregory? But how can the Great Love be passed by one selfishly clinging? Her hands are encumbered.]*

I have continued to think and act as if I'm being coerced by moral standards that have to do with the situation and other people's needs, not my own. Not true. The "sin" lay not in causing harm—I don't know if we did or not—but in doing and continuing to do that which I *believed* could cause harm. So the fault lay in going against my *own* beliefs, commitments, and vows. It's this that I must see as I continue to look in the mirror.

•

[The long winter beings to yield up its lessons:] Tonight Greg told me he had reached resolution. I feel his clarity, see my wavering. I see that dedication is hard, and that I am not yet truly dedicated; I sometimes want to be and sometimes, like tonight, see how much of me doesn't yet want to be. Tonight my only prayer is that Creator help me truly want and truly *will* to do what is good for all beings. *[Clear perception of the gap between aspiration and willingness shows where the work is. There is nothing unintentional about profound purification.]*

Maybe morality will begin here, in seeing my frailty. Maybe dedication can begin here, in seeing my lack of it.

I think it is actually through seeing my faults that I am learning to love myself, as an ordinary human being. I love even my clinging, selfishness, resistance—they are human, I am human. Perhaps some learn compassion from seeing the suffering of others, but I think I'm learning compassion through seeing my *own* suffering. I couldn't feel real compassion for others' emotions, ignorance, dramas until I had perceived these things *as suffering*, and this I have had to realize first with myself. The Dalai Lama says, "If you can't help sentient beings, then please at least try not to harm them." Here is a place from which to begin.

This is a human woman in the process of realizing her buddha nature. I affirm that in this lifetime I shall learn to love others, all sentient beings, as my own beloved children. I begin with myself.

Forgiveness and compassion can grow from this soil. And these plants can feed many. My suffering and ignorance, my moral weakness, my selfishness and pride, clinging and aversion—all this is good manure, good fertilizer. I am thankful.

This, the living experience of the pure lotus arising from the mud of the swamp.

May

> The greater the intensity of pain or passion the greater the potential of creative expression and pure pleasure; but although pain and passion are not to be rejected, neither are they to be cultivated. . . . The middle path is maintained in the experience of excessive passion and over-indulgence by practising the precept "neither cultivation nor rejection but identification with the nature of being" . . . When incisive insight into the nature of mind, from which emotion is inseparable, removes the sting of passion, passion becomes an inexhaustible source of energy, power and awareness." [115] *[Nothing to grasp at or push away—simply observing mind's pure play.]*

Passion, a wind of fire, a fire of wind. To *be* that fire, that wind—passion with no point of reference, no personal attachment, just desire, empty, primally pure. I am burning—burning is. Ah. *[The primordial purity, isness, stands clear and unimpeded to the gaze that does not condition the object, the experience, or the one who gazes. Awareness shines forth. Ah.]*

---

115. Dowman, *Sky Dancer: The Secret Life and Songs of the Lady Yeshe Tsogyel*, 236–37.

All day I have felt happy. I am healing. I can't help it, I just feel happy.

This evening I am praying, "Let me love the good because it is good for all." I see the gap between belief and action, the gap between my formal spiritual practice and the way I actually live my life. *[In this fertile gap is found the very stuff of spiritual work.]* I choose impeccability then fall back again. My mind is made strong by practice, then I weaken it by not practicing what practice has shown me.

Traveling to teach, flight filled with marvels—the phenomenal world as manifestations of Guru Rinpoche: clouds, sun, rain, fields, birds. Planes coming in to land, headlights suddenly appear like angels winging in—and around the wing of our plane is dancing a moth. I weep with the isness . . .
     . . . and in instants succeeding each other like lifetimes I experience longing so intense that I actually imagine giving in to it, allowing this passion to be the wind that carries us both away from the path—and then clarity of purpose that makes me gasp, "Oh, Beloved, I forgot my purpose: to attain enlightenment in *this* lifetime, in *this* body."

It's not that *wanting* is bad or wrong; I am human and humans want. It is what I add onto the wanting: attachment to the object, clinging to the wanting itself. Yet, how to transcend without *suppressing* desire?
     The corrections all seem, today, to boil down simply to this: self-discipline. And I am looking at the extraordinary degree to which I lack it. It's peculiar, because this is one of the qualities others think I have in abundance. Yet I suspect what they've seen is really rigidity, the moralistic, self-punitive stance that is meant to control the thirsty, hungry child within. *[That grubby little girl whom I want not to know, to touch, or to see, who keeps turning up uninvited, needy and importunate. My teacher of love.]* Right action is just simpler, more direct. But without denying or suppressing feelings and thoughts. To *transform* them—through conservation of energy, choice of what to energize in the thought-stream, the stream of karma: virtuous or non-virtuous actions, generous or selfish thoughts. The enormity: simply transcending the personal. In any given instant.

Beloved, how is it that I maintain this mind of separation from you, my spiritual friend, *you*, who hold me with your great kindness and compassion, *you*, in whom I slowly-by-slowly traverse the treacherous seas of samsara, *you*, Beloved, who hold open the gate for me?

Praying that once and for all I be healed of dualism. Let me *be* the sacred bundle. *[As the Sufis say "the longing is the love," so can I say of this fresh longing to move beyond duality: This is the non-dual, the One, calling to me within my own heart.]*

At 2:30 a.m. I go to the temple, sit before Beloved's place, speak to her in my heart: "Just as I am, Beloved, with all my faults, I offer myself. Not as a warrior, just as an ordinary woman. Slowly, with reluctance, bit by bit. Grant me your blessing, please."

Gregory: "Go. Manifest my love for you. Make something of beauty and give it away—to someone other than me."

June

Everything falling away, the Great Unraveling—

Beloved said, "For me, duty is just *being*. If you feel differently, then half of what I say must be confusing for you." *[Only half?]* She added, "You really need to be teaching regularly. It's your function. And besides, when you don't teach regularly you get . . . distracted." Made me laugh. I told her, "After fleeing in terror from the open doorway, I am now wanting to go through it."

July and August

❖ Beloved and the lama are checking us for blocks; for a number of us, including me, the work in this time is to resolve karmic patterns of longstanding duration, some from the early Middle Ages. This is told in order to explain why for some of us the movement is not easily and simply just forward in this time. ❖

Tonight in meditation I learn that I will not fall apart or explode if I allow my emotions simply to *be*, for these emotions are not I.

My morning baths in the stream are a beautiful gift. Today I met the rising sun on the way home. At the end of a five-day fast I feel cleansed inside and out. There's healing and rebuilding to be done, slowly by slowly, here in this body-mind, which has been wandering in the Swamps of Self.

Karma yoga. All the overwork, the demands I've felt surprised by—I think Beloved has been, for years, giving me repeated opportunities to work off negative karma. From now on *[seeing the pervasiveness and power of my negative karma!]* perhaps I shall be able to meet these opportunities more gratefully. She shows me, in this time, the vastness of her compassion.

On the eve of my departure for a month of retreat she said several times that the work I have contributed *[compiling some of her lineage teachings]* is beautiful, very significant: "It is an honor to be so close to the stream of such sacred teachings. It accumulates much merit for you." I thanked her. "You're welcome. I'm a lifesaver," she said, smiling, and held out her hand to me, answering my persistent thoughts about death.

Retreat at the Shrine of the Tsawai Lama

It was like the bardo all these months—lured by the soft light of personal love, needing an effort of will to choose instead the bright, clear light of truth. I see that this is how the transmutation will occur—just like this: by practice, inch by careful, determined inch. *[The holy, faultless, generous inchworm path.]*

I feel safe only when I'm practicing. Otherwise my senses all key to the phenomenal world, the world of sensation and appearance. Even on the journey here to the retreat center, even to the last minute, crossing the bridge near where Greg was haying his uncle's fields, even then I hoped and feared I might see him. *[And didn't know if even then I would stop the car or keep driving.]*

Milarepa: a great sinner who became a great saint. There seem to be many who've been great sinners and who then have seen the light, found and followed the Dharma. Are there any like me? Who have been in error and ignorance, then found the way, made their vows and shown great potential—and then turned away from the path, walked sideways? Any who have done this and *then* become saints?

Grasping, clinging, attachment—doesn't matter "to what": it's the clinging itself that's got to go! Gratify desires, desires increase.

Dreaming I am revealed as unfit to be with others: ❖ I've been exposed to rabies, am locking myself into my house so no one will catch it, sealing it up like a prison tower. ❖

Prostrating with *joy*—gratitude for the blessing of refuge in this lifetime, for the never-ending compassion and welcome of the gurus, for the strength and steadfastness of the sangha, their pristine example, all the buddhas and bodhisattvas who began, like me, by taking refuge—and now light the way to enlightenment. I am throwing myself at their feet.

I write about what's more mundane, more easily put into words, not about the sense that I am slowly being permeated and transmuted by blessings and grace, from the inside out.

Deep remorse at the suffering I have caused.

The ripening of my karma—good. Just as Lama said: "If I get what I want, good; if I don't get what I want, good. In the first case good karma is ripening; in the second, negative karma is ripening. In either case, keep the mind always open, not grasping, clinging, or holding to cause, effect, phenomena. Look innerly, always look innerly; watch your own mind. Know the emptiness."

As the ego dies it will keep grasping for whatever will feed it, keep it alive.

Work on *pride* has begun in this retreat.

This morning, prostrating, a moment of lucidity: If I were offered the possibility of enlightenment in this lifetime, would I give up everything for it? Shock—the answer was yes. And then I realized that I *have* been offered this possibility, was told "the door is wide open for you in this lifetime"—and I *fled*. I panicked, ran craving after distractions, excuses, delays. The choice is mine only, and it is made in each instant.

(End of Retreat at the Shrine of the Tsawai Lama)

September, October, November, December

> When one has lived a long time alone,
> one refrains from swatting the fly

and lets him go, and one hesitates to strike
the mosquito, though more than willing to slap
the flesh under her, and one lifts the toad
from the pit too deep for him to hop out of
and carries him to the grass, without minding
the toxic urine he slicks his body with,
and one envelops, in a towel, the swift
who fell down the chimney and knocks herself
against window glass and releases her outside
and watches her fly free, a life line flung at reality,
when one has lived a long time alone . . .[116]

Cabin Retreat

[Here begins the semi-retreat into which Beloved places me on my return from retreat away: intensive practice in my cabin in the woods near the ashram, much solitude, not taking part in community activities, once or twice a week crossing the mountains to the city to see psychotherapy clients. But it isn't till near the end, some five months later, that I realize this has been a retreat. I think it is exile.][117]

My teachers shine on the crown of my head, my true nature is like the empty sky, intrinsically pure, and in that natural mind I am one with the only Teacher. All else is distraction.

Following the disarray of seeing Gregory unexpectedly after more than two months, in meditation I ask to see the roots of my grasping. What comes: "There is no grasping." I find this response peculiar and suspect, then understand: I am working now with recognizing the *essential* self—this is the subtle knowing that filters my experience these days, surfacing at unexpected moments to remind me of What Is. [118] And in this essential self there is, of course, no grasping. So the antidote to grasping is to recall and to center firmly in that essential nature—clear light.

---

116. Kinnell, *When One Has Lived a Long Time Alone.*

117. My retreats in this and the coming years, starting with this Cabin Retreat, are intended to bring me down to bare bone, to naked reality. I am not looking for a time of respite but for liberation. Retreat is not this for everyone, and has not always been this for me, but in these years retreat is where the fabric of contrived reality shreds for me, not to be rewoven.

118. "In preparatory tantric practice, refuge is taken in the natural mind of enlightenment, which is endowed with three qualities—entity, nature and compassion. Entity is the wisdom of emptiness; nature is that of clarity; compassion is the all-pervasive wisdom." Sangpo Rinbochay, *Tantric Practice in Nyingma*, 117.

I have yet really to do the work with self-forgiveness, and it must be done. Better to focus on practice as *purity* instead of as purification. Purification: need to be purified; purity: intrinsically pure.

Thoughts of impermanence and death are with me a lot. Today, stirrings of a more urgent motive to realize enlightenment this time around, in this body, in this lifetime, when "the door is wide open" for me. Is it still? I have no real option but to proceed as if it is—and so I practice.

An extraordinary rawness is surfacing. Perceiving what Buddhism is actually referring to in talking about our "insanity"—we really *are* insane, every one of us!

•

Pain still coming up in waves, yet a clearing today as I perceive the confusion itself as part of the necessary progression, the falling away of ego's shackles—the fall preceded, of course, by pride *["that fallen light being," Beloved called it]*—necessitating the loss of *all* held most dear by the personality self. *["Everything she has held dear I have taken away," said Beloved of me earlier. Since I am still holding dear, she is still taking away.]* What truly is precious, luminous and illuminating, is unchanging and unmoving at the center.

Recently am aware of my mother's pure love for me, like the pristine blue of the enamel bowl she gave me for Christmas many years ago. *[Matte black iron without, clear cerulean within—like this time, like the shell of ignorance opening to reveal the pristine nature.]* And feeling the great earthquakes in the southern hemisphere as messages of the Mother's love—it seems like catastrophe, yet it is deep healing, out of profound, always existing, unalterable love.

Well, Greg's wife and I are certainly connected in some way that I don't understand but am unable not to register! About midday I felt I absolutely had to go to bed; as I climbed the ladder to the loft I felt coiled, about to pop. Looking at my female body, touching my vulva: "My female organs have never even been used, except for sex; there's something less than real about these compared to hers, which bring forth children—*that* is real." Fell into a deep sleep, awoke, found a note from sangha neighbors saying Greg's new baby is being born. Deep wrenching of self-grasping arose in me like spasms—pain, remorse, fear, jealousy, despair, longing. I went back to my loft and just practiced, practiced. *[Gregory's wife, giving birth. When I learn of the pregnancy I feel betrayed and humiliated; when I now learn of the birth I feel like the thief I am.]*

"Me, me, me"—that's all my emotional spasms are about. And since each one eventually passes, no matter how acute the anguish at the time, of what possible usefulness is it to talk about the "issues"?

•

I think I've turned a page—not a new chapter, nothing that definitive, but something different is happening. *[The inner work generalizes further now. Processing—mentally, emotionally, spiritually—the relationship with Gregory, I am driven by the need to understand my "fall," wanting and willing to see the crevasse into which I have fallen, that "deep, archaic split in my nature," love vs. duty, spiritual vs. secular, altruistic vs. personal. Confronting the effects of obsessive attachment will bring me face to face with the delusion of duality itself.]*

I'm thinking about "attachment hunger" as deriving from insufficient maternal nourishment for security, love, touching, and holding, and from inadequate paternal support for individuation with a solid sense of self. This isn't new insight, but this is the first time my defenses have been permeable enough that the raw emotions and bodily feelings are really accessible. There's certainly some—not relief, but something like relief, maybe objectivity—in having the information surface so baldly. [119]

How to transmute something so fundamental? How to go on from a point that has not yet been reached? Feels like climbing a ladder that's missing rungs: I'm hanging on for dear life. Must have felt this same

---

119 Psychologically, a *serviceable* sense of self is essential for healthy development, while spiritually, a *solid* sense of self is precisely our problem. Notions of inherent self and solidity of any kind misconstrue the nature of reality, in which everything arises from causes, dependent upon conditions, in some way composite and thus empty of inherent existence, inherent "selfness." But the psychological and the spiritual views of "self" are not contradictory. Rajneesh pointedly remarked (source not noted in my journal) that if you have not an intact ego, in the psychological sense, and you try to "transcend" the ego, what you get is arrested development. You can't transcend what you haven't got. (Unless, of course, you are one of the rare and lovely holy fools, dysfunctional to this world, at one with the One.) While there is no conflict between the psychological concept of ego, necessary for psychological and psychosocial wholeness, and the spiritual concept of ego, source of all our confusion and suffering, there is definitely a conflict between egocentricity and liberation. Devotion to the well-being and liberation of others, bodhicitta, the Great Love, is the Liberator.

way as a little girl. Shaky, brittle, as if I'll literally fly apart if I don't hold on. Gregory got pulled into my pathology. So have a lot of other people. Maybe I can at least project less now. The possibility of forgiving myself seems closer now, when I realize that in fact it was a little girl, not an adult woman, who was creating all that havoc. [120]

That little girl deserves to live, to grow up, to be happy. How can I be a good mother to her, a good father? And this healing contains within it, somehow, a healing of my relationship with children, as I heal my relationship with the child within myself. And somehow, too, a healing of my creativity, long tamped down and suppressed. Perhaps its energy is the energy of the child—whole, beloved, and free. [121]

•

The world of appearances—or the essence. I am being *driven* inward. Essence is a seed within me; only I can choose to nourish it. Ultimately samsara, in either its suffering or its pleasure, will never satisfy. It is only illusion that I can "do it over again and be healed" in the phenomenal world. Phenomena are substitutes. What is real is the natural mind within, the true "face I wore before."

If the healing can go even half as deep as the pain . . .

---

120. Fundamental" here means fundamental to the infant's healthy maturation, not fundamental in the sense of basis or ground, although I probably couldn't have said this then. The ground—insubstantial and all-pervading—is the true nature itself, the true nature of all beings and phenomena. Experiences of the personality complete old karma and create new, but I think there is no actual reservoir of emotional affliction or mental confusion that must be somehow discharged in order to resolve. Our work would never be done! What we commonly think of as emotional residue might be understood more accurately as *habitual patterns* of body, speech, and mind. These may lay down cellular imprints, including synaptic pathways in the brain, that can appear like mental or emotional residue at the experiential level, or that can appear to influence experience and behavior as if they have the weight of residue. The weight I think they have, though, is not the weight of residue but the weight of karma: effect and predisposition.

121. Repatterning is so easy, really, although it may be hard to believe that. Spiritual practice, like a new broom, sweeps clean. I do not even remember much now about the sorrows of the child I was; spiritual purification and insight have given a fresh childhood, different events recalled, different memories evoked, and a different present and future nourished by them. But here I was still inquiring, examining. I needed and *wanted* the wisdom of particulars.

Beloved: "Do inner work, fulfill your vows, be strong." Doubt comes up, yet also firm resolve and faith. And I return to the cushion.

My heart may be becoming more peaceful. Yesterday I went up to bleed into the moss on the ridge. There were birds all around me, including my signal of peace, the woodpecker; today a dignified, majestic V of wild geese flew directly over my head, and I saw ten wild turkeys and a beautiful red fox.

•

Something strange is happening. I am out of synch with the community, feeling they share a private language I don't understand, a rhythm I'm not part of, a subtle network of knowledge, assumptions, values, expectations I'm not meshing with. It's not overt conflict—more subtle, indefinable, as if I am in a foreign country where I thought I could function because I spoke the language, only to discover that the dialect is all the more incomprehensible because it sounds familiar but is not. The sensation is almost of being in a different *medium*.

> Two templates, like continents
> of the mind, float
> in vast, empty space.
> The closer they come to perfect
> synchrony, the more jarring,
> discordant and harsh
> when their edges
> meet yet do not mesh.
>
> It is like this with me
> now. My spine is out of whack,
> seeks yet does not quite hold
> the true plumb line.
>
> Yet in the solstice fire
> I see only emptiness
> and luminosity. I know
> that fire-clear light,
> that arcing, inky sky.

Beloved, on my resistance to seeing emptiness: "She desires union so much she fights it—ain't that funny, girl?" Well, maybe a little.

How am I going to get through this day?

She tells me, "You don't have to *swim* in the lake of causes! *[That is definitely what I am doing, as I continue to probe mind, emotions, and behavior for their causes and conditions—sometimes meditating, more often ruminating, self-absorbed.]* If the water is undrinkable, boil it. Immediately apply the antidote. *[I am still more interested in anecdote than antidote. I feel impelled to see and to understand, at the level of phenomenal reality. It is as if I need to walk this part of the path stooped over and twisted around to examine my own footprints. There is nothing wrong with doing so—it does yield information about how I've been walking—but it makes it difficult to see the path ahead, the beauty around, the sky above.]* Affirm beauteous essence of self. Don't make the practice into a weapon to punish yourself. You're not being punished; it's an opportunity, it is care. Yes, it *was* 'spiritual life or death,' because of the vows and commitments made in this and previous lifetimes; it is good that you see this." "I feel as if I'm not cooked yet, Beloved." "And I'm turning up the heat, girl! You're not going to blow it, don't even energize that thoughtform. You're almost out of the tunnel." *[The last statement stuns me.]*

I think the fault of my involvement with Gregory lay in turning away from the teacher more than in what I was doing with him. That was what contravened my inner vows, that was where the spiritual danger lay. And underlying that was pride, a refusal of my bodhisattva vows, a desire to gratify the personal self even at the cost of harm to others. Panic at the thought, "Oh, I'm going to have to give up *selfishness:* the choice, large or small, based on personal taste, desire, 'need.'"

What still confuses me, though, is that my corrective motivations are still somehow external to me, rather than springing spontaneously, wholeheartedly from compassion, from unselfish care.

A trembling sense of panic, just below the surface.

•

If I let go of the pain, what have I got, who am I, what am I? *[To release the continuous creation and re-creation of the constructed self is the choice—made over and over, lifetime after lifetime, year by year, moment by moment.]*

Beloved: "You need laugh injections. When heaviness starts to come over you, lighten up, look to the positive. Your practice should be a *happy* offering. Happiness is your sacred duty." *[Happiness as duty? How can I understand this when I feel duty the opposite of what I take for love? Caught in self-clinging and duality mind, the "this vs. that," I cannot rest in the Great Love that includes all.]*

Meditating, I experience myself one with space—simply contain all, so no struggle, resistance, or reaction—no aversion, attachment, or ignorance—spacious like sky—clear, bright.

Yesterday, out running, chest pains that actually took me to the ER. The night before, or was it the same morning, somehow got stuck going up or down the loft ladder, just sat on the edge, dazed and weeping, thinking, "My heart is breaking."

Last night I really called out for help, to Beloved, to Guru Padmasambhava, in letting go of Gregory. That I've done this before seems probable, but perhaps there was something different this time: I was crying out not from the place of "I ought to, have to, must do this," but acknowledging that it must be done and that I cannot do it alone. *[Mental choice and deep-rooted emotional wanting, as empowering affirmation—both are needed.]*

And this deepened in morning meditation to seeing attachment truly as a *poison*. *[Attachment itself, whatever the object—Gregory, food, praise, father, teacher, love . . .]* To acknowledge that I am *sick* is a step toward clarity—toward a genuine, self-empowered motivation, rather than whining notions of external coercion. I *choose* to heal this sickness, to transmute all grasping, clinging, selfishness, pride, because they are *untrue*. They are illusions that block my perception of *what is*, they are obstacles to my enlightenment—and thus to my being able to help others.

Slowly by slowly, bit by bit, step by step. Nothing dramatic. Just release attachment as it comes up, each time. And each time I'm not successful, acknowledge it and move on. It's not a one-time event—more like every minute, every choice-point. Coming to give thanks for the pain and panic when attachment hunger rises, for it shows me where the next step is.

Yesterday, for the first time, I actually said good-bye to my father.

In meditation, a commitment that seemed stronger and surer than anything I've known for a very long time—to cleave to the Dharma, to realize enlightenment now, in this body, in this lifetime, to drop the bonds that tie me to samsara: my desires, hatreds, opinions.

[The deep, inexorable inner momentum—like an undersea current, irresistible once engaged—is throwing up on the shore of my conscious awareness, one by one and in orderly progression, the specific elements of disorder, the detritus that must be purified. The delusions of the constructed self give way—not easily, not without struggle—before the vow to liberate all. This commitment cleaves the seas.]

Thanksgiving Day. Reach for nothing, neither push anything away.

•

Rills of panic. I feel vulnerable now to the faintest vibrations of those things I have so long denied or defended against—as if I'm shedding an *inner* skin, one that shields me from *myself.*

Jeez, these things are impossible to write about.

Virtually all my tension is from trying to hold a boundary between "me" and . . . anything else, everything else: the tension required to maintain the illusion of separateness, the idea of a separate self, the illusion of "I." To *maintain the illusion*. Meditating, reached the point where that was the remaining obscuration. I was unable to release it.

What helps? Only remembering who, what, I really am, only remembering the spacious, empty sky, only remembering to anchor *there* my identity—not in anything outside that great, pure stream within.

The three and five poisons *[passion, aggression, and ignorance are the primary three, pride and jealousy make the fearsome five]*: they are not in themselves evil, the person afflicted with them is not evil—they arise naturally; they are the human condition. Though not *necessary* to that condition, for they can be transmuted.

[For aggression:] In my heart I ask Grandmother Bear how to transform the roots of aggression. "Eat roots!" she says, grubbing in the earth. Eat the roots of aggression, digest them into good food, to nourish a mother of all. (Now I am eating roots: beets, carrots, onions.) And practice compassion; consider whether the words and actions will be beneficial to all beings. Take into the heart the objects of aggression. Now I am literally placing people visually inside my heart; it is a strong transforming practice.

[For attachment:] The more I release attachment to Gregory, the more

fully the love flows—first with joy, then giving rise again to the impulse to cling. *[So I make a give-away in the forest for him, enclosing a prayer in a small leather pouch and burying it beneath a pine tree, tall and straight like Gregory.]*

[For ignorance:] An abundance of lessons about where to take refuge: only in the unborn and undying, the I AM. Like a ship on dangerous seas I seek good harbor, I anchor in that which is indestructible, eternal. Let the waves still, waves and sea become one, true mind of enlightenment arise in me.

The mystery of emptiness becomes less mysterious as I begin to understand that emptiness is not an "experience"—it is the nature of what is.

(End of Cabin Retreat)

YAY, I had my hair all cut off today! Let this whole past year and all its pain, insanity, selfishness, and ignorance, all its suffering, be offered up.

•

Year Eight

Laughter innocent, riotous, huge ·
Reach for nothing, neither push anything away
Traversing the barrens · The liberation of desire
A living morality · City MANI · Only the naked, tender heart
"I don't remember who you are but I remember that I love you"

January

Landmark! Went to a wedding party, had a wonderful time, and it was okay, really, that Greg and his wife were there. Seeing her happier now, I understand better our choice to part.

Greater harmony—I am more in harmony—I *wish* to be in harmony—I *desire* what is good for all.

❖ One of those dreams where I am laughing, laughing—so hard I can't move—caught and held by laughter, innocent, riotous, huge. ❖

•

Am I suited to community life? I am so self-centered and removed. "What you do not know, is how to love one person among all the creatures in the Universe, and then how to love all the creatures in the Universe, and then go back to loving them again in one single person." [122] *[It will be with Marianne that I will learn this, years from now, in a moment in which love for all and love for one become one.]*

I see how my ignorance, suffering, and exile are yielding good fruits for others. Seeing two students wavering at the place where I panicked and fled *[facing emptiness and the bodhisattva commitment]*, I am able to give reassurance and encouragement not to back away, as I did.

❖ Asking Beloved for instructions. "Forgiveness," she says. ❖

---

122. Bellesi, "Happy Crossing, Good Luck Little Uli."

[224]

[I doubt that I then understood who or what I was being guided to forgive, but I now see tender intimations of self-forgiveness—shaky and inconsistent, but there.]

I've been setting up the "love vs. approval" dichotomy for a long time, I think. It's gotten exalted, of course, into love vs. *duty.* I even repressed that I was seeking approval, seeking *anything* from anyone else, including affection.

"Reach for nothing, neither push anything away." I remember, I forget, I remember again. These words are moderate, gentle. They suggest standing tranquil while emotions simply arise within me and pass away again. I have not actually, purposefully, diligently, mindfully *practiced* this yet: *applying* the principles of nongrasping.

And remember this, Barbara: It is not true, as I sometimes think, that I am nothing *but* grasping.

> I acknowledge the winds of change:
> they blow.
> I acknowledge the purifying fires:
> they burn, they burn.
> I acknowledge the forgiving waters:
> they flow.

February

❖ Journey across a terrain of crags, cliffs, fantastic rock and mountain shapes—remote, barren, desolate, hard. I kept thinking, "I don't like this, it's not beautiful, welcoming, soft"—yet I proceeded. ❖ *[As I am, yes, proceeding, traversing the barrens and hard places, across bridges I sometimes can't even see until I have crossed them.]*

❖ White deer! ❖ *[A dream sign of purification.]* And after three days of not being able to meditate, today I sit—and I'm emanating rainbows!

Directly in front of me I see a small figure streaming golden light rays in every direction, like a sun. It is myself. When I draw it into me I know that I myself am radiating golden light, in all directions, like the sun.

❖ A man intimately known to me reaches to grab me—and I can't tell whether it is the one I love or the one I hate! ❖ So much for attraction and aversion. The same thing is happening with sense experiences—I find myself thinking or saying, "ouch, too hot" when really it's cold, or "mmm, salty" when it's actually sweet. "Conceptualization falls apart with the abandon of a madman." [123]

Reach for nothing, neither push anything away.

March

Thoughts of moving away, of living in a city; a growing feeling that it's coming time for me to leave here, for something larger, more peopled, more active. Maybe it's March blues, as a long winter opens into spring. I imagine what it would be like to have central heat, running water, nurturing, stimulating connections with people. Suddenly, a sense of freedom: Oh, I could *leave* here, I could go where there are people I feel close to, I can give myself this if I really want it! And, of course, Gregory—it would be a lot easier to be far from Gregory. But I also have a sense that there's something not yet done for me here, related to my sense of separation in the community, where I feel nourished on a "spiritual" level but truly not on a personal level.

[If you are caught, as I was, in the persistent duality of "spiritual" vs. "personal," I earnestly encourage you to pray, pray for its dissolution, and in every moment to examine mind, speech, and activity for its confounding seeds and weeds. The spiritual path is undertaken and accomplished by persons. Spiritual work pulls and weaves the most personal and secret threads of our intention and manifestation. At whatever level we experience spiritual mastery it reveals, within the phenomena of appearance and experience that constitute the personal, full knowledge of the sacred. Truth is One.]

[In the next short section, insight flings out into light the banner of a hard-won, small, powerful victory. Though much undergrowth yet obscures, this particular, visible instant is a floodlit clearing in the forest.]

A lot of the work for me right now must be about simply knowing and acknowledging *desire*—for if denied, suppressed, unacknowledged, it will surely surface to drive me once again around the wheel. [124] So

---

123. Dudjom Rinpoche, "Calling the Lama from Afar," *The Preliminary Practice of the New Treasure of Dudjom*, 8.

124. "Denied, suppressed, unacknowledged." I mean slightly different things by these three: *denied*—blocked from reaching conscious recognition; *suppressed*—nudging conscious recognition but consciously prevented

whatever the desire is—loving friends, passionate sex, enlightenment, a pretty body—simply draw it into the stream of inner light; let it flow in that clarifying fire, to become a jewel to pass to others.

Highly developed mentally, pretty retarded emotionally. Wanted father *[his love, nourishment, choosing and cherishing me—and simply his life continuing with mine]* and suppressed not only that wanting but *all* wanting having to do with men—so this wanting *must* come up, *had* to come up. The purpose was appropriate and so was the vehicle: desire for a man; what was distorted was the object choice, determined by compulsive addiction to unresolved desire. Now I'm free to wonder: What would it be like to want a man and have the wanting be truly fulfilled in a wholesome relationship? [125]

And of course this helps me understand better why I am somehow goal-less and unambitious: All goals and ambitions are based on desire, on wanting. *[I am goal-less in the relative sphere only, where indeed goals arise from wanting; spiritually, however, I am committed to the ultimate goal, which uses wanting for fuel but which arises from aspiration.]*

And this helps me understand, too, "the great split"—secular-sacred, private-public, personal-political, love-duty. To choose the side away from the personal, emotional realm felt like death—could only live publicly, sacredly, dutifully at the cost of "wanting"—can't quite get this into words—it's as if I've always seen clearly where I am to go—sacred,

---

from expressing; *unacknowledged*—felt but not recognized directly, not "met," not "owned." These three mental operations have an important factor in common: they each rely upon the decision neither to be with nor to look directly at what is arising in mind or emotion. "Being with" one's experience is simply experiencing it, letting it be, just as it is, without grasping, repulsing, or elaborating. And looking directly at one's thoughts and emotions reveals their inherent emptiness as they arise and dissolve, of the same nature as mind itself. Thus, whatever the character of the experience (even when injurious), there is no fixation, no reification—and so, by definition, no reinforcement for psychological habituation or trauma. (A contemporary clinician, Janina Fisher, writes of these matters with great compassion and clarity; see her "Working with the Neurobiological Legacy of Early Trauma.")

125. These psychological, developmental explications have validity in their own spheres, and the inquiry was undeniably useful to me at the time, elucidating the relative reality in which I was so confused. But this elucidation pertained not to causes, only to conditions. Karmically, I was like a hungry ghost, lost in a realm of craving that could not be satisfied—because karmically it had nothing to do with what was craved and everything to do with the *predisposition to crave* and the *habit of craving*.

public, duty—and yet have always known that there was something profoundly significant that had not yet been resolved on the secular, personal, emotional side.

Free choice is *possible* when desire is acknowledged. Then I can *choose* what desires to fulfill and what ones not.

It feels as if simply the acknowledgment of wanting *is* the resolution. Can it really be so simple? *[Yes.]*

Wanting *itself* is now freed.

Before, I couldn't *trust* my wanting: I believed wanting *itself* was wrong, would always lead me to forbidden places and desires. Now I am free to want *whatever* I want, and I come to see how naturally, how simply, how freely arises desire for the good, and for other people's happiness. No wonder I've always been envious, angry, resentful; if I couldn't have what I couldn't even acknowledge I wanted, how could I rejoice in other people "getting theirs"?

Even my cells feel as if they are breathing in new life. I feel stronger, more buoyant, fuller *inside*—"plumper." What a fresh breeze this is, blowing through all my being—just see the clouds and mists disperse, flying, dancing, spinning, whirling! This is the *liberation of desire*.

The work with "liberation of desire" now becomes highly specific and practical. A remarkable fresh energy of affirmation flowing through. When working with my therapy clients, an amazing new immediacy, presence, and availability. When reading the criteria for mastery as a spiritual teacher, instead of "Oh, I'm not good enough"—now, "I *want* to attain mastery." When feeling grasping for Greg, instead of conflicted affirmations of "May he be happy"—now, "I *want* Gregory to be happy, and his wife, his children." No difference—except *all* the difference. I am *one* with the prayer now, I AM affirmative.

All my love—oh, I meant to write "all my *life*"—all my life I have been interrupting this creative life energy, damming it up, pulling it back—yes, "all my *love*," all my *loving* has been withheld. Now it can flow free. Wanting arises now from direct experience—it is not abstract, vague, arising from obligation—it arises from my *essence*. This feels very different, very significant, very creative. As if the energy is for the first time allowed to arise from *true source* and flow into a true channel of manifestation, power, creation—one with life. As if all my life I've been *stopping* this natural flow within and through myself—I know I have, I know this is so—and I know I am no longer caught in the knots that created that pattern. I am free to *be* who I am.

I've always seen my ardor, my passionate nature, as both my greatest gift and my greatest failing. So I've always known what I am now in the process of discovering. *["We already are what we aspire to become."]*

April

Moving away *[to a large city in another state—my plans are made now]* is partly about expanding to greater complexity. It's so simple here *[rustic cabin, wood heat, much meditation, a few psychotherapy clients, tiny local sangha, small rural village]*. Now I'm choosing to live simply amid complexity. And the inner message: Just go, just be there—take as little as possible, don't worry about money. Do it like a pilgrim.

Yesterday, on Rattle Mountain, Gregory and I: resolution. We gave our love away on the winds. Beloved said to him, when he told her we had reached resolution and yet longing and pain still arose: "Resolution doesn't mean everything is perfect; it just means you can go on living your life, doing your duty."

May

From "looking outside," from even thinking there *is* an outside, arises suffering. Nothing from the phenomenal world can satisfy; I reach, I am unsatisfied, I turn inward, I know peace—and then craving arises again and the cycle resumes. This morning I learn the lesson from a grapefruit. *[Not a bad description of the "karmic predisposition to crave" and the "habit of craving."]*

I feel as if I am more seeing things simply as they are—and "seeing what is" is not the mysterious thing I'd conceived of it as. It's not "piercing a veil" but simply seeing what is, in each moment: Oh, now I'm feeling sad, now I'm feeling desire, now I let go. I take a step, joy arises; take another, pain arises; another, and hope arises. Reaching for something, I push it away; pushing something away, I grasp it—and the grief and pain are just, again, the strivings of attachment, clinging. "My" love for Gregory is now free to nourish all. I am empty, I am full. We are letting each other go *and* we love each other. We are parting in love, *because* of love.

When I leave I must really *leave*. I *need* this freedom, I *want* this courage.

Whew, it is taking a fair amount of courage and trust to be doing some of the therapeutic work I'm doing these days with clients—trust that they'll get through their process, trust that they'll decide to live, courage to go with them into some very dark places. I see over and over again the fruits of my own inner work. I am thankful.

•

In my cabin tonight, aware of how my heart jumps with joy and kinship—with love—at the sight or sound of any live thing: ant, moth, mouse, fly, mosquito, hornet. I greet them with gratitude for their *being*, and for their being here with me.

Self-denial is not renunciation. Self-denial is negative, life-denying; renunciation is positive, affirmative, enlarging life for all. It has been essential that I move from self-denial to renunciation. This lurching, painful, ungraceful process is the way I've done it. Now, out of my own faltering, fallibility, and failures, I am harvesting the lessons, forgiving myself, reaffirming clear intention, and changing my behavior.

Morality grows from this soil, a *living* morality—not of abstract ethical principles but springing from lived experience. The teachings are becoming real for me through the falterings of my will, the waverings of my intention. It seems there are rules I've lived by that I haven't actually believed in, have only subscribed to. Now I have some better basis for understanding them, and ever less and less ground from which to judge another. My behavior has been far from impeccable. Now my impeccability will lie in the care and honesty with which I allow my failures to teach me what I can use to live better and to help others live more wholly and happily.

My birthday. I ask Beloved if I completed the work of the year, if it was a good year. "The year wasn't good but the outcome is." What is not yet complete, what is yet to do? "*Certainty*—unity of heart and mind. It's just about there, but because the potential is so great it's obvious that it's not there." How to work on it? "Practice."

June

[I am deeply inspired and directed *by Beloved's instruction on "certainty—unity of heart and mind."]* Yesterday I saw a small V of geese flying high. "I love you!" I cried out to them—"I love you!" And wept, for the ineluctable imperative of their flight. Living arrows springing from the divine bow, the flight of the geese is absolute. From the ground where my walk is hesitant and lurching, I fling my heart out to the geese: "Carry me with you, teach me your flight." There is drama in the sky, in my heart. I can only love the geese for their implacable, unwavering flight.

Eager to be gone now. I choose to go, I want to go, I go with joy, it is time, it is good. I do not doubt, I am certain, I am wholehearted. *And* this certainty, this wholeheartedness, includes grief. My heart feels as if it is breaking, ever so quietly now.

Very tenderhearted this last evening and night alone in "my" cabin. "My"—nothing is "mine"—in fact I am leaving easily, for "I neither leave nor did I ever come."

The nestling birds on my porch fly from the nest all at once, in an instant.

July

Popped through a portal. *[Now living with friends in a large city, distant from the ashram, where I go from time to time to visit, practice, do work for Beloved.]*

In meditation this morning, as many, many months ago, when I did not feel free to act on it: Let me not teach now until I *embody* the teachings. That feels right. *[I tell Beloved, "I don't want to teach again till I'm enlightened." "We might have to call on you a bit sooner than that," she replies, smiling.]*

•

The momentary confusion of the boat that has slipped its moorings—no longer tied to the shore, not yet full in the current.

A lot of shaking and quaking going on, very deep. What I am aware of is "cutting through" energy: CERTAINTY. *[Though I am now living away from Beloved, still she is speaking in my heart, mirroring my mind, holding*

*my feet to the fire of sacred purpose. This is the compact of teacher and student; it
has nothing to do with time or place.]*

Ever subtler disharmonies of thought, word, or action are registering
with me more quickly. It's as if the system is so sensitively tuned to
go forward now that even a momentary distraction is keenly felt as
disharmonious. *[Such registrations on consciousness are always there, just not
always recognized. In these times I am looking innerly, the inward attention like a
lighthouse beam, scanning, scanning for signals rising from the deeps.]*

A channeled communication sent by the person who had received
it for me: "Remember whose path you are following and never stray
from it, for in doing so you shall walk far this time." I ask, "Whose
path?" and receive, "The Tathagatas." [126] A freshet of tears, signaling
recognition—and the image of "cutting through" became like "warm
knife cutting through butter"—immediate, direct, simple, effortless.

Meditating, I become aware of a sudden dramatic heightening of sound
in the environment: city noises, a cardinal right outside my window
loudly calling, fire engines roaring, sirens sounding. Mind registers all
this as *life*.

City MANI [127]

Sirens
rend the night.
That's what compassion
sounds like
in the city,
hear the city
chanting MANI.

August

Visiting Mother in her nursing home across the country, I'm as insubstantial as a feather, dropping, leaving no trace, floating on to another
place . . .

---

126. Tathagatas: the "thus-gone" ones—gone to precious, unsurpassable,
perfect, complete enlightenment.

127. MANI: short name for OM MANI PADMA HUM, the mantra of Avalokiteshvara
(Sk.), Chenrezig (Tib.), the deity of compassion.

New Moon. Thinking of vacation, resting, idling—but the reality is, I am happiest and have most energy to draw upon when I am actively serving, helping, transforming for others. *[I see this over and over, act on it over and over, yet still there is this longing for idling. It is, purely and simply, the longing just to* be. *It is definitely not going to be satisfied by vacation.]*

Feeling deeply disheartened in interactions with my sisters while here visiting Mother—seeing the unloved and unloving aspects of my personality. All that hateful personality stuff: a slab erected over essence, a defensive structure.

It's all about love. What is to change is the *source* of confusion: the thought of not-love. If this tangle of living—cars, pigeons, sand—is all the guru's mandala, then truly there is nothing that is not-love. Not even me. Something must shift inside. Innerly I *am* love, love is what I AM. So I have only to go naked in the world. *[The thought of not-love throws me around and around until penetrated by direct knowledge of love's nature, not other than my own nature and the nature of all phenomena. The thought of not-love dissolves in an instant.]*

I weep easily at signs of compassion or need. As the flinty stuff falls away there is only the naked, tender heart.

On this visit I loved my mother more spontaneously, fondly, compassionately, unconditionally than I ever have before. *[She is in a nursing home, at her own request, instead of with one of her three daughters. The tension of trying to maintain a coherent social self as her Alzheimer's Disease progressed—she knew what this entailed because she had seen her own beloved sister go through it. "I just want to be able to let go completely," she had told me.]*

•

[Visiting the ashram.] Beloved. All storms calm in the twinkling of her eye.

Simply reminding myself of what I know to be true: The past is done, the future I know nothing about, it's only this moment that contains the entire Mystery, revealing itself instant by instant, millisecond by millisecond. Oh, to have the concentration of the ant! *[Or my old friend the inchworm.]*

Well, no ups without downs. Ran into Gregory and wife today at the ashram—it wasn't entirely easy; longing arose, it was acknowledged, it passed away. In the moment, of course, everything is fine, the world is not caving in, my heart is entire, all is well. *[That's it: the inward attention allowing recognition of the arising, the acknowledgment allowing it simply to be, the resolution, the dissolution, flowing naturally from the moment of naked, unadorned awareness. In natural mind, open like the sky, empty and brilliant, everything arises fresh, spontaneous, just as it is, and again dissolves into mind itself . . . when we don't react. Reacting, involving ourselves with what arises in awareness, turns flow into cause, freedom into karma.]*

What a beautiful offering it is given me to make! Something really precious to me, to which I am deeply attached—*this* I have the opportunity to offer up for the benefit of all beings! I am thankful, I pray to give it completely—as I think I do over and over again and then keep finding out there's more. Well, keep giving it over and over again—finally one day it will all be given, it is sure to be. *[And if not? If not, then what has been won is the incomparable, irreplaceable gift of always giving.]*

All these tears: polish for the love offering!

September

I am much preoccupied with questions about marriage, families, relationships. Sitting on the toilet, my housemate reminds me that it's not the *what*, it's the *how*. "What's a good family?" I wonder aloud. "Probably the one that keeps the shit moving," she says as she flushes the john.

Meditating, I feel, hear, sense, see the "sounds of resolution." As I hear grief's sound, I immediately feel, hear, sense, see the tone that resolves it to serenity; same with loneliness, aggression, fear. It is *wondrous!* And later, this dream: ❖ Two times I see someone who says to me, "I hurt"—each time I sing their pain to resolution, once with vivacity and verve, the second time sweetly, slowly. ❖

October

The fire-clear light within the spine grows stronger and brighter—like a molten flow, the sun, the sun in me. Where once I was seeing the vastness of the empty sky within, now it is this fiery core I see—and experience an inward pull, to see with the inner eye, while living, look-ing, thinking in the form-world. *[To apprehend the absolute while living in the relative—this is ever my deep challenge, ever where my resistance burgeons, ever where the small victories are taken, ever where my failings cut into consciousness deeper grooves of habit, clinging to the world of appearances—and ever where truth flashes through, flashes through . . .]*

Earlier it was the hard, flinty, rocky, metallic stuff breaking apart around my heart; now it's the brittle, fragile glass, splintering sharp shards—yet glass reveals the light behind it, so I'm getting closer to the light source itself.

Undefended now, my "stuff" about feeling unloved surfaces and I become more and more sensitive—to love coming in, open to receive it—and to criticism, disapproval, or rejection; it makes me want to kill myself. "Perfection's all I've got—if I'm not perfect I might as well die." *[If I'd ended that last sentence at the halfway point I'd have gotten it right: Perfection* is *all we've got, and we've all got it!*

The deluded, despairing litany—perfection or death, enlightenment or death—is distorted aspiration, grasping instead of giving, grabbing for result without yielding myself up to the necessary discipline, carried forth with right motivation: love and compassion for all. And the duality—enlightenment or death—will play itself out. My very lifelines will play themselves out.]

World Series playoffs on TV, watching as if meditating—very intense— the ballet of the game, the beautiful heroes in their youth, strength, beauty, grace—the diamond, the DIAMOND—the Vajra—the playing field, the Field of Mind—

November

❖ Something about refusing to nurture a little girl, who then moves away from me, and when I entreat her to come close again, understanding now what it is she was wanting from me and ready to give it, she is very mistrustful and stays away. ❖

Image of a feather being drawn, wrong-way-to, through a narrow tube. It is extremely uncomfortable. The feather is, of course, myself. What's the tube—the "straight and narrow"?

My mother died tonight.

Mourning my mother, I catch a glimmer of what it means to know that all beings have been my mothers, and to desire their enlightenment: "All beings throughout space are my parents . . ."

This morning my mother was cremated. As on one coast her body was being offered to the purifying, transforming fire, on the other I was praying that she release all attachment to her form. Ha, me too! Let *me* release all attachment to her form, to this particular version of "mother."

This afternoon, weeping: "I want my mother, I want my mother!"— her executor talking about her estate—"I'd rather have my mother!"

On the sixth day after my mother's death, reciting the *bardo* readings,[128] I perceived that my mother attained liberation, became one with the wisdom light. This I registered at that very moment as an event of the most wondrous and significant joy. Today on the phone Beloved confirmed this, said that my mother, perceiving in the Christian terms familiar to her, recognized the unity of her mind with the wisdom light; that though she will be reborn she will spend a long time in the realms of pure light; that you can't always predict who will attain "a surprising great realization after death"; that the prayers of myself and others did help her. I am suffused with the wonder and power of it, the beauty, the grace—my mother, my own mother, has realized, and I witnessed the very moment. So though I wasn't a good daughter to my mother, I have been given the opportunity to be a good spiritual friend to her.

December

"Count the gifts your mother gave you," Beloved told me. *[I am still counting them, all these years later.]*

[From my eulogy for my mother:] Mother had Alzheimer's Disease. We know this disease's great burden of suffering, yet it also gave blessings to her and to those who loved her. There was a period when she was very anxious and frightened, but when that time passed there occurred a relaxation, a softening—and, most wonderful, a great opening of heart. Always warm to others, my mother now allowed others to be tender and loving with her. The healing this brought to my relationship with my mother was a dear and precious gift.

My last visit with my mother is a jewel in my memory. Although she

---

128. Padmasambhava, *The Tibetan Book of the Dead.*

appeared to be recovering from her recent heart attack, I wasn't so sure; there was something very of-the-essence in the way she was speaking that day. At one point she looked up at me and exclaimed, as if I were brand-new, "Oh, I love you!" And, looking out at the magnificent trees, "Isn't that tree beautiful!"—as if she had received it that very moment direct from Creator's hand. This luminous, joyous effulgence, making everything new. And late that afternoon she said something I had never heard her say before. She looked up into the space before her, her face just shining: "I'm so happy," she said. "I'm so happy."

This gift: the happiness of my mother, poised on the threshold.

[And this one: One day, swinging on the backyard swings at the care home, waiting for my mother, I saw her walk toward me, her face open and curious, bright like a child's. As she reached me she held out her hand and said, "I don't remember who you are but I remember that I love you."]

•

YEAR NINE

"It's really all or nothing" · The Big Give-Away
Rebirth · The sweaty tangle of human life

January

Reach for nothing, neither push anything away. "All substances are my own mind, and this mind is emptiness, unarisen and unobstructed."[129]

❖ Someone's hands and feet have been amputated; in order not to be wasteful, my companions are grilling and eating them for dinner. I was attracted to the fine-smelling, succulent meal until I learned what it was, and then I was repulsed. Attraction, repulsion. Neither is to be trusted. ❖

Remorse for my actions during the ashram years that disturbed the harmony of individuals and the sangha. What surfaced to be seen this morning was the pattern of subservience, craving approval, propitiating authority—giving over my own sense of right and wrong, doing things that did not spring from *inner* authority. Now, not rebelliously but simply and directly, I choose to take responsibility for transforming that mind. *[Rebellion, disrespect, recklessness—as in the drama with Gregory—more visibly disturb the outer harmony, but both my subservience and my rebellion arise from deep undercurrents of confusion about responsibility, power, and integrity. Outer authority, inner authority: these threads are tangled and must be freed. It will be in the Teacher Mirror that I will see them most vividly.]*

•

In the Temple of Records I met a large angelic being, shining with light, who enfolded me in his wings. I received the message that my journey in this lifetime would be ending soon. In a way it was chilling, in a way gently, factually confirming. There are numerous internal signals

---

129. Padmasambhava, *The Tibetan Book of the Dead*, 86.

about this, particularly figures of speech I hear myself using, about completion, bringing things to order, letting go of attachments. Later, some other sense was prominent—not of mortal demise, perhaps, but of a significant passageway in consciousness.

I want to stay longer, yet of course I accept this movement to completion if that is what is most beneficial. I say that easily, yet I *don't* want to leave. I want to realize this life's purpose—Tathagata realization—for the sake of all, to liberate all from suffering, to establish all in perfect buddhahood. *[There seems at this time to be no particular attachment to life, in a personal sense—just this aspiration. My own suffering—seeing it, acknowledging it, discerning its true causes, not in circumstance but in karma and consequence—is slowly opening me to the suffering of all, and to the desire to lift it.]*

Today received news of my Tsawai Lama's death. I realized that the day before he died he had come to me in my meditation, here before my shrine—suddenly, without knowing why, I was weeping, touched by his presence and by some sense that he was leaving, calling out to him, "But I love you, I love you!" I feel empty, drained, sorrowing. Full, too; he is the essence of my own mind, nothing is lost. And yet, and yet . . . something there was that comforted me simply in the knowledge that he was in a body here on the planet with me. It's a little as if my father has died again, or my lover.

February

"It's all or nothing," Beloved told me during my recent visit. *[We choose the path and it leads us to this choice. All or nothing.]* "No more struggle, no more resistance. Just give. Forget about 'your portion'—of rest, food, money, whatever. Look to see what you can offer for the good of all. Duality mind: it's your illness. It's at a crisis state for you, it's depleting your life force. Replace the habit of suffering, fill up with luminosity. You have not yet generated bodhicitta, have not yet attained the first *bhumi*.[130] You still panic and fear lack; that shows you have not yet attained. If you had you would feel joy and never lose it—might feel momentary doubt when your airplane's shaking in a storm, but once on the ground, joy again. Think only of what you can give, not of what

---

130. The *bhumis* are the stages or levels of bodhisattva realization. See Gampopa, *The Jewel Ornament of Liberation*, ch. 19.

it costs you, not of what you need or want. That's the bodhisattva's vow. Think 'communion, communion.' Call forth bodhicitta."

In confusion I whined, "But you tell us to take care of ourselves, to rest, to be happy, to do what gives us ease and joy." "Not for you!" she said sharply. "The bodhisattva looks to care for *others*, to give *others* rest and ease, to establish *others* in true joy and happiness."

This lifelong illness *[illness of lifetimes, really]* now has a chance to be cured. It's as if she's trying to pull me through a keyhole and I keep thrashing and flailing, trying not to be pulled through. *[Ah, the dream-feather being pulled through the narrow tube . . .]*

Truly, the medicine is badly needed: I am more concerned that I'm not up there with those who have generated bodhicitta than I am concerned with actually developing bodhicitta! *[That day I laughed at this, today I laugh again. The first laugh was rueful and edgy, the second lighthearted and loving. The difference between the two is the joy Beloved was talking about.]*

March

❖ I am wondering what became of my body—was it cremated, buried? Then I realize I'm dreaming so I must not have died yet. ❖

Don't look back, don't look back—breathe, be present in *this* moment, in *this* moment make the choices that further your true purpose.

"When you show someone the clear light three times and they don't recognize, then they must take the gradual path," Beloved tells me. *[In those previous "showings," I had recognized what I was seeing—the clear light, emptiness, true nature—but hadn't understood how to abide in or practice on that state. And though I have been seeing for a long time that mine is a very gradual path, I am still grasping at the idea of swift accomplishment, mortified to be trudging, not soaring. So my striving is still selfish, not yet fully aspirational.]*

Seems as if a significant part of my learning is about trying and failing and trying some more: "going on with my head held high," as the last advice in the *Book of the Dead* says—not pridefully attached to glamorous, dramatic realization, but humbly, simply, keeping on. [131] Let me pass through the door she told me is wide open for me in this lifetime—and let me approach it very carefully, each step an offering

---

131. Padmasambhava, *The Tibetan Book of the Dead*, 92.

for all my precious mothers, that they may move through before me. *[Here, aspiration's loving note gently sounds.]*

Beloved showing me how little I know—my emotional immaturity, my confusion when I "don't know," the feeling that I *should* know—as when, years ago, my inmate therapy client immobilized me with a blade held ready at her own throat and then jumped headfirst through the prison window, glass flying all over the place, sirens, chaos, and I kept saying, "I don't know what to do, I don't know what to do"—*that* was the source of my panic!

"Why is my jewelry falling apart?" Beloved: "The stones of your ignorance are shaking loose." "Shall I have it repaired?" "Better wait till everything's shaken loose." ❖ I go to my jewelry box—it is empty, everything of value is gone—"Oh no! No, no, no!" I cry out. ❖

•

[Gregory has now separated from his wife and we are communicating again, gingerly.] Looking at a possible future with Gregory—the sweaty tangle of human life that I don't really know; commitment to build lovingly with another; immersion in a family; loving daily, being loved. This feels like the next step: this man, these children. And yet, and yet—is this best, especially for the children? And I feel Beloved is telling me, this way, that way, and every which way, that it's better not to think of a future with him.

The roar and chirp of spring—

❖ A teaching situation. People bow to me, I stiffen: "I'm no one to bow to." Then I allow myself to relax, allow the bows to be to the perfect buddha nature within. It is easy and simple and I am transparent, unmoving. ❖

April

Beloved is asking me to come back, to work closely with her again. Do I want to? Working with her feels like what's important to me, yet it's a lot more fun here in the city, in a personal way—am I ready to let go of that again? *[Is this not exactly the either-or with which she is confronting me: what I want or what's good for others, my portion or what I can give?]*

Told her yes. Can think of no rationale for being anywhere else on the planet if where she wants me is there with her. Don't know why it's me she sees doing this work that I neither perform well nor enjoy, but she said, "You're the only person whose mind works so well with mine, the only one whose work the teachings come through so clearly"—so here I come. I have been blessed this year. It's all love. Now let me return it in service.

Possible futures—labeling none impossible: just looking.

I awake with stomach hurting—too much thinking of past or future.

My thoughts on waking were for Greg's wife, feeling love for her, feeling her pain, her panic, as they end their marriage. I'd never even spent an entire day with the man and felt as if I were dying when we were sent apart. It must feel like the end of the world to her. I don't know how we survive these losses, we humans.

May

Recurrent anxiety, the persistent sense that I am making a mistake—yet I feel now that I need to, wish to, choose to go *into* the relationship with Gregory. A long time ago she said to me, "You stepped into a snare—just step out of it." Wasn't able to, so am choosing to enter it, choosing to *choose* it, really, for the first time. Ever since we've known each other I have been resisting, struggling with my feelings—never have I been *in* the relationship, wholeheartedly. I am now choosing to be where I find myself. *[But to be there only for a moment, apparently, for I then write:]* Now I must go *through* the relationship to get out the other side.

I've made Beloved and Gregory represent two poles of my consciousness. Now I am choosing them both.

June

Cancer.

[Years of premonitory dreams and physical symptoms discounted by doctors, and now this diagnosis—very shortly before I return to live near Beloved and the ashram.] I offer this illness as a healing for all beings. This was absolutely my first thought upon receiving the diagnosis. Second thought: "Oh good, I'm going to die, I'll never have to go to the dentist again!"

Meditating, I see: there is no difference between health and disease. *[One taste.]*

A beauteous net of love and caring is unfolding all around me and under me. Maha: "We'll get through this." *[Ah, this heart-lifting "we."]* Beloved: "Come back, start work. I'm supporting you wholeheartedly." Cancer is yet another bridge across the waters that divide.

The creative nature of mind: this bodily event in my womb whence flows the transformational blood. I have resisted deep transformation of mind and womb has been trying to do it for me, shedding and shedding and shedding. Well, beloved body, *I'll* do it now, with awe at the sacred power and its ever flowing to harmony. I'm in charge again, the I AM. Already this bodily event is such a blessing, such a teacher, such a doorway.

Healing ceremony—immense heart, pulsing, radiant—and laughter. I was a brown hawk, spreading her wings over Earth and all her children. This morning, passed through the vagina three small pieces of black carbon-like matter, crumbling into ash at my touch—the cancer passing from my body—the healing is complete—I AM HEALTHY, I AM WHOLE, I AM HOLY.

I awakened this morning stretching and smiling, thinking, "Oh, it is good to be healthy again!" And then my visit to the medical people seemed to reify it all, shaking my confidence in the healing. Yet when the root causes in the mind of dis-ease in the body are transformed, the process must still be drawn to completion—and if the discordance has actually come to the point of manifesting as bodily disease, the healing of the physical body will be the last to occur. So, though I am fully healed at the source, it may be that cancer will still be found in my physical body and I may need to go through the envisaged medical treatment—as the sacred vehicle of the healing process. So I am to see *all* that occurs from now on as manifestations not of disease but of wholeness, articulating throughout all densities and frequencies of vibration of the entity that I AM.

Surgery, macrobiotics, spiritual healing: There is no either-or here—it is all a process, each of these elements can play a healing role. *[Powerfully beginning: the resolution of duality mind.]* My purpose in this time is to bring forth the Wisdom Child from my womb of spirit-matter. I call upon clarity, courage, and compassion, that I may engage this labor gracefully and joyfully for the benefit of all.

[I move from the city to live again near my teacher. She comes to see me, bearing

three cookies on a plate. We sit at my little shrine under the eaves and speak of living and dying, and of choice. I tell her I have seen, innerly, that I could die now, ask her whether it would be better for all that I live or that I die. She says, "Better to live—give people the example of profound transformation." So I choose to do everything in my power to live.

*Thus does cancer become a spiritual rebirth for me—this time a conscious one, ever remembered: choosing to be here, for love of all, here in life, here in the world. Later I will make a painting about this portal, this choice. Around the painting, as a sacred frame, these words: "*THEN HER WOMB *was buried / in a sacred manner / beneath the beauteous mountain / and nevermore was she a stranger / to the people or the land / but now a mother to all creatures / within the arc of heaven / daily birthing* LIGHT */ to warm and feed each one."*

Love is my healing practice. As a mother loves her unruly, panicky, overwhelmed child, I whelm with love the disorganized, overwhelmed cell that has lost its original instructions.]

I burn as a spirit fire. I am as if on vigil. There is a doorway opening before me, I am walking through it one step at a time. To establish all beings in enlightened mind, I now liberate myself from suffering.

July

Seven days to surgery date.

I can hardly believe this: I am more stressed over whether I'll do the "right" thing or the "wrong" thing in choosing surgery vs. not-surgery than I am over receiving a cancer diagnosis! I fear failure and being "wrong" more than I fear death! This is *funny! [That resolution of duality is entrained now throws its manifestations into sharp—and sometimes comical—relief. What a relief!]*

This thought of failure has been with me all my life—from birth, even: the thought that if I were perfect I wouldn't even *be* here, wouldn't have had to be born again! And yet I discovered on the last turn of this illness-healing spiral that I have *chosen* to be here. It is not failure that I am in this body. It is about wholeness—not this or that, but the *whole*. The hand of the surgeon and the leaf of kale are both the touch of God—all is God, there is nothing that is not God—even the metal scalpel going into my body is God, God's beautiful minerals shaped into an instrument to heal. All is an articulation of the perfect healing that has already occurred. That belief is the golden thread weaving together spirit, mind, and body and all that touches them: my delightful doctor's instruments wielded carefully, respectfully, compassionately *["The body is my temple," he tells me, and operates on me wearing pink Argyll socks and Birkenstocks]*, the pure rice steaming in the pressure cooker, the sacred practice of chant and dance and prayer and contemplation, the healing love of friends and family, the blessed flow of generosity and eros with Gregory, the radiance of this precious countryside—there is nothing that is not God here, not the x-rays, not the scalpels, not the dye in the veins, not the bee, not the sanitary pad, not the bills—it is all part of the healing, all a manifestation of the Whole—and I AM THAT. No personal vs. impersonal love—it is all One, and I AM THAT.

Surgery. The body-mind's response is occasionally tears and mourning, but basically "YAY! Let's get on with it!"

[The Big Give-Away. Signing my will on the way to the hospital. Mandala offerings while being wheeled into the operating room: "The bodies, enjoyments, possessions, and glories of the succession of all my lifetimes I offer to the Three Jewels."[132] My doctor telling me, "There is no bigger surgery a person can have than this, this is the big one." And now an empty pelvis, the fertile void! Almost dying on the operating table, waking up choking on respirator, furious, get this thing out of me, I can breathe! Rebirth. Sangha members practicing for me in my room, outside my door, in the hallways. The sound of the pump—whump, whump, sshsshssh—drawing the flux from my body, all that blood and pus filling and emptying and filling again—just like the river, just like the heart. Horrors, hilarity, and holiness.

Then months of slow, gradual, up-and-down healing. So grateful. So weak. Wanting to walk outside, falling down by the side of the road, crawling the few yards to the front door. Friends helping, my clothes falling off me, Beloved by my bedside, her husband bringing me a poem he wrote for me, lifting me in and out of his truck so I can attend a ceremony. Lama coming to see me. Greg moving in with me; the children coming to visit, to play, to pray, to stay. Sledding, laughing, cooking, cuddling. Months of home life, domestic, intimate, daily.

Gradually increasing strength and health. With Gregory, gradual distancing, emotional confusion, and numbing, both of us. Greg needy, depressed, I self-absorbed, feeling suffocated—loving him and waiting for the relationship to be done. As

---

132. Dudjom Rinpoche, "The Accumulation of Merit: Mandala Offering," *The Preliminary Practice of the New Treasure of Dudjom*, 17.

when we were not together, again now: unable to end it. Even Beloved now saying, "Stay, do not hurt the children, they have never met anyone like you."

Increasing pressure and unhappiness working with Beloved, she mirroring to me my hardness, my self-involvement. Caught in relationship and work demands, unable to recover my energy at the end of the day, the end of the week, always starting again on empty. Desire to take care of my health, feeling I had to fight for that against Beloved's demands on my time, attention, energy. She challenges me: "I've had surgery, Ruth has had surgery, why are you so tired?"

I never write in my journal during all the complex, joyous, confusing, challenging year following the surgery. I am living my life.

And then comes the long cycle of Hard Times with The Teacher, my mental demons projected onto the clear mirror she holds unwaveringly before me.]

•

YEAR TEN

The Third Poison
"If it can be destroyed it's not really you"
Rebellion · Creation Elation

August

Projecting onto the teacher the scenario of rejecting mother, infantile despair, the unworthy self. With the surgery, spiritual rebirth—and now this old story again. Here is the opportunity to heal this charge against the self, definitively.

[What I have seen, in my experience and with others: Our personality issues and dynamics—our karmic patternings—present themselves at each turn on the spiral of transformation, to be resolved at the next higher level. The scenarios may look the same, but for an authentic practitioner with authentic aspiration, authentic practice, and an authentic teacher, the process is one of authentic transmutation. It is usually gradual—even when, in a given lifetime, it looks instantaneous—because it must be specific, precise, in the present. This is in the relative dimension. In the absolute, nothing is happening. It is ever the magnificent, inconceivable, effulgent majesty entire, displaying freshly again and again, evanescent in the play of appearances.]

September

The healing of this ancient, profound experience of a core flaw in my nature, the "hole in my heart"— this morning I see it's not just to heal it, it's to leap right through! And I now begin to experience it as a "whole" in my heart—through which I see the luminous, empty, vast, clear sky, spacious and shining.

Then tonight Gregory and I separate. "It has evaporated," he says. I have been choosing this for months, yet it had to be that he chose it for himself. "Letting go of Gregory" has been on the agenda for me ever since the beginning, but I have clung, with his help. This time, because he has already let go, I will be able to. I am shocked at the sudden chill; at the fire of his love I have warmed myself for years. At the same time, I am happy and energized. I sense my lifework waiting expectantly. *[Still, I grieve, especially for the relationship we never really had, the fruit of desire plucked past its season, sweet only for a moment. And now I taste the bitter fruit of anger, the other face of passion, the other heat. Whether desire or anger: hot self. I work my way through the emotions, calling on compassion and gratitude to be my guides; gradually the waves calm, and I am able to write to him, "I can not begin to count your many kindnesses to me, your generosity and courtesy, your gentleness of speech and action. You treated me like someone precious. In your hands and eyes I was beautiful and cherished. I am thankful." We never cease to love one another, in gentle friendship, loyalty, and respect, through his coming remarriage and relationships, and through and beyond his death some ten years later.]*

❖ Greg is leaving. He has completely emptied the barn and painted it a bright white, floors, walls, ceiling, with a bright green mat on the floor. Thank you for freeing me so decisively. ❖ He is in my dreams, a kind, helpful presence, solid, strong, generous, caring—just enduringly there.

•

With Beloved, I am feeling battered. What is difficult is to reconcile my feelings toward the human being who acts harshly toward me sometimes with my feelings and respect for the enlightened being whose actions are at all times meant for my benefit. "Good mother/ bad mother." That's how folks go crazy. I can twist and turn in these tight little circles forever and not attain clarity. Guess I'd better just leap right through the center.

[This time finds me in a bewildering and mostly silent inner struggle with my teacher. She is bright and sharp as a cautery, cutting away at my ignorance. It is what I have asked for, and I am grateful; it is confusing and painful, and I am resentful.

I seek respite, a few days on an island sanctuary, where I go at lengthy intervals to reflect and repair.] Debris on the beach reminds me that there is no place on this planet immune to the effects of human rapaciousness and degradation. A dead seal gives the message: "Wake up, wake up, you are killing your children, your aunties, your mother." I could barely tolerate the clamor of sun and sea, longed for the woods. Yesterday's deer leaping across my path, a sweet reminder of silence; I felt in my body the drumming of hooves, saw only a dun blur off to my right— then definition: the deer!

I am not the young woman I was when I last came to Cliff Coast Island, leaping and dancing over the trails and rocks. I am stiff, sore, labored. Yet this time last year I was just beginning to walk again—so this is youth and health, after all.

Oh, it makes me so *angry* to think about the derisive tones and words my teacher sometimes uses with me. She told me, "Don't react, just listen." "You have all the power," I said. *[Oh, my dear, student in power struggle with teacher is complete absurdity—there is no winning that struggle, there is only losing your heart's desire: the very annihilation of self that frees you from suffering.* Desire *the true teacher's power over you,* long *for it,* pant *for it, do anything and everything to secure her victory! That is your best and only hope—her victory over you is your victory over illusion.]*

The only changes that matter are the ones I make in the quality of my mind. WAKE UP, PAY ATTENTION, THINK CAREFULLY, MASTER ATTRACTION AND REPULSION. And now, this season, the flowering of the Third Poison: ignorance, confusion, bewilderment. When I've exhausted all three, will I be still?

> Out on the cliff edge, vast sea, empty sky:
> > Why did you ask me to come back, Beloved,
> > if only to destroy me?
> And on the wind comes the reply:
> > If it can be destroyed, it's not really you.

October

Yesterday I silently poured out my heart at the shrine, expressing to Beloved the confusion and frustration that have been running obsessively in my thoughts and feelings about her, ending with "and I do not know how to resolve this." As I closed the shrine and prepared to leave I received this, very matter-of-fact, as if conveyed by her directly: "There is the level of personality interaction and that of relationship as spiritual teacher and student. I can choose where to focus. If I focus on the personality level I will continue to be frustrated, angry, and deprived—because whatever choice or change she makes will be because she wills it, not because I do. If I focus on the spiritual relationship then what I see is: 'I have simply been showing you your own mind.'"

It came as a mild shock—"showing me my own mind"—the thought that she has been treating me so harshly because I have that also in me and have been treating others that way. Last autumn she said, "I am just watching you, Barbara," as in "You are being tested." I had asserted that through the cancer experience there had been a decisive shift, told her, "I gave everything away and I'm not trying to get it back"—and proceeded to indulge in a frenzy of selfishness and willfulness. No wonder she's been being hard; so have I.

November

The end of my job at Beloved's office! Adventure! *[I leave the office, not the relationship.]*

Painting. I am focused, one-pointed, fully present, happy, joyous. CREATION ELATION! *[Thus I begin to paint—for five energetic, happy, confident, generative, generous, collaborative years. An artist from childhood, untrained and untamed, I now give myself free rein, and it is a glorious time. Over an extended period I am aware of an ongoing inner work that I think of as "tying off in beauty" threads from earlier times, perhaps earlier lives, and this is one of them. When it is done it is done, and I move on.]*

December

More and more clearly all the time I see what Beloved means when she tells me I put myself and my own feelings, needs, and desires first, and how I must learn to put others first.

❖ Message comes, innerly: "You are one of those who will have a second true teacher in this lifetime." I am upset then see it's really fine, there is only One Teacher. ❖

A dear elder asks what my paintings are like; I describe them as bold, vigorous, energetic. "That's you," she says, and I realize yes, they are showing me myself. *[I am walking in a house of mirrors—my teacher, my paintings, my mind.]*

•

YEAR ELEVEN

Putting the past in its place · Stones rolling away ·
A double dorje spinning in the sky
"A True Sacred Site Can Never Be Destroyed"

January

❖ I tell someone that working for Beloved was a powerful working off of karma, saying it's just as well she never told me at the outset that it would be so—that might have increased my resistance *[surely huge enough as it was]*. I hung in through the most challenging part, thinking I was doing it for the sake of the work and Beloved, not at the time realizing it was also for me. As I describe this Beloved sparkles and beams, says it was good I managed to get through that phase, "until the indissoluble merging" took place—and it is clear from her manner of speaking that the indissoluble merging has indeed taken place. ❖

I am deeply engaged in painting, and at an interesting point: The first fury of creative juices has boiled up, frothed, and spilled over, and now the discipline begins—like a musician practicing scales, so when the beauteous understanding arises in the heart the fingers are ready to express it. Now is the moment when I can choose to move beyond naive enthusiasm, into glibness or into discipline, control, depth, mastery. *[The same moment occurs again and again in the inner work, as some of the journal entries in this year show: certainty penetrating the recurring displays of ignorance and confusion.]*

❖ I am bowing, taking refuge. I experience the prayerful bowing as soft, flowing, buttery, like the surfaces of my richest paintings. I am one with it—no obstacle, no hindrance—bowing is. ❖

February

Putting the past in its place. The power of naming the childhood event: molested, wounded—without attachment to story line, drama, emotions. I have related to my "personality stuff" as characterological rather than etiological and thus have continued in self-blame. *[Seeing it as "I am" rather than "I became" means seeing it as static and solid rather than processual, dependent upon causes and conditions and thus void in its nature.]* So now, without making myself a victim or anyone else a persecutor, I acknowledge: When I was a young child, too small to protect myself, some things hurt me badly, and in recent years, in relationships with spiritual friends, some things have hurt me badly—and I am now in the process of healing those wounds.

Acknowledging the solidity of fact—*and* it is past. I seem to have needed *not* to acknowledge that others have hurt me or behaved badly toward me. Simply letting it be what it was is allowing it to recede more into the past. *[I am helped at this point by attending to the apparent "solidity of fact," acknowledging the effects and consequences of events without attributing blame or causality. This is a skillful way to work with karmic fruition at this stage—but facticity is not solidity, and later it will become crucial to recognize karmic cause and effect as not solid at all, simply as appearances arising and dissolving.]*

❖ I walk through wooded fields, see a path up a canyon, an open field. I start to go there, am assailed by panic, feel clutching at my throat, spirit beings threatening to grab me, attack me, rising around me like angry hornets. I want to flee before I am caught and can never escape, but as I turn to run I pause, remembering who I am, remembering our practice—then I begin reciting Vajra Guru Mantra, OM AH HUNG VAJRA GURU PADMA SIDDHI HUNG, over and over and over, praying that these beings may have everything they need, be peaceful and at rest. When all is well I am free to leave. I keep the mantra going even as I slowly awaken. ❖

March

❖ Beloved and I—gold threads link us—she reaches out to touch me, our hands are interlaced, like friends—she is saying, "When you are dark and heavy I can't make contact, energy not free to flow—when open and light it is easy, as is always the case, and *with someone like you,* especially so." At this she throws her head back, laughing—at the irony of light appearing dark. ❖

There are more paintings in my head than I am finding time to paint, more ideas in my fingers than I have hands to paint with! The tap is open—and just look at the flow!

•

Today I *experienced* how anger comes back to one—directly. Whatever mirrors it is irrelevant. It comes back. It is cause and effect.

"Hate and anger are the same energy, and you and I still have some things to work out in this regard," Beloved said to me. Later I just fell apart, weeping, shaking. [*Reading this today, I am wishing I had simply been less afraid, less defended, able simply to say to her, "Teach me what you can, and tell me how to learn,"' as Sadik Hamzani did.*]

Stones are rolling away from my heart.

[*No journal entries for three months. During this time I am painting, painting, painting, turbulent emotional experience, joy in life, and spiritual insight pouring out in paintings, not in words. "Human states," I hear, when I ask innerly what I am exploring and showing in my art.*]

July

A cancer scare—the mole on my chest enlarging, sending out spokes— fear arises, anxiety icy, like waves—I apply the antidote of self-lessness, emptiness, and what I see is this: Illness and death are simply opportunities for practice, generosity, enlightenment—death will be not even an interruption—"I" will still be dedicated to realizing enlightenment for myself and all beings. Oh, *this* body, *this* personality, *this* life—just the forms of the present moment; in other flashes of light the crystal of "my" continuum will reflect other moments, other forms—all dedicated to establishing all consciousness in true enlightened state. It is a glorious realization. [133]

---

133. This is how I think of the apparent succession of lifetimes we live— nothing solid, not the bodies, not the experiences, and certainly not the dimension of time in which they shimmer for a moment, like clear crystal in the light.

And last night in the dream: ❖ Beloved performed a wonderful healing ceremony for me, waving lashes and whips over and around me in the air, chasing away all malignant or demonic spirits. I heard her crying out, "Barbara *has* to stay, she *has* to receive these teachings." ❖

Little Big Heart, small wild bird, fragile and fierce, living here with me and my cats—tonight he died in my cupped hands. As his spirit left his little body I saw him fly straight into the heart of Buddha Amitabha. *[And before dawn the next morning I padded barefoot down the stairs to my icy studio and, on the painting in progress, painted the form of Little Big Heart on the right shoulder of the Buddha.]*

Said my name aloud in the community circle. DORJE, VAJRA. Initiatory name, received from Vajrasattva. Recounted the story of the cliffs from which I cried out to Beloved, "Why did you bring me back if only to destroy me?"—and returning on the wind, the reply: "If it could be destroyed, it wasn't you." In the circle Beloved leaned forward, looking into my face, nodding gravely, with utter love and truth shining in her face. Facticity. Sacred suchness.

In tonight's ceremony, a double dorje spinning in the sky—

August

The only thing between me and certainty is—doubt! *[I remember sharing this sudden, startling insight in a community gathering, just undone with hilarity at the suchness. I couldn't understand why my sangha companions weren't laughing, too, with relief and joy—at the blessed* certainty*! And now I remember that for a long time I, too, didn't laugh at this fact that leaves no room for evasion. Our minds are our responsibility, no one else's. And there is nothing solid to be found. Certainly not in doubt!]*

October

Last night was no dream: I'm lying in bed, sound asleep—a tall, thin male lover stretches himself along me, embracing me warmly, and slowly, carefully, deliciously enters me. I am concerned about pain to my vagina but there is really no pain; it feels wonderful to be full again with a warm, erect, loving man. I am also concerned about how this can be happening, who is this man, how did he get into the house—but fleetingly, for his presence, touch, and energy are for me, not against me. I wonder if it's real, am I dreaming, and know it *is* "real," I am "dreaming."

December

I'm looking again at *fear:* to transform fear—of all kinds, at all levels, for all beings. Practicing, I experience many little spirits—demonic, wrathful, devilish, mischievous—later, wraithlike, wispy, sad—then, last of all, a starving baby—all sliding down through an interdimensional vortex, through my crown—dancing within my heart—then like leaping flames they become one with the fire, a circle of fire in the heart.

❖ I send my painting, "Sacred Site," to a photo lab for the exhibition catalog. When I go to pick it up I find it has been cut into slices, bent open, as if for technical reasons—yet it is nonsensical, absurd. They have *destroyed* my painting. I howl like a mother whose child has been murdered, in unassailable anguish, as if my heart itself has been ripped open. I go to demand an explanation, insist on talking with the technician who actually did this. I stand before him with my ruined painting and ask, "WHY?" He says nothing, simply smiles—and I immediately see: he is evil incarnate. I am totally chilled—and instantaneously I understand: There is no reason for his destructive act; it is simply his nature and his purpose to destroy beauty and holiness. So I say, "Ah"—and I stand before him, confront him with my painting, and I am completely restored. I say to him, over and over, "A true sacred site can never be destroyed"—and he simply evaporates in a puff of smoke. I then take my painting and hang it in the exhibition just as it is, in its ruined state, with all its inherent beauty and dignity—and with its new title: "A True Sacred Site Can Never Be Destroyed." ❖

•

YEAR TWELVE

False foundation falling away · "Drowning in yin"
Sister Bodhisattva · Nothing to hitch the confusion to
I have waited all my life to hear these words

January

❖ "Planetude"—"attitude of plenitude" for Planet Earth. ❖

I am appalled at the extent of the internal damage, the panic and flight and grasping, the embeddedness in old pain and neediness. Shame arises in waves. This morning I recall that each contraction is preceded by and followed by an expansion. What was the last one? Ah yes, it was, of course, about *relationship*—how everything is related, how all my confusion arose within relationships. The disturbances are to the *sense of relatedness*. To test the liberation that understanding gave me, I must pull through all the layers the sure knowledge of oneness, relatedness.

Astrological consultation, sitting in my painting studio, looking out on the mountain. The astrologer: "Your art—crystalline energy, sparkling, refracted light, like high, clear mountain air. You're finally being able to radiate this as you've always wanted. Looks as if this is the path you walk toward the end."

The foundation has fallen away from beneath the edifice of separation, control, fear—hallelujah—

March

In teaching last weekend I directly experienced myself as deity. My co-teachers also perceived it; one said that she became quite confused, trying to figure out how I was managing to sit on my cushion with one leg in the dancing posture!

June

Important conversation with Beloved. *[The incisive, profound oral instructions that follow will continue to unfold in my understanding throughout the years to come. Here is the Physician, offering medicine to her patient.]*

I expressed remorse at my part in a sangha mate's rage toward me. I didn't have the skill to help him transform his unacknowledged rage, Beloved said, because I still have so much of it myself. That surprised me *[my surprise in that moment strikes me as astonishing in this one]*. She says it is in the body, still, as habitual patterns of reaction. The medicine: cultivate silence and restraint. *[Same instruction all our mothers have taught: 1-2-3-4-5-6-7-8-9-10.]* I think it's okay to be tinder for fires of transformation in others, the lance of their rage's releasing—but in clarity, with compassion and skillful means, not out of my own confusion. *[Here is Beloved's teaching on the question of how past suffering affects us in the present, as residue or as habitual patterns. She's saying it's both. Of course: she was always pointing through apparent duality to the nondual.]*

"The disturbances are to the sense of relatedness." Beloved's Rx: to reparent oneself, spiritual practice the ongoing way to do that. Peel away the lies of this and this happened, so-and-so did this—"they increase enmeshment in materiality, so there's no ethics."

[Relative truth and ultimate truth both are; we are of the ultimate and we live in the relative—except when at rest in our true nature. Driven by self-grasping, imputing reality to illusion and thus ruled by karma, we are indeed enmeshed in materiality. Our condition is aggravated not by acknowledging events and experiences in their simple facticity but by reifying them—elaborating upon and around them, in mind and action, stories of cause and consequence rooted in delusions of duality, self, and other. "Facticity is not solidity."

Working with these patterns over many years, with myself and others, one thing I see—so obvious, so easily missed, and so evident in these journals—is the direct connection between our ordinary human behavior and our confusion and suffering. I remember saying to Beloved, in one of the many conversations in which she was pointing out a fault, "Please tell me how to get enlightened, but please don't tell me how to live my life!" So comical! For this is precisely the point. How we live our lives, what we actually do *with body, speech, and mind, is the stuff of virtue and nonvirtue. This is the ethics of which Beloved spoke. This is what sows the seeds of karma—either laying down layer upon layer of confusion, illusion, delusion or cutting the root of suffering, opening our minds to the true nature of ourselves and all phenomena, the true nature of reality.]*

She talks to me about the dangers of lethargy: "drowning in yin, the cold water that doesn't move, body lacking inner fire." She says, "The medicine is faith—yet the obstacle is the energy that belittles faith, blames the teacher for demanding too much, moving too fast. People reach a certain level and then, 'Oh, it's too hard.' This is a dangerous point of complacency in the inner development, similar to illnesses of self-esteem. Feeling unable to address directly the light within, one blames others, blames the teacher." *[She was speaking directly to my condition, as the Quakers say. This vitally important teaching is still unpacking itself in my mind, penetrating in tiny increments, ever more subtle and precise.]*

Oh, what a mirror this is, what a teacher! So it's up to me. Do I choose to go all the way in this lifetime, or not? It's fine either way—but I must see that I am *choosing*. It is not at all about incapacity. It is about whether I am willing to exert the necessary effort. Starting with *this* moment.

Please help me abandon false refuge in the illusion of materiality. Emptiness *is* the joyful nature of my mind—oh praise, oh graceful praise—I vow to liberate myself and all beings, we are free, we are free.

July

A lot of shaking loose for me; I wept most of the weekend. *[All this weeping, all these years! I dedicate it now, this very moment, for all who weep and all who cannot weep—our tears, our tears, springing forth like mountain streams in spring, fresh, solacing, forgiving, melting our hardness, confusion, and loneliness, canyoning dense misery into broad, sweet plains, deep, fecund soil for happiness and love.]*

This is it—will I or won't I? I recommit to *do it in this lifetime*—and this image comes, making me laugh: I am on my belly, literally *crawling* to the threshold of the Enlightenment Door that Beloved told me is "wide open for me in this lifetime." I throw myself across the threshold, hanging on to it by my fingernails—but *I make it, I get across, I do it!*

About to begin two large canvases. One is the last time I saw my father, being carried out on a stretcher; the other is a big four-panel painting—of this moment's opportunity to kindle the fire, to jump through the open door. I am thankful, thankful, thankful. *[Completed the first. And the second? Almost done, threw it into the dump on my way out of town, heading west, long time later. Time to do it, not paint it.]*

❖ I'm sitting with a large, flat bowl between my legs, filled with warm water. With another small, beautiful bowl I scoop up the water and pour it back in. In both dream and physical body there comes a lovely orgasm with the moving waters. ❖

August

❖ I'm with a group; we've learned that we are to die—those with power over us will administer our death through one of our own, who will give us poison. All seem to passively accept this fate. A young, plump, blond woman walks among us, hands cupped, outstretched, holding soft blue fabric sculptures of sea creatures. I realize she's the one. I say to her that she doesn't have to kill us, all she has to do is simply not administer the poison. She looks at me as if I'm crazy, says they'll kill her if she doesn't kill us. I ask her, "Wouldn't you rather be killed than kill us?" She says no. I am stupefied. I explain to her that if she refuses to kill us they can only kill her body and that if she kills us they will have killed her soul. No success. I certainly am not going to hang out there waiting for this bizarre fate to overtake me, so I split—cut off my hair so I again look boyish and young and take off by train, lighthearted and devil-may-care. After all, what's the worst that can happen? Only that they may still kill me some other way! But at least not with my connivance—and I'll die a free woman. ❖

So what did I learn during this night at the vigil fire? That I and the fire are one, that I can ask the holy beings to help me with any and all things, that humility and humiliation ain't the same thing, that there is still a lot of NGE *["not good enough"]* to be transmuted and a lot of faith yet to be generated. I left before the sunrise, walked home in the cool dawn light.

Expansion is going big and fast. I am feeling overwhelmed and panicky, calling for help. Generate faith, courage, and commitment! *[Calling on the teaching about "drowning in yin."]*

November

[I am now in my new home, just a short way up the welcoming country road from my teacher, purchased with the intention of planting myself in our spiritual community physically, like a prayer stick. The day I move in—with my new companion, Sister,

a true bodhisattva wearing the body of a beautiful dog—a large quail flies hard and fast into the picture window, breaking her neck. Sister and I place her still warm body beneath a high pine, on the welcoming boughs.]

Big winds during the night, and strong rain—and these moments remembered from the dream: ❖ Tsawai Lama is with us. I recall the nectar of devotion, the ardor of delight and gratitude that arose in me, the haste to see him, hear him—"Oh, he's coming, oh, he's here!"—the breathless joy, attending upon the arrival of the guru. Waking either in the dream or from the dream, I call out, "Guru, please bless me that this perfection of devotion may arise in me for my teacher, Beloved." ❖

Is it possible that I am sometimes actually reacting with aversion to the light itself? To those who show me my ignorance? As if I want to stay in the dark! How can this be? Just lethargy? *[Beginning to experience consciously what Beloved told me about "drowning in yin."]*[134]

The wounded child—no story line—nothing to hitch the confusion to—

Beloved tells us a dream she's had: We are helping people reach the mountaintop, enter the field of light; beings from deep space saying our prayers are resonating through many realms. I hear her say, "We are being asked if we are ready and willing and able to take and wield the staff of initiation. This is the time." When I hear these words I stir—in my mind, this: "I have waited all my life to hear these words."

---

134. Lethargy connotes not only lassitude (tiredness) and slackness (neglectfulness, suggesting perhaps even some aversion to activity), but also forgetfulness, in its etymological relationship to *lethe*. So "*just* lethargy" is a real misunderstanding. Lethargy, as Beloved spoke of it, is clearly of major significance for the spiritual practitioner, "a dangerous point of complacency in the inner development." In the Christian tradition, spiritual lethargy is often called *acedia*: "When a person is freezing to death, he feels a pleasant numbness . . . But when heat is applied . . . pain immediately occurs. [T]he pain is indicative of rescue and cure. God sends a prophet to people who are cold in their relationship with God—spiritually freezing to death . . . The prophet turns the heat on, and they become angry with him when he is actually working to make them better. He is often accused of causing their pain." (Cutts, "Acedia and the Good Friend.")

December

These days it's the content of my mind, not the process, that catches my attention.

[Significant shift. I had always been more interested in process than in content, in all aspects of my life and work. In social science and clinical theory, I elected to work with qualitative, inductive modes of inquiry and analysis, and while there were excellent scientific and creative reasons for these choices there was also a subtle, unacknowledged element of subterfuge. Focusing on process, I thought I couldn't be evaluated on content. Now, with Beloved, no more outs. She is nailing me on content, holding me responsible. The journal notes show that I am resisting; they also show that I am responding.]

I've been going through some kind of hell—seeing unworthy me—at the same time, seeing inherent divinity, in fleeting glimpses—at other moments, doubting light's the truth. At one point, thinking, "I'm in disarray," saw my confusion and corruption falling off me like clothes, and from the heap of defilement on the floor arises Yeshe Tsogyal, pink, plump, smiling.

A little whirlwind came and lifted away the anguish—I called out, "Guru, guru, guru"—and it was *she* who came, Beloved. *[I've been surprised like this before, calling for help in a dream and finding it's Beloved who appears. Am I expecting someone else?]*

The world prepares for war. I observe within myself grief as the youngsters are sent off, and I see the warlike impulses in my own mind.

So much ambivalating—be a peace pilgrim, paint up a storm; retreat, dailiness; spirit, world. Ideas, ideas: mind of dualism. As long as this mind is, suffering is. I have a sense of being on vigil, that there is now the opportunity again to meet the clear light—a sense of waiting actively, attentively, alertly, for information, insight, illumination: to see my next step.

•

Year Thirteen

The sound of truth · Looking for clues
Going back to go forward · A house close to the tide line
Calling my mind into the world

February

Seamless: spiritual practice and painting are not two. I have held myself away from both these last months, and pined—now, returning to the studio, I at the same time become more regular in formal practice.

[Assaying for a new leach field, I become fascinated with this:] Pebble dropping into dry well: it hits bottom or it doesn't. THUNK—the sound of truth. That is the tone I'm listening for now. In my words, my work, my motivations, my actions—everything—I'm listening for that.

March

The movement of love so strong now that to experience what gives the appearance of not-love is intolerable. Next: that the river of love be so vast and profound that the illusion of not-love moves as part of that inexorable flow. Next after that: that there arise no longer the thought of not-love.

November

[After a long gap in journal writing:] Rereading the pages preceding this entry I am astonished. My memory of last winter is of the hell realms—I'd remembered *none* of the insights, illuminations, transformations. *["Enmeshed in materiality," we glimpse and then forget or turn away from that which has so sweetly, clearly been shown to us. But it will be shown again, we will see again—because it is what we are.]*

First appointment with psychotherapist *[finally decided to get some personal, psychological help here in the relative world of material delusion]*—ready confusion rising up to meet her clarity, fear that my shameful secrets will show, and my shameful ways of trying to hide them—manipulation, slyness, seduction, brilliance. Here is potential for help. Take it, Vajra Babs!

Last night a phone conversation with a relative—compassion for him as he described his lifelong depression—then awoke this morning from ❖ a dream of him slashing my vagina with a knife, stabbing over and over. ❖ Awaking, I thought, "Oh, was it he?" And then, "Oh, that couldn't have really happened, could it? If it had, there would be scar tissue and there's no scar tissue." *[There was plenty of scar tissue, as this record shows—and yet "no story line, nothing to hitch the confusion to." At the relative level, I am amnesiac for my early childhood; at the absolute, there is no story.]*

Shall I construe these past years as spiritual failure? Yet I have had to come to this, actually to *see* the contents of my mind—and could not, as long as I was "being good, doing the right thing, being perfect." I think maybe I had to fall in order to get up and stand on my own two feet.

I feel little and wild and confused and frightened. But I am calling forth the courage to see my mind. The teacher is the mirror of my potential; to the extent that I am shrinking from 100 percent commitment to realizing my full potential, to that extent I will recoil from the mirror. Some have *left* when their negativity arose and they projected it onto the teacher. At least I'm still here, at least I'm still here—

Still limping, but with every practice I am at least, at last, honoring my vows.

Therapist says she doesn't think the two-year old had the intent to kill her mother, says mingle with little kids, see what they're like. It never occurred to me before that maybe it was just my interpretation—I always believed that I *was* trying to kill her, and held that close as dramatic charge and proof of my evil. *[My mother told me many times, always laughing, the story of how at age two I had seen her leaning out the second-story window and, running full tilt, had pushed her, hard. She caught the window ledge and just managed not to fall; when she could speak she said to me, "That was very dangerous. I could have fallen out the window." My reply, which I always took to indicate that I had acted with intent: "Mommy go squash?"]*

December

Awake at 4:30 as the big storm swept in—what a blow! One of my porch doors is blown out and the top of the Peace Tree main trunk, the leader, lies just north of the porch, like a fallen angel—like the *kouros* lying in the wild field on Naxos, that beautiful boy, broken warrior youth *[with whom I briefly lay in the golden Aegean luminosity, his marble warming, my heart warming, in the sunlit January chill.]*

Yesterday my therapist emphasized the need to *see* the environmental influences I experienced as a child—likening the visible damage *[my personality confusion, disorder, flaws]* to a room devastated but by means unknown. The damage is there, so something has caused it. I'm looking into my behavior patterns, thought patterns, emotional patterns, for clues as to what *happened* to me in this lifetime.

I heard myself describing my mother's and my teacher's mockery as "mortal wounds." I felt annihilated, literally reduced to nothing. But here I am, still breathing, still laughing, still working . . . *[The words of my mother and my teacher didn't cause my suffering, they were the circumstances that allowed my suffering to be experienced—and its seeds, thereby, to be purified. So far from adverse is the apparently adverse condition! For the daughter, a long-painful wound has healed in the mother's transfiguration. For the disciple, eventually there will be understanding—and always gratitude, even when being "reduced to nothing." It means reduced to essence. My essential aspiration.]* [135]

---

135. SELF, TRAUMA, AND BEING: REFLECTIONS ON PSYCHOLOGY AND ONTOLOGY. (a) A child's complex reaction to harsh treatment or abuse by a parent figure or close adult frequently includes both a sense of panic and a sense of shame. It is almost impossible for a young child to discern wrong action by the adult as having to do with the adult; the child will normally interpret it as "something wrong with me." (b) One who has experienced early hurt of this kind can still react with a hot flash of panic or shame to unkindness, harshness, or abuse in adulthood, the "something wrong with me" thoughtform restimulated in the current situation. Restimulated and carried forward. The nature of trauma is encapsulation and habituation, and thus maintenance. (c) Psychologically, the persisting, intrusive "something wrong with me" ideation is disturbance deeper than low self-esteem; it is disturbance to selfhood, to the actual sense of self. This is the ego that *must* be intact: coherent and flexible enough for maturation, integrity, creativity, and wholesome relationship (and not to be confused with the deluded self-grasping that for spiritual realization must be liberated.) (d) If selfhood is not intact, even what is given for one's benefit can be taken as confirmation of one's *essential* shamefulness or perceived as an *existential* threat. (e) Essence and existence are the language not of psychology but of ontology. Ontologically speaking, the panic or shame we are considering may be pointing beyond what is felt as "wrong" to what is inwardly known to be profoundly,

It's all such a tangle, and I hate that I have to go back when I want to go forward—but I have seen that I *can't* go forward. Going back is the only way I can imagine finding out what's back there. So GOING BACK is the next step. I fear it—but more, I fear *not* doing it.

And yet . . . intimations of another way: simply saying, STOP! Not in denial, but in acknowledgment that the past is past and passed and gone and I can go forward—

NO!

I want to know.

And I have *not* been able to go forward—it's like trying to swim with lead weights on—

I'll do both at once—I'll keep moving with the practice *and* I'll go back.

The nation is indulging in a media orgy of sentiment and recrimination about Pearl Harbor. Talk about clinging to old grievances!

I awake in unease, think "Oh, am I making it all up about childhood abuse?" And I am very uneasy writing about all this—words limit, fix, distort, and then what is recalled is the way the experience or insight has been expressed in words, rather than the essence of itself, its

---

ultimately, absolutely right: that very essence, the essence of existence. *Being.* (f) When we somehow participate in violation of *being*—whether in self, another, or the fabric of life itself, and whether our participation is willing, ignorant, or coerced—it must and will register in consciousness. We are in essence one with truth—authentic *being* and *interbeing*—so at the core we are always resonant to it, and can thus be profoundly wounded by even an involuntary experience of negating it. This is one of the reasons that warriors can suffer such acute, persisting, and sometimes catastrophic mental, emotional, psychological, and spiritual trauma from their participation in war. Most humans do not return unhurt from causing hurt. (See, for example, Robert Jay Lifton, *Home From the War: Vietnam Veterans—Neither Victims nor Executioners* [New York: Simon & Schuster, 1973]). (g) *Being* is intrinsic and intrinsically good, and intrinsically we know this. Thus *we* are intrinsically good, and intrinsically we know this. (h) Though this goodness may be violated, the violation occurs only at the relative level. In the absolute, no harm can come to *being*. Our sense of self can be hurt, but no harm can come to the intrinsic sacred template that is our true nature. (i) Love, compassion, and prayers for those with violated or damaged sense of self and its attendant existential panic, despair, or shame always have benefit, because love and compassion are all-permeating. And since true nature is ever present, access is *always* possible. Learning how to recognize even a fleeting glimpse will purify and heal.

suchness. Don't know if it's really being helpful or not, to be writing at this time.

My life's feeling like a house of cards constructed on a windswept beach, close to the tide line. When I look closely at it, its carefully constructed form appears to dissolve. *[Yes, just so.]* Oh well, the better to perceive the innate nature, emptiness—but first I've got to penetrate the walls of defenses I've erected, inside and out. It ain't pretty to look at, but maybe there's greater freedom just around the curve.

❖ I'm flying, swooping and soaring, up through an opening into a room where men are demonstrating what seem to be yogic techniques. An elderly man drums on his chest and his chest quickly drums and hums on its own. There are other people there, ordinary people who've arrived in the ordinary way, apparently by climbing steps. ❖ *[Like the dream, years before, about the elevator, with its ordinary and extraordinary levers that give access to ordinary and extraordinary experience and perception, and the dream about a young woman trapped in a house that I can leave and enter at will. I think these dreams are about the non-dual, the Two Truths, ultimate and relative, mutually interpenetrating.]*

Two parallel streams of truth—do they ever intersect? *[Never apart.]* On the plane where I live in this body-mind-personality, I want information and understanding about the *reasons* for my personality disturbances and character faults. On the other plane I am simply seeing what is: These are traits or aspects of my *mind*—I simply need to see them clearly and name them for what they are.

Therapist: "Your only flaw is not loving your flaws."

It's very bad out there—disintegration—people are really suffering—and there's tremendous insanity. *To the cushion!*

Well, I don't remember the dream, but the message was clear: ❖ I run the risk of increasing entanglement, enmeshment in material illusion, by this focus on "going back," recitation of the unhappy family, etc. Okay to be in therapy, but focus on the moment. If there's relevant historical information, it will surface. *This is important.* ❖

Why can't I live what I know? Some have visions and their lives are then guided by them, while it seems I have a vision or glimpse of truth and then fall away from it.

Oh. Just pray to do God's will. That's all. I've been tormenting myself because I haven't been able to align my will with what I think is my purpose. That's off track: I need only pray that my will be aligned with God's will, that my purpose be God's purpose—and for willingness to follow what is shown me. *[A few months later my sister will tell me, in a dream, "Just put God first. That's all you need to do—just keep putting God first."]* [136]

All my life I have been trying to fling my body, my life, and the whole world out into the realm of the Ideal, where my mind is rooted. Now I think I am calling my mind *into* the world, into my life, into my body. If enlightenment is to show itself, its radiant face will simply be my face, however I *am*.

●

---

136. Even well into my years as a practitioner of Buddhadharma I continue to refer, in my journals, to the Named God. This is not the "personal" God of my childhood and youth, Creator and Heavenly Father, but the absolute, the One, apprehended in the most personal of ways while known as reality itself, What Is, that within which we "live and move and have our being."

YEAR FOURTEEN

*My mind rooted in that sky-like nature · Shapes subtly shifting
Stir the fire of truth within · Take nothing with me*

January

A long, loving day at the studio—and on TV a close-up of a Russian missile—the screws, the metal plates and their joinery, a beautiful, carefully made disc, ornamented and polished, shining, like a work of art. I can feel the handiwork, the careful, meticulous attention to detail, the absorption, the intense concentration, the creative process of the artisans—like me in my studio, my hand loving every surface of a painting, all the convolutions and textures and colors and shapes. Same, like, common. Love is work so absorbing, total, engaged—one a research into life and its complex texture, the other an instrument of abundant death.

Things so obvious now arising in me as *understanding.*
     Why make myself so important? I am only one cell in the body of this planet—a necessary cell, for a moment—that's all.
     Why keep looking to events and experiences to explain to me my confusion? It arises from seeds within my own mind, from causes I myself have set into motion by my own thoughts, words, and actions—so, "going back," I should be going back to those *primary* causes, within myself—not as more self-blame and self-loathing, but as the clay artist seeking to make a smooth clay body, so it can be fired at high enough temperature to hold the truth.
     Let the negative karma ripen this time, so I can be free to be *free* next time.

Maybe I misunderstood, only *thought* my purpose in this lifetime was enlightenment.
     I don't think I misunderstood.

[268]

February

A very healing meditation Beloved gave us: in the womb, then coming through the birth canal out into the world. I could not, could *not*, find the trauma back there. What I found was impatience to *get out of the womb*—then, once out, great interest and curiosity, eagerness to explore—and when I was shown the sky for the first time: "Oh! That's it! That's home!"—and an intense desire, a *drive*, to go there. My mind is rooted in that sky-like nature while my body is here—and this illusion of separation, *this* is what is to heal—and *is* healing—I know it, I can feel it—

April

Truth is within me, *is* me, and my work is to continue clearing away whatever obscures it. Shapes subtly shifting position within, and the thought coming, gently, "Oh, maybe I will be able to leave here sometime," as I sense the very subtle healing edge, the growth of independence through the throes of my counterdependent struggles of these many years—and in all my life.

May

❖ Beloved is driving my car—she is all over the road, while lecturing me about "being one with your vehicle." *[Later this also happened in waking life.]* When we stop I take both my keys and the driver's seat. It may be crazy to take the direction away from my teacher, but I'm going to *drive my own vehicle.* ❖

Emotional deprivation, the condition of my childhood. Seeing this, somehow a fulcrum on which I have turned. I am grateful, I am *hopeful.* I was emotionally deprived then—but I'm *not deprived now.* All the feelings I couldn't have wholesome relationship to then are available to me now, pristine, colorful, flavorful.

In my mind I see: "I don't want to take anything with me." Resolve it *this* time. *[A marker event: recognition and affirmation of purpose.]*

September

Beloved: "Place the impression of joy, unconditional love, and awareness every place you've been in these years. Release any patterns of another time. Let all fall away so light is revealed. Just *be* completely who you *are.*" *[Like a Cézanne apple: the essence of the thing and the thing itself, not two.]*

November

Reading *Daughter of Fire*, Irina Tweedie's spiritual autobiography of her training with her Sufi master. She's very upfront about her resentments toward him, lets us see how his "action upon her," as she puts it, stirs up confusion. Why is it not okay with me simply to know such things about my relations with Beloved? Instead, I make it into something, think "I hate her." *[The turbulence in relation to my teacher is in my thoughts and emotions, only occasionally spoken of in the journal, in extremely brief, sometimes coded, notations—acknowledging negativity and gratitude, doubt and confidence, love and hate.]* Mrs. Tweedie speaks so matter-of-factly about "hating everyone," including the guru—and she quotes him as saying it is natural, just a stage: "I don't want your mind to be clear. I want confusion. If you are in the mud, you try to get out." He also told Mrs. Tweedie, "And if you don't hate the guide, you hate yourself." [137] *[This compassionate teacher—stirring, stirring his disciple's samsaric pot to purify hatred, willing to be hated himself so the one in his care does not hate herself. I pray, I aspire, I commit to love so pure.]*

And this just about says it, really, doesn't it?—"I cannot haggle about what he said or did not say, what I can accept or not. One cannot surrender to a Great Being . . . and criticize the man as imperfect. . . . Only by accepting everything . . . there is a slight hope to surrender this devil, the mind . . . Otherwise I will haggle till doomsday and get nowhere." [138]

Beloved said many months ago, about my pain, "I understand, the longing is so great." She did understand, and I did not. Can I accept her, love her, surrender to her, follow her all the way? Only by her grace, I think, not by my own will.

•

137. Tweedie, *Daughter of Fire*, 731–32.
138. Tweedie, *Daughter of Fire*, 490.

Year Fifteen

Deity Retreat · I wave in the wind like an old tarp
This boat self sail away · Enlightenment or death
There will be a girl buddha born · Cut through, cut through
Bleached, bare bones, tk tk · To be well used

January, February, March

Deity Retreat

[Identified with forms and the substances of forms, we easily miss the pure essence charging them—though it is always right here, accessible and alive, at once empty and brilliantly, dynamically displaying. By turns captivated, betrayed, and silly with fear, we who have the innate imperative to cleave to essence turn again and again to craving for form. The skillful tantric method of deity yoga, divine union, halts this helpless turning, dissolving duality itself.

The many deities in the Tibetan Buddhist pantheon mirror the enlightened qualities already ours as potentials: primordial purity, love, compassion, power, wrath, wisdom, knowledge, accomplishment. As we "practice on the deities," contemplating and identifying with their pristine nature, qualities, and powers, they become familiar and dear to us. We relax in their presence—and, relaxing, recognize their qualities in ourselves, our nature one with theirs. With divine confidence, we take ownership of our spiritual legacy.[139]

While it involves creative imagination—visualizing and meditating upon sublime form—deity yoga is not making something up and pretending it is real.

---

139. Tibetan Buddhist deities are not creator-beings, like the Judeo-Christian God, nor are they beings to propitiate and pacify. These deities pacify *us*. And though Dharma doesn't posit a creator as first cause, it definitely addresses cause. Everything that arises within mind is potentially a seed of cause, and everything that arises in phenomenal reality has arisen first in mind. Further, each moment of mind can be seen to arise from the preceding moment of mind. This means that *we* are the creators of our reality, moment to moment to moment.

No, this is cutting through *our fictions. This is not theater but yoga: union with essence. The all-freeing yoke of love.*

Deity practice reveals: reveals our true nature, reveals what obscures it. The deity's radiance can be experienced as effulgence, with contemplation ecstatic and sublime, or gentle, even tender, and that baring light can also be disorienting, shocking, even shattering—driving us inward.

My journals during this retreat record swings of mind and mood that are exaggerated by the retreat situation and practice, and by the examiner's microscopic lens, but it is probably not an exaggeration to say that our common state is something like this. Yet here also can be seen the transforming aspirations. We plead and call for the ego to dissolve: "Oh, pride, house, money, sorrow, youth, fame, beauty, fear, let them all go, let me be free." We seldom pray, "Oh, me, let me go." But when we do, it does; when we pray for the constructed self to fall, and hold purpose and love steady through the falling, it falls, it falls away.

This retreat stripped me bare. By its end, Project Barbara was in shambles. For the practitioner, this is grace itself. If "I" am here, deity cannot be seen. Strip me bare, let me go naked.

Naked truth. Deity and I, deity and you: not two.]

•

I feel so confused by . . . oh, can't remember *what*!

How grateful I am! It is as Beloved says: the ashes can accumulate, and when they are swept away there is still an ember waiting to burst into flame.

Sore, uncomfortable, heavy body, "impure clinging to substantiality" *[same meaning as Beloved's "enmeshment in materiality"]*—and in the midst of physical exercises I see: body is just light, organized by sound.

"In non-dual mind we take refuge"—Tsawai Lama showed me, and then by my own actions I lost touch with that sky mind, Dharmakaya. *[Yes, by my own actions—and it is also completely normal. I do not yet understand that realization must be fostered, taken as practice, taken as path. I think it means, "Ah, I'm there," and that I can then just live, just be. "Ah, I'm there" is true—but then comes "Ah, I'm fogging up again, can't see the 'there,' too caught in the 'here and there,' the 'this and that.'"]*

Take it all away, body, speech, and mind—tired of the burden of it, having to clothe and feed and water it according to my desires. *[This plea is directed both to deity and to teacher, whom I know as one. It sounds like surrender, but it isn't; it is ego, exhausted but still clinging, now pleading for relief and rescue.]*

And in *this* mind dwell buddhas and bodhisattvas! The seed of enlightenment! The means to liberate all beings from suffering!

Nothing to protect—I wave in the wind like an old tarp.

Something critically important: to transform *in the moment* the thought-form of spiritual failure.

"Remembered glory," or something like that, makes me this arrogant. I somehow remember that the pristine state is my true nature—so I think that just as I am I am a candidate for enlightenment and clamor to be *endowed* with it, as with a hat or cloak, something external, conferred like knighthood.

•

Thinking of asking her, Is that door still open for me in this lifetime? *[I never ask, never. Don't want to know. Yes would heighten the internal pressure under which I reel, my fear that I will not fulfill my spiritual potential, and no would end all my hopes for this lifetime. I have not yet fully comprehended that we practice not for this lifetime but for liberation.]*

I don't think I'm really cut out for this gradual path of many practices combined with a life in the world—I'm too undisciplined, too impatient, I fall into the abyss of self-doubt. If you say to me practice this, purify that, I feel like a failure, I despair. *[This is an example of what I mean by saying that "if self, in the psychological sense, is not intact, even what is given for one's benefit can be perceived as threatening." But in the spiritual sense something far deeper is involved: I am in this time approaching the true cure for all damage to the constructed self. I am approaching abandonment of the construction project itself.]*

❖ I dream that I kill myself, bloodily, visibly, here in retreat. ❖ *[It is true, of course. I am trying to kill my "self," the illusory I both attacking and grasping to the illusion as the illusion itself is shattering. It is not "like" a death, it is a death. Longed for, actively sought, and terrifying.]*

Yet *all* this is marked with the seal of emptiness.

[My inner travails and the drama I create with them may be extreme, but they are not unique to me. Reading this now, I think with love of Milarepa, my

saint, my saint, brought to the point of suicide by his own longing and despair. [140]
At the time, I felt very alone. But I was willing.]

Innerly I ask Beloved, "Am I making *any* progress?" She answers:
"You're almost there." [*Her "almost" penetrates like lightning the darkness of my
despair, and for a moment I lean back on her knowing what I cannot possibly know.*]

•

This morning, what appeared and felt like pure offerings with my
body, cutting open the top of my skull and offering her my brains to
chop up, stir, and eat. It was funny, and also very real—I truly *meant*
those offerings.

> KUNTUZANGMO!
> Bring me into the vast primordial space
> natural unfettered mind
> establish me in nowhere/everywhere
> silence
> sparkling clarity and luminosity
> vast empty open
> sky mind
> Dharmakaya Mother Buddha
> bring me home
> leaving nothing behind
>
> TEACHER, HOLY GURU!
> Take me with you into the land of
> completed vows
> Whatever I must do
> however I must do it
> only you know
> Remember your promise
> *Hook* me now
> I abandon my self
> I have no further use for it
> only to cross the sea in
> this boat self sail away

140. See Lhalungpa, *The Life of Milarepa.*

[Now I am throwing myself into the vast aspiration, abandoning myself to it, just surrendering to my longing.]

I am willing to let go of *whatever* obstructs the flow of wisdom, love, compassion, joy, enlightened mind, enlightened activity. Though I don't really think I understand what it is I must release *[yes, you do, my darling; that's why there's all this desperation]*, I am willing—

3:30 a.m. Tsawai Lama calls me to come close, puts his head and mine close—so caressing—

•

Thirty-one days to go. One minute it seems short, every moment a precious opportunity—the next, oppressive, hardly to be borne another second. *[Just like life, just like samsara.]*

All, *all* can be fuel for a fire of desperation, rebellion, and despair—or for practice. It's as if the flame is artificially inflated—too quickly it dies out again after a brief, bright flare-up. What are the fuel and method that will maintain a strong, steady fire for the entire winter, until the spring of enlightenment dawns? *[Here, right here, just a crack, a tiny opening: the freshness of insight, the good question.]*

"Enlightenment or death"—the *epitome* of grasping and repulsion! I haven't been *applying* the teachings—I've mostly been grasping at them and then recoiling, falling away. It *is* like a pitiful bird in a cage, I. Hear my cry, Precious Guru! Please give me the key!

Ah, I think *this* is the key, *this* is the basis of my pattern of recognizing and falling away: I see light / I grasp for it or push it away / I fall into ordinary perception: confusion / I get discouraged and desperate / I seek again, again I see, / again I grasp or repulse, again I fall away.

Oh! To practice without grasping, to live without grasping—that *is* the way!

> Much harm befalls those with little forbearance
> And those who want results without making any effort.
> While clasped by death they shall cry like the gods,
> "Oh no, I am overcome by misery!"

Relying upon the boat of a human (body),
Free yourself from the great river of pain!
As it is hard to find this boat again,
This is no time for sleep, you fool. [141]

Reading descriptions of the ways suitable to the "superior," "average,"
and "inferior" practitioner, it seems to me that my aspiration and potential
(what I *could* do) are superior, my motivation (what I *will* to do) average,
and my activity (what I *do* do) inferior—and in the gaps between them
I flail and thrash around in grasping, recoil, and despair, in frenzy and
apathy. But gap means *bardo.* And in the bardo the instruction is to see all
as display, arising from one's own mind's unceasing activity—intrinsically
pure, effervescence of enlightenment, natural state.

After meditation, as I walked I could feel fire moving around me.

Others are saying, "We've been in bliss!" Not I. I'm always going for
Absolute Reality.

The truth that I seek, that I see
feels hard and bony,
bleached and dry—

•

Today sadness arose: that I didn't meet the Dharma when I was young,
that I am so troubled, even deranged sometimes, so much potential
and so obscured—then the thought arose in me: "Oh, there will be a
child born someday in whom all these sacred potentialities will bear
fruit. How wonderful!" [*A flash of lightning in the dark of night.*]

I feel as if I'm confronting the wreck of my dreams:
union, enlightenment,
in this lifetime.
    I never even thought of such a thing
before I met my teacher.
She said, "Why not now?"

141. Shantideva, *A Guide to the Bodhisattva's Way of Life*, chapter seven
("Enthusiasm"), verse 88.

Since then that has been my beacon,
my only aspiration.
    And now I am passing it to the girl child
I see in the future,
The girl buddha
Who will arise from these ashes.
May I purify all for her
May I be faithful for her
May I persevere for her
May I have courage for her

Something is cracking open around me.
The girl buddha is within me in this very moment.

•

❖ Someone suggests that the bird I used to keep, Thrinley, is probably still around and might come if I called. He does come—a little brown sparrow-like bird, like Little Big Heart. I prepare a cage for Thrinley. He flies around it, becoming smaller and weaker, and sad. I understand that I am to let my Thrinley fly free. *["Thrinley" in Tibetan means enlightened activity, to benefit and liberate beings. I am to let my enlightened activity fly free!]* ❖

Practicing intensely, I fell over into a deep, deep sleep—chanting mantra the whole time—and something happened to me in my sleep, like being suddenly and sharply hit on the head. I hope she hit me *hard* on my hard, hard head.

> . . . hopelessness is the essence of crazy wisdom . . . The process is one of going further in and in without any reference point of spirituality, without any reference point of a savior, without any reference point of goodness and badness—without any reference points whatsoever! Finally we might reach the basic level of hopelessness, of transcending hope . . . we still have all the energies; we have all the fascination of discovery, of seeing this process unfolding . . . deeper and deeper and deeper. This . . . is the process of crazy wisdom, and it is what characterizes a saint in the Buddhist tradition. [142]

---

142. Trungpa, *Crazy Wisdom*, 10.

At one point today, briefly, I caught this thought moving within: I can make it—I have what it takes—I can do it.

Cut through
        cut through
                to the bleached bare bones
                        dry
                                tk tk tk

I am hope-less
        GOOD   hear those bones rattle
I am broken
        GOOD   the fire is crackling all around me

She tells me, "In your life, in your work, fulfill your vows."
        Here's how I understand it:
        Live your little life in the biggest possible way—as a BUDDHA.
        (End of Deity Retreat)

April and May: Post-Retreat

❖ In the dream, something "wrapped around a death rattle." ❖ *[The catabolism of intensive practice, cauterizing, purifying, shaking away, down to the ground, to the dry, bare bones, tk, tk—and post-retreat reveals the skeleton dancing on the charnel ground.]* [143]

I am in a bardo, a gap. I no longer know anything about my life. All feels imaginary, illusory. My house in repairs, I am living in other people's houses, almost can imagine simply moving into one of these other lives—it is as real to me as my own, maybe more so. I have no anchor, I am adrift. I was going to say I don't even have a compass, but that's not really true, is it? I have a bead on TRUE NORTH. I call to be used for supreme enlightenment.
        Somehow my present exertions in the material world *[house repairs,*

---

143. Reading this, I am reminded of Dudjom Rinpoche's marvelous aspiration prayer, "The Heart Nectar of the Saints" in *The Lamp of Liberation*, 43–67—this verse in particular: "This form of greatness, like dogshit wrapped in brocade, / If it's obtained that's all right, if it's not that's all right. / Having smelled the rot of my own head, / May I constantly practice the Supreme Teaching."

moving a lot, hauling and toting] are building a strong *spiritual* foundation for the work to come. In some way it is the exertion that is the point, not the problem, not the solution. "Cleansing the impure clinging to substantiality" seems the keynote of this moment.

> I *rejoice* in the apparent dissolution of my little life—
> Charnel grounds abound
> Bones are many
> tk   dance
>   tk   dance
>   tk   dance

Wondering if I am making it all up. *[Well, yes . . .]*

Sat in a field this afternoon, drawing, tracing the intimate calligraphy of the beaver ponds. None of my "doing" has significance today. Would that I could live like Sister *[my bodhisattva companion, in her dress of lovely dog]*, hungry, playing, watchful, resting—simply, directly.

Yesterday, the thought: "I want to live for others—now I want to live for others." What a relief. No longer preoccupied with grasping for my own enlightenment, I am free to desire and work for the enlightenment of others. I am on the alert for signs and signals. What next? What am I to do with the rest of my life? How can I give my life away? Everything that comes, I check: Is this the direction, is this the call? Somalia? Bosnia? How to be of use?

> If in this lifetime
>   PRIDE
>   is somewhat diminished in me,
>   maybe that's enough—just that.

There is nothing here to hold on to. The refrain keeps running through my head: "leftover life to live." May it be "leftover life to *give.*" *[Hearing now, faintly, the tones of true renunciation, in this moment registering emotionally as loss. This is the door I must go through, to freedom.]*

"Go on with your head held high."

"I have already died," said the shaman.

What am I to do with my life?
  Whaddya want, Babs?
  To be well used.

·

Book·Three

Waking Light

WAKING LIGHT

*I*F SPIRITUAL PATH HAS A BEGINNING, *where is that? Is it located in suffering, seeking relief? In inspiration, seeking fulfillment? Does it arise from knowing or not knowing, from certainty or doubt?*

Perhaps it is different for each one. In this lifetime, from early childhood I had been seeking, seeking. The search looked and felt different at different times in my life, but I was never not searching. What was it I sought? I always called it truth. I sought it everywhere, looking, touching, sniffing, tasting . . . and especially listening, listening for the sound of truth.

So the beginning was knowing, but inchoate.

Now I have compassion for that seeker, intense and intent, willful and willing. My seeking was sincere and good—and yet so subjective, so unfocused; blind, really. In everything I saw reflections of truth, but I did not know where or how to look directly for or at truth itself.

Seeking led me toward but could not yield me what I sought. Eventually the seeking itself hid truth from my sight.

We long for and seek what we think we are not, think we have not, think we have lost or are separate from. About myself and truth, I thought all those things, and the more I thought those thoughts, the more useless my seeking became. How could it be otherwise? Thrashing the waters obscures the deeps. Truth is the only source of truth.

The thought of separation is the original lie. Perhaps the only one. I believed my inconsolable longing meant there was something wrong with me, something missing in me. It was the opposite. It was wholeness itself, holiness itself—truth itself—calling out its own name in my heart. This it always was that drew me, that would not, could not release me. I could be met by nothing less or other than direct experience of this, direct knowledge of this—that never was, not for one instant, other than my own being—and the being, the essence, of all and everything, ringing out, "Come, come, come—wake, wake, wake—sing, sing, sing—holy, holy, holy—praise, praise, praise!"

The spiritual path: its ground is truth, its method is truth, its fruition is truth.

My longing for truth? Truth itself, forcing me, as a plant is forced in darkness, in deep winter, to awaken in spring.

•

YEAR SIXTEEN

I want to go unadorned

October

It's raining—softly.
I am more and more who I am,
I know less and less about it.

May Sarton's *At Seventy*: I'm irritated by her giving her time away to visitors and then being resentful and harried about it, yet admire her commitment to creating and maintaining place, and to a creative life lived in continuity. I'm a writer who doesn't write, a painter who doesn't paint, a practitioner who doesn't practice. I, for whom definition is so key, live an undefined life, have an undefined character: amorphous, improvised. If at the end I and my life reveal their lines, it will not be because I have consciously shaped them. The best I can do, it seems, is just show up, be here—knowing very little about it. *[Not consciously shaping this life's definition, at the point of this writing, is very propitious. Eventually, though, I must claim authorship.]*
      In my life there is a clear pattern of abandoning ship after the initial glorious launching and highly successful first voyage. I complete projects, some very long-term and demanding, but I don't show a history of completing *lives:* continuing to be a U.N. officer, a psychotherapist, a scholar, an artist. I start, I'm hot, and then I don't go all the way. Also true with formal spiritual practice—seems like. But *is* it like? This pattern is too consistent to be a pattern of failure; I don't believe I came into this life in order to fail, so it must be something else. *[Aha! Here I explicitly* disidentify *with the thought of spiritual failure!]* More and more I think I'm gathering threads, weaving and reweaving, not building anything permanent by way of a worldly identity. As soon as it begins to reify, I'm outta here. *[Spiritual purpose itself is shaping my course, lifting me out of each promising identity before it can harden around me. "As soon as it begins to reify, I'm outta here." YES!]*

The activities I'm helping Beloved with are so clearly *her* lifework.

What mine is I have no idea, but I sense it may be more about dissolving structures than about building them—structures of mind, habit, belief, illusion. So for now, at least, when I see nothing ahead of me that's "my" work, except the coming winter retreat, I'll do my part in helping my teacher, who gives me everything.

My lifework, my spiritual purpose: to help others realize theirs. *[Insight comes to me sometimes just like this: one phrase, limpid and freeing.]*

November

This is the most glorious autumn in my memory, one long, slow, pristine, warm day after another, crystalline light, deep burnished colors now turning to heathers, grays, browns, punctuated by the bright jay's wing.

And I, slowed by injury, bemused by my flawed character, wracked by deep, painful ambivalence. I remind myself: This is the process of *certainty* arising within pristine mind.

It seems to be something like this:

> I want to go unadorned
> with role or practice or title
> (or even guru?)—
>
> naked truth
> walking in the world.
>
> Is that possible?
>
> Let it be:
>
> Put it all down,
> everything
> but the practice of
> awake mind,
> loving kindness.
> Even that.
> *Just be.*

AŠILA

Bare bones
clack clack
dry

•

YEAR SEVENTEEN

Winter Retreat · Liberate all from Demon Fear
Trust-mistrust · For the first time the pure yearning
To tame those hardest to tame · Train or churn
"Oh, happy are the myriad manifestations!"
She dances, she dances, unceasing, unmoving
Well, then, think another way · Unbearable compassion
Waking up · Africa

January, February, March

Winter Retreat

[The deity retreat a year earlier saw me enter inflated and exit deflated. This is different. Outcome isn't really on my mind. I just know I have to practice—alone, for an extended period. I deeply sense that anything I and my life might now become they will become only on ground cleared by practice.]

On the eve of retreat, a little scared as I close down to the world, yet utterly sure. The shrine is so glorious I laugh out loud—it is a *celebration.*

The remembered body travails as practice begins: an agony of waking up. The peace of sitting *[Sister enjoys the reversal: I on the floor, she on the settee]*, the loving kindness of the buddhas and bodhisattvas, my gratitude *[ah, gratitude, that opens the doorway to the spiritual dimension]*. I just want to practice as well as I can, with no expectations.

Praying to soften, to melt in love for my teacher. I vow to redeem her faith in me.

"Gimmee the beat, boys, and free my soul / For I wanna get lost in your rock and roll / And drift away-ay."[144] This continually arose in my mind while I was drifting away during practice this afternoon . . .

---

144. Words and music by Mentor Williams, original recording 1972 by John Henry Kurtz.

[288]

I am sure I have never really practiced before. This is practice because I *want* to—it is what she said it should be, a "happy offering."

•

The disaffection, the resistance—no mystery, just causes and conditions: my own "mountains of nonvirtue"—and remedies at hand, in fact in my hand, now. It is I who have made myself a holey vessel from which have leaked the blessings, merit, and realizations, and it is only I whose efforts can rebuild a whole and *holy* vessel. There is no other way.

I'm thinking that all of my "spiritual failings and failures" are really the *opposite* of incapacity: they are my attempts to flee, elude, avoid possession by my spiritual destiny. There have been signs and graces too numerous to count, and too mysterious and all-encompassing in their apparent implications to bear, to bear—they must be borne by someone in surrender—and I haven't been *willing*. Even back in my twenties and earlier I was aware that I was fleeing the hounds of heaven. They're a-gonna git you, Babs, one day or another, one way or another. Turn around now, face them, offer yourself, for whatever you may be worth at this point.

Potent image of myself at brink of yawning abyss, wild beasts snarling below, Guru Rinpoche in the sky above—and no escape. Buddhas and bodhisattvas swept across the night sky, terrifyingly wrathful, terrifyingly ephemeral. I ended up finding this detail comical and laughing at it, but at first it, too, was terrifying: *all* the buddhas and bodhisattvas were wearing Beloved's face! She was everyone, everywhere, sometimes with fangs dripping, sometimes with smiles. Terrifying because I couldn't get away from her, or from the nonduality, like vertigo, though not so much vertiginous as encompassing, immense, vast, formless, black. It is *this* that they're galloping across with their terrifying vajra visages.

Easily discouraged, I must strengthen my determination to succeed for altruistic reasons, not in order to feel better about myself.

I think, "I don't want necessarily to live by Buddhist forms, like a monk." The response, innerly: "These forms and practices are to free you. Are you free yet?"

Sister and I took a walk through the woods, air fresh with dawn, arrived at the pond to find the sun about to crest the mountain—we sang her up, clouds like silk billowing up from south to north, trailing scarves of mist.

[This same morning, or it may have been another, Sister and I stroll down past the pond to the brook. I on a log bared by the sun, Sister belly down in the snow, we happily contemplate the white, sparkling landscape, water briskly flowing, ice lacing stream edges, grasses, rocks. Pristine purity within and all around. And as we meditate on the purity, suddenly, appearing from nowhere as in a dream, bobbing merrily along on the rushing stream, comes a round, pink, perfect little pig corpse, intact and bright, legs stiff in the air. Sister is up in an instant, agog, and I almost fall off my log, laughing, laughing. Pristine Purity and the Pig!]

BIRDYCHITTA! Finches, grossenbickles (grosbeak), chickadees, woodpecker (downy), blue jay and little monkbirds (junco-monkos). BIRDYSATTVAS!

•

I feel trapped in my own mind's display. Fear is everywhere, about everything—the wind, night coming on, Sister running off, Sister bringing back a rabid animal, falling asleep, staying awake, being near Beloved, being away from her, being alone, being with people—it is everywhere! I don't feel safe, but I never have. I'm going to have to transcend or transmute this basic fear sometime, might as well be now—to flee is not it at all. And if the fear is the lion I dreamt about last night, well, we're in the cage together, and my running away only leaves the lion in control of the premises, not I.

Self-cherishing *[fixated notions of self]*—or else there would be no fear, right? It is the *view* that needs to be purified.

Is this all about emptiness, that which I long for and fear? And Beloved—after all these years of pushing her away, how to capitulate, fall into her terrifying vastness?

Took a nap with Sister, sweet and peaceful, and the instant I got up I was just clenched in fear, gut wrenching. So many beings of all kinds live ruled by fear, ruined by fear, controlled and condemned by fear—the children in our cities, in Africa, the mothers, the men in war and on

U.S. streets—it is everywhere. By meeting it in myself, even if I never master it, I pray that all others may live safe from fear—from the roots of fear, from the fruits of fear. All buddhas and bodhisattvas, all who have conquered DEMON FEAR, please help me tame this mind of terror, liberate all beings from DEMON FEAR.

In the middle of the night *[not a dream, I was awake]* the lama was telling me, "Someone has a contract out on you." I responded, laughing, "Well, I hope the contract includes enlightenment!"

Do not hesitate, do not doubt, do not be afraid. See all as your own mind's various and varying display and he *[Padmasambhava]* promises we will be enlightened. Okay.

•

Guru Rinpoche told me, in actual words, to read his pith instructions aloud, and gave me book and page numbers; I did go right to the book, right to the pages. [145]

I love these slow, deep practices outside, with the sky, critters, everything so simply *being*. Me, too.

•

Maybe all this lifetime is about, in fact, is purification of pride. *[About pride Beloved told me once, "It is the last."]*

I suppose the simplest way to say it is that about ten years ago or so, or perhaps gradually, I lost faith and devotion, practice became hollow. But that is only part of the story. The other part is that awareness has continued to sparkle forth, and somehow the hook of Beloved's compassion has brought me to this retreat. And of course: *illusion* that I have ever for a moment been separate, my mind always one with the mind of the true guru.

---

145. At that time his instructions were "self-secret" for me: though I could read and be inspired by them, neither as concepts nor as practice were they really accessible to me. When they became accessible I turned to them; it is then that I wrote them out in my journal (they appear later in the book). This helped me learn how to "let the practice lead me" to what I need and how to use it.

The woods, new snow coming down—millions of Vajrasattvas drifting down on all sentient beings—

Astonishing hatred arising during practice—flash intensity. This is a part the teachers and the books don't talk about, isn't it? How if you really practice you're going to have to look at *everything*. That the only way to see the absolute, for most of us, probably, is by seeing *through* the relative. And that the relative, for many of us, includes what's inside that may be terrible stuff. Purification isn't just about the light flowing through and carrying the gunk away with it. *["There is nothing unintentional about profound purification."]*

And with the hatred, projections of Beloved severing ties with me. *[About projecting onto the teacher one's own ignorance, permit me to speak directly from my own intimate experience: Don't do it. Don't project your "stuff" onto your teacher. Don't contaminate this most precious of relationships, imperil this most critical of opportunities. Recognize and take responsibility for each and every one of your thoughts and emotions or you* will *project them onto the mirror-like screen of mind, where they will appear as friends and foes, feeding your confusion. Each moment in which we treat our mental-emotional-psychological-situational-historical ephemera as solid is a moment lost to delusion. See your mind's condition as the dream it is, arising and dissolving even as you watch. And know that the dream is your own and of your own making. If the wave is breaking on your shore, it is your wave. Be brave. Let it break over you, dive right through it, surf it, stand steady and watch it dissolve—just don't think it into an illusion of solidity or it might knock you head over heels. Thought is to mind as wave is to water.]*

Well, hello there, JUDGMENT, RAGE, RESENTMENT, RANCOR, REACTION, AND REBELLION, and how are we all this fine day?

THE IMPURE HAS ITS BASE SOLELY IN THE PURE.
THERE IS NOTHING ELSE.
ALL CONDITIONS OF BODY, SPEECH, AND MIND
ARISE FROM AND ARE OF THE ESSENCE OF THE
UNCONDITIONED.

•

I note increasing openness to the emptiness—and with that: grasping in belly, mind, skin, emotions, eyes, ears. Looking at my flesh, touching it, feeling as if almost beginning to see through it—and tears come, body sadness. Yet the thought, "Oh, what freedom!"

I think we may have a little breakthrough here. I cannot fight off the guru, get her away from me, no matter what I do. She is not other than I. And of course the thought that I've been pushing her away is incorrect—I've been pushing *myself* away, with results that are clearly evident. She never comes or goes, is always there, unchanging, just as she is. It is we who approach or withdraw, open to her light or—as I have seen—try to shield ourselves from it. Today I am wondering, do I even know *how* to open? That will be my prayer.

Experienced for the first time the pure yearning for oneness with Guru Rinpoche *[the "how to open," right here]*—like song calling to song, light to light . . .

•

This morning remembering Beloved saying, long, long time ago, "You are the most difficult person to get to the other shore that I've ever known." Then, that gave me a perverse pride. *[What conventional pride is not perverse? Only divine pride is pure, seated on the throne of the true nature.]* Recalling it this morning I am assailed by sadness—Oh, please, don't let me be the hardest—then, *suddenly*, a complete shift: YES, *let* me be the hardest—let all others be easy, let them all cross over right away! I am suddenly just *keening* with sorrow for those who are so hard to tame: some who long for enlightenment, as I do, and fight it, as I do; some who fight the ones who would help them, as I do; some who want only to be good and aren't; some unwilling to be willing. And this arose, so strongly, in my heart: When I become a bodhisattva I promise to help all beings like me, who are their own worst enemies. When I become a buddha I promise to tame those hardest to tame, I promise to rescue them and bring them to enlightenment.

The view changes so easily, from vast to minute, and how *solid* everything seems, so quickly. I rely on the practice to show me the way.

Shantideva (as if I could single out one stanza from the compendium of perfect stanzas): "What is enthusiasm? It is finding joy in what is wholesome. Its opposing factors are . . . laziness, attraction to what is bad and despising oneself out of despondency."[146] Sound familiar?

Actually, it's pretty amazing that I'm even still *on* the path, considering my lack of realization—I mean, given no fruit, why continue to water the tree? Because I see that it bears fruit in others' gardens and hope that it may, eventually, in my own? *[Well, I haven't been so much watering it as shaking it.]*

It seems that what we're dealing with here is a deeply flawed personality and character. With the kind of intellect I have, I have felt driven to find and understand the causes. That has proved impossible, essentially. Oh, there is this and that, in this lifetime, that I can point to—but no *answer*. And this pursuit tends to *solidify* things. I think this is what Beloved has been trying to tell me over the years.

Guru Rinpoche: "I do not have, I do not understand, I do not know. Repeat these unceasingly."[147]

The *instability* of the mind—one week ready to give up everything to the teacher, in total surrender; the next thinking, "I don't believe a thing she says." I am just amazed when I read all the devotional stuff—Khyentse Rinpoche on guru devotion, Jetsün Mila's beautiful songs of devotion and realization.[148] WHAT IS THAT ABOUT? HOW DO THEY GET THERE? It sure seems a long way from here, don't it now?

•

Tomorrow begins the period of strictest retreat. "Just abandon yourself to the practice," she said. Of course, I have no idea how to abandon myself to the practice. I'm not sure I have ever abandoned myself to *anything*—not even sloth, because I keep arguing with myself about it. *[What Beloved called "the Two-hearted Disease": mind that argues with itself.]*

The thing is, I can make whatever I want. If I want repetitive tor-

---

146. Shantideva, *A Guide to the Bodhisattva's Way of Life*, chapter seven ("Enthusiasm"), verse 2. I have rarely encountered in the Buddhadharma references to self-hatred (here, "despising oneself"), which is so common among Westerners, perhaps especially Americans, and was so strong an affliction for me.

147. Padmasambhava's "Advice and Admonition to the Revealers of Treasures," in Tsogyal, *The Life and Liberation of Padmasambhava*, 635.

148. Khyentse, *The Wish-fulfilling Jewel*; Chang, *The Hundred Thousand Songs*. See also Du Bois, *Devotion*.

ment, that's what I'll have. I can choose to change it in an instant. It's all about what I do with my mind. Train or churn.

•

Mandala practice makes me delirious, *drunk*—all those buddhas and bodhisattvas, all those worlds, all those offerings, all those offerers—all that big SPACE filled with this mandala of mandala offerings—transparent, luminous, sky-like—[149]

By afternoon things got back to normal—even flatter than normal, I'd say. So often my experiences of the subtle and vast are followed by ego's attempts to grasp and solidify them. Today's experiences were waves of grace, showing me—and now it is for me, through dedication and diligence, to *realize* what has been shown.

A little chickadee whammed into the southern window and sat, stunned, for a long time absolutely still on a branch of the shad tree. Quite soon a Doctor Bird came to take care of it—a larger chickadee, who seemed to communicate with the injured bird and flew from branch to branch, always very near and always facing the hurt one. After awhile the injured bird seemed more still, smaller, as if dying. Then a second Doctor Bird arrived, flew right at the injured chickadee, seemed actually to peck him. Then the two caregivers seemed to have a consultation, after which they both flew directly at the hurt one—who up and flew off the branch!—alighting just a few branches over, and soon joined by the caregivers. It seemed he was going to be okay. The two caregivers were clearly professionals; this was their *job*.

Sister kills and eats a critter. I am angry at her. Wanting, as with Marianne, to repulse the dear friend who kills, I see how little developed is my compassion, how tenuous, how fragile, how very conditional. *[Though it seems simple and obvious, this experience gives me practicable insight into the actual character of relative compassion, fueling the intention to attain ultimate compassion, free of these sad limitations.]*

Well, all this is okay—we have the medicine to deal with it. I say let it come, the more the better:

---

149. Mandala practice: offering the universe and its contents to all buddhas and bodhisattvas, symbolized by ritually strewing precious objects, such as rice and jewels, on an offering plate. It is an opulent, vast practice that can generate immense merit for the practitioner.

Oh, happy are the myriad manifestations!
The more ups-and-downs, the more joy I feel.
Happy is the body with no sinful karma,
Happy indeed are the countless confusions!
The greater the fear, the greater the happiness I feel.
Oh, happy is the death of sensations and passions![150]

•

*[Bodhi days in Retreat Land—can't be created or contrived, can't make it happen
or not happen. The grace of the guru. Ah la la!]*

Dancing: The Eagle soars, leaps in the air and pounces—she flows
with the eddies, rides the wind's currents, strong or sweet—cries out,
calls her mate—they dance, they dance—

And it is Vajrayogini,
    dancing for us all—
And it is Yeshe Tsogyal,
    dancing for Guru Pema—
And it is I, dancing, dancing—
    setting the Eagle free
    Oh, she is joyous,
        strong
        & proud
            Vajra Eagle
            Wisdom eye
                Vast vision
                Clear perception
                Unerring aim

SHE DANCES, SHE DANCES
UNCEASING, UNMOVING

---

150. Milarepa, "The Song of a Yogi's Joy," in Chang, *The Hundred Thousand Songs*,
75. Translator's note: "The one who practices Mahāmudrā should know that, from
the ultimate viewpoint, samsara is nirvāna, evil is good, kleśas are Bodhi. The up-
and-down feelings, or the vicissitudinous emotions occurring in meditation, do not
in their ultimate sense differ from Mind-Essence. To an advanced yogi, the greater
the kleśas that arise in his mind, the brighter, deeper, and better his illumination as
to Reality" (86). For the practitioner, then, the worse it gets the better it is.

Seemed there was nothing to purify out there with the sun shining on the snow and I cocooned in the duvet, all the little birdysattvas flitting and twittering around, Sisterdogini snoozing at my feet. Seeming to see the void nature of things, pure in emptiness, all things inherently pure.

•

Milarepa: "Easy it is to glimpse the Dharmakaya, / But hard to stabilize its realization."[151] I didn't know that. I thought that my earlier "glimpses" should have continued as my always-view, that it was my *fault*, somehow, that I "lost" it. But he is saying the glimpse itself is not a sign of realization but rather a more or less ordinary experience or accomplishment. *[Of course it's ordinary. It's our own face. How could it be extraordinary to recognize it?]* Oddly comforting. He goes on to say, "Hence, one is still beset by the Five Poisons."[152] So, there can be glimpses of Truth, as I have experienced, and one can continue in error, as I have experienced—and that is *normal*. Now the question becomes: how to stabilize?[153]

Guru Yoga ended with a sort of sad yearning, then sudden sharp weeping and the cry, "Oh, please don't send me away again! I never want to be separated from you again!" I didn't know I felt *that* way. And of course, it's not just about Beloved—it's the cry of the heart

---

151. Milarepa, "The Gray Rock Vajra Enclosure," in Chang, *The Hundred Thousand Songs*, 101.

152. The three and five poisons: "passion, aggression, and ignorance are the primary three, pride and jealousy make the fearsome five."

153. "Even after kensho, when you perceive that everything is one and are no longer confronted by an external world, you still cannot live in and through that experience. Somehow you keep returning to the previous state of mind. [Through continuing practice] that experience is reaffirmed and you return to the world of non-duality with greater clarity. Gradually the clarity and the ability to live in this world of oneness improve." (Kapleau, *The Three Pillars of Zen*, 63.) See also Anila Rinchen Palmo: "Because the basic clinging to the reality of ego and phenomena is undermined by the realisation of emptiness . . . , there is no longer the same foundation for the emotions or concepts which appear in the mind. . . . However, this realisation, although authentic, will only be fully developed when one reaches Buddhahood, and for this reason one must continue to exercise and affirm one's realisation until that moment." (Palmo, *Cutting through Ego-clinging*, 5.)

for oneness with the absolute. (And my confidence in the self-arising American popular song as indicator of my state of mind is no longer to be relied upon, with this morning's selection: Sinatra's "I get along without you very well.")

Later. Well, I guess that song *is* accurate to my current state. A little reaction setting in. In the middle of practice up come very painful thoughts about the ashram years, thinking everything solidified for me then, when it was supposed to be becoming more transparent. Where I got left behind *["Bye, bye, baby, go on home now"]* was when she began introducing people to emptiness. Thinking about this, I am overwhelmed with grief.

I need to see the void nature of all this.

This morning, as this stuff shot up into my mind from wherever I keep it stored away, I thought, "It is so painful to think this way." And immediately the thought arose, "Well, then, think another way." *[No storage place, just habituation—hence the simplicity of the solution.]*

That is acknowledging voidness, even if not "seeing" it. *[And that is taking responsibility for oneself. The instant the story line is dropped, there is original mind.]*

•

My terrible, terrible temper—
Like my father's, they told me.
Well, Pappy, let's both take refuge
In Dharmakaya's changeless expanse
And offer our terrible angers up
As part of her ever-changing display.
When I become a buddha I promise
To rescue all beings from the fiery hells
Of rage and hatred.

No wonder I'm so paranoid about rabies—"LA RAGE."[154]
To the tune of Gershwin's "Our Love Is Here to Stay":
♪ —it's pretty clear
Who is the MAD DOG here! ♪
♪

_____

154. *La rage* (French): rabies.

This is where people who feel terrible about themselves (and therefore, of course, about others) find it almost impossible to do spiritual practice, accept help, and so on—because inwardly they think they're a pile of shit. And they know you don't take *that* and dump it in front of a shrine and make nice prayers.

While prostrating, caught a glimpse of Milarepa on the shrine and said to him, "You can't tell me you never felt hateful and shitty toward Marpa Lotsawa!" Milarepa instantly responded *[in these actual words]*: "Not really, because by the time I got to Marpa I *knew* I was just a pile of shit—whereas you still think you're *hot shit!*" I collapsed mid-prostration, laughing, laughing. *[Jetsün Mila, my saint, my saint. Lama Laughter, my friend, my friend.]* [155]

Suddenly I find myself in a charnel offering ground. I recognize it, have been there before. Beloved is the one to whom all are making their body offerings, so I do the same—and in very comical ways she reveals the emptiness of every body part, mind part, or speech part I offer. She takes one set of parts, shakes them out like garments, and then holds them up as if hanging them out to dry—and they are, of course, totally transparent. My brain she mushes up, eats, and spits back in my face!

•

Though my concentration is poor, my motivation weak, and my devotion terribly flawed, from my heart to the heart of Guru Pema a pathway of light opens for all beings to rise into his heart.

•

155. Marpa Lotsawa, the Great Translator, Milarepa's guru, put him through terrible trials to purify the terrible negative karma he had accumulated by his terrible deeds. Milarepa said that the reason he was able to realize enlightenment in one lifetime, despite his past, was that no matter how he suffered under his guru's treatment he never once had a negative thought about him! To me, astounding! On my shrine Milarepa looked like a bronze statue, but clearly he was alive—and had my number.

Marianne

Any insect beneath my careless foot
Could be you, dear friend—
Any bug I slap or curse, any poor thing
Wandering homeless in the streets,
Some cur or slinking garbage-eater,
A brute driven by a brute,
A child starving or alone, a woman
Raped and thrown aside like offal,
Any boy forced to die for words
Some old men ejaculate,
Any green living thing that rejoices
The eye or brings good air, any fish
Or bird that gracefully glides,
Any sweet mare galloping her foal,
Or young deer startling itself
Playfully in the fields, watched
By its hovering doe, caring only for
Its safety—as mothers do,
Dear Marianne, as mothers
Always have and will, as you did,
Friend, for all the years of their
Precious childhoods: watched over them.
     Ardent, fierce and tender you were,
Like a mother in a dream: so dear.
Marianne, the same hand that took
Their lovely lives away caressed
Them as newborns and fed them
Good food for lifetimes. They will not
Forget, nor will I, nor will it be
Forgotten how you loved those two
Dead girls. Someday you will stand
At the doorway of your own
Perfection, and those white stones
Will count.
     Marianne, any creature I encounter
Could be you. For you I promise
I will love each one and bring
Each one to buddhahood.

[Here, one last time, tolls the bell that has been ringing for me down the years. Marianne's gift to me: in this moment, to know the one and the many as One.]

•

Grasping isn't a sign of being bad or sinful. Arising from and solidifying confused notions of the nature of things, it is simply an obstacle to perceiving and realizing the true nature of reality. *[Constantly feeding the illusory self feeds illusion, and the tendency to create it, believe in it.]* In the same sense, "pure" and "impure" aren't value judgments, they're simply descriptors. Pure = the natural state, impure = anything that qualifies, obscures, distorts that state or one's realization of it. Useful concepts for those of us who tend to define ourselves as "in deficit." *[Even the apparently benign and minor attachment thoughts, wanting something, just some little thing, even slight craving or grasping, obscures the wisdom eye. I think we Westerners sometimes hear teachings about things like non-attachment as moral injunctions. It turns out they are technical information. I remember how I experienced shame upon receiving correction from Beloved about grasping; I thought it confirmed I was faulty. She was just telling me: "If you put that blindfold over your eyes you won't be able to see where you're going."]*

Tonight I am quite clearly remembering some of why I stopped practicing for so long: the sense of surfeit—surfeit of activities and symbols and requirements and words and images that lack inner life, vividness, and meaning for me.

•

I'm really spacing out over here—can't remember my song to Guru Pema, left the shed wide open, completely confused the time this morning and lost an hour's practice because I thought—looking right at the clock!—it was an hour later than it is. It's so light out, don't know how it happens: you get up every morning, poke around in the dark, and finally the sky begins to lighten—and then one day, seems like overnight, you're sitting here eating breakfast with sunlight pouring across the field. *[Yes, and this is just how IT happens, too.]*

goldfinch	blue jay
purple finch	downy woodpecker (male)
brown sparrow?	red-breasted nuthatch
chickadee	grosbeak
junco	

The next step is the impossible, undreamt of, inconceivable—DEVOTION. I know the seed is there because I have recognized devotion in others, particularly in India, seeing the old Tibetan men and women at their prayers, circumambulating the Dalai Lama's temple—and I wept to see it, my heart just tore open. A tentative sense of joy arising—that I am at this threshold, and asking for help in stepping across.

Practiced outside in the early afternoon sun. Concentration wasn't great but enjoyment certainly was—it was just a riot of lust and longing and sexual titillation out there in Birdland—the evergreens waving and bobbing, light snow puffs scattering in the air, sounds so intimate and beguiling from the inner branches, all twitter and chirrup and mew. There's lots of snow on the ground and anything can happen in the weather department, but spring is definitely here. I feel as excited as a little bird! Soon I'll see what my gardens have been dreaming all winter.

•

Whether I ever achieve realization or not, it is a gift just to be able to practice these luminous pathways. The inner channels are so beautiful, like flower petals, like the softest, most delicate skin. My tears become nectar—drawn in through the breaking heart, they drip and flow through the channels, clarifying, purifying, cleansing, renewing; and into the sacred prismatic fire, feeding, building. What was sorrow becomes light, pain transforms to bliss, and the too-solid-to-be-borne flows into all-pervading emptiness, to manifest as compassion for beings suffering in the too-solid-to-be-borne.

Padmasambhava must have known that the vessel was faulty when he blessed me, blessed us all, with the signs of his presence in the temple for my bodhisattva vows with Beloved—and yet he came anyway. With his omniscience did he know that I would then fall, wander lost for ten years? Or was that fall just a potential, and he saw and blessed me to bring to fruition other potentials, positive ones? How to understand these things? Is his love so vast that my falling or my walking straight are the same to him? *[There is a powerful heart-knowing embedded in this last question.]*

1 robin!!! 2 grackles, 2 doves

•

The Dalai Lama:

> It is said . . . that it is necessary to accumulate infinite merits for innumerable kalpas in order to accomplish Buddhahood. Let us not be dismayed by this, thinking, How could I ever accumulate so much merit? Instead, let us make the wish to lead infinite beings to the infinite qualities of Buddhahood by carrying out the infinite activities of the Bodhisattvas over an infinite period of time. . . . So let us not be influenced by the laziness of being discouraged. [156]

In the last years I have abandoned *myself* in the face of danger—the danger of completely falling away from the teacher, the teachings, the community, and the path, out of what the Dalai Lama is saying is the "laziness of discouragement," the laziness of *losing courage*—which means *losing heart*. That is exactly what I lost—I lost heart. [157]

Shantideva: "How will those who leave the struggle, lily-livered, ever free themselves from such debility?" [158]

I think it is only now that I am seriously considering the possibility that I might try to *control my mind*. There will always be little biters and big dangers and petty annoyances and an incomprehensible guru and rejecting friends and family and snow to shovel and a house to clean and a living to be made. *None* of this is bearable unless I discipline my intense emotional reactivity. *[Surely one meaning of "exhaustion of dharmas" and "karmic exhaustion" is the simple fact of exhaustion itself: running out of repertoire, unable to keep on keeping on in the same old way. A saving grace!]*

•

---

156. Dalai Lama, *A Flash of Lightning in the Dark of Night*, 81.
157. The etymological root of "courage" is the Old French *corage*, from the Latin *cor*, for heart.
158. Dalai Lama, *A Flash of Lightning*, chapter 7 ("Endeavor"), verse 53.

Longing for emptiness, for stability in the view, for realization of the void nature of myself and all things, as a beached whale might long for the sea. *[The view: conceptionless, knowing, luminous expanse of absolute truth. Even one glimpse can liberate completely. Though thoughts, speech, and acts might err, longing for truth is truth itself, unerring.]*
Meditating outside, so beautiful, very warm and full of spring—just celebrating the voidness in all its lovely display—then I open the sealed envelope sent by Maha—EMPTY!—then, passing a mirror, I glance at it to see myself: NOTHING! VOID! *[Voidness "in all its lovely display"— recognizing this—oh, how fortunate a practitioner am I! Praise, praise, praise!]*

Blackbird!

The quality of renunciation is very rudimentary in me: "I don't really *want* to give up the world, Guru Pema—please bless me, that I may become perfect in renunciation." And then: Oh, renunciation means, yes, I choose no longer to be a part of samsara—in order that samsara and all beings may be a part of *me,* that my liberation may truly be theirs.

LOTSA CRAVING
Me too! Gimmee! I want! Where's mine?
[Renunciation reaction.]

[Inner experience, arising spontaneously in meditation:] Full moon night. I go to the Temple of Records—there I find only light, can see no images or things, no conventional forms. Myself: naked, empty, VOID. I then ascend further, to the Temple of Realization—night sky black; subtle, refined energy just above the light. Higher still, I enter the Temple of Ultimate Realization. Here I meet the gurus. I ask Guru Rinpoche, simply, "How?" "You'll be guided," he replies. Tsawai Lama says: "*She'll* tell you what to do." And she does: "Go back down and work your butt off." Went back and forth three times, so I'd remember the way. If this is not just a Fig Newton of my fevered full moon mind, if there is still a possibility of realization in this lifetime, it will certainly take the entire Guru Team, pulling from one side and pushing from the other, to get me through. The tone was casual, almost flip, totally without drama.

Four-and-twenty (well, maybe five-and-twenty) blackbirds sitting in a tree, and today a daylily coming up! I think every blackbird and graaaaaaackle in the neighborhood is at this moment making splendid cacophony in my north woods.

❖ A colleague, suggesting that I am not the best person for a certain project, comments, "You tend to want to review the conflict"—stay focused on the conflict rather than focusing on solutions. It is true, of course. ❖

As if to prove the point of the dream, I am blindsided by an onslaught of painful, intrusive memories of past suffering and confusion. Only stabilizing the view can resolve this: going to the absolute. *[Banging shutters, that's all: the repetitive, noisy back-and-forth. Ambivalence, doubt in myself, and most especially the habit of doubting keep those shutters banging. Only certainty will still them. Milarepa: "Only through cultivating Bodhi-Mind / And contemplating on the Void / Can Karmas, troubles, hindrances, and habitual thoughts be killed."]*[159]

•

Longchenpa describes the qualities of the student for whom the ultimate teaching is appropriate: "Those who are very trusting, vigorous, and committed; / Who are sympathetically compassionate and do not change their minds; / And who would offer their body, offspring, spouse, and wealth / Trustingly and joyfully, yet without desire. / Such students are characterized by their trust and commitment."[160] I have none of these qualities. *[Oh, yes I do. There is confusion's profligate display, but to truth my commitment is true. And I am willing to suffer—to endure—the confusion and its clarification in order to be free. Whatever it looks like moment to moment, that certainty is commitment, that willingness is trust.]*

[And then . . . the justification for everything:]

Tasting *fearlessness*, unassailable *courage*, intrinsic to recognizing voidness. And a sweet, quiet, all-loving happiness, intrinsic to recognizing voidness. And sensing the infinite play of appearances—never-ending and infinite in variety—arising from the stainless, the lovely, the DHARMAKAYA.

159.Milarepa, "Guiding Instructions on the Bardo," in Chang, *The Hundred Thousand Songs*, 342.
160.Longchenpa, *You Are the Eyes of the World*, 25.

Transparency
Leela
Appearances ceaselessly arising
Spontaneously self-liberating
Pristine awareness
Playful display
The all pervading, all illuminating
All manifesting
All liberating
DHARMAKAYA
VOID
THOU
We are all one
Like flames and the fire, one substance
Like waves and the water, one
Ever moving, ever changing
Changeless and unmoving
Arising freshly,
Each experience
Each moment
Each appearance

It is beyond words
Untellable—

And how LOVE pours forth
Intention to awaken us all

Guru, Guru,
Praise, praise, praise
Let my heart break open
For everyone

[*Here, waking up. Here, bodhisattva. The longed for, the promised. Direct experience and recognition of true nature. Primordial Purity.*

Seeing nakedly, set free. In an instant, sorrow disperses, doubt dissolves, striving releases. No past, no future, no this, no that, no coming, no going, no self, no not-self. Joyous serenity pervading, love's wisdom effulgent, clear light unimpeded. Pure being, pure awareness. The peace that Is, and is Knowing.

More will yet come to pass before I take firmly into my hands the staff of spiritual sovereignty, to wield for the benefit of all—but here is certainty.]

•

Taking the ritual wine as the nectar of nonduality—and the chocolate as Miss Piggy!

Sitting for afternoon practice, calling for my heart path to be shown to me clearly, and for the courage and commitment to walk it straight ahead, all the way to the end, I suddenly remember that I have received my instructions already, from Guru Padmasambhava, in his actual words, telling me to read aloud his pith instructions, the ones I went to unerringly:

> Although there are many key points of body, rest free and relaxed as you feel comfortable. Everything is included in simply that.
> Although there are many key points of speech such as breath control and mantra recitation, stop speaking and rest like a mute. Everything is included in simply that.
> Although there are many key points of mind such as concentrating, relaxing, projecting, dissolving, and focusing inward, everything is included in simply letting it rest in its natural state, free and easy, without fabrication.
> The mind . . . is utterly empty and completely awake—that is the nature of your mind.
> Having recognized it as such, to become certain about it, that is the view. To remain undistracted in that state of stillness, without fabrication or fixation, that is the meditation. In that state, to be free from clinging or attachment, accepting or rejecting, hope or fear, toward any of the experiences of the six senses, that is the action.
> Whatever doubt or hesitation occurs, supplicate your master. Don't remain in places of ordinary people; practice in seclusion. Give up your clinging to whatever you are most attached to as well as to whomever you have the strongest bond with in this life, and practice. Like that, although your body remains in human form, your mind is equal to the buddhas'. [161]

This is the path I wish to follow, this the practice I wish to master. Absolute truth practiced secretly in the world. *[Here, path certainty.]*

---

161. Tsogyal, *Dakini Teachings*, 153–54.

My nature, indestructible like a vajra, manifest now. *[Here, pure prayer. No bemoaning, no beseeching, just truth calling to truth.]*

•

Occasional glimpses showing me I'm really right there all the time, then losing that view, having to rely on intellect to remind me of something I am not presently experiencing—feeling trapped in dualistic separation—nothing that I can do to get out of my cell *[that's true: it has nothing to do with doing]*—and yet I know there is no guard outside, only my own mind. What I need to remind myself is that practice must become for me a way of *living*, not a way of getting somewhere or getting something, not even getting some enlightenment.

[Natural state, wisdom nature; normal state, ignorance; co-emergent, existing together in sentient beings—and discernible one from the other. That discernment, the principal activity dimension of awareness meditation, opens the door to abiding in wisdom nature. Having directly experienced the natural state but not knowing how to rest there or to engage it at will, I am in some moments tranquil, confident, and in others self-doubting. Recognizing is easier than abiding. "Easy it is to glimpse the Dharmakaya, / But hard to stabilize its realization."[162] Process of attaining view certainty.]

•

The Dance of Dharmakaya this morning—appearances arising, flashing, glowing, sparkling, then returning to the void-luminosity—

It seems as if rainbow light is playing across the face of Guru Pema's portrait.

Quieting, slowing the pace, loosening the structure. Gorgeous spring day. I am ready to be out working with the land, the gardens, the rocks, Earth and sky.

What energizes me to keep going is the glimpse, from time to time, of the stainless, luminous lake of truth. I am also motivated by commitment to others' well-being and enlightenment. And by recognition

---

162. Milarepa, "The Gray Rock Vajra Enclosure," in Chang, *The Hundred Thousand Songs*, 101.

of how much worse off I am when I don't practice. And by this stark fact: It ain't gonna get better on its own—the contrary, in fact—and if I don't stay on it now, when will I? *[Retreatant preparing her mind for re-entry to world.]*

Last day. Holding the energy right through to exact completion. Morning practices, breakfast, vacuum, clean shrine, fire and feast, opening gates. And a lovely end-of-retreat snowfall. Retreat Complete.

(End of Winter Retreat)

•

April, May, June, July, August

Post-Retreat: Africa

[A few days after Retreat Compleat I receive a call from the director of an international agency, asking me to go to Africa—to create a women's peace movement in a country convulsed by a highly politicized interethnic civil war that has by then taken more than 100,000 lives, sent thousands fleeing to neighboring countries, internally displaced massive numbers, and devastated social and economic infrastructure. "I want an army of Lysistratas," he tells me. [163] *I am very shaken by this request:]*

I can't think of a single reason not to go, except that the idea of going terrifies me and I want to watch my flowers come up. As soon as I said yes, the waves of fear and weeping began. At first I thought it was just my cowardice. Then I saw that I am being pried out of my little self, my little life, my lethargy and self-absorption—and jolted into SERVICE. So often, thinking about people risking their lives for others, I have wondered where their courage and selflessness come from. Without their qualities, I am going—perhaps only because it is given me to go, and because I can. *[So, with a last glance at the spring flowers shining in my gardens, I go. Beloved strongly, warmly encourages me: "If tested by violence, no fear: only love."]*

[I had lived and taught in Africa twice during my twenties, more than thirty years before this moment, and had loved what I then experienced of her. I saw many beautiful faces

---

163. He was referring to Aristophanes' comedic drama "Lysistrata," in which the women of Athens refuse to make love with the men until the men make peace with Sparta, to end the Peloponnesian War.

of love, humor, intelligence, and kindness in people I met; wondered at the scale and power of African lands and skies, at once domestic and impersonal; and experienced both my own resourcefulness and my insufficiencies, in skills and character, in work and relationships. All of this arises in a gust of love as I return to Africa.]

At dawn, banking in over the dark plains, the enthralling high mountains of lake country at sunrise, love flooding my heart with newly remembered scents and sights and sounds: the air fresh and clear with morning, the close hills, the dusty plains, trees I didn't remember remembering—in that very first moment of seeing Africa again all my love rose up. Almost, I could have gotten back on the plane right then and something worthwhile would already have been accomplished. How could I have forgotten how much I once loved Africa?

[I enter a situation—like life—that has been going on a long time before I enter and will go on a long time after I exit. I will be there a bit more than three months, it will feel like three years, and in the rapidly unfolding course of events will signify about three minutes. Though I quickly become aware of an absence of fear in myself, fear saturates the place, the people, and the time. This is a war of intimate violence—in terms of who is killing whom: relatives, friends, neighbors, co-workers, companions; and in terms of how the killing is being done: some by air, tank, and large weapons, but much, perhaps most, by knife and machete, close up. And in such beauty:]

This dreamtime is strange with stark contrasts: paradisiacal beauty and burning, smoke black and thick; the nights and early mornings filled with sounds so different from the colobus monkeys, elephants, and birds that I have heard before in Africa: machine gunning, grenades every night. I shall long remember the grenade so close that it shook our window panes, rocked me into an additional little creative step in the sacred dance, and then resolved, eerily, into the gentle thththth of dust falling back to earth. *[Like a touchstone I turn over and over again Beloved's words: "Remember the insubstantiality of all appearances."]*

[Swiftly my work takes hold. I begin meeting with the women who will initiate the peace project, and within a few weeks we hold a national conference of women, from peasants to parliamentarians—who immediately jettison the nice plan we have prepared and simply sit down to talk together. Out of this emerges a fledgling national women's peace movement: lifted by need and hope, riven with the very political conflicts that fuel the war, and sustained by determination and courage. I move into providing support for their work with one another, across lines of class, ethnicity, politics, age, and education.

Happiness characterizes the initial stages of my endeavors with these brave women. I am happy to be in Africa, happy to be with them, sharing their fears, commitment, and humor, and happy to assist them in weaving the peace they long for. Not for themselves, they tell me: "For us it is too late, our lives have been ruined, but for our children . . ."

However, wherever we go there we are, and of course my personality faults must crop up, creating difficulties for me. Due to my agency affiliation I am accountable to excellent, dedicated men whose guidance I must follow but whose ways of working are not mine, and particularly not in working with women.]

My way of working is close up, through relationship; I can't imagine working with women and not going into their homes, which I am being told I must not do. I am chafing at the restrictions on my freedom of movement and association—but I also see that these are ways to be experiencing *with* the people here, who are facing those factors much more than I, and in life-threatening ways. *[I feel confined: they are confined.]*

[At the women's conference I witness a sharp instance of the tragically foolish aspect of this war:] Some women were talking about who was of which ethnic group; one mentioned that so-and-so was of one group, the other expressed surprise. It was a scene I've witnessed several times, conveying the absurdity of 'ethnic hatred' when the adversaries themselves can't tell who is who!

Realistically, I think of my work as planting seeds that may take a very long time to sprout; the soil looks fertile, but sometimes I think it is too saturated with blood to bear good fruit. It may need to be turned over and over for a long time to come.

And the spiritual moment? An opportunity for nonjudgment and unconditional love. I am fully here, wouldn't want to be anywhere else, and am grateful for the moment, whatever it brings. A co-worker, smart, dynamic, sassy, awake, commented as she told me her age, "Here, that's no longer considered young; our life expectancy is so short now." We smiled together in recognition of life's fragility and beauty and of our good fortune in being aware of it. How wonderful—all appearances arising afresh, sparkling with the dew of voidness.

[As in retreat, I laugh with pleasure as I catalog the morning bird symphony—]

chuckle   whoop
crow   clunk
hoot   toot
whistle   clang
chirrup   tweet
caaaackle   chortle
twirp   ker-lunk
cheep   ooooh?

•

[Everyone refers to what is happening in the country as "The Situation." Since my arrival The Situation appears to be deteriorating, my work seems more urgent, but my stay in the country is soon to be curtailed by my project administrator, citing the increasing risks.]
Last night, machine gun fire in the city—on and on, sounded like one gun, firing and firing, as if to slaughter one cowering family. Imagination is a hindrance in this situation. Last night, my first flashes of real fear and the thought, "If I lose my nerve I'm no use." And it's becoming personal, taking on a face—the beautiful, sublime face of bodhisattva Pierre, killed last night or early this morning, his body stuffed into a toilet. I am remembering "the insubstantiality of appearances," and I am remembering Pierre's face.
[As I begin to feel more vulnerable I also become entangled in self-grasping—or, more likely, the other way around:] When the talk began about sending me home early, I think my focus shifted from the work itself to whether I would be here to do it or not: I got snagged on self. I think I also got too pleased with me, me, me, open-hearted, expansive, clear-sighted, unafraid—now I'm feeling tight-hearted, contracted, fuzzy in vision, vulnerable. Everything surely does turn into its opposite, yeah, Babe.

[At another level, what is happening with me is just what happens in war:] . . . encapsulation of trauma so you can keep on going, then at some point, unexpectedly, it just pops and you are momentarily overwhelmed. Massacre at the university, just down the road from where I stay. There is something sacred about a university and students; they symbolize freedom of the mind, respect for difference. The numbed city was shocked by the murders, but there are so many, so often; this event, too, quickly seemed to become one of the many. It had been followed by days of

very heavy gunfire in my immediate area, which had me spending tense hours flat on the floor behind the thickest walls of the house several nights running—after which I was a little more brittle, mistrustful, and defended than usual. Gradually seemed to be coming back to balance. Then today, sitting quietly in front of my shrine, I started to cry, and it was about the university students: they were my children, both the killers and the prey, and my heart ached for them all.

[There can be trauma for those directly involved, and secondary trauma for those involved with those directly involved. By the last weeks of my work in this beautiful, sorrowing country, I myself am caught in confusion, frustration, helplessness, and anger.]

❖ I'm having to swim through water that is like a sewer outlet, literally filled with shit. Other people see no way to the other side except *through* that shit. I am sure there is another way, just haven't managed to find it yet. ❖

•

[In this circumstance I have great compassion and commitment, a paucity of skillful means and equanimity, and a surfeit of self-concern and emotional reactivity. I have come to Africa, into the war, still raw from retreat, and as time goes by The Situation degrades, within and without. In a phone consultation Beloved says to me, "How can you help other people transcend their stuff if you're stuck in yours?"

Now, when I look back on myself and these events, I see a beautiful generosity and caring, abundantly expressed and realized in some moments and in others limited and distorted by my human limitations, both of quality and of circumstance. I hold this time of my life gently in my mind, as I would hold an old photograph in my hands, yellowing and soft, a little crumbly at the edges, showing me dignity and goodness in the visages of those with whom I engaged in works of love. All our successes and all our failures weigh the same in my heart.]

•

YEAR EIGHTEEN

Letters to a Spiritual Friend · Storm-tossed and sublime
The dance floors of our minds
Like my own ignorance, this spring snow
I still think the climbing is the thing
How light, how insubstantial the burden · Giddy with freedom
In the midst of the Ten Thousand Things
Only my own answers now

Letters to a Spiritual Friend

[In this year my email correspondence with a Zen practitioner whom I meet in an online Buddhist forum replaces my journal writing. There is a different quality of voice in these letters. The journals were never intended for others, while here I am speaking to someone, in my first experience of unguarded, free-ranging peer communication about spiritual experience. We are not known to each other in any other way than this, which lends to our exchanges a freeing anonymity. Our conversation is in many tones—playful, mannered, serious, intimate, provocative—and always fresh, spontaneous: emails dashed off in the moment.[164]

Throughout the years the journals themselves are so very raw; perhaps it is with some relief that I find this correspondence providing a way to frame personal experience, allowing me a different angle of view—not more distant, but maybe on occasion less subjective or myopic. Rendering some of my life narrative, I find myself not so much elaborating or rehashing as seeing through it in a new way. "Through our communication," I tell her, "I am enabled to know more consciously and explicitly what I Know." My messages to her reveal awareness's messages to me, shimmering within and radiating through the conventional appearances of mind and activity— showing me the necessary, freeing integrity for which I long: absolute and relative, One.]

January

Perfect. There we were in the boat house anchored just offshore, the city on the sloping hill visible to port, and to starboard the spacious

---

164. Only my own communications are included here.

lake bordered on the far side by high mountains. Yesterday, intense rainstorm, turning first to sleet and then to heavy, driving snow as evening came on—and today, bright hard sun, stiff wind churning whitecaps on the steely lake, huge chunks of ice banging the hull, the sloughing and groaning of the vessel rising and falling on the swells. It was dreamlike and impeccable—the shrine with its fresh flowers, photographs of masters, statues of deities and bodhisattvas, cloudlike silken prayer scarves, elemental offerings; sweet perfume of incense; the sangha murmuring, laughing, chanting, praying, listening, shining; the teacher on her small dais, funny, loving, embracing, encouraging, radiating, inspiring, perfecting. To meditate there was to experience the insubstantiality, no solid ground beneath, everything in motion within and all around. I would look up from time to time and tears would flow—for the beauty and holiness of the moment: we with our precious teacher, riding the waves, safe in our sacred vessel, gathering all beings to us with our practice, rocking, cradled, storm-tossed and sublime.

I love your observations on the immense value of a real-life working relationship with my teacher. I know you are right, especially about how she thus prevents me from walling off a section of my life to "spirituality" and not having to integrate it. It's exactly the medicine I need for the disease of duality mind—but there are times when I think, ah, getting up at 3:30 to go to the monastery, as you do, wouldn't that be lovely.

One of my friends has decided to take nun's vows. I am deeply happy for her, and . . . a wave of longing arose, for that kind of total engagement. I think that in this life for me it is more like this: nothing to hold on to, nowhere to hang my hat. No hat! No defined, visible, or nameable path, no robes, no trappings, no this, no that, not even "Buddhism," not even "this lineage, that lineage." Naked truth. Secret path. Just: ah, here I *am*. *[Yet I keep forgetting this clearly seen luminous truth of my path. Out of habit—the habit of doubting—I long continue to strive for reassurance, definition, identity.]*

When I was young I, like you, thought of becoming a nun, but the tone wasn't quite right. Later, at Quaker boarding school, I rejoiced in our silent meeting for worship in the bosom of an intimate working community of students and teachers, took to it like a silver fish gliding silently into cool, shadowy depths. I am sure that in those fertile silences I re-membered myself as meditator and contemplator—then in the

Christian idiom, longing for union with God, for unimpeded service, for humility.

I set both liturgy and belief system aside my first year at college. It wasn't the encounter with humanism, intellect, and sex that did it, it was this: One day in my freshman year I entered the science building, for astronomy class.[165] At the top of the steep stairs, looking down into the lab, I was suddenly stopped, as if with a hand to my chest. There was no sound around me and strange sound at the same time, people milling about, finding their seats, but I could neither see them nor move. I stood planted, staring straight out over all those heads into the space directly before me, where the eyes of God looked into mine and the voice of God said, "You must now leave the Named God to walk alone for a time." I flooded, bereft, and fled. Alone, shaking and sobbing, I wandered for hours. When I came back to my dorm my entire life had changed. I entered the world. *[That time I was required; later there would be many opportunities, several of them recorded in these journals, freely to choose. In Alice Bailey I read that a disciple, at a certain stage, must learn to stand completely alone, though only apparently and only temporarily: "Circumstances are staged to bring this condition about, and if they are not so staged by the disciple's own soul, then the Master acts to bring the circumstance about. The disciple must be thrown upon his own resources."[166] It seems that this was the experiment into which I was cast that day in the university science lab. It would last more than twenty years . . . and it would not be the only time.]*

In the first year I worked with Beloved she asked me for my ideal, my aspiration. I told her, "Union with God, the divine." "How will you find that?" "When I die," I answered. "Why wait?" she asked; "why not do it now?" And there she was, holding open the door I had closed behind me at age eighteen. Still is.

---

165. I took astronomy to fulfill my natural sciences requirement because other students told me it would be the easiest for one with my sorry mathematical skills. Imagine my shock, confronted with mathematical formulas for the half-lives of stars! Ever hewing to the qualitative, even in this rarefied company, I wrote my term paper on the potentials for life on other planets. This was well before the topic had any scientific credibility; there was virtually no scholarly literature to serve as foundation or doorway; and I quite rightly earned a low grade for my paper, the one and only D of my life. However, some years later, watching the film "Close Encounters of the Third Kind," with glee I espied in the credits my venerable astronomy professor: scientific advisor to the film! Did my speculative undergrad disquisition plant an unruly seed in the Shades of Erudition?

166. Bailey, *Discipleship*, 593.

No hat, no robe, no monk, likewise no nun, no school, no home, and likewise no extinction of these, the wild invisible secret practitioner "relies upon the Prajnaparamita and mind is no hindrance, without any hindrance no fears exist . . ."[167] Where will I find the courage and discipline for this wild and joyous ride into absolute liberation? I can't even make myself sit on the darn cushion every day!

February

I am convinced that most of the time we haven't the faintest idea what is really going on, how very much help, support, guidance, and protection we are receiving. Reminds me of a lovely story someone told me years ago.[168] She was a flower sensitive, one who communicates with flowers. One day in Scotland, walking in the woods, she came upon a little glen filled with flowers, like a tapestry. The only way to pass through it was to walk through, literally to walk *upon*, the flowers. She could hardly bear it, they were so fragile, so sweet, looking up at her with their lovely faces. She tried to walk without stepping, to step without crushing, and as she tiptoed across the flowery pathway she became aware of the many little flower voices calling out to her. "We love you, we love you," they sang. My friend, touched, asked them lightly, playfully, "Is there anything you *don't* love?" There was a little silence. Then one flower voice spoke for them all: "What is . . . 'don't love'?"

What I want us to communicate about is this utterly critical question of integration, ordinary life, being awake. Minute to minute, day to day, week to week, how to live what we know to be true, the pure light of awareness not a remembered experience but a door open in every moment, for ourselves and others. I want truth to so permeate my being that the distinction of ordinary-extraordinary simply dissolves.

Had a little taste of that today. In the bank I was speaking with one of the officers, pictures of his family all around, my wonderful dog, Sister, sniffing at the tennis balls on the floor and the bagels on the table. It couldn't have been more ordinary, yet this subtle sense was creeping through me: "We are divinities clothed in human form, ours

---

167. From the Prajnaparamita (Heart) Sutra.
168. Loving thanks to the one who told me this story; its meaning informs my life.

a meeting of sublime with sublime, our speech really mantra, holy sound, praise, praise, praise. We are flames of one fire, lights of one light. Our meeting has nothing to do with the business that brought me here. In a moment before the beginning of time we agreed to meet in this way, to shine forth the glory of WHAT IS in this ordinary place and moment."

Awaking is one thing, Being Awake is another. Here's a useful insight: "The issue is only whether we're awake in *this* moment. And this moment. And this moment. And having been awake [at one point], perhaps so awake you were given a title, doesn't mean you're awake [years later], or in all situations. . . . [C]hances are, even if the curtain goes up, it's going to slowly come back down, into your clouded ways of seeing things."[169] This practitioner also says, of an experience of insight, "I spent . . . two years trying to recapture that historical moment."[170] I did that, too, after my winter retreat, and blamed myself: "See, you woke up and then went back to sleep." So my glimpse of truth served to separate me further from truth. *["Eventually the seeking itself hid truth from my sight."]* Talk about amalgamating new insight to the old paradigm!

Of course what you're telling me is true: "Once you have seen you don't un-see; still you know what is." Yes. Even when I was trying so hard to hold on to it and confusion became again the predominant mode, I never forgot. In the moment of awakening in winter retreat, all that you say about innate purity was resplendently obvious. Warts and all, I knew, *knew*, because I *saw*, that I and all beings, and all the ten thousand things, arise immaculate from the luminous emptiness, and return, immaculate, to the immaculate. Primordial purity our innate nature, we *are* that. Joyous certitude.

•

Absolute, unconditional love: this is *the* work for me in this time. I

169. Elizabeth Hamilton, in Friedman, *Meetings with Remarkable Women*, 130–32. Another comment: "The Enlightened Person. Good riddance! Maybe now we can get out from his or her shadow and see that there has never been an Enlightened Person. There are only enlightened activities—that is, activities (or words, or thoughts) that do or don't reflect a direct experience of the non-dual nature of reality." (Kjolhede, *Tricycle*.)
170. Hamilton, in Friedman, *Meetings with Remarkable Women*, 131–32.

am so grateful to be able to speak of it. Yesterday, walking along the road with Sister, I thought, "Ah, the person who can be so harsh and the one who shines like the sun, these are not two." Isn't that the Mystery? Divinity and humanity are not two. Makes me weep, so sweet this truth, so forgiving. I am not other than that which I long for and fear.

Today I realized that I am coming to love my teacher. I am so thankful. *[In fact, I love her from the beginning, right through the troubled times, and to this very moment. As she loves me. Is the sun extinguished by passing clouds and storms?]*

Your story about transmission with the "holy hug"! I've seen similar things happen with just a glance—and the recipient is transfixed, sometimes arising from that moment, as in your story, transformed, redirected, ennobled. I have even experienced it happening with me. I remember once a young woman said to me, "I want everything you've got"—and instantly there poured forth from my heart to hers grace waves of a fine, subtle energy, rose and gold in hue, that flowed in a steady, perceptible stream. I never thought of it as having to do with "me"; it was at once intimate and impersonal, specific and universal. That is the nature of enlightened mind and activity. Spacious, precise; all-encompassing, distinct. Like the eagle—from the height of its flight in the vastness, plunging unerringly to where the tiny mouse awaits its release from mouse-mind.

Some of the teachers I have sat with have taught as you describe your teacher doing, one with the group, the individual minds and the moment, satisfying each one's questions or stirring each one's pot, with humor, ease, spontaneity; also, often, sharpness, sometimes shocking. Beloved teaches like that. And she speaks in circles and spirals, utterly confounding linear mind. She pours and pours, overwhelming the full cups we bring to her. And she radiates, confusing the defended and warming the chilled, a fire that stirs, animates, vivifies, tears down, builds up, refines.

Today many things, people, and moments revealed themselves in beauty. Drinking from a glass: water into water. Walking on snow: light and air on air and light.

It's cold, definitely still winter. Spring here usually lasts about twenty minutes, but once we had a true spring, just blissful, a slow unfolding of color in mountains, trees, fields, and forests, the changing scents and sounds—subtle wave upon wave, over weeks instead of hours and days. Especially I remember the wildflowers and forest groundcovers. That spring the season of blossoms just went on and on and on, and we saw delicate flowering things we'd never seen before: leaves showing their sexy little propagating organs, bushes putting on the most frivolous of displays. It was prolific, extravagant, and astonishingly sexual, just everything flowering, blushing, blooming—swelling and opening like a ready woman.

•

You describe the "cooling of relationships." Yes, I think this does occur with practitioners, as attachment, grasping, and clinging begin to be pacified. Love becomes less personal, more objective. Sometimes it's hard on one's friends and family who are not practitioners, for it can feel like abandonment, loss of interest. But really, it's just that the practitioner's mind is revealing its natural amplitude, spacious to contain all beings in the love and care formerly reserved to a few.

Sometimes I ache with longing to follow my love of Dharma all the way. I know it is only in my mind, but at times I feel I must make a choice between the Buddhadharma and my teacher's tradition, as if I will never go beneath the surface if I don't go one way or the other. But there is no call for that, really. It is all right, quite all right, really. Perhaps when I am able to truly taste the One Taste I will no longer feel it even slightly as conflict, but for now I acknowledge some envy of the simpler form: one lineage, one teacher, one practice. *[This correspondence clearly shows the experience of tasting the one taste; it is stability that is not yet established: relaxing into being and resting there, not just extolling its glories. Although that, too, is good practice: praise, praise, praise.]*

Your sweet note: expanding awareness of bodhi. Very goodhi. Wish mine were. As I sat this morning I found myself musing on just how *solid* things are feeling and appearing to me these days. Well, that, too, is awareness. Not badhi, not goodhi: intrinsically bodhi.

Today it's foggy and drizzly, creating a strange luminosity between sodden earth and frothy, low-hanging clouds heavy with rain. The snows are gone now; there is distinct warmth in the air, and as I brought firewood in today I saw new green in the daylily bed: they are the first, always; I always think they'll get nipped in the bud by returning freezes, and by July they are always confounding my pessimism with their brilliant, wavelike display.

"Africa?" you ask. Perhaps the biggest lesson was this: Shortly after I returned, one day I was standing at a window, looking out at the flower gardens in my cousin's yard—and realized that the work I had just done in Africa, in a situation of danger and suffering, and the work I had done the summer before, developing flower beds in my wild little yard, were Not Two. One was not more or less valuable or important than the other. They weighed the same. One taste. I am no longer driven to save the world or longing to be quiet and alone, no longer swinging wildly between the personal and the political, the private and the public, the spiritual and the material. Truth is nondual. *[Healed now, that archaic split in my mind, my character.]*

MOVIEYANA! Yes! The Celluloid Vehicle, Dhramarama Dharma, Perfection of Illusion, Video Verity, the Reel Truth! Ordinary, extraordinary, ghood, bhad, ugliness, beauty, all void in their nature, arising from the all-ground, returning to the all-ground. [171]

You describe reentering apparent limitation from the spaciousness of the absolute. The bodhisattva's gift to all sentient beings.

Apparent limitation is where this particular sentient being is living every day. I am in the moment where memory of the view must nourish faith that it will become, eventually, lived experience, and infuse every moment. I am remembering and anticipating—therein duality, hence suffering. *[The view is infusing every moment. It is inseparable from every moment. In many of these moments I am, again, recognizing. That the recognizing is occurring not in meditative concentration but in the context of active life makes it perhaps more slippery and difficult to affirm, but it is still none other than the perfection that is . . . and awareness of that.]*

Let this stand as one of our communications that upon re-reading causes infinite compassion to flow forth like a woodland spring, as now from my eyes, unstoppable. If even I, who have received all the gifts

---

171. The all-ground: sometimes called the *alaya* consciousness or the storehouse consciousness.

and sit at the feet of a master, and have seen truth, am still groping and lurching around as if blind, what must be the loneliness, doubt, despair, and weariness of beings who have never even glimpsed the possibility of freedom?

•

Snow's falling off the warming metal roof in huge, luscious glops. Sister's dozing in the sun, belly in the snow bank. Nothing juxtaposed, everything just so.

Keen awareness of the phenomena of the world, endlessly arising and falling away, forming and dissolving. Beauty and suffering, wind and sun, house and forest and vehicles and thoughts.

The intersection of world and wisdom is where practice makes perfect. You asked how I help people "know how to know." I show how to see oneself knowing, how to see thoughts and emotions arising and dissolving, how to look right at them, how to see in between stimulus and response, between in-breath and out-breath. Not so many are ready for that, in psychotherapy or in spiritual practice—but when it clicks, there it is! *[I don't see it at the time, but here it's clear: I already hold the method for which I think I am still searching.]*

I got a lesson the other day from a local sangha member who occasionally visits the online forum you and I play in. She told me, "Tremendous compassion is just *pouring* out of my computer whenever one of your messages is on." Good reminder for *moi:* we already are what we aspire to be.

March

This afternoon I stepped out into a golden landscape: blonde grasses waving, light slanting across the field, illuminating hummocks and hillocks, clouds bright in the great blue sky—all seemed ablaze with the light of creation, and I moved through this fiery, bright world like a gentle breeze, barely touching the Earth, only stirring slightly the little bushes and branches as I passed.

How will I perfect the jewel of pure awareness when so active in the world? It's the other face of your dilemma: how to function in the world while perfecting the jewel of pure awareness? *[The jewel of pure awareness needs no perfecting—it is perfection itself! What I am needing to perfect is my willingness, in each moment, to look within, see what is coming and going in my mind, and* leave it alone—*instead of doing what we virtually always do with every thought, perception, emotion: grasp it, push it away, or elaborate it. When we do none of those things, what arises in mind, lacking any nature of its own, simply dissolves back into mind itself. "A beginner does not believe it, but this dissolution is Buddhahood."*[172] *To reveal the perfection? Simply allow the appearance of imperfection to dissolve. Thought is to mind as wave is to water.]*

Now when I am with Beloved sweet smiles pass between us, bright joyous glances. This is new for me. Always before when I heard the word devotion I felt a little sickish, seeing in others what I myself was incapable of, and from the outside it sometimes looked to me like slavishness. But now it looks different, because I'm not looking at it from the outside.

Though it is, of course, "not about the teacher," in some mysterious way that I cannot explain but deeply, mysteriously comprehend, for some the teacher also *is* the way. For me, the entire mysterious, mystical, tortuous, ineluctable, beautiful, terrifying, sweet, simple, direct path is mediated through my relationship with my teacher. As soon as I arrived I was placed right next to her, in the space of skillful activity in her mandala—and struggle though I have, and mightily, that is where I have continued to find myself through these many years. Now, this time, by free and loving choice, with a sense of gratitude and wonder at the opportunity itself, as well as recognition that the principal beneficiary of my presence there is me myself.

A few nights ago I found myself in a bookstore, in front of a rack of Dharma books. I started to cry, the longing was so intense, so unexpected. It was total, took me over completely, I wanted to prostrate, place the books on my crown. It's not that I particularly want to read, mind you, but that the books *are* the Dharma. Yeah, yeah, I know, so is everything. And you know I'm not into religious trappings. But I want IT. "She's gotta have it." What am I going to do? I've seen truth. How am I to live like this, remembering and not having access to the direct experience? I feel . . . oh, who cares? I said I was going to fall back on

---

172. Garchen Rinpoche, "A River That Cannot Be Frozen."

what I know, not on what I feel. And of course what I *know* is that I am not other than IT, not separate, no way to be separate.

Boy oh boy, this is very painful.

Bodhi's pissed off at bodhi for hiding bodhi from bodhi, while bodhi is turning inside out trying to uncover bodhi. I am alternately pissed off, amused, despairing, and serene.

April

The light is tremendous.

It is seeing what is true, and seeing that this is who I *am*, that has changed my life. There's nothing to hide from; I've seen the worst of myself and knew it wasn't me. But what really shifted things was not seeing what *isn't* me but seeing what *is*—the clear light, primordial purity, void nature of all things, empty me, no me. Oh, what joy it is! Even to remember the seeing of it fills me with laughter, like birds suddenly lifting up in flight in my heart, like praises.

•

Personality and enlightenment. Since I came out of last winter's retreat I have had countless opportunities to look into the mirror and see, flinchingly or un-, one of my least attractive and most problematic personality aspects: anger, hostility, harsh speech. It has caused pain to everyone who has ever associated with me, I think. Not to mention what it's like to live with it! I have learned to be a truly graceful apologizer, spontaneous, prompt, sincere, loving, remorseful, all those good things. I'm so good at it because I've had so damn much practice. If it's a day when I've had contact with other human beings it's a day when I've had need to apologize. What's different now is that now I know what's true, so my remorse and apologies tend to be given with laughter, and the post-dereliction phase doesn't find me reeling with dismay, cringing in shame, recoiling from the person or situation I have offended, but rather taking the lesson and bringing it out to others.

There appears to be some truly decisive turning point when we choose to withdraw the projections, to *welcome* seeing ourselves in the mirror, to *actively* ferret out the little sneaky places where some idea of self has managed to get itself ensconced. The hardest work for the teacher is probably helping the student get to that point without turning away. After that it's not "if" but "how," and the relationship is more of allies, sharing the open secret.

We don't have to have perfected our personalities in order to realize enlightenment, so apparent personality glitches and faults are no obstacle to enlightenment and no justification for discouragement. They are simply displays of pure awareness, occasions for piercing the veil of appearances to reveal What Is.

I am not directly perceiving emptiness, but that doesn't change the fact that emptiness *is*, and I Am That. Primordial purity *is*, and We Are That. I don't have to look into the mirror every day to see if I am still me, nor ask myself my name every day to be sure I still know who I am. No more do I need to be *in* the experience of IT to know that IT IS and I Am That. Not making two out of One, but finding the One in the two and the three . . . and in the Ten Thousand.

[So it seems that this is my way: not sublimely meditating, just seeing and being. *And loving and praising.]*

•

Too much: pressure, work, blame, anger, frustration. Too little: support, appreciation, rest, good food, recreation, solitude. Just enough: guru showing me where I lack equanimity, serenity, unfailing recall of emptiness.

Humongous snowstorm, apple tree lost a graceful limb, spruce trees and white pines stand like ladies in ermine at a lawn party. But it can't fool me: like my own ignorance, this spring snow hasn't got a chance when the sun really starts shining.

Last week, on one of our teasingly springish days, I went out to peer at what will be daffodils and iris soon, beneath the apple tree. Standing there, I felt a soft touch on my cheek, so tender. Only recently have I begun to open to tenderness. This touch, by the flower bed, was infinitely tender. Yet was I not alone in the yard that day? Surely I would have heard or sensed if someone had walked toward me, or Sister would have barked. Without turning my head or saying anything, I just leaned into the caress, softly returning it with my cheek. Such love flowing along those touching membranes, suffusing the day with sweetness. It was the apple tree itself, leaning down one of its branches.

In another time I would describe my life right now as "not practicing, caught up in everyday events, too busy." But this is this time, and I see it differently: Everyday events are the stuff of enlightenment. Did a fair amount of driving around this week and at one point had a little highway insight that is very, very useful. Was in a bit of a rush, wanted to barrel along out there on the road, and of course found myself behind an old feller pokin' along, familiar little pressure of impatience mounting in my head and gut—when suddenly the thought came, "Ah, in this moment when I can't have my own way, in this moment enlightenment could arise." Did that ever transform the highway experience! Since then, every little obstacle appears as a luminous, spacious, empty sky. Talk about pure perception! *[And talk about ephemeral realizations!]*

May

You ain't kiddin' about sense of humor as indicator of path. Really, if you ain't got it, you ain't gettin' it!

Beloved could talk about canning fruit and it would still be about the Mystery. Yesterday the utterly perfect young woman who is our office secretary reported the plumber's saying the resolution of our water problem would be in the central channel. I burst out laughing, as did Beloved, who jumped up, dancing and singing, "The central channel, the central channel!" Delightenment!

Melting, you say? Here, feels like hardening. Not just the weather. Me. Am in struggle mode, face to face with my resistance to *doing* all that helps me experience *being*—the many and various practices I have from both traditions, this ritual, those exercises, these prayers and offerings, and on and on and on. I don't *want* to. What I *want* is simply to BE. Simply to *be*, and to *be* simply, one with WHAT IS, in the state of I AM THAT. *[Later my lama will say, "The only effort we need to make is the effort to do nothing." This invitation rings unceasingly in my heart, as plentifully evidenced in the journals—but really, I do not know how to "not do" and "just be." As the not knowing can be key to the just being, I am confounded. I have not yet fallen into the irresistible crevasse in the unscalable glacier. I still think the climbing is the thing, not the falling.]*

Suffering never ends until eradicated at the root. That is where I want to go.

It is very interesting to have reached a longed for state of love and confidence in my guru and now be thinking of leaving her immediate tutelage for immersion in another phase of my path. For the moment I am watching closely the operations of my own mind. This is one of those narrow defiles in which a wrong step could flip me from rumination to ruination without my even being aware of it.

One of the ways she teaches: My ignorance comes up and then lessons abound, flashing from every rock and rill, everything within and all around mirroring both the ignorance and the resolution. She doesn't have to say a word.

You erupted in rage at a human colleague insufficiently awake to animal suffering, and now here's my version of that: Rescuing from her porch a blue jay that my elderly neighbor was trying to kill, I terribly offended her. What's going on here, you and I with our compassionate care of the little critters and our offenses to the human ones? Maybe something like this: that every duality we set up is going to end by giving us the finger? This is known, in *Dr. Dorje's Book of Laws for the Slow to Learn*, as the Law of "Watch Out, Here It Comes!" and enunciated thus: EVERYTHING THAT HAS A FACE HAS AN ASS.

It snowed all last night and the ground is covered again, the trees luscious—apple blossoms pink and white and tender green in the creamy white snow.

June

It's like a Charlie Chaplin sequence—everybody's mooning dreamily around in Buddhaland, the sun is shining, all is glorious and blissy, and then BAM, a speed-up! Movements become jerky, things drop and fall and fly out of people's hands, machines overheat and explode, the assembly line piles up on itself, neckties catch in the cogs, people fall into vats. That's what Beloved's office has been like for a few days. Not to mention that at my house the grass is growing about five inches a day and the dishes are piled so high they are *out* of the sink. Let's not even speak of what awaits me at her office, or what is not getting done at all. But somehow, panic and despair included, it is quite all right. Inside the sun is shining, steady and serene.

As to what you call your critical mind and pedantic speech: me, too, as you know. That's the person I call the Meddling Fool, the one who thinks she knows what's going on with everyone and what they ought to do about it (blue jays) and doesn't really understand why everyone isn't just prostrate with gratitude and delight at her limitless stream of helpful suggestions and interventions. The two principal injunctions I'm currently receiving from the universe are: DON'T MEDDLE and DON'T DEFEND. Not bad precepts, huh?

July

Oh, life overflows with jewels. Today they sparkle, diamond-like, on every tree, bush, flower, and blade of grass as rain drenches the landscape, weighs down the lupine so there is a carpet of purpose (of course I meant to say "purple," but isn't it wonderful to think we can walk on a carpet of purpose?) and deep rose blossoms mingling with delicate white potentilla and perky yellow Creeping Jenny in the garden bed.

I am feeling quite sad this last day or two, a little tender, a little raw. As one relationship after another falls away, I am freer and freer of the kinds of ordinary ties that limit one to time, place, obligation. There is no one who really needs me, in fact, except Sister. That is a remarkable freedom. *[A slight misconception here.* Everyone *needs us.]*

I told Beloved that in my heart of hearts mine is a secret path, no one would ever know; that it is always a shock to my system to be called upon to pray in public and such; and that at the same time I am aware that countless beings are as thirsty spiritually as I have been, and I have had the unspeakable good fortune to stumble upon a spring of living water—and I know I am a cup. I told her I am thinking about retreat.

How light, how insubstantial, the burden
Of my ignorance, once having seen
THAT
From which all things arise, pure,
Pure, primordially pure!
Praise, praise, praise!

August

Here is the color of the day: green, at its most lush after a sweet late-summer rain in the night. In the woods the greens are deep black, brown, red-black, and shiny gray-green on the poplar branches. Little sparkles dance on field grass, and the great white pine behind my house is like a comforter, green, plump, and holy, the Great Tree of Peace. The sky holds promise of more rain to come, deeper greens.

I gave up my college teaching job on Monday, seeing clearly the internal message that had been coming for weeks: "Do nothing that you do not do with your whole heart. Put your spiritual purpose first. Drop everything. Just do it." So I said farewell to colleagues and students, stepped into the car, turned on the ignition, and drove away. Liberation flowed around me like silken scarves, joy surged through my body. Every piece I put down returns as immense energy. I feel as if I'm leaping off the cliff, doing loop-de-loops in a plane of light, going to sea, joining the circus, running away from home with a gypsy band. Nothing's the same and everything's the same. There's a sense of hilarity, joy, tears, and laughter indistinguishable. Falling in love, singing old songs: "You've got all of me," "Waltz me around again, Buddha," "Singin' in the light, just singin' in the light." I'm a postmenopausal girl, giddy with freedom, Dharma's embrace.

Barbara, remember this: Fall back on what you *know* to be true, don't get caught in eddies of confusion and emotion. Remember this.

Aware of choosing not to follow the emotions and thoughts but rather to bring mind back to simple truth. This makes life *really different.* It also means that in those moments when I at some level choose not to be awake I am choosing simple and complex *untruth*—such as "I am angry," "she's a pain," "the world is a mess," and so on. Beloved said the other day, "Ifs and buts are just excuses; the first thing is simply to be honest." I put that together with something she said to me years ago: "Just stop telling lies." I asked her what she meant (of course I pride myself—there you have it—on being a truth-sayer) and she said, "Lies like 'I'm like this because such-and-such happened to me,' 'I am a this or a that,' 'This is the way I am,' and all that crap. Just tell the truth." What she meant was tell the Naked Truth.

I am saying YES to the only thing I have ever wanted in my whole life, from early childhood right to this very moment.

Dearest friend, how wonderful! Everything is just popping up out of the luminosity in response to our thoughts, words, and actions. Forms arising, spontaneous, fresh, utterly humorous. Ain't it a *hoot*!

September

My good friend's mother-in-law came to visit. Each time I saw her I completely blissed out, with that skin-tingly feeling I get when I've been outside all day in the sun and just feel languorous and happy. This sweet, round, soft-skinned mother's heart is so radiant, so clear, that even I can feel it! I said to her, "I'm so happy I've met you. I just love you." She replied simply, "Everyone tells me that. When you have a good heart, people feel good." *[We like to call It by the Big Names—enlightenment, awakening, realization—but I remember my lama, when first meeting us, asking simply, "Do you have a good heart?"]*

I spend so much energy girding myself 'round. I am clenching my teeth at night, my back and shoulders are tight as steel, not to mention my facial muscles, and definitely let's not talk about my gut. I am tying myself up in knots of resistance and defense—against . . . ? The emptiness itself, I think. That which I AM. It is the stupidest paradox imaginable. It is *the* paradox upon which all other paradoxes are predicated. You and I have laughed about it: remember bodhi peeking out at bodhi who's looking for bodhi? I know I have and I suspect you have cried about it, and I'm sure both of us have cursed about it. When I am not frustrated I find it comical beyond words.

I had a very interesting experience on the road the other day—the kind that's so quick, so subtle, that if you don't have someone to tell it to you might forget it even happened—but I have you, so here it is. I'm driving along, mind doing its usual 85 mph frolic. Coming toward me is a monster truck—huge, bright red, silver chrome. Bearing down on me. Fast, heavy. The road's very narrow; if I have a moment's lapse of attention or swerve even a little, WHOMP. And then it happens: the thought manifests in this experience that occurs in mind, body, energy, sky, Earth, somewhere, nowhere. I and the truck meet head-on—and we drive right through each other! I feel it, see it, hear it. The molecules interpenetrating then separating again. The materialization dissolving into energies just zooming, literally, *through* one another and out the other side. Nothing passing through nothing, the uncompounded interpenetrating the uncompounded. The main sensation is a big WHOOSH, and the truck opening up, molecule by molecule, all in an instant. When I'm out the other side I am just calm, clear, and very *interested*: "Oh, this is how the old ones walk through walls—because they understand emptiness, the insubstantiality of forms, the appearance as display, no ground or substance. This is how it's done."

Cool, huh? Your friend Dorje doesn't get to hang out in the emptiness but she gets to see it, taste it, hear it, feel it in the midst of the Ten Thousand Things. *[Oh, how fortunate a practitioner am I! Praise, praise, praise!]*

In the days since I last wrote to you what I have been most aware of is the radiance. Light is flooding, flowing, filling, radiating, expressing, healing, marrying, *being*. There is nothing that is not That.

I read recently the phrase "core belief," and that night as I was falling asleep I asked myself what my core belief is in this life. Instantaneously the response was, "That I am one with God, the divine, the One." I was startled, then realized that absolutely, that is it, exactly, and has always been. And that my Great Suffering in this lifetime—the thought that I am *separate* from God, truth—has been actually the *proof* of that inner truth ever shining in my heart-mind. If I didn't absolutely know that *It Is, I Am, We Are One,* there could be no thought of separation, no pain of separation, no longing for union. I, and we all, have never been other than whole, have never *not* known what is true, have never wanted other than that, in our deepest core. *["The longing is the love"—that is what it means.]*

•

Perfection is the natural state, and I know that I shall stabilize in view, but in this time I am heavily involved in things of this world: working with Beloved, community building with the sangha, renovating my cottage *[for the extended retreat I have been planning for a long time]*. These activities are directed to spiritual ends, and yet they all concern forms, forms that will fall away. I imagine the forthcoming retreat as the time this mind relaxes into its natural state. What if I never attain that? Will I then have wasted these weeks, months, years of activity that might instead have been devoted to contemplation, quiet, rest for the weary mind? These questions are what arise for me. Don't think, dear friend, that you must answer them. Only my own answers can help me now.

•

YEARS NINETEEN
&
TWENTY

The Hauling Rocks Retreat · Karma 101
The real work begins right here · I am willing
In the odd flatness of this retreat · Cut through! · Sacred sewer
On the rack of their suffering · My ally, my best friend
Bridge of hair · "To B or Not to B" · She burns down my house
The precise point of tension · Free fall

The Hauling Rocks Retreat

[Now I enter retreat, for three to six years, perhaps more. I have loved the careful creation of the retreat place, my cottage near my teacher now a bright, clear space for practice, secluded and comfortable for Sister and me, looking out on the lovely little meditation park I have drawn out of our forest glade. [173]

In the preceding months, however, I have become a pustule of pride and rebellion. I know in my heart that I should not go into retreat in anything but a state of harmony with my teacher—but I also feel, keenly, that I can do nothing now except go into retreat. It is an inner imperative: go practice in seclusion. Though disquieted, I proceed.

It is like dying and being born simultaneously as the gates close behind me. And if Beloved and I hadn't already seen innerly that this retreat might be a bit unusual, what happened with those gates would have been a clue. Heavy, solid, custom-built cedar gates, to seal me off from the world. Three times great winds burst them open, blow them flat; two times I have them repaired; the third time I leave them where they fall, to be covered by leaves, pine needles, snow, and dust.]

---

173. In the East, the tradition of years and decades spent in solitary retreat is alive and well, and there are Western practitioners, too, in them thar hills. For me to envisage a retreat of three to six years or more was thus neither unheard of nor impossible. To do it alone rather than with a group was perhaps less common at the time in the United States; I was very fortunate to be with a teacher and community who understood and supported this intention.

November and December

Beloved reassured me of her blessings and they were very present: lovely, fresh, joyous, the outrageous snow dropping in great bursts. Her last words to me: "I pray your practice will reveal those habitual patterns that obscure the true nature of your mind." *[A potent prayer, indeed. This retreat will be my Karma 101—intensive, intimate study of karmic cause and effect, and my salvation in this time.]*
      My heart is heavy—"wherein the salt has lost its savor" comes to mind—but the burden is light: "The obscuring patterns have no substantiality," she reminded me. *[How I and those who rely upon me rely upon those words.]* Even with this heaviness, when I sat to practice it was as if I were continuing directly from last retreat—uninterrupted practice, continuous attention. *[And the same in all succeeding retreats: one continuous thread.]*[174]

I have vowed to realize absolute truth, so why snivel and whine at what displeases me, and rejoice and grasp at what pleases me, in the realm of relative truth? What she keeps giving me are guideposts for the absolute.

Am physically quite awkward, clumsy—knocking things over, bumping, spilling, dropping, lurching. So much chafing and rebelliousness. Energy not caught up in emotional storms, mental confusion, is available for practice. And for *compassion*.
      Maybe beginning to understand something about what I often preach to others: that real spiritual development begins when we choose to take responsibility for our lives, our minds: our karma. *[And our aspirations.]*

I would like long to remember tonight's vast starry new moon sky, the ground shining white, the canopy inky and deep, and the stars *blazing*— glory, glory, glory—phenomenal reality surging forth like a torus ring with enormous energy, wrapping back again into the vastness-emptiness—the grace of the guru streaming compassion, activity unceasing, display ever new, and I both observer and a part of it all. *[In this moment I see, Oh,*

---

174. My practice in this time: meditation, recitation, prayer, contemplation, study—and looking at my mind and my conduct, searching out the patterns that obscure.

I could simply relax into this "other" reality—and I draw back, not willing to abandon clinging to conventional perception and experiencing. Like the day, early in my time with Beloved, sitting by the bay. She asked, "What do you see?" "A pathway in the light." "Are you ready to walk that pathway?" "I don't know." That meant no. Doubt is a locked door, willingness the key.]

•

As the teachings about karma sink in, I am relieved of some of my sorrow at thinking I have wasted this life's "open door" opportunity—for no matter the potential, potential is only part of the picture. Karma shapes dispositions *[tendencies]* as well as actions. Understanding troubling experiences as karmic effects evokes acceptance, compassion—and *optimism.* The traces are maturation *[karmic seeds ripening, coming to completion],* and their information can be useful, now, in creating future effects by present actions.

Well, I have *no idea* how anyone really practices in ordinary life—I could pass the entire day at all the things that appear necessary before even entering the shrine room! *[And most of us pass entire lifetimes at all the things that appear necessary before turning our minds to truth, our hearts to the Great Love.]*

In this lifetime my greatest suffering has been the sense of spiritual failure and despair. Never do I want another being to experience these sufferings. *I will walk beside.*

It is the shadows that reveal the great beauty of the mountain in bright daylight. This evening I just wanted to honor the light in its stately passage toward dusk and night, its painterly passage across the face of the mountain, its elegiac passage from the land, from the peak, from the sky itself. This was a way of honoring Luella as she approaches death, her stately passage. *[Luella is a community member with cancer. At the onset of her illness she asked me to accompany her to the end, "no matter what happens," and I agreed to do so—if I were not in retreat. However, about two weeks before I enter retreat her condition sharply worsens, she enters a residential hospice, and I am "it," her designated caregiver. Thus, right from the beginning, as Beloved and I have seen, the retreat does not look quite the way we might have anticipated.]*

•

The disrespect I have shown Beloved, from ignorance and pride *[and perhaps also from not really understanding how to be a true practitioner, a true disciple]*—thinking of this I become despondent. I don't know if I have ever totally opened my heart to her, allowed her blessings to enter and soften me. *[I am forgetting the early part, where all was new to me in spiritual relationship and practice; where I myself was new for a moment, like a child, in wonder and gratitude. Before the real work began: walking and falling and standing again. Seven times fall down, eight times stand up.]*

There's some fear here, not far below the surface. I am seeing, in me, doubt in the teacher. It is my own vision that is at fault here, for in truth she is a buddha, effulgent and all-embracing. *[Doubting self, doubting others: same. I must recognize the habitual tendency to doubt as my own mind's production. Here, I am still conceptualizing, intellectualizing. Seeing it nakedly will demand far more of me.]*

> Sun on new snow
> Remember now!
> The pristine nature

Seems she's shining her intense light into the dark corners where PRIDE has been hanging on—stiff and ugly, pitiful, unnecessary. Thank you, Beloved.

Is it just PRIDE that forms my aspiration to enlightenment, that makes me practice, keeps me on the path? Do I have time to purify this, sufficient courage and commitment? It's almost as if I am starting from the very beginning here, as if I have never yet taken on the project of myself. *[That is exactly what pride is, isn't it? The "project of myself."]*

•

> Outrageous expectation is aspiration without creation of the cause
> … It is self-cherishing which produces outrageous expectation. [175]

I'm in a state of shock and dismay as the *nature of selfishness* is revealed.

---

175. Dharmarakshita, *The Wheel of Sharp Weapons*, 58. This was my primer in this time, like a grammar of self-grasping and karma, bringing me needed conceptual understanding and vocabulary with which to mine my mind.

As long as there is self-grasping we can't really see *anything* as it really is, can we? It infiltrates every relationship, every thought, every emotion, every bodily act, every word, every dream, every hope and fear. *But not every aspiration.* If my aspiration prayers are somewhere recorded, there is a record of my buddha nature singing out, calling me forth.

[*This is looking directly at the root of our suffering. We* must *look right at it, see it naked, unadorned—just like this—appearing yet empty. Ignorance is illusory. Truth is the only source of truth.*]

❖ Dreams in which I'm being given a chance to see how a *selfless* person thinks and behaves. ❖

The glimpses of the absolute, the Dharmakaya: my only moments of true peace and ease in this lifetime. I never thought about it as karma before, the profound, pervasive mental conflict, pain, doubt, and torment I have lived with. What is it like for others? Do some people actually move through life with inner peace?

Yes! The real work begins right here:

> We should think in this way: "Previously I had not recognized this energy of self-cherishing, but through the kindness of the guru and the Dharma I have caught him. I have now apprehended the thief who had been sneaking into my thoughts and stealing my wealth of positive karma. I have finally caught this worst of the worst enemies, for the worldly enemy steals merely the materials of this life, but the self-cherishing attitude steals the opportunities of eternity. . ."[176]

●

It seems I am needing to be more honest here. I think I am wanting to move on. My *attachment* to this form of relationship with my teacher, this "identity," has gone on longer than the *reality* of it, I see. So just let it go. Let the veils fall away, revealing the true nature. That's all.

Bringing firewood in—walking, felt as if body had lost something—some solidity—felt light like air, air moving through air.

---

176. Dharmarakshita, *The Wheel*, 54–55; Geshey Ngawang Dharghey's commentary to stanza 49.

January

All form   purity
      all sound   primordial
           all thought   arising from

I take refuge in this truth, its simple facticity.

Eye infection. Illness makes practice more urgent—and more difficult to accomplish. But I have already said I would give everything to attain buddhahood, so what is there to fear at the possibility of losing another body part—or the whole body itself? *[Or the teacher?]*

Just returned from seeing the doctor, shaking, tearful, contracted. I want to say it's just hypersensitivity because of intensive practice—and what I really think is that *this is the way we really are*: incredibly sensitive, touched in every nerve in our interactions with one another. *Interbeing.* Exquisitely tuned to one another, even when we are doing our best not to be, *nous entre-sommes, j'entre-suis, vous entr'êtes.* [177]

I was really terrifying myself there in the shrine room this afternoon. All felt dead, like ashes in the mouth, thinking of "moving on" and feeling what it would be like without the heart of my heart, Beloved. But I am *willing* to go through this. I am willing to go through whatever it takes to get to the other side, beyond delusion and duality. *I am willing.*

The incalculable blessing—to be on retreat, to have such a teacher, to let these poisons come to the surface to be boiled off. Anything that comes up is calling for purification *now*, and is therefore *possible* to purify. First thing: stop reacting to this "stuff" as if it were solid. Just let it come, let it go.

Without getting involved in shame and guilt, just recognizing: In this life *[the only life I can see, and that only in fragments, but it's true of every life, for each of us]* I have committed many wrongs, "defective actions." They give rise to inner torment, from little contractions to large waves of reaction. I know the karmic consequences are my own—but I am wanting to dissolve the reaction.

---

177. We inter-are, I inter-am, you inter-are. See Thich Nhat Hanh, *Interbeing.* See also The Order of Interbeing: www.orderofinterbeing.org.

[Here is a key to working with karmic fruition: Grasp nothing, neither push anything away. Create no new cause as old cause resolves. Let it come, let it go. And rejoice gratefully, sing songs of praise: the worse it gets, the better it is. Padmasambhava told Yeshe Tsogyal, "When the lake of misery overflows while you try to engage in spiritual practice, it is a fact that your evil karma and obscurations are being purified."[178]

And here is a key to this strange retreat: an ordinary person beginning to understand the workings of karma. Practice, study, and close examination of my own mind and life, pointing through *material illusion, begin to shred my conventional notions of cause and consequence. Like a chilled, lumbering planet, my thinking begins slowly to turn on a new axis. I begin to take responsibility for my mind.]*

It's so completely simple, once I see it: *All* my sufferings, doubts, violence, torments, inner anguish, and outer disharmonies—*all* arise from my own deluded thoughts, words, and actions, *all*. There is no "one" and no "thing" to blame, no mysterious "cause" or "something wrong with me." It's that I've *done* wrong, knowingly and unknowingly. What I didn't know, or really understand, was what that meant.

In the odd flatness of this retreat this simple fact emerges. In a more dramatic and arresting landscape, it might not ever have caught my attention.

I could get discouraged or dramatic at this point, or even take on an identity as "one with heavy negative karma." Let's not. But really, I had *no idea*! How could I not have seen this before?

•

So vulnerable:
    fragile, like a baby.
Yet within, some tiny spark:
    resolve—
    endoskeletal strength,
    not just exoskeletal,
        morally speaking.

Dangerous moment. Facing the opportunity, now, today, this very moment, to make *the* shift: from self-grasping and ego-motivated practice

178. Tsogyal, *Dakini Teachings*, 67.

to practice motivated by commitment to *others'* enlightenment. "If I'm not going to become enlightened, why bother?" We've been here before. Even when very young: If I'm not Rembrandt, why paint?

The potential is vast. So is everyone's. *That's* why continue. *[Yes, this is the shift, the one that opens the path beyond individual liberation: the ultimate path, the path to buddhahood.]*

Memories of Beloved telling me to teach and me begging her—yet again!—not to, not fit, still too coarse, too filled with ego. "Teach from your experience," she says. *[Motivated by great love and compassion, we can offer even our ignorance to free others from theirs.]*

Can I, will I, persevere? Praying for courage, commitment, devotion, dedication.

•

I wish I'd done more questioning at an earlier period so that now, doubts satisfied, I could just settle down and move forward. *[But it isn't about* doubts, *it is about* doubting: *not about a fault perceived or imagined in myself, my teacher, or anyone else, but about the habitual tendency to look for one—what my Zen correspondent described as my "remarkable gift for finding the imperfection in the perfection."*

This "gift" is a karmic tendency in my mindstream, as well as an artifact of undeveloped practice: not understanding how to look directly at truth. As a gift, however, yes! To be able to see the imperfect in the perfect is a gift, powerful and precise: mind's awake, vivid clarity, its vajra quality. What recognizes imperfection is perfection: what sees confusion is wisdom.

The recognizing is the thing: this is what we must cultivate, repeatedly. To recognize what arises in the pristine purity of natural mind, to recognize its nature as one with natural mind, to recognize it dissolving like water into water: this is uncontrived practice on natural mind.]

Prayerfully, innerly, I asked for her help with this. Came the unperturbed reply: "All this is just the manifestation of your doubt in yourself. Don't doubt yourself. Just keep going." *[Ah, such compassion and patience with this recalcitrant disciple. "Just keep going" is a wisdom blade, and in the coming short, intense period that blade will lay open to daylight what I need to see.]*

•

Luella seems to be preparing to die like an ordinary person—social visits, refusing to hear or utter the D-word, reading novels. [179] Of course, this is just appearance; her inner reality may be quite different. My job here is to dissolve all preconception and judgment, love her for who she is, and help her in the best way I can. *[Truly, I know nothing about Luella's inner state or her realization. She will die like an eagle: powerful, certain, unerring. And reading novels now seems to me a fine way to enjoy a leisurely approach to death. Opening and closing books of fictive lives—isn't that exactly what's happening?]*

The stove and I, both burning these days as if the wood is wet. My heart isn't in it. I feel sad and despondent and dis-*courage*-ed, dis-*heart*-ened. Even my pens are running out of ink! Is this PRIDE?—so ugly, like a dirty sock stuffed in the throat, smoldering, damp. Funky.

Talk about self-doubt! I've got about 3,000 recitations to go and I'm thinking, "Why bother? I'll never make it." That's it! That's just exactly what's eating at me! That thought! Banish it, banish it, stomp on its head! Trample it, trample it, pay it no heed! It is not the absolute state—so CUT THROUGH. Bodhicitta is the medicine here. To give up on myself is to give up on a sentient being, and I *will not.*

Doesn't anyone ever write about this stuff *[self-doubt, teacher-doubt, discouragement, resistance]*? And how it plays out in the relationship with the guru? I mean, concretely and graphically, not prettying it up as a "hero" story but showing all the hideousness, the evil thoughts? Oh yes, one has—a woman, of course: Irina Tweedie. I disdained her, old weeper like me, but kept the book, just this minute ran to get it, the first words I read are: "I could not face [looking at my diary] before . . . It was like a panic; I dreaded it. Too much suffering is involved in it; it is written with the blood of my heart. A slow grinding down of the personality is a painful process." [180] Yet she had courage and faith enough to go through it. Will I?

Pride. The battle is joined, the enemy is named. If I don't go through this, how can I ever help others?

---

179. The D-word: death, that is, which I never once heard her say, Luella-just-as-she-was, who spoke of cancer only as "my alleged disease," never once taking it on even as it was taking her out, unwaveringly asserting her path defined solely by herself.

180. Tweedie, *Daughter of Fire,* ix.

•

During these heavy, leaden, bleak, desolate days, the bodhicitta rising in my mouth when I recite—sweet, light, nectar-like.

It is not really that I desire to leave my teacher—it's that I want OUT OF THE BOX!

I am praying for surrender, and . . . I DON'T TRUST HER is what comes roaring to the surface.

This is terrifying stuff.

If I am unable to go the next step, what will happen? I will leave her? She will, finally, kick me out? I will die? I will search for another teacher? It will be as vapid, without heart and breath, as this retreat seems to be, because of broken or damaged commitments? *[Looking back on this record decades later, it seems to me this retreat is anything but vapid. It is more like a power mower! But I, pushing the mower, am choking on the fumes, blinded by the debris flying up in my face.]*

All these years I have thought that I trusted her deeply, completely, on the inner plane. I thought my resistance was just my personality reacting to her personality. I am seeing that it is much, much deeper than that—it is very deep—I really don't *trust. [She who pours out the teachings, the blessings, she who took me in, she who guides and forgives, who loves and corrects—how can I not trust her? But how can I trust her, or anyone? I do not trust myself.]*

Suspicion. Is this a closed door—or a window?

If all along, hidden in the depths, there has been this profound mistrust, lack of faith and confidence *[in myself, in life, in other people—and in recent years projected onto the pristine mirror that is the spiritual guide]*, it would have to surface eventually, wouldn't it? No better time than on retreat. Anywhere else, unsafe. (Well, it *feels* bloody unsafe even here.) It was already surfacing, all along, like the ooze of a failing septic system; by this fall it was getting pretty florid, in outright disgust and rebellion. Well, it is now up, so thickly coating the ground that even I cannot deny what I am smelling and stepping in. It is the ooze of my own foul hatred and mistrust, my suspicion, judgment, disgust, paranoia, self-interest, and on and on—*[I am HOWLING with laughter as I transcribe this from the handwritten journal—what a HOOT! This is WONDERFUL STUFF, this is IT—the GRACE OF THE GURU, this is the SACRED SEWER boiling over, the very STUFF OF ENLIGHTENMENT!]*

Everything is so obvious once you let yourself *see* it! With this mistrust eating away at the very foundations, *how* could I build anything wholesome? So I am *blessed* to see it, *grateful* to see it, thanking you on my *knees*, Beloved, for letting me see this corrosive, corrupting, contaminating, destructive, erosive, explosive, vitiating, inimical, maniacal, hysterical, florid, septic, seeping, weeping, DISTRUST, MISTRUST, lack of faith and confidence, paranoia, hatred, aggression, aversion, repulsion, revulsion, disgust, dislike. *[My all-time favorite negativity litany—I just let 'er rip, laughing and crying my way through this outrageous outburst.]*

Good God, I am insane. "Well, so is everyone else," she has frequently replied to me when I've claimed this insanity as, for example, a reason not to teach.

Today's the day to CLEAN THE BATHROOM! UNPLUG THE DRAIN! GET IT ALL MOVING! Now I don't know what happens, but at least I'm seeing the hairball in the pipes!

This morning: an ecstasy of relief to see and say what's been going on in me.
    This evening: so now what happens?
    Does this mean I have lost my faith? Or never had genuine faith?

As I entered the shrine room I wanted to back away, turn and run. But I went in, and what I found was that somewhere in heart-mind-consciousness there is, not faith, but Knowledge. I know the absolute state, the primordial purity, exists within and all around. I rely upon That.
    And when I went out to place offerings on the ground, on this crystalline, below-freezing, absolutely clear night, I was calling for the help of all buddhas and bodhisattvas in fulfilling my buddhic aspirations in this lifetime. Whatever motivation, faith, belief, and commitment are dying or peeling away, or have been corrupted in me with pride and its murderous hatreds—whatever has gone—this pure aspiration and intention remain: a diamond light at the very core.

This buddhic aspiration—it is not at all about thinking I *can* realize in this lifetime, it is because there is nothing else for me. What else could there possibly be?

There is nothing to fall back on but truth. If I lose the teacher, too, there is still that: the absolute, revealing itself directly.

•

A brief flash, this afternoon, of how it might be—to hold all suffering and confusion as positive, as *blessings*, each one bringing me closer to absolute truth. I felt like a bowsprit when I was thinking like that, waves and wind breaking around me, flowing swiftly, cleanly forward, nothing holding, cleaving samsara's ocean.

❖ Dreamt of "living waters"—water bearing the imprint or blessing, the "enlightenment quality." ❖

•

> Let it all go
> no teacher, no sangha
> no buddhas, no bodhisattvas
> no practice, no enlightenment
> no nirvana, no samsara
> no grasping, no repulsion, no bewilderment
> no truth, no not-truth
> no I, no you
> no nothing, no something

I feel as if I am dying—torn apart—oh, wonderful, if "I" am dying! Let no idea of self remain, just let them all dissolve—including "too late," "still okay," "keep on," "service," "panic," "self, not-self." And "progress"? That, definitely, can go. How *could* I have been making any "progress"? The work is to become free of self, and all my efforts have been bent on *maintaining* self. Now, for a little moment, at least, I am going to rest here in this bardo of no goal, no teacher, no measuring stick, no enlightenment, no practice, no service, no retreat, no nonretreat.

•

These friends in the samsaric web—it's like a rack. I pray, "Break my hardness of heart on the rack of their suffering."

We're actually *unable* to be in right relationship. With our beautiful gifts and potentials we are tripping over ourselves, hitting ourselves in the face. We build monuments to our injuries—then we worship the injuries, as if they are the reality. *That* is what cripples us: not knowing where to turn for healing and truth. Remembering this, may our minds turn towards the Dharma.

I feel as if I've been hauling rocks all day. This is what it's like in the self-prison. Free, one can walk through walls—I already know—but it seems I'm serving another term—and still looking for the damn wall-switch! Where *is* it? Not to mention the key to the cell door, which I've got somewhere. I've really got to improve my housekeeping. But look! High up there in the wall there's a tiny window—I can see a little patch of sky! Is it enough? Can I get out through there? Bring it in here? Oh yes, seems to me I remember something about that . . .

I just saw an *ermine*! At the suet feeder! Pure white but for tiny black tips. I am breath-taken, trembling with astonishment and joy, my body hairs standing up all over!

Unless I am directly seeing, contemplating, or cognizing the absolute state, anything I am thinking is delusion. So what's a girl to do?

> Let it go,
>   let it go,
>   let it all go.

•

Sacred outlook—last time I was on retreat it seemed to arise spontaneously, warmly, often hilariously. This time I feel very rooted in relative reality, phenomenal appearances: hauling rocks, hard time on the chain gang. It seems this is the level of work I *need* to be doing right now, I with my tendency to fly up to the ideal realms, to long for "spiritual" home, to chafe and pull away from material life. Very good for me to engage my own efforts, not just be carried along on the outflow of divine effulgence. I keep on keeping on—that's my commitment. Hauling rocks!

It is *pride* that has me wanting everything, even the guru, to be just ordinary *[and doubt, pride's other face, that has me wanting to remain so myself]*—and pride can be incinerated: in the fires of devotion and longing. Let self dissolve, melt away: in the fire of bodhicitta.

•

An arrow of anger from Luella when I visited, and now I am as if sundered, weeping in my woodshed, practically doubled over in pain—"This seems hopeless, doesn't it, this project of dissolving the ego?" I *threw* myself into practice with this pain, and as the breath was drawn in the heart seemed to crack open a little more—the pain like a hot wire to the quick—seemed I had never really allowed any pain to get that far in before—but maybe it was already there—don't know which was from out and which from in—

Feeling much appreciation for the many who have remained my friends for so long, and better understanding of those who have not.

❖ I'm being hired by the police department. Someone asks me how I work and I explain that the work happens through me: I'm like a fire always burning. ❖

•

February

> Oh, empty, empty, empty,
> Full, full, full—
> Give it all, all, all,
> Hold nothing back,
> Hold nothing—

This is the bridge of hair across the chasm of fire—the very moment that the guru is a dire necessity. [181] This is the invitation to the dissolution of the constructed self, without which the true nature cannot be realized, and the self cannot dissolve itself, vanquish, conquer, tame, subdue itself—*cannot.*

---

181. "The path of love is like a bridge of hair across a chasm of fire"—see Tweedie, *Daughter of Fire*, v.

I see your face on the other side, lit by the fire below and the fire within. You are calling to me, "Keep coming, keep walking, keep moving, don't give up now."

There is no drama here. There is no time for drama. This is truly life and death. *[Beyond the physical, so far beyond.]*

Is this even possible? When I am still fighting her as if my life depended on that instead of on surrendering?

But she is *on my side,* my ally, my best friend, helping me do what I long to do. Oh, Beloved, my best friend!

I know nothing here.

Would like to think these are the ego's death throes, but I think it's really our first face-to-face meeting.

[This next paragraph, written near the beginning of retreat and then forgotten, was placed in the unwritten journal on this particular empty page like a little terma, *to be revealed when needed. How precious was the moment, in the midst of this great suffering, in which I turned the page of my journal and found this mind-treasure.]*[182]

To remember the Dharmakaya, the void nature, the Absolute,
the True Nature, is to have a Teacher within, ever accessible, ever kind,
ever relieving fear, suffering, grasping, shame or doubt.
This is the kindest of gurus, whose perfections are ever evident
and ever consoling, who always understands and renders understandable,
who is the essence of forgiveness and compassion,
whose every manifestation is compassion.
This is the jewel, the pearl beyond price, the heavenly nectar,
the sweet crystalline water of remembrance.
I don't have to be seeing this Truth with direct perception
in order to be in pure and whole relationship with it—for it is who I AM;
and simply by remembering it I am freed
from doubt, shame and torment,
and delivered into the chamber of primordial purity and peace.

182. In texts and objects placed in the Earth and in the minds of certain disciples, Padmasambhava hid away teachings to be revealed in later times, when most needed. Such treasure objects, treasure texts, and treasure teachings are called *termas* (Tibetan), and those who find them are called treasure revealers, *tertöns.* Termas and tertöns are still today doing their profound, liberating work.

Can't get anything right. In the kitchen, thinking, "Oh, I'm about to do something right!"—and poof! it was wrong. I don't want to get dramatic, but this is really how it seems here in samsara. *[These ups and downs, from mind* terma *to kitchen clutching, seem so compelling, as from one minute to the next sense experience swamps direct inner knowing. But this is just perceptual and conceptual habit. The subtly known will endure; the sensory will not.]*

•

Bodhi making offerings of bodhi to bodhi. I am placing my heart at the feet of the guru.

Inner scenario arising spontaneously during practice tonight: Beloved beats me mercilessly, friends looking on aghast—then she calls me a dog, ties me up, makes me eat dog food and sleep on the floor. Throughout, I am laughing at us both and playing the dog quite wholeheartedly—and the dog food turns into nectar!

I made an aspiration prayer of pure longing, to embody the true nature, to liberate all beings—and the prayer rose straight up, like a clear note of light, was immediately received—and blessings descended through the crown, stilling me on the long-working cushion.

I am bursting with energy—joyous effort—moments of remembering emptiness—

I am in Guru Rinpoche like the clapper in the bell.

An *inward* gaze that is new to me—probably everyone else has known it for years, but I just found it. Allows me to perceive the deity within. *[The inward attention, yes—seeing the inner sacred space, recognizing the luminous nature within, empty yet vividly appearing, fresh and radiant.]*

Yesterday's mandala offerings were like shoveling heavy sand uphill— could hardly lift my hand, the offering plate was so heavy—once lifted, I couldn't remember what I was supposed to do with it. I think it was Yeshe Tsogyal who got me through it, as I recalled her accomplishment, imagined that even with her superhuman dedication and great realization there must have been times when continuing to practice called for simple endurance and commitment through deep exhaustion, discouragement, and—well, perhaps not in her case, but certainly in mine—doubt. And I got through it yesterday—to reach this day on which, if conditions remain favorable, this practice I've been doing for thirteen years shall be complete. May the merit cascade down upon all wandering and floundering here in the samsaric wilderness.

Tremulous, eager, reluctant, I step slowly into the practice—weeping, my heart lotus soft and moist, my voice trembling—oh, oh, oh. The same quality that yesterday was heavy, exhausted, grueling, today was like honey in the veins, languorous, warm, caressing. And the practice is complete.

What'd I think, there'd be bells and flashing lights? Next . . .?

•

I'm in a bardo, no idea what to do with myself. *[The thirteen-year practice commitment completed, what now?]* Breathe in whatever is not the absolute state, the true nature—breathe out the absolute, the true—always, for everyone and everything—

[In this gap, this opening, I reach deep within to speak from my heart in a letter to Beloved—resigning my position as a teacher, resigning all my "roles" in her spiritual organization.]

Something is definitely different—as if a layer has been removed—from the inside. I went into the shrine room and couldn't find the light, or herself. Panic just below the surface: Have I ruined everything? Has she cut me loose, turned out the lights, pulled the plug, rolled down the blinds? Reminded myself of *her* vows, and of all those who've come and gone who are still held in the net of her love and compassion. *[Innerly I hear her say, "But you will want to teach again someday"—and my immediate response: "That will be then, this is now."]*

Let it go,
    let it go,
        let it all go.

I think I am *choosing* to travel this way—all the minutiae of inertia, resistance, ego, duality, the Three Poisons: I must experience them in order to free others. She is ever reminding me of what I *know*—with humor, exasperation, disgust, anger, love—but always reminding me. I do know. Now I must pull it all the way through every fiber. *[This, this is the work, in this time, in every time: pulling all the way through every fiber truth and the knowing of truth. Unmistaken, immediate, right now: this moment, then this one, then this one. Seen through this emotion, this thought, this confusion, this merriment, this sorrow, this courage: this, here, now.]*

•

[I sense that it is time to come out of retreat for awhile, and as I await Beloved's response to my request, this little theater spontaneously frolics out onto the page, wry and compassionate.]

TO B OR NOT TO B, IS THAT THE QUESTION?
(A Monologue in Four Voices)

Barbara	(Pacing around the room, muttering to herself) Hmm . . . Wonder what I should do. Does she mean for me just to come out when I'm ready?
BABS	What's the hurry? You only wrote to her a week ago.
Barbara	Yes, but . . .
Babzilla	Oh yeah, she's wanting to "know" something! (Making "screwy" gesture at her forehead)
DorjeB	(Smiling) Just B . . .
Barbara	But how am I supposed to know what to do? When I do what I think is good it seems to displease her, when I ask her I often don't understand her answer or misapply it, and displease her, when I ask others she seems displeased . . .
BABS	(Laughing) Pretty cranky lady, huh?

Babzilla	HAH! Can't win for losin', is that it?
Barbara	No, but ... **(on the verge of tears)** In the practice it's easy—whatever I ask, she's right there, and I always seem to understand…but in ordinary life, whew! I'm always getting into trouble! How am I supposed to approach her?
DorjeB	No separation, no "approach."
BABS	Just B! **(Whirls around, buzzing like a bee)**
Barbara	**(Ducks and swats at the "bee")** But what do I decide about and what do I ask her about?
Babzilla	**(Exasperated)** We need a B-B gun, shoot some holes in her head so she can get some kinda View! Just B, stoopid b, or we'll B-B you!
Barbara	You old hags sure are full of advice! I know you mean well, but really, the only advice I want is *hers*!
BABS	But-but-but! You sound like an outboard motor!
DorjeB	She knows what you need. Just keep practicing . . .
Barbara	But what about my cousin's funeral, my taxes, my broken gates, my—?
Babzilla **BABS** **DorjeB**	**(All together, shouting) Just B!**

•

Of course, doubt. I am working to dissolve pride, ego, self-grasping—and isn't self-doubt the other face of pride? Why *wouldn't* my greatest weakness be encountered here as the Tempter?

I VOW TO CUT THE NET OF DOUBT
FOR MYSELF AND ALL BEINGS,
TO ESTABLISH US ALL IN JOYOUS CERTAINTY.

[See the poison, distill the nectar. Take your own suffering, offer it for the liberation of all, and it will liberate you.]

Do I not have to give up attachment to *all* conceptuality? In some way this is like "abandoning homeland and relatives." [183] I didn't think it would include abandoning teacher, teachings, sangha, and practice, but in some way it does: those concepts, and my attachment to them, whether positive or negative.

I have served the teacher for twenty years, well or badly. It would have been more meritorious and efficacious had I served her for twenty minutes, perfectly.

And then there was the observation, arising in my mind, in her voice: "It's just doubt—it doesn't *mean* anything."

> Put it down, put it down,
>   Put it all down
> Let it go, let it go,
>   Let it all go

No teacher, no teachings, no practice. I am in my cave in the Himalayas, there is no one around, my teacher is dead and left me no instructions, I don't know where my next meal is coming from—and I am vowed simply to practice.

March

I awoke thinking, "Well, here it is, what you most fear: not fulfilling your life purpose and spiritual potential. Looks as if that's the case—and now you get to learn how to live with it."

Just thoughtforms, not the absolute state—just keep practicing.

---

183. "Abandoning homeland and relatives": a reference to the *Thirty-seven Bodhisattva Practices*, verse 2.

Nothing to "make" of it all:
when thoughts, opinions, evaluations arise,
don't go there—
just look 'em in the eye . . .
and don't blink first!

Padmasambhava's blessings! Sweet balm to my heart.
    Rainbows! The grandmotherly protector deity picture in the front
    hallway is emanating a complete rainbow.
        Blackbirds! Their strange, sweetly beautiful metallic call: spring's
        bell.

The stories of spiritual masters: tale after tale of *power*. Energy, voltage.
I see in myself the inertial vector—sleepiness, stasis, desire not to move
or be disturbed. Remembering how Irina Tweedie's master spoke of
the teacher "quickening" the individual, and seeing my desire to control
the speed, slow things down. The "Bye-bye, baby, go on home now"
dream was partly about this—"It's too hard, it's too fast, it's too . . ."
And resenting attempts to stir me up, get me moving—resisting, wanting
to hunker down. How do I think we come to enlightenment? *Gathering*
energy and power, not sitting on it. There's a word I'm looking for;
what is it? Sloth, laziness, indolence, torpor, sluggishness, listlessness,
inactivity, passivity, apathy, languor . . . LETHARGY—that's it. *[The
"yin disease" about which Beloved spoke to me years before.]*

•

In this morning's practice the work, apparently, was to relax—face,
head, jaws, ears, eyes, forehead, back of head, top of head. It lasted
three hours! The OM on Guru Rinpoche's forehead at one point blazes
forth and I feel my own OM light up. At another point I feel a light
touch there; thinking I am once again contracting my forehead, I
relax—but it isn't me, it is the guru's touch. This instant—and it is only
an instant—is such solace, reminding me that the blessing is no further
than my breath, always there, I have only to open myself—and only I
can do that. Oh, I can be taken over, as I have been, by the grace of
the guru, but only I can do the gradual work of *changing my mind*: how
I breathe, how I sit, think, speak, act.

April

Today Earth, sky, and I have been melting—she with soft, soaking spring rain, I with gratitude and longing. It is enough, today, simply to round the beads, one by one, with the mantra in its unceasing rounds in my heart-mind—

Laying bare: Seeing that memories, seemingly so solid and present, can dissolve, do dissolve, shows me that the "real" event, in time and experience, was just as insubstantial as the memory.

"The door is wide open for you in this lifetime, Barbara," she said to me early on. Instead of asking, "How do I go straight through?"—and doing that—I have seemed driven to explore every error and downfall. And it seems as if, somehow, that's by *choice*—not choice to do or be wrong, but choice to test, experience for myself, not just to do what I'm told. Something like that.

All the stuff I am so exercised about is the world of *appearances*—and she keeps giving me the highest teachings: emptiness.

At the end of my practice session—Tsawai Lama's photo on the shrine—he was looking right at me, his eyes were *alive*, he was *there*. Such compassion in his gaze, a look of infinite tenderness—and an almost quizzical cast, as if, "Now really, my dear girl, what are we making such a fuss about, after all?"

In youth I saw this life's task: purify pride. So if I do fail in meeting this life's highest opportunity, that might be the way I succeed in meeting its task. Failure, success—same, when it comes to pride, humility, ego.

I am a fortunate woman, indeed, to have my negative karma being skillfully stirred like this.

•

First daffodil today. And spying Alchemilla's new wavy tendrils of lovely leaf peeking out from beneath winter's debris: "Like that! The true nature so near, inseparable, and all covered with old stuff!" So I go to it, poking, pulling, clearing, doing mantra the while. Clear away the old stuff!

❖ In a book I'm working on for Beloved there is a blank space where the work had been. The message, clear on awaking: let the blanks stay blank, don't fill 'em up. ❖

•

What a tizzy. Kyabje's training course starts in June, on the other side of the country! *[The lama, the lama, my saint, my saint, whom I had met before entering retreat, in whose comet-like tail stream of blessings I am already being drawn forward.]* I want to do it. But what about Luella? If she's still alive, am I free to go or not? When I went to the cushion and called for help all I got were *lines* tying me to Luella! I tugged this way and pulled that way, but I was tied. I felt like crying—in chagrin, frustration, resentment—but I burst out laughing. What a spin! I get to choose: *study* Dharma or *practice* Dharma!

❖ I am standing in a room with an Oriental man—elegant, strong, hair pulled back like a yogi. It is my Tsawai Lama! I go to his room; there is an eyeglass case with small crystals inside, into which I place some crystals of mine. All the crystals break up and intermingle, inseparably. ❖

I want to end retreat. *[Beloved agrees.]* And sometimes it does seems as if I am preparing not just to end retreat, but to leave—just leave—go where I know no one, and just *be*.

•

May

Luella died yesterday.

> Splash of crimson across the road.
> Sparkling blood—deer?
> Shining maple buds—spring!
> Life,
> Death—
> Inseparable

Luella's cremation. *[I sat by the open oven door the whole time.]* Hard: putting her into the oven—that body she fought to hang onto, no longer of use, into the fire! Interesting: the intense purification energy at the beginning. Spectacular and awakening: bodily remains in the roaring inferno, body as light and heat and wind. To see the fire and the ashes, the skull, sternum, and long bones of the legs still intact, was to glimpse emptiness in pure incandescence and dust, a bodily child of Earth and sky returning to light.

Tomorrow I begin three days of completion practices to close this very odd "retreat." I guess I'll keep doing some kind of practice, but without any expectations of spiritual accomplishment. I am sad, deeply so, that I find no window open to rest in the true nature, but I pray that I am planting good seeds that will bring forth good fruit for me and others in some future time.

[The accomplishment is too deep to see. As in the early meditation image of the clockworks, the small wheels whir quickly, flashing with light, while the large wheels circle slowly, solemnly, their movement virtually imperceptible—and their long, invisible turning charges the entire mechanism. The surface turbulence of emotions and ideations has my attention, while the activity of karmic purification is dredging in the deeps. What I have been seeing and experiencing—just as Beloved prayed I might—have been my habitual tendencies of thought, emotion, speech, and conduct: karmic causes, consequences, predispositions. I have had to confront them this starkly in order to recognize them as causes—and to release them. Willingness is key. I am willing to recognize in my own mindstream and actions the faultless, precise play of cause and effect.

The contemplation and practice are purifying, no doubt about it: light banishes darkness. I think that in this instance, though, the suffering itself is also profoundly purifying. Beloved taught that suffering is unnecessary, and I have seen the truth of that, in the absolute. But it is in the relative that we create cause, and in the relative it is usually some form of suffering that purifies our negative karma. Perhaps our own suffering is what allows us to learn fortitude, courage, and compassion for the suffering of others. It has seemed so, for me. And though I'm not qualified to know, I think this strange retreat may have closed the door to the hell realms. If not? Then it has girded me well to penetrate them with love and compassion.]

(End of The Hauling Rocks Retreat)

•

Post-Retreat: Bardo

> [Remembering the Creator's instructions,] they understood that
> the farther they proceeded on the Road of Life and the more
> they developed, the harder it was. That was why their world was
> destroyed every so often to give them a fresh start. [184]

Beloved calls me on the phone, very early in the morning: "I want you
to separate yourself from the community. *["Separate!" Astonishing to
hear this from her mouth, she who taught me "there is no separation"—so I cleave
not to the narrow word but to the vast teaching, through everything to come.]* You
have caused harm—to the community, to me, to yourself—by your
disrespect and negativity. I cannot allow you to continue creating these
heavy karmic consequences."

Words of truth. I am grateful, Beloved, for these words of truth.

"I don't know if you can correct this, Barbara." Me, too, Beloved.
But that feels more real than the inflated expectations and defective
actions of the past.

> Wonderful! She has burned down my house! [185]
> Praise, praise, praise.
> Now let's go weed the garden.

Mind keeps returning to "you have caused harm." I'm sure I have no
understanding of what this means. I am also sure that the most important
thing is not that I have caused harm in the past but that I have the
opportunity now, and from now on, to cause no further harm.

*[This understanding and determination: fruit of Karma 101. As to the harm:
At the time of my expulsion I don't know, specifically, how I have harmed. I don't
yet understand, precisely, the harm that one's own doubt, negativity, and disrespect
can cause to others; at some level, I still think that though they might be annoying
to others, they are actually harmful only to me. I don't create a façade or pretend
I am someone I am not, so nothing is hidden—but with what a friend called my
"devotion, directness, humor, and love," it is easy not to see the unease and doubt
aroused in others by my own. Now, decades later, it is this seeding of doubt that I*

---

184. Waters, *Book of the Hopi*, 22.

185. There's a man whose house burns down. When he comes to Guru
Padmasambhava, devastated, Padmasambhava gives a shout of joy: "Wonderful!" That's how I felt. She torched my house! Wonderful!

think was my harmful activity of body, speech, and mind during these many years.
And doubt, Beloved had told me, is the "most poison of poisons, the most destructive
of energies." It undermines the faith and devotion that open us to the blessings ever
raining down—so to shake the devotion and faith of another is one of the most
grievous of harms. To purify doubt in oneself requires utmost diligence, and though
diligent in many things, I had not uprooted the habit of doubting.

To protect us all, I have to go. By her decisive severing, I am freed to go. Regret
and sadness withal, I am glad to go.]

Here's a good one! ❖ An event at the ashram. The Dalai Lama is there;
he and I laugh, as always. He offers me a massage—he is stripped to
his blinding white Jockey briefs and socks, preparing to walk on me.
Everyone is looking on amazed, none more than I. ❖ Classic sign of
purification in a dream: Tenzin Gyatso to the rescue!

My home—how lovely, how perfect, how shocking to leave it. I wanted
to live quietly, simply, here in my little paradise, learning with the seasons
and cycles of Earth and sky, making gardens, working the land. But I'll
have to leave it some day, so why not now?

In the midst of all this, I am keeping my seat; I believe this is Beloved's
grace, calming, steadying. And really, there seems to be nothing here
to get upset about. I grieve for the harm I've caused and for being
an unworthy student, the loss of community and friends. I am sad
to leave the generous canvas of this land that has been my studio for
ten years. And I rejoice! I am still in the care of my teacher, in every
moment there is the Law *[karma and Dharma]*, there is renewal, there is
generosity, there is transformation—and there is emptiness. Nothing
comes or goes, leaves or stays, grieves or rejoices.

Looks as if I'm *fired*, but really, I'm being *re*-fired, like a worthy pot!
Wonderful!

If she hadn't given me the boot, would I ever have left? And I needed to
leave, for everyone's good —the relationship was unwholesome, riddled
with my egregious ego-grasping. How long has it been too long? And
because I didn't trust my own judgment, didn't allow myself to "know
what I know"? *[Yes. But really, her timing and mine are at one, and perfect.*
She holds me until I want to go—100 percent—then releases me as the archer the
arrow—sharply, purely—at the precise point of tension for swift, unerring flight.

But even that understanding is at the level of personality, interaction, event: relative reality. There is no need to struggle with this and that explanation for what is void in its nature. Dudjom Rinpoche: "One need not erect a fence around a mirage of water."[186] *Nothing comes or goes, leaves or stays, grieves or rejoices.]*

Probably the only thing she could have said to push me out of here was what she did say: "You are causing harm."

June

I told her my deep sorrow and regret at having been a viper at her breast. She replied, "I knew the condition of your mind when I started." Oh why, Beloved, why? *Why* did you let me come close to you, be at the center of our community, occupy positions where I could cause harm to you and the community, and ruin to myself? How, Barbara, how? *How* would this great edifice of ego and pride crumble if it were not exposed? Is it not all just as needed for the work that must be accomplished?

•

There is no ground—I am in free fall.

It appears to be disgrace, exile—but months ago she assured me "there has never been any separation," and I will rely on that. It may look like ruin, loss—but it is the path, and I will rely on that. *[I am stable and certain, shifts in mood and thinking no longer the swinging of the old shutter, the turbulence of the clogged streambed, or the roller coaster's asphyxiating rise and fall—bright and dark dance together now, in mind looking through them to its own nature.]*

> Amazing!
> Greatest hope and aspiration dashed,
> Greatest fear realized—
> And all is well.

[Glancing into the past, now not for trouble but for truth, I find this:] Journal notation from thirty-two years ago, so perfect a reminder right this

---

186. In Ngari Panchen, *Perfect Conduct*, 127.

moment: "Courage sustained / on a high, clear note, / rising and holding, / its trembling / the sign of its strength."

Failed every test
Until this one
Meeting it directly

Let it go,
  let it go,
    let it all go.

•

EPILOGUE

NATURAL LIGHT

EPILOGUE

Natural Light

*L*EAVING HOME, POSSESSIONS, ART, FRIENDS, *everything I have planned and created, the community I thought to grow old with, the teacher herself, the visualization of my life to that moment falling away behind me, none arising before me, suspended in time while moving through space—Sister and I, in a Toyota packed tight as a tick, drive down the lane one bright fall day, and simply head out.*

The next decade or so sees the coming and going of familiar "stuff," human condition and experiences, but I and they seem to become more and more less and less. As in a dappled glade, shapes and shadows dance in the light—natural light, simple awareness—and this long laboring woman begins to relax.

•

The northern countryside beautiful in the autumn sun, wind, and rain, then the Poconos, the Delaware Water Gap, leaves and clouds scudding, whitecaps on the river, western Pennsylvania utterly lovely—and then there I was, entering West Virginia, even the name Wheeling on the highway signs homely, evocative, compelling, feeling like my mother—so I wheeled in, some sights unfamiliar, some intimately recalled in the body's memory though long gone in the mind. I felt tight-strung, as if I had been awaiting this return for my whole life, holding my breath till I could find my way home. The Ohio River, the Narrows between Wheeling and Moundsville, the mills, steel, coal, Fostoria signs—grimy facades, coal slags, abandoned factories, small houses. How I had been visually, esthetically, viscerally conditioned, somehow, to these narrow, crabbed, gritty spaces and surfaces—how I longed for this, to be in it again. Moundsville—dreary, left behind, yet on Fifth Street our old house, yellow and white, a beautiful Victorian home, immaculate and luminous. The Mound now has its own museum, and the state penitentiary, now closed, hosts tours of its horrifying self.[187] I released

---

187. The Indian burial mound and the prison held strong memories for me,

a long, shuddering breath and a few tears, climbed the Mound, made offerings and prayers, sat awhile—then west into friendly hills, open and inviting to move, breathe, expand. What I come from is not where I am heading. *[Geographically, that is; spiritually, what I come from is precisely where I am heading.]*

Ohio and Indiana, "amber waves of grain," fields in harvest, autumn colors turning to winter-ready gold-brown fields of stubble, wide rivers rolling with sudden, surprising deep glades, black-green shade. Then Missouri and Arkansas, the Ozarks breathtakingly lovely, welcoming, at once spacious and intimate. If it's not clear where I'm to be I'll think of this again, maybe. Today Oklahoma, down along the Illinois River, and in the Cherokee museum young Beulah from Texas with her great green eyes and the kind aunt and uncle who care for her, her father dead, her mother recovering from drugs. The blazing afternoon sun just fried me in the car and I bolted for the first exit that offered gas and lodging, so here I am in Henryetta, where I bought two gallons of water at a tiny Wal-Mart and plan to spend the rest of the day and evening curled up with Sister on our bed at the Pakistani-run RelaxInn, reading a novel and watching TV, if I can find the remote somewhere. *[The "remote somewhere"—exactly what I am looking for!]*

Laughing as I crossed the Texas panhandle—three improbable, actual road signs:

1. "Hitchhikers may be escaping inmates." *[Splendidly ambiguous syntax.]*
2. Museum with "Devil's Rope" exhibit—I'm curious—there at the entrance, where one is used to seeing the *lions couchants*, two huge, maybe eight feet 'round, balls of rusted barbed wire: the Devil's Rope—the museum a tribute to barbed wire!
3. An enormous white cross advertised thus: "The largest cross in the Western Hemisphere—RV accessible."

How the fenceline loves the land . . .

---

the prison siren rending the quiet of the small town when an inmate escaped, the Mound holding mysteries and secrets within—and opening them one day to the subtle sight of the small child I was, skipping down the large, flat, stone steps, in an unbidden, undeniable, unimpeded view of carefully tended bodies and their tenders within, in long white robes.

•

Oh, West, don't crush me with your bigness. Keep me high and strong for the struggle.[188]

I am confused by this country: limitless, dangerous, hard. Sorrowful, elated, frightened, brave, standing on a rim at sunset, looking out over the canyon bowl, something like vertigo, my awareness beginning to, wanting to, fearing to expand out into the huge spaces. Mountain roads taken at speeds that daunt me, chasms opening out beneath—afraid to look but I will have to, and have to get bigger, braver, to live here. For long years I've cozied into little spaces, enclosures, nests. Small challenges. The inner challenge now is matched by the outer. No limits. *[The past challenges may have looked small to me that day, as I gazed out on the immensity of the western sky—but I hadn't read the journals yet. In them it is unmistakable: let it go, let it go, let it all go.]*

Touched by the pueblos and by the red rocks, those great spirit beings, and by the love *in* the land—vast, impersonal, weightless and immense, warmth aglow in hills and sky, irradiating the landscape, grasses alight, distances shimmering, above and below. Prayers here in Indian Country—the wind stirs right away.

Hopi. Doors opening one by one. Prophecy Rock at dawn. Nothing spectacular, no visions, no revelations—just the perfect intention, the perfect sun rising in the perfect dawn sky over the perfect desert and the perfect mesas, the perfect prayers and the perfect understanding: For this perfect person, the perfection is not other than here and now, not about emergence from Fourth World to Fifth, not about vibrating into another dimension, but about doing it, being it, right now, in this world, in this dimension—revealing and living the inherent perfection.

•

The most egregious *apparent* disrespect for her as teacher, the most faithful *inner* respect for her as guru—her teachings and the gifts of practice permeating my mind, clarifying all.

---

188. Vreeland, *The Forest Lover*, 291.

Not sure I ever recognized how rebellious I am. Whatever I "have" to, I don' wanna!

•

Kyabje, Compassionate One, I am here placing myself in your hands.

When I told him the outlines of what happened and then said, "Yet, really, nothing happened"—"That's it!" he cried, big smile, two thumbs up. "That's wisdom! No matter what anyone says to you, even the guru, if you recognize that nothing happened, knowing it as mind, the bond is undefiled, intact. When you react, then it becomes 'real.' Negativity doesn't come from outside; it can be transformed. Take all faults as your own, all wisdom as others'—and you are doing this already. At the same time, pay attention to your own certainty." [189] *[In the perfection of What Is, no meeting, no parting, no confusion, no awaking from confusion, no respecting, no disrespecting, no harming, no not-harming. "Emptiness cannot be harmed by emptiness,"* [190] *the unconditioned cannot harm the unconditioned.]*

The bodhicitta gently disperses, settles like a warm, refined nectar in the channel linings—blissful, intimate, luxurious.

•

Identityless and unattached. In every moment I'm living my life, doing my practice. There is nothing to wait or prepare for; it is all here, now.

I'm staying in a town through which pass 129 trains a day, whistling, clacking, roaring, humming, full of personality and pzazz, unique and colorful—one mournful and longing, another boasting, then another spunky, streetwise, rebuked by the elegant, ladylike moan coming along soon after.

❖ Beloved is teaching; I'm tucked in next to her. Amused, I think, "Oh,

---

189. He was here giving me one of the most profound, penetrating teachings of the Dharma: "Of all the profound teachings I have read, this only have I understood: that all harm and sorrow are my own doing and all benefit and qualities are thanks to others. Therefore all my gain I give to others; all loss I take upon myself." Langri Tangpa Dorje Gyaltsen, in Khyentse, *Enlightened Courage*, 50.

190. Padmasambhava, *The Tibetan Book of the Dead*, 69.

I am banned—but here I am, tucked in under her left wing." At that instant she turns and lets me know I'm to leave! I find it so comical: just the *thought*, then there it is comin' back at me. So I'm smiling as I rummage around, getting my stuff together, moving first to the front then all the way to the back, chuckling all the while. She looks sideways at me and growls, "So you think this is funny, huh?"—and I just have to laugh out loud—"Yes, I do think this is funny, very funny." I have no idea if she is amused or annoyed, but I am enjoying the moment, enjoying the irony. ❖ *[That's just what I did, isn't it? Coming into her mandala, I moved right to the front, then all the way back! I just forgot to chuckle all the while.]*

I sense that the opportunity for me now is to inhabit ordinary circumstances with extraordinary mind. *[Funny use of "ordinary" and "extraordinary," since awakened mind is our ordinary mind.]* Such a sheltered life I was leading back "home." Now I'm out here in the world with no mooring, no harbor, no rudder. I get to look at my mind freshly, not in a "spiritual" but in a secular context—so I get to see "how it works." I am now out from under Beloved's wing and having to make all decisions, great and small, without external guidance. It's all in my heart, including my relationship with my teachers—but especially my relationship with truth.

Really, I wish never to be attached to anything again in this life.

Chemical toxicity has driven me from the ranch where I've been staying. But this suffering of chemical poisoning and homelessness is not "mine" in any way that is unique; it is our condition. Our environment that we degrade, desecrate, and poison in turn poisons us, we flee our homes or are driven out, many wander the Earth, the beautiful, poisoned land, and for so many lifetimes I have caused this kind of suffering—ants, roaches, spiders, mice, bees, wasps, snakes. So now, with this ripening, may the suffering of all instantly be relieved through my own.

With my aloofness and withdrawal, my shielded heart, I never really felt the Earth's sufferings before. It is rough here—and we have all ill-used this land, its energy, beauty, vastness, resources—still are.

Remembering Beloved saying, about awakening, "It was your *wanting* that allowed it." Not grasping but aspiration. I have been ambivalating for a long time about how and where to live, not wanting to plug back in—so really, *not* having a home was what I wanted. Then snow and ice, freezing temperatures, unable to practice or work or feel clean—so yesterday I wanted, not for selfish reasons but so I could get on with it—and then I received. I asked, and then I received.

Dawn spilling in over the countryside, pouring in from the eastern doorway, first warming Hopi, now flowing down to us. Driving to my temp job, seeing all as display of primordial pure wisdom light, thinking, "The activity isn't what matters—it's the seeing through to reality, the true nature."

•

Have begun transcribing the journals I've been keeping since I stepped onto the formal spiritual path twenty years ago, began working with Beloved. It is stirring stuff up—but I feel I am to do this work. *[Abandoning homeland and community, moving to an unknown land, I have come to a critical turning point. I need to see what I have been living for the last twenty years*—need *to see, the way a blindfolded person on a precipice* needs *to see.]*

•

The desert, saguaros, ocotillos—all the great, flat sky—oh, the desert! Winter heat, dry, penetrating, body soaking it up, eyes anxious, light too bright—yet softer here than at 8,000 feet, more atmosphere. Northward again, a pecan grove, bare trees in their careful long rows, like a Rembrandt etching, the trees dark, pewter, dry, dry bark, silvery wood, the ground beneath them dry, crumbly, silvery-dun—but it was the light around them that captured me: caught in the bare, thin, feathery branches and twigs, this silvery-gray light, domesticated, stilled, quieted—unlike the wild desert light, brazen, all-revealing—the pecan grove was decorous, ordered, placid—modest, subtle—the trees so calm, carefully ranged, somehow settled the light, turned that Southwest spotlight of the sun into something gentler, moister, quiet. It reminded me of plane trees in Normandy, of Vermeer, of November's silver light in the north. For the first time I felt something in my blood stop, shift, turn toward home—something like longing. Memory.

Probably it is always wiser to think in terms of effort than accomplishment.

How ill I have been, so terribly sick, for so long. There was fear—oh, I can see how I could lose my grip on life, just not make it back from this illness. Quite the discipline, just to keep mind clear of the impetus to decline—remembering purification: exhaustion not of life force but of karma.

Ah, beginning to recover—everything looks and sounds and tastes so sweet, emerging from illness into life, tasting the isness: *this* day, *this* sky, *this* broccoli, *this* dog tongue, *this* music . . . *now*.

What if I could just accept myself simply as I am? A person who deeply loves the Dharma, who has formed the highest aspiration, who will surely fulfill it one day, who in this time in her life is not particularly inclined toward formal practice except in retreat, and so on—just stop arguing with myself about what I think I *ought* to be doing and let myself simply *do* what I *do* wish to do. *[Remember the Two-Hearted Disease: could and should but won't and don't, and constantly arguing with self about it? Here I'm seeing how to cut through it, not with grand philosophy but with simple acceptance of myself as I am. Letting be.]*

As I work with the old journals, perplexity. *What happened?* I think it is this: From the beginning she took my aspirations seriously, as they matured she held me to them, and as they became only one aspiration, the highest, she took the cleaver and started actively cutting away the obscurations, the impediments to realization.

So it hurt. So what?

•

I am wondering if I should just no longer think of myself as a Buddhist, or even as a spiritual practitioner. Feeling lost, vulnerable, anxious. Praying for guidance: what to do, how to serve, how to live, how to practice? The ices are melting, spring is coming, the waters are flowing—and more layers of the constructed self peel away. I love the cushion, the formal practice, but what I *must* practice is this moment-to-moment awareness—cutting through all appearances to the true nature.

Over the last weeks, flutterings or hints:

SWEET
   WILD
      FREEDOM

Today, *two* emergency dental surgeries. Am I going to become a toothless hag? Didn't Kyabje say, "Be happy for all purification, especially illness"? Okay, I'm happy. In fact, it was comical. Remembering emptiness, interdependent arising, and the fact that we manifest whatever we want, I thought, why would we manifest tooth abscess and root canal? Then, laughing behind my dental dam: Well, as long as I'm manifesting *that* I'm glad I'm also manifesting *this*—modern dentistry, including anesthetic!

•

Driving through Indian Country, bemused by the fantastical landscape formations, like huge architectonic dream images suspended between Earth and sky, now radiant, glowing, later cool and distant, hinting of a scale so vast that in it they are atom-like and delicate. Stupendous structures, with ephemeral life forms that seem fragile, like the powdery, crusty soil, but really they are *tough*, shallow-rooted and resourceful: one drop for a crop. Everything seems brand-spanking new, appearing just in that very moment, and at the same time ageless with wind and sun and dust. It's like the enlightened view, 360 degrees of luminosity, clarity, space, emptiness, interpenetrating the highly specific event of fauna, flora, great rock hands running geologic time through outspread, eloquent, absolutely silent fingers. I feel I'm wandering a new planet, in a state of ceaseless worship at the shrine of Our Lady of Perpetual Astonishment.

Some kind of inner learning is being drawn from the mundane circumstances of my life and activities. Perhaps it is something as simple as participating in the human condition without restraint, or at least with greater simple willingness, and accomplishing both basic human things and enlightenment itself through my own efforts. I am calling on my teachers, innerly, for help in bearing up, seeing clearly, staying steady, having courage, compassion, and commitment—but I am not even asking for teachings, only for support in living them.

Homage to Escher

Downtown,
bright afternoon:
out of the corner of my eye I see
a school of fishes, silvery gray,
teeming in a pretty arc
from beneath my car—
suddenly they rise
into the air—birds!
banking and wheeling,
fishy shadows
of my mind.

Whatever state of mind it is that holds one activity superior to another, I don't seem to have it anymore. I am as happy cleaning toilets as writing poetry. That is, surely, a happy state of mind. *[Convenient, too, in this period of taking whatever temporary work is available, wanting and revealing no professional identity. Later, while working temp at a university, I will blow my cover and function again for awhile, also happily, as a social scientist. Yet when that identity, too, dissolves I dance a merry little jig in the cinder-dust roadway with Sister, singing out, "We're free, we're free! We can go, we can go!" And we do, heading north through vast new country before perching awhile on a remote mesa with a pack of dogs needing a caretaker. They almost kill Sister, but we all end up in love with one another before she and I take off again.]*

•

I have found in myself an immense *willingness* that I never knew I had, and I love myself for this quality that allows experience to rise up in and around me like joy bubbles, unpredicted, unowned, enchanting. *[Throughout the journals the signs of willingness are as prolific as the signs of resistance, but for a long time I was more willing to see the resistance, more resistant to seeing the willingness.]*

[A series of cancer dreams over a year or so, and then . . .] Colonoscopy this morning: large polyp, "one degree before frank malignancy," the doctor said, and recommended surgery to remove part of the colon. Flashes of

the cold gut-wrench heart-chill that is dread—yet I am at ease, tasting the one taste: cancer and light.

Thus concludes perhaps the most extraordinary week of my life. One taste, mind stable in clarity and luminosity, recalling emptiness and impermanence moment by moment. Unceasing appearances that would usually cause suffering—and no suffering, liberated from suffering. No grasping or repulsion, no ignorance—so no suffering. Remembering What Is during the surgeries—no fear, no recoil, no desire for another to take responsibility, no abnegation of my own—fully present and accounted for, alight throughout with joy, gratitude, and awareness, energy boundless, wisdom mind revealed in the gritty circumstances of life. Nothing grandiose or great, just living this specific moment and condition, embodied. Alive, awake, aware: liberated from suffering.

Kyabje, when I told him that I was not doing the formal practice he had given me to do: "Perfect! Practices are means. When the result is achieved the means are no longer necessary."

[Years ago I laughed out loud when I heard the country song "Drop Kick Me, Jesus Through the Goal Posts of Life."[191] Just the title was enough! This period of my journey, inner and outer, reminds me of it. Forms dissolving, structures of thought and activity falling away, many challenges on the physical plane, with money, living conditions, work, health—the karma popping like corn in hot oil. And I? Amazed and grateful actually to witness this being becoming ever clearer, lighter, and more loving. Beloved had not just kicked me out, *she had kicked me* up—*arcing right out across the field toward the goal posts.]*

The poignancy of the setting sun, the soft approach of autumn. Surrendering over and over just to what is in every moment. Releasing pain, fear, sadness, desolation, inviting consciousness to root itself in every cell and atom of my physical being. Alive, awake, aware—not wanting, not *not* wanting—fully present, experiencing it all, *willingly*—encapsulating nothing, letting it all move, letting it all *be*.

•

The roiling tempest within *is* the purification process, and my responsibility

---

191. *Bobby Bare Greatest Hits*, Bareworks Inc. (CD, BWCD-040292); words and music by Paul Craft, 1976.

is to let 'er roll—and contemplate mind. With this understanding comes a timid flicker of the joy fire.

I have prayed that my karmic propensities be exhausted and my prayer is being fulfilled. I'm walking through a field of ripening karma. Oh, yes, ripening, ripening—karma ripening like corn, tasseling, tossing in the winds of change. Sometimes it feels like a minefield—HA! a *mind*-field!—my character faults, negative behavior patterns, egotism, as Beloved had predicted, flying up in my face. I start to get confused by shame, regret, sadness, then remind myself what this really means: opportunity to see the harmful patterns and release them, exhaustion of karma. The guru's blessing—and a burst of joy in the armpits, in the throat, in the feet, in the stomach, in the mind, in the heart. All is well, all is well, even down in vajra hell!

I am weary of conflict, at last I am weary of conflict. Avid now to learn how to be a person who does not cause harm, I am soaking up feedback from environment, from people—and when I think I have destroyed my life and relationships, when I think this is the wreck and ruin of great potential, reminding myself this is no such thing. This is not about failure and ruin, it is not "about" anything. *This is the path clearing before me as I walk.* I must just keep walking, holding my compass steady. Unwavering commitment, courage, and compassion. And over and over again offering myself, my ignorance, confusion, nonvirtue, suffering, as ransom for all suffering beings. I pray for us all.

How often I remember the six realms in my belly, in my heart—and remember that in each one there is stationed a buddha. No one, *no one* is without help. We swim like blind fishes in the waves of karma, but the sea is the stainless, the lovely, the most pure.

Smiling, vajra thumbs up, the guru told me, "Developing bodhicitta—this is more important than the calluses on the butt, more important than the cave." *[Milarepa's last teaching to Gampopa was to lift his own tattered robe, showing his callused derrière—fruit of long hours sitting, sitting, in profound meditation. This day's Milarepa, my saint, my saint, points me to the* essence *of practice: bodhicitta, the commitment to free all.]*[192]

A dear young friend, in her early twenties, said to me today, "The one

192. See Chang, *The Hundred Thousand Songs*, 495.

thing I truly love about myself is my mind. Growing up, they taught me racism, they taught me hatred, they even taught me violence—and I never took any of it."

•

In meditation I see: The door that was "wide open for me in this lifetime"—it is much closer now. Oh! *I am standing in it.*

Reading through the journal volumes I begin to get a sense of how finely the wheels have been grinding. Though it looks like nothing, like the *opposite* of accomplishment, it is as Michelangelo said: the work of the sculptor is to release the image from the stone. *[We already are what we aspire to become.]*

❖ Beloved comes to visit. As we are walking together she says, "Every single hole in your mind has been sealed." ❖

No ground	Om gate gate
No past	paragate
No future	parasamgate
No this	bodhi
No that	swaha

A walk with Sister in the forest in my new hiking boots—Perfect Ponderosa Peace.

Behavior increasingly nonmotivated *[arising spontaneously]*—doing is becoming like *being.*

The medium is love.

•

[Exuberant joy and a subtly pervading, evanescent sense of permeability as I wander through time and the western landscape—often with no one on this Earth knowing where I am, I myself knowing less and less about me and my life. I sometimes feel light and insubstantial enough just to rise up off the Earth like dust, as if I am dissolving in this brilliant openness, only occasionally marking turns on the spirals of the freeing dance.]

In a canyon sanctuary, peaceful, perfect praise.

> The canyon embrace,
> sky nipples, motherly
> bovine white belly up—
> gaze, love, sky:
> soaring walls
> wheeling eagle
> valiant pine.
>
> Her love does not know
> even one limiting bound:
> every wall is an invitation to lift,
> to *rise*.

•

> I am pierced
> I am penetrated
> I am sundered
> I am not separate
> From you, world
> From you, life
> And all your 10,000 things,
> Holy, holy, holy.
> I weep, I am keening
> My song of praise.
> Unbearable presence,
> Leave nothing
> Of me in your
> Implacable wake.
> Life, holy, holy, holy,
> For not one instant's
> Hot breath am I other
> Than you.

•

[Beneath the big sky, Sister and I sit with horses on a broad hillside, full of feeling, empty of knowing, shaken by a swift squall—then sent aloft on this gust:]

I want—I am
wild and free
Full exposure

[Then we go quiet for a few years, briefly settled in a small log cabin in high-desert ranch country, among cactus and piñon, rattlesnakes and road runners—time on the cushion and in the countryside, riding warm, fragrant, dusty horses, walking the strange land, teaching a little, helping another friend die in joy.]

It all looks perfectly ordinary—and it is. Ordinary perfection, Great Perfection. "Open and empty like space, neither center nor circumference"[193]—I open my eyes and it's *this*, this right here, just this—not some mysterious "other" state, not something within my head or heart—just *this*—loft, altar, cushions, window, trees, sky—*this* is open and empty like space, *this* has neither center nor circumference—crisp, clear, sparkling, vivid, fresh—just plain, simple, direct—available, accessible, present—now—here—*this*.

Nothing to grasp at
or push away—
simply observing
mind's pure play

I see that my whole life has been one continuous, uninterrupted prayer for oneness with my divine nature. Now, today, simply acknowledging, here in the presence of my lama: I have already Seen, so I Know. Now, today, I dedicate what remains of this lifetime to helping others attain this.

•

I am helpless against this roaring, raging, rampaging river of love that surges through me—I can't help myself—confronted with the unlovable ones I am undone, overborne, all I can do is ride the terrible waves of this mighty river. The terror-striking boys, the sad, furious girls—where what we think of as love won't go, there I must go.

193. Padmasambhava, *The Tibetan Book of the Dead*, 35.

The "door that's completely open for me in this lifetime"—I am still standing in it—and now I'm turned 'round, facing back into the world, streaming down upon all beings the vast, indescribable, blazing light.

•

[My darling dies now, my longtime companion, the bodhisattva and great being: my beloved, my friend, my girl, my girl.]

Sister

I rest my great sorrow
in her great
emptiness.

That raw, grand fineness:
magnificent,
adorable and sublime—
pure presence, pure *being*:

I feel her
dispersed
among the stars.

•

America has gone to war. Before my shrine, from deep in my heart I am startled to hear myself saying to the beloved lama, "In this situation I don't know right and wrong—I only know love and compassion." *[Startled—because in this moment I remember myself in the era of "right-wrong," that deep searching out of my integrity. The bright burnished axe of love cuts at the root the duality tree, and its fruits of war and peace fall to the ground, barren of seed.]*

Our resonance to truth stirs within us as the great sea mammals stir within the deeps—slowly, powerfully, in curves and spirals so huge, so silent, we rarely even discern them.

•

The kindness of the lama is absolute.

Still clinging to samsara, the "human position"—but a sense today of slipping quickly now along a secret passageway—from "here" to "there"—beginning—oh, just beginning—to long for the boundless.

Intimations of matrix. No self, no container, no contained. Yes, *let me* give up all my versions of reality—they are heavy, onerous, laborious— have to keep them going all the time—and though day by day I more see how terrifying it is, I am *ready* to go without—*I want to be free!*

Deconstructing.

I don't even know if I'm practicing or not.

No external frame of reference. No internal frame of reference, either. Raw, as if flayed, then LOVE—oh, let it all be love—and love pours forth, expands to all worlds, to all of *being*—and I love even the confusion, the breaking up of limiting certainty—opening to freedom.

•

The longing is the love.
When you can't find the love, burn in the longing.
I burn as a spirit fire.
I am consumed.

•

Feeling frightened of this book, its rawness, its nakedness. The majesty to which it points. But this fear is not fear—it is the shaking, the deep tremors, of standing clear. Rock face cleaving. Elucidating.

•

The door, the door—
no longer standing on the threshold,
light streaming down me to the world—
I am turning from the world—

I am going through the door.

But oh, let me never for an instant
be separated from the suffering of beings!

This, my one great act of love.
This, here, now.

•

COMBING THE PRECIOUS TEACHER'S HAIR

Notes on Method

I LOVE THINKING ABOUT METHOD, in research, writing, painting, teaching, spiritual practice. It brings me close to thinking about *knowing*—what knowing is, what is to be known, how we know. This is a way of thinking about both methodological enterprise and spiritual path. Epistemology and ontology. Knowing *being*.

With this in mind, I offer a few notes on how this book has taken form.

•

This work consists of material from my journals together with commentary and annotations made in the course of transcribing and editing the material. The journals themselves cover twenty years; the Epilogue touches very lightly on the decade or so following that period. During the primary twenty years I sometimes wrote daily, sometimes throughout a day, and sometimes very infrequently, so there are periods in this history that are rendered in great detail and others that appear sketchier. Even so, the book does not include everything I wrote during this time, for which we can all be thankful; transcription from twenty-seven handwritten volumes yielded 1,225 single-spaced typed pages.

At first I was transcribing the journals just for myself. *[I needed to see, "the way a blindfolded person on a precipice needs to see."]* That first close reading showed me the unmistakable directionality and momentum of the lived process, and it was then that I started cutting, cutting, cutting, to reveal its essential nature, structure, and textures. Only very gradually did I begin to think this record might be of value to others, and to work with that in mind.

In cutting and editing I removed many words but I changed nothing essential to what unfolds in these pages. What I do speak of I treat as honestly as I know how, always seeking essence.

I pruned and condensed the journal material, sometimes lightly restructuring for readable transitions and occasionally rephrasing for clarity. Surgical intervention was needed, at times, to spare the reader at least some of the repetition that characterizes the slow process of penetrating ignorance, gaining insight, generating clear intention, falling again into confusion, recalling insight, testing experience against understanding, and so on. I was encouraged in this effort by a friend's admonition: "You can't make people wade through what you waded through." Forgive me, please, if you have found yourself from time to time wanting your high-waders—or a helicopter evacuation. [194]

Information about people, relationships, organizations, situations, and historical events is sparse, as it is in the journals; I develop neither characters nor story lines (except about a college at which I taught for some years, whose own organizational crisis was the occasion for a significant ethical and spiritual crisis for me; and just a bit about several people with whom I was close). Everyone mentioned in this book has a pseudonym except me, animal friends, and a few people who are no longer living. [195] Names of most places and institutions are invented, until the Epilogue, and the narrative makes no reference to dates, nor even to years or decades. In addition to respecting the privacy of individuals, these considerations place focus accurately, on *meaning* rather than on history, places, personalities. This occasions some loss of specificity in context but not in content—as this is a tale not of persons or places,

194. I have not spared the reader all of this repetition, because for most of us the process of waking up is, in fact, repetitive and cyclical (until, suddenly, there it is!). This itself tends to renunciation, as the hollowness of appearances and experiences gradually yields to the luminous transparency of insight. Irina Tweedie comments on the repetitive quality of her spiritual diaries:

The pupil has to learn the lesson again and again in order to be able to master it, and the teacher must repeat the lesson . . . many a time, but each time it triggers off a slightly different psychological reaction leading to the next experience, and so forth. I . . . expected wonderful teachings, but what the Teacher did was mainly to force me to face the darkness within myself, and it almost killed me. In other words, he made me "descend into hell," the cosmic drama enacted in every soul as soon as it dares to lift its face to the Light. (Tweedie, *Daughter of Fire*, ix–x.)

195. The sex of several individuals has also been changed. Two dreams name public figures.

the world of appearances, but of how one person comes to realize the sacred nature of reality pervading all appearances.

There is no information here about spiritual teachings or practices that should rest between teacher and student or in the secrecy of one's own mind. There is also no personal or historical information about the teachers with whom I worked during these years. The relationship between spiritual teacher and student is by nature not personal but impersonal. Though intimate in ways no other relationship can ever be, its purpose and activity are directed wholly to helping us *see through* the personal constructs, habits, and attachments that are the stuff of conventional life and relationships—to see through the conventions to reality as it is.

A word about dreams. Reading the journals all the way through for the first time, I was surprised to see how frequently and in what detail I attended to my dreams during these years, and more surprised still to observe their relationships to my waking life, relationships that were seldom visible to me at the time. Rare in the journals are what I call psychological dreams, which process events, deal with day residue, and so on. Instead, most of the dreams directly reflect inner spiritual challenges, deliver insights and learnings, facilitate transformations. A remarkable number presage future events or inner developments, and many are themselves actual spiritual visions, events, or teachings.

•

In the decade I worked on this book the manuscript itself became my teacher—exigent and generous—whose long hair, tangled by her labors, I had the privilege to comb. Drawing the comb of mind through the mane of experience and reflection, pass after pass after pass, gently, firmly, quietly, I came into a state of bemused gratitude and trust. Tangles released, knots opened, ratty snarls relaxed. Health and wholeness gleamed—and natural holiness, the holiness we all share, the holiness of *being*, luminous and self-aware, shone for me in these pages. It is shining the same way in everyone's mane, tangled or smooth. Just comb your hair.

•

ACKNOWLEDGMENTS

To Tsawai Lama, Kyabje, Beloved, and all my teachers, who by love lay me bare: praise, praise, praise.

To the dear spiritual friends who allow me to companion you on the path: I bow to you for your courage, commitment, and love. Special bows to the Garchen Assembly of Kindness and Love and the Garchen Institute for tireless enthusiasm and generosity.

To all who generously encouraged, criticized, and helped in many ways with this work, my love and appreciation—and especially to these individuals:

Cherilyn Parsons understood from the beginning what this work was and what it might become. Throughout the entire process I continued to take courage and guidance from her comments on the very first draft. I could not have had a more gifted, astute, constructive, generous, faithful literary friend.

Mary Dumas, Sue Favia, Moon Teitel, and Regina Sara Ryan provided close critiques that gave me insight into how this chronicle could become useful to others; the comments of Kim Agullard, Jan Walker, and Patricia Lamb were also helpful in this way. Teri R. Freeman shared perspectives about psychological trauma and sense of self, in a fresh reprise on conversations we have been having off and on for many years.

Peggy Dority, Kim Agullard, Lance Sandleben, and a kind gentleman at Lucis Trust cheerfully corralled bibliographic references for material read decades ago. Stacey Lynn and Harrison Shaffer of Green Sand Press were very generous with their time, skill, and counsel.

Robert Ewing provided space for writing, plus excellent provocations and laughs. Sandra L. Pickens, Teri R. Freeman and Ava Greenspun, Joan D'Aoust, and the Angel Canyon Sangha (Kanab, Utah), gave valuable financial assistance at the publishing stage.

Walton Mendelson expertly, lovingly crafted the beautiful look of the word.

Amanda Amos, Skywalker, helps me and many others in every possible way, each instance fresh with the dew of bodhicitta.

•

REFERENCES

Aiken, Robert. *The Mind of Clover: Essays in Zen Buddhist Ethics*. San Francisco: North Point Press, 1984.

Bailey, Alice. *Discipleship in the New Age*. New York: Lucis, 1944–55.

———. *Esoteric Healing*. New York: Lucis, 1953.

———. *Esoteric Psychology*. Vol. 1. New York: Lucis, 1962–70.

———. *Glamour: A World Problem*. New York: Lucis, 1950.

———. *Initiation, Human and Solar*. New York: Lucis, 1979.

Barks, Coleman. *The Essential Rumi*. New expanded ed. New York: HarperSanFrancisco, 2004.

Bellesi, Diana. "Happy Crossing, Good Luck Little Uli." *Conditions VI* 2, no. 3 (Summer 1980): 58–67.

———. "Human Word, Sacred Word." *Heresies*. Special issue, *Third World Women: The Politics of Being Other* 2, no. 4 (1979): 11.

Bhagavad Gita (The). Tamil, India: Sri Ramakrishna Tapovanam, 1982.

Blofeld, John. *Bodhisattva of Compassion: The Mystical Tradition of Kuan Yin*. Boulder: Shambhala, 1977.

Boyd, Doug. *Rolling Thunder*. New York: Dell, 1974.

Browning, Robert. *Paracelsus*, part 1. www.bartleby.com/100/473.html.

Caddy, Eileen. *The Spirit of Findhorn*. New York: Harper and Row, 1976.

Castaneda, Carlos. *The Fire from Within*. New York: Simon and Schuster, 1984.

———. *The Teachings of Don Juan: A Yaqui Way of Knowledge*. Berkeley: University of California Press, 1968.

Chang, Garma C. C., ed. *The Hundred Thousand Songs of Milarepa*. Boston: Shambhala, 1999.

Chidbhavananda, Swami. Introduction, *The Bhagavad Gita*. Tamil, India: Sri Ramakrishna Tapovanam, 1982.

Cravens, Gwyneth. *Speed of Light*. New York: Simon and Schuster, 1979.

Cutts, Jiko Linda. "Acedia and the Good Friend." *Wind Bell* (San Francisco Zen Center) 34, no. 2 (Spring/Summer 2000): 39–46. www.

whiterobedmonks.org/macedia..html [© 2001 White Robed Monks of St. Benedict].

Dalai Lama. *A Flash of Lightning in the Dark of Night: A Guide to the Bodhisattva's Way of Life*. Boston: Shambhala, 1994.

Dallas, Ian. *The Book of Strangers*. New York: Warner, 1973.

David-Neel, Alexandra. *Magic and Mystery in Tibet*. New Hyde Park, N.Y.: University Books, 1965.

Dharmarakshita. *The Wheel of Sharp Weapons: A Mahayana Training of the Mind*. 2nd rev. ed. Commentary by Geshey Ngawang Dhargyey. Dharamsala, India: Library of Tibetan Works and Archives, 1994.

Dowman, Keith. *Sky Dancer: The Secret Life and Songs of the Lady Yeshe Tsogyel*. Boston: Routledge and Kegan Paul, 1984.

Du Bois, Barbara. *Devotion*. Prescott, Arizona: Laughing Vajra Press, 2007.

———. "Passionate Scholarship: Notes on Values, Knowing, and Method in Feminist Social Science." *Theories of Women's Studies*, ed. Gloria Bowles and Renate Duelli-Klein. Boston: Routledge and Kegan Paul, 1983.

Dudjom Rinpoche. *The Lamp of Liberation*. New York: Yeshe Melong, 1988.

———. *The Preliminary Practice of the New Treasure of Dudjom* [*Dudjom Tersar Ngöndro*]. New York: Yeshe Nyingpo, 1984.

Ellsberg, Robert, ed. *The Duty of Delight: The Diaries of Dorothy Day*. Milwaukee: Marquette University Press, 2008.

Fisher, Janina. "Working with the Neurobiological Legacy of Early Trauma," 2003. www.janinafisher.com,.

Friedman, Lenore. *Meetings with Remarkable Women*. Boston: Shambhala, 1987.

Gampopa. *The Jewel Ornament of Liberation: The Wish-fulfilling Gem of the Noble Teachings*, trans. Khenpo Konchog Gyalsten Rinpoche. Ithaca, N.Y.: Snow Lion, 1998.

Garchen Rinpoche. "A River That Cannot Be Frozen," trans. Khenpo Konchog Gyaltshen Rinpoche. Gar Gön, Nangchen, Tibet: August 1995.

Haich, Elisabeth. *Initiation*. Palo Alto, Calif.: Aurora Press, 1974.

Harvey, Andrew. *A Journey in Ladakh*. Boston: Houghton Mifflin, 1983.

Isherwood, Christopher. *A Meeting by the River*. New York: Simon & Schuster, 1967.

James, William. *The Varieties of Religious Experience.* New York: Harper and Row, 1976.

Kaplan, Abraham. "Hasidism and Zen-Buddhism." *Inner Paths* (May/June 1980): 6–13.

Kapleau, Philip. *The Three Pillars of Zen.* New York: Anchor, 1965.

Khan, Hazrat Inayat. *Mastery through Accomplishment.* New Lebanon, N.Y.: Sufi Order Publications, 1978.

Khyentse, Dilgo. *Enlightened Courage: An Explanation of Atisha's Seven Point Mind Training.* Ithaca, N.Y.: Snow Lion, 1993.

———. *The Heart of Compassion: The Thirty-seven Verses on the Practice of a Bodhisattva.* Boston: Shambhala, 2007.

———. *The Wish-fulfilling Jewel.* Boston: Shambhala, 1988.

Kinnell, Galway. *When One Has Lived a Long Time Alone.* New York: Knopf, 1990.

Kjolhede, Bodhin. Responding to Brian Victoria, "Yasutani Roshi: The Hardest Koan." *Tricycle*, Fall 1999.

Kongtrul, Jamgön. *The Torch of Certainty.* Boulder: Prajna Press, 1977.

Lame Deer, John (Fire) and Richard Erdoes. *Lame Deer, Seeker of Visions.* New York: Simon and Schuster, 1972.

Lao Tzu. *The Tao Te Ching*, trans. D. C. Lau. Baltimore: Penguin Books, 1963.

Lhalungpa, Lobsang P., trans. *The Life of Milarepa.* New York: E. P. Dutton, 1977.

Lifton, Robert Jay. *Home from the War: Vietnam Veterans—Neither Victims nor Executioners.* New York: Simon & Schuster, 1973.

Longchenpa. *You Are the Eyes of the World.* Novato, Calif.: Lotsawa, 1987.

Lorde, Audre. *The Cancer Journals.* San Francisco: Aunt Lute Books, 1980.

Lutyens, Mary. *Years of Fulfillment.* New York: Avon Books, 1984.

Matthiessen, Peter. *The Snow Leopard.* New York: Viking Press, 1978.

Merton, Thomas. "New Seeds of Contemplation," *New Directions* 1972, quoted in *Co-Evolution Quarterly*, no. 40 (Winter 1983): 126.

———. *The Seven Storey Mountain.* New York: Harcourt Brace, 1948.

Midwer, Gesshin Myoka. *Primary Point: Journal of the Kwan Um Zen School.* February 1985.

Mishra, Ramamurti S. *Fundamentals of Yoga.* Monroe, N.Y.: I.C.S.A. Press, Ananda Ashram, 1985.

Ngari Panchen. *Perfect Conduct: Ascertaining the Three Vows.* Commentary by Dudjom Rinpoche. Boston: Wisdom Publications, 1996.

Padmasambhava. *The Tibetan Book of the Dead (The Great Liberation through Hearing in the Bardo)*, trans. Francesca Fremantle and Chögyam Trungpa. Boston: Shambhala, 1975.

Palmo, Anila Rinchen, trans. *Cutting through Ego-clinging: Commentary on the Practice of Tchod*. St. Léon sur Vézère, Montignac, France: Dzambala, 1988.

Pollitt, Katha. "In Horse Latitudes." *Ploughshares 1*, no. 3 (Winter 1972).

Postle, Denis. *Fabric of the Universe*. New York: Crown Publishers, 1976.

Rajneesh, Bhagwan Shree. *I Am the Gate: The Meaning of Initiation and Discipleship*. New York: Harper and Row, 1977.

Rama, Swami. *Himalayan News*, September/October 1983.

———. "The Nature of Avidhya and Maya." *Himalayan News*, January/February 1982.

Reps, Paul. *Zen Flesh, Zen Bones*. New York: Anchor Books, 1989.

Sahn, Seung. "Three Letters to a Beginner." *Primary Point* 4, no. 1 (Winter 1987).

Sangpo Rinbochay, Khetsun. *Tantric Practice in Nyingma*. Ithaca, N.Y.: Gabriel/Snow Lion, 1982.

Sarton, May. *At Seventy: A Journal*. New York: W. W. Norton, 1984.

Shah, Idries. *Learning How to Learn: Psychology and Spirituality in the Sufi Way*. 1978; San Francisco: Harper and Row, 1981.

———. *The Way of the Sufi*. New York: E. P. Dutton, 1970.

Shantideva. *A Guide to the Bodhisattva's Way of Life (Bodhisattvacharyavatara)*, trans. Steven Batchelor. Dharamsala, India: Library of Tibetan Works and Archives, 1979.

Spalding, Baird T. *Life and Teaching of the Masters of the Far East*, vol. 2. 1927; Camarillo, Calif.: DeVorss & Company, 1986.

Srigley, Michael. "Hamlet: An Esoteric Approach." *The Beacon* 28, no. 8 (March/April 1980): 230–35.

Storm, Hyemeyohsts. *Seven Arrows*. New York: Ballantine Books, 1981.

Suzuki, Shunryu. *Zen Mind, Beginner's Mind*. New York: Weatherhill, 1970.

Tart, Charles. *Transpersonal Psychologies*. New York: Harper and Row, 1975.

"Ten Oxherding Pictures (The)." Paintings by Yokoo Tatsuhiko, commentary by Kubota Ji'un. www.terebess.hu/english/oxherding.html.

Thirty Seven Bodhisattva Practices (The), trans. Acharya Rigzin Dorjee and Bonnie Rothenberg. Sarnath, Varanasi, India: Central Institute of Higher Tibetan Studies, 1988.

Trungpa, Chögyam. *The Collected Works of Chögyam Trungpa*. Vol. 3. Edited by Carolyn Rose Gimian. Boston: Shambhala, 2003 [© 2003 by Diana J. Mukpo].

———. *Crazy Wisdom*. Boston: Shambhala, 1991.

Tsogyal, Yeshe. *Dakini Teachings: Padmasambhava's Oral Instructions to Yeshe Tsogyal*. Boston: Shambhala, 1990.

———. *The Life and Liberation of Padmasambhava*, Part 3. 1978; Berkeley: Dharma Publishing, 2007.

Tweedie, Irina. *Daughter of Fire: Diary of a Spiritual Training with a Sufi Master*. Inverness, Calif.: Golden Sufi Center, 1986.

Usharbudh Arya, Pandit. "Samkhya Philosophy: Meditation and Karma." *Himalayan News*. January/February 1981.

Vreeland, Susan. *The Forest Lover*. New York: Viking, 2004.

Waters, Frank. *Book of the Hopi*. New York: Ballantine, 1963.

Wilber, Ken. *One Taste: The Journals of Ken Wilber*. Boulder: Shambhala, 1999.

Yogananda, Paramahansa. *Autobiography of a Yogi*. Los Angeles: Self-Realization Fellowship, 1971.

———. *The Movement Newspaper*. November 1980, 5, issue 11: 16.

•

COLOPHON

The text was set in Garamond, named after Claude Garamond (c.1480-1561). Most versions of Garamond are based more on the work of Jean Jannon (ca. 1580 - ?). Jannon began designing his alphabet in 1615, when his type was wearing out and replacing it was difficult and expensive. He based his alphabet on fonts designed by Garamond. The italic fonts in the Garamond family are based on work by Garamond's assistant Robert Granjon.

The display type is Requiem, an old style serif type family, designed by Jonathan Hoefler in 1992. Hoefler's inspiration for it came from a 1523 writing manual by Ludovico Vicentino degli Arrighi.

•

Made in the USA
Charleston, SC
15 August 2011